RADIO
VOICES

RADIO VOICES

American Broadcasting, 1922–1952

Michele Hilmes

University of Minnesota Press

Minneapolis

London

Portions of chapter 3 appeared in different form in *Critical Studies in Mass Communication* 10, no. 4 (December 1993): 301–21, published by the Speech Communication Association. By permission.

Published by the University of Minnesota Press
111 Third Avenue South, Suite 290, Minneapolis, MN 55401–2520
Printed in the United States of America on acid-free paper

Library of Congress Cataloging-in-Publication Data

Hilmes, Michele, 1953–
    Radio voices : American broadcasting, 1922–1952 / Michele Hilmes.
      p.   cm.
    Includes bibliographical references and index.
    ISBN 0-8166-2620-0 (hc : alk. paper). — ISBN 0-8166-2621-9
(pb : alk. paper)
    1. Radio broadcasting—United States—History.   I. Title.
PN1991.3.U6H56   1997
384.54′0973—dc21   97-394

For Red

Contents

Acknowledgments

This project began as far back as the early 1980s, when, much to my surprise, I found my dissertation research turning to a medium to which I had given virtually no previous thought. It never crossed my mind as a cinema student at NYU that radio would loom on my research horizon—I'm sure it never occurred to my professors, either. But in the course of piecing together what became my first book, *Hollywood and Broadcasting: From Radio to Cable*, I realized that the story of the relationship between Hollywood and its chief ally and competitor began long before television, and a whole new territory opened up to me. As a baby boomer born in the year of TV's big boom, 1953, I had never listened to radio myself as anything but a medium for Top 40 and news. How strange, then, to find myself joining arcane organizations like SPERDVAC (the Society to Preserve and Encourage Radio Drama, Variety, and Comedy), renting *The Lux Radio Theatre* and other radio classics from its immense collection, and being drawn into a world, both contemporary and distant, that I hadn't known existed.

I soon realized that the academic sphere had little space for radio. Study after study of early television appeared, with barely a backward glance at the thirty years of direct influence that preceded it. I began to feel like a one-woman crusade to expand academic collective memory; my students and colleagues became inured to the phrase, "Well, of course, in radio . . ." that preceded so many of my comments in class and colloquia. If this book begins to put that phrase into the mouths of others, I will consider it a success.

I would like to thank those colleagues and students for their immense help throughout this project. At the University of Wisconsin-Madison, I thank especially my colleagues Julie D'Acci, John Fiske, Mary Anne Fitzpatrick, Tino Balio, David Bordwell, Vance Kepley,

Lea Jacobs, Don Crafton, and J. J. Murphy, all of whom have aided me through departmental support, discussion, or just listening to me go on over the past three years. Among the graduate students, I would like to thank in particular Matthew Murray, whose own research contributed some key elements to this study and whose critical reading helped to shape it. Lisa Parks, Donald Meckiffe, and Jennifer Wang also supplied important pieces of the puzzle; many thanks to them and to our other talented students for their input in classes, seminars, and colloquia. My work would be far less rich without the critical questions, interesting ideas, and sometimes amazing details their work has unearthed. Our Communication Arts Department staff, especially Linda Henzl and Mary Dodge, assisted with many crucial tasks. On the computer front, those anonymous student wizards at our DoIt help desk bailed me out more than once. My undying gratitude goes to Fran Breit, who miraculously recovered for me a chapter I thought had been lost, representing months of work. Thank you, Fran.

Without generous summer support from the Wisconsin Alumni Research Fund, I would not have been able to complete this work for many a long year. I also appreciate the key research grant from Duke University's John W. Hartman Center for Sales, Advertising, and Marketing History, which allowed me to spend a vitally important week of research in the J. Walter Thompson Collection.

The other crucial site of research for this book exists at the State Historical Society of Wisconsin—an unparalled archive of material on radio, television, and film history, including the early NBC collection along with many other indispensable records from this vital part of our cultural past. I'd like to thank Peter Gottlieb, archive director, for overseeing it all; Harry Miller, head archivist, for his assistance and advice; along with the staff in the Archives Reading Room, who have been unfailingly helpful and informative. Maxine Flexner-Ducey provided invaluable insight into the sound and visual collections. At Duke, Ellen Gartrell was a font of information and encouragement; I greatly enjoyed spending a week there and appreciate all the courtesies extended by her excellent staff. At the Broadcast Pioneers Library, formerly in Washington, D.C., but now relocated to College Park, Maryland, I thank Catharine Heinz, long its director, very warmly for letting me have the run of the collection; she possesses a knowledge of the archival history of radio unrivaled in my experience. Michael Mashon, head of the library in its new location, has been an invaluable source of help and information, not only to me but to others I have directed to this fascinating collection. My thanks also to the archive staff at the Manuscript Collection, Library of Congress; the N. W. Ayer corporate archivists, who sent me much useful material; and the archivists at the University of Southern California.

Many thanks to William Boddy for his encouraging and perceptive reading of the manuscript; also to Christopher Anderson for his early comments. At the University of Minnesota Press, I thank Janaki Bakhle for her initial interest in the book and Micah Kleit and his assistant, Jeff Moen, for their efficient and beneficent shepherding of the book through the complicated process of editing and production.

At Spring Hill College in Mobile, Alabama, I want to thank my former colleagues Tom Loehr and David Sauer, who heard a lot about this project in its early stages and offered their encouragement and support.

A good index contributes immeasurably to a scholarly book; thank you, Laura Gottlieb, for the very best.

And finally—isn't this always the way?—my husband, Bruce Croushore, and daughter, Amanda, can never escape their responsibility for making it possible for me to exist in this world, as well as write books. Mere thanks are not sufficient.

Introduction: The Nation's Voice

Traditionally, histories of broadcasting begin with technology: the telegraph begat the alternator, which begat the audion tube, and so on, and we are led into the seemingly natural and heroic march of technological progress led by great men as an admiring nation watches in awe. By the time Edwin Armstrong arrives with his superheterodyne receiver, the course of radio is set; strangely, by this time, it seems that a whole industry has sprung up around magical transmitters and tubes that somehow spoke for themselves, or at least left their operators little choice. Luckily, they managed to say exactly those things that most pleased the hearts of the American public, and the rest is . . . history.

What if, instead, we regard radio not as a collection of wires, transmitters, and electrons but as a social practice grounded in culture, rather than in electricity? What if the history of broadcasting, properly construed, lies not in a succession of technological developments but in a series of small crises of cultural control, of sometimes minute and sometimes groundbreaking decisions made, often at the last minute and without much forethought, by the varied custodians of radio's infant voice? What if it is social currents, running through the voices in the air and fingers on the control boards, that flow out or meet with resistance, not so much in the "ether" as in the studio, the boardroom, the headphoned circle around the crystal set?

This vision necessitates a whole new approach to radio's roots, one that attempts to locate them within the matrix of opinions, feelings, and interests within which radio developed as a technology, as a practice, and as a part of lived daily experience, both for those who listened in and for those who experimented with its production: what Pierre Bourdieu might term the cultural "field" of radio's origins.[1] Though no discussion of radio's social/cultural context can be comprehensive, there are certain major tensions that run through the period during which broadcasting, and ideas about broadcasting, took shape and began to flourish. These tensions indicate areas of change that radio, among other developing social phenomena of the twentieth century, would help, hinder, or redirect, and with change comes conflict. Indeed, it is conflict that exists as a necessary precondition for any kind of technological or other development. As a previous technology's weaknesses or incapabilities begin to emerge—and as interested groups struggle to impose different uses for technology through which they can better profit or dominate—the initial impetus for further experimentation is produced.

The technology of radio developed from one such set of tensions;[2] the ways in which radio was utilized, discussed, understood, and experienced grew from another. The social conflicts most relevant to radio's "soul" obviously involve those conditions most affected by its presence:[3] the emergence of so-called mass culture, and the crisis in national identity from which this notion arose and that it engendered; the twentieth-century transition from a culture based on conservation to one of consumption, and the shifts in relations of power and social distinctions, particularly around race, gender, and ethnicity, that this process implied; and the changing role of women in American society, linked to an inexorably altered concept of the distinction between the public and private spheres upon which so much of American self-identity had been based. These overarching social processes form the backdrop against which radio's first antennas went up and voices ventured into the night. They would significantly influence the definitions of what could be and would be said—or sung, or played, or performed—over radio in its early years, of who would be put in charge and who banished from the airwaves. These are decisions that continue to influence our lives today.

Asking these questions should, I hope, produce a small shock—radio? No other medium has been more thoroughly forgotten, by the public, historians, and media scholars alike. Despite its dominance of America's waking hours and public consciousness from 1922 until its apotheosis in television in the early 1950s (and despite the attention that media such as film, television, and the press have received academically), radio remains a dark and fading memory somewhere between vaudeville and *I Love Lucy*—without the benefit of cable-channel reruns. The fact is, however, that television grew directly out of three decades of radio broadcasting, from which it carried over not only its economic, regulatory, and institutional structures but also its familiar program forms, even to specific shows and personalities. From 1922 to 1952, most of broadcasting's basic definitions, functions, and uses were struggled over and set into motion, producing an enormous social investment in the novel and extraordinarily influential narrative forms and genres of radio. This neglected body of texts and cultural tradition has become the "repressed" of television studies, occupying a position similar to that of the silent film era in film studies twenty years ago.

Though it is true that the developing television networks made it a high priority in the early 1950s to induce audiences to forget about radio in favor of the new and more profitable medium, it is not only in industry accounts and those reliant on them that radio as a social and cultural force is overlooked. Much has been written, for example, on the role of the immigrant press in ethnic preservation and transformation, yet almost nothing on foreign-language radio, on representations of ethnic immigrants and their assimilation in the mainstream of broadcasting, or on the role that radio might have played in the assimilatory process, though evidence exists to show that radio rivaled the movies as an influential cultural form.[4] Similarly, in the recent outpouring of scholarship on television in its early decades, attention has been drawn in particular to TV's construction of gender and address to women,[5] yet almost without reference to the long history of programming by and for women, and narratives dealing with women's roles, that filled the majority of radio's hours from the 1930s on—many of which carried over directly from the original medium. And though some excellent recent studies trace broadcasting's underlying regulatory and economic conflict between forces of "high culture" and education and those behind radio's overwhelmingly commercial function,[6] little exists for those who wonder what effect, if any, such a permanent and deep-rooted contradiction might have had on the programs actually experienced by audiences—most of whom remained blissfully unaware of the struggles being waged behind the announcers' round tones and bursts of organ music.

The reasons for this neglect are many and deeply tied up with the cultural function of radio itself. What I am attempting to create here is an argument that radio must be resurrected as a field of study, not only because it underlies most directly the forms and structures of television—which almost everyone agrees occupies an important enough space in our cultural preoccupations to warrant study—but because in speaking to us as a nation during a crucial period of time it helped to shape our cultural consciousness and to define us as a people in ways that were certainly not unitary but cut deeply across individual, class, racial, and ethnic experience. Radio was in many ways unique: significantly different from any preceding or subsequent medium in its ability to transcend spatial boundaries, blur the private and public spheres, and escape visual determinations while still retaining the strong element of "realism" that sound—rather than written words—supplies. And its institutionalization as one of our central social structures for transmission and control of information about the world we live in makes its study relevant to almost all aspects of American social history—hardly anything that has happened in or to this country since 1922 has not been shaped by radio or television in one way or another.

Yet we cannot take radio's influence fully into account when so little is known about its thirty-year reign over American consciousness. As usual, the writing of history is limited by the materials available—and here radio presents a unique challenge. So much of what was actually broadcast—the sounds and stories actually experienced by listeners—went out live, unrecorded, and with little record keeping. Many—the vast majority—of broadcast hours are lost forever; others must be pieced together out of scripts, press accounts, and reminiscences. What does exist tends to privilege the dominant and centralized sources. I have drawn heavily on NBC records for this study, because they make up a very large proportion of what has been preserved and is accessible to historians. Likewise, records and accounts of the larger and more successful stations, programs, and performers are more likely to survive than those that actually may be of more interest to the poststructuralist scholar: those small stations providing a different service to a more marginalized audience, those programs deemed of specialized interest or least appeal whose scripts and records have long been destroyed, limited regional and local broadcasts, those efforts that never made it to realization precisely because they went against the grain of dominant practice. Much research needs to be done in these lesser-known areas to bring them to other scholars' attention and to reflect more fully our diverse and conflicted media heritage.

I have chosen to focus here on mainstream, hegemonic practices not only because, despite their material availability, they have not been adequately explored, but also because I believe that there is value in bringing an informed cultural studies approach to the dominant discourse. Of course, the writing of history is also shaped by the ideology or national narratives surrounding its project, as Warren Susman has argued.[7] If broadcasting history has been shaped up until now primarily by "consensus" narratives, we are currently in a cycle that sees more value in marginalized discourses than in the mainstream—in the resistant, "deviant," or popular construction than in the official, dominant, or "sanctioned" representation. However, dominant forms also take shape as sites of cultural tension and conflict, with some channels of meaning promoted and idealized while others are cut off and pushed to the sidelines. Though consensus history has worked to obscure these aspects, that is the fault of history writing, not of the discourse itself as a field of study. As Michel Foucault has demonstrated, dominant discourse when subjected to reversal reveals not the smooth face of consensus but the ruptured and seamed lines of tension and resistance that consensus seeks to conceal.[8] In fact, I would argue that one reason for radio's neglect as a field of study is precisely that close analysis of radio begins to unravel the mask that U.S. commercial media have created for themselves: as a naturally arising, consensus-shaped, and unproblematic reflection of a pluralistic society, rather than the conflicting, tension-ridden site of the ruthless exercise of cultural hegemony, often demonstrating in its very effort to exert control the power and diversity of the alternative popular constructions that oppose and resist it. Power to dominate such a field as radio also brings with it its own power to shape the outlines of historical perception.

Thus the task here is to examine U.S. radio's construction of itself—institutionally, in the texts it created, and in the space it opened up for listeners to construct themselves as an "imagined community"[9]—as a structure in tension, significant for both what it includes and what it excludes, for those things it identifies as important and those it denigrates as simply not worth saying. To call radio broadcasting as constructed by major national institutions "the nation's voice" is to refer not to one uncontested discourse, but to the one that dominates out of the many competing, often conflicting, voices that make up the whole of broadcast experience. We must look for those elements that are silenced and muffled within the voice that speaks the loudest.

One way to begin is to look at some of the very earliest attempts to speak and the conditions and expectations that motivated and constrained them. Chapter 1 opens by drawing attention to the weight placed by early radio on the assimilationist drama, exemplified by the innovative and influential show *The Rise of the Goldbergs* and the career of its creator, Gertrude Berg. This leads to a consideration of radio as it helped to build the "imagined community" of the 1920s United States, using concepts developed by Benedict Anderson to examine radio's early concern with the problem of national unity and identity in a diverse and conflicted society. Utopian predictions for radio as a unifying and culturally uplifting medium collide with dystopian fears surrounding its unique ability to transcend traditional boundaries of time and space, and the social distinctions that these boundaries maintain. Pierre Bourdieu's theories on the work that cultural distinctions perform in creating and stabilizing social hierarchies supplies the framework for a consideration of the historical context of radio's initial development and uses. Assimilation, "Americanism," and the complex functions of racial and ethnic "difference," along with the rise of commercialized mass culture and its creation of a preferred, yet feared, buying audience of women, form the backdrop that informs radio's earliest definitions and practices.

Chapter 2 takes these social tensions into the field of early radio experimentation and the development of a framework of gradually naturalized structures and practices. Starting with the work of key inventors such as Reginald Fessenden and Lee DeForest, I bring to the fore the important but too often overlooked contributions of early radio amateurs, focusing not only on the practices and problems that influenced early commercial stations, but on the regulatory conflicts and disputes over "good taste" in the ether that had far-reaching effects. In particular, the amateurs' use of jazz records and the racialized cultural hierarchies challenged by this emergent musical form provoked restrictions that helped to separate legitimate from illegitimate interests even as the first stations began to broadcast. Pioneer stations such as KDKA and WJZ benefited from the cultural distinctions encouraged by early regulators, and influential practices begin to emerge. The announcer became the personification of radio's brash voice in the mid-1920s. Two groundbreaking programs, the National Carbon Company's *Eveready Hour*, with Wendell Hall, and WEAF's *Capitol Theater Gang*, with "Roxy" (Samuel Rothafel), deployed what Warren Susman identifies as the "culture of personality" to introduce the expanded and newly constituted listening public to the experience of radio. Finally, I consider Chicago as a fertile site of radio innovation, notably through its two great newspaper-owned stations, the *Chicago Daily News*'s WMAQ and the *Chicago Tribune*'s WGN. These important early stations, practitioners, and emerging forms set the scene for the dramatic debut of radio as a national medium as networks spun their webs across the country in the late 1920s.

Chapter 3 focuses on the development of radio's influential narratives of national definition, again drawing on Benedict Anderson, with particular attention to the characteristically American tradition of the minstrel show and its influence on U.S. radio. The history of the innovation of radio's most representative textual form, the serial/series narrative, is traced from its beginnings in the blackface program *Amos 'n' Andy* to its eventual domination of network schedules. Within the context of Chicago's melting pot of ethnic groups and Jazz Age culture, the serial comedy/drama provided not only a uniquely useful textual format for radio's technical, industrial, and economic structures, but also created a new kind of relationship between audience and medium. Drawing on the work of theorists and historians such as Homi Bhabha, Toni Morrison, David Roediger, and Ann Douglas,[10] I reveal the central role played by race in radio's early narratives and address, constructing a national norm of "whiteness" that emphasized the differences between "black" and "white" while working to erase distinctions between groups of European descent. The fact that radio was an aural medium meant that it had to work harder than its comparable national form, motion pictures, both to depict and to define racial differences, and thus a consideration of the specifics of radio's narrative constructions works particularly well to reveal the hidden workings of race behind naturalized conventions. As radio grew from a local novelty to a great national institution, it built on the forms and tensions exemplified by this extraordinarily influential program.

Chapter 4 looks at the offshoots of the *Amos 'n' Andy* phenomenon: the explosion of serial dramas and comedies that debuted in the early 1930s and the cultural tradition on which they drew. This includes such innovators as Bernarr Macfadden (*True Story Hour*); Marian and Jim Jordan (*Fibber McGee and Molly*); Chester Lauck and Norris Goff (*Lum and Abner*); Louise Starkey, Isobel Carothers, and Helen King (*Clara, Lu and Em*); and Myrtle Vail (*Myrt and Marge*). I place the success of these shows within the context of the transformation of networks from cultural arbiters providing programming produced in-house to sellers of airtime to advertising agencies and their clients. In particular, I use the conflict between one of radio's largest program suppliers, the J. Walter Thompson agency, and NBC to illustrate the economic and cultural pressures that shaped radio as a national medium in the 1930s.

Chapter 5 turns to the suppressed history of women in radio, tracing the efforts of women's voices to be heard. From the female amateurs of the 1910s through the debate over the suitability of women announcers in the 1920s, to the creation of the daytime network schedule as a "ghetto" for feminine audiences, producers, and concerns, this chapter begins the process of reexamining the construction of radio as a medium targeted primarily at women, but preoccupied with containing the transgressive potential that such an emphasis presented. Key female innovators in radio, such as Bertha Brainard and Judith Waller, are exhumed from historical neglect and evaluated for their contributions to radio. The ways in which these and other radio innovators began to define women's interests on the air and to develop programs that spoke, often in subversive and controversial tones, about women's experiences begins in chapter 5 and carries over into chapter 6's focus on the oft-pilloried daytime radio serial. Drawing on Nancy Fraser's theories of "subaltern counterpublics,"[11] I place daytime radio dramas within their context of schedule differentiation and tensions surrounding radio's perpetual conflict between public service and private profit and the gender assumptions behind such terms. A closer look at the work of key originators, such as Irna Phillips, Jane Crusinberry, and Frank and Anne Hummert, along with the discursive strategies that worked to denigrate this popular form—and its audiences—reveals what was at stake in the creation of a separate place for women on the airwaves and how audiences used and responded to the potential for resistance and transgression that the serials provided.

In chapter 7, the focus shifts to radio at night, and I examine four of radio's most popular and prestigious programs: *The Jack Benny Program*, Fred Allen in his various settings, *The Lux Radio Theatre*, and Orson Welles's *Mercury Theater of the Air*. These two forms—the comedy/variety show and the dramatic adaptation—represent prime-time radio's most popular genres and the ones that most clearly mark the differentiation between nighttime and the disparaged daytime. Employing Lawrence Levine's analysis of cultural hierarchy, I show the concepts of the disciplined audience and the controlling author to be hard at work in these popular programs.[12] Radio drew a fine line between "highbrow" and "lowbrow" forms, with radio hosts assigned the formidable task of walking that line before live weekly audiences of millions. While self-consciously challenging social pretension and lampooning the institutions of culture, these programs built on and reinforced other social distinctions, notably along the lines of race and gender. And it was precisely these lines that would come under heavy scrutiny and conflict as radio entered the decisive national identity-defining period of World War II.

Chapter 8 traces some of the contradictions in radio's embrace of the war effort, including the organization of the Office of War Information and its internal disputes. During this period, radio played a crucial role in the newly urgent task of mobilizing national identity and recruiting excluded groups to the idea of "Americanness." Programs designed explicitly to advocate ethnic unity and interracial solidarity worked simultaneously to draw attention to radio's complicity in the conditions that made such appeals necessary in the face of the Nazi threat. Similarly, radio proved an important aid in recruiting women to war work by expanding the theretofore limited range of female representations and modes of address. However, this expansion also served to indicate the nature of the previous limitations, and ultimately would necessitate strong measures to recontain the marginal voices that were given new space on the airwaves, even if in contained and partial forms. In my concluding essay, I show how the historical amnesia surrounding the career of radio personality Mary Margaret McBride, particularly as concealed beneath the historically foregrounded practices of Sylvester "Pat" Weaver in the 1950s, reveals this containment process at work in the definition of the emerging medium of television.

As the sweeping scope of this study clearly implies, only a very partial and selected range of concerns can be covered out of the immense and virtually unexplored territory that radio occupied in the American psyche for more than thirty years. Much has been omitted that would greatly reward further study. For instance, in my effort to draw attention to lesser-known radio programs, I have given short shrift to the two narrative forms that, although not dominant on radio, would prove extremely influential for television: the domestic comedy (sitcom) and the detective (action/adventure) show. Another telling and very fascinating chapter in the history of radio might concern the border radio stations in Mexico, where such colorful personalities as

W. Lee "Pappy" O'Daniel, later governor of Texas and U.S. senator, "passed the biscuits" for Hillbilly Flour and where Dr. John R. Brinkley purveyed his famed goat-gland therapy. Literally marginalized—pushed over the border by developing U.S. restrictions, not all of which would bear scrutiny today—these border operations blasted a concentrated violation of cultural standards into U.S. airspace and defined daily the limits of the permissible in radio.[13] Black broadcasting pioneers such as Jack Cooper and the early black-format stations in Memphis, New Orleans, and Atlanta have been discussed by a few historians but deserve, along with overlooked ethnic broadcasting stations, a much more prominent place in a reconceptualized broadcasting history.[14] And the list goes on, inevitably. I sincerely hope that the following chapters will awake an interest in this rich and rewarding period in U.S. broadcasting and stimulate further research along these lines and others yet to be discovered.

► ONE

Radiating Culture

I want to talk about the America I've discovered on the air—Radio America. Columbus discovered just a rock-ribbed continent, but if you want to discover the real heart and mind of America, you've got to look for it on the air! The programs of all the broadcasting companies are like mirrors held up to America's soul. They reflect what people are asking to hear and wanting to know.[1]

With the same warm tone of buoyant Americanism that characterized her thirty-year serial, *The Rise of the Goldbergs*, Gertrude Berg editorialized for the *Cleveland Press* in 1933. Her article expresses the kind of sentiment about radio broadcasting so frequently heard in its first two decades: a utopian rhetoric tied to nationalism that glorified radio's special properties and emphasized its uniquely "American" character. More than any other medium, radio seemed in its early days to lend itself to association with ideas of nation, of national identity, to "the heart and mind of America," its "soul"—and not just in the press releases of networks and advertisers, who might be assumed to have an agenda, but in the popular press, in sermons, speeches, and songs, from radio enthusiasts' magazines to farm publications, in the opinions of factory workers and of U.S. senators.

In our current dystopian times, when everything from violence to family fragmentation to tooth decay is blamed on television, this enthusiasm is hard to account for. In today's light, such typical 1920s assertions as Senator James Watson's that radio supplies "renewed evidence of the sublime fact that 'God moves in mysterious ways his wonders to perform,'" or Joseph K. Hart's triumphant declaration, "The day of universal culture has dawned at last!" seem either cynical or hopelessly naive.[2] Yet this type of discourse dominated broadcasting's first three decades, becoming especially strident—in the face of mounting disillusionment—during television's early years. Is this merely a fluke, a quaint and charming but now outdated rhetorical flourish of

1

a time and a medium now largely forgotten? Or was there something about radio, something about what it did to us and how we used it, that truly did result in a changed America, that both helped to define us as a nation and itself shaped that definition somehow? To understand the roots of the revolution that was radio, we could do worse than to examine the career of Gertrude Berg.

The Immigrant Saga

In many ways the program that Gertrude Berg devised in 1928 and sold to NBC the following year was anomalous; no other daily serial drama reflected so explicitly its creator's own ethnic background, and few other creators retained such close control over their work. Until the late 1930s, Berg wrote all the scripts—five fifteen-minute stories per week!—and performed the role of the main character herself. Yet in other ways "Molly" Berg's story reflects early radio the way she claimed radio itself reflected the soul of America.[3] *The Rise of the Goldbergs* had grown out of skits that the young Gertrude used to write for the entertainment of guests at her father's resort in the Poconos. Catering to a largely Jewish clientele, the resort gave Berg a captive (on rainy days) and appreciative audience for her first efforts, a series of monologues delivered by a character she called Maltke Talnitzsky. Gradually Maltke modulated into Molly and Talnitzsky into Goldberg— "And Talnitzsky was no longer suitable. It was too much, it was trying too hard, and I couldn't take my character seriously. I changed the name to Goldberg because it sounded right and that was the only reason" (177)—and Gertrude Berg, by this time married herself with two small children, began to search for a wider market for her talents.

But before the newly titled *Rise of the Goldbergs* would get an audition, Berg's efforts to find a connection in radio led to two other writing jobs—interesting, in light of the nature of the popular entertainment of the period. As she recounts it, her first assignment consisted of writing the continuity for an "African" road show called "Boomalay"— "Mostly it's dancin' but I need woids between the dances," as small-time producer Willie Kamen explained it. When she worried that her background might not provide suitable authenticity, Kamen explained:

> "What's with you? You think any body in Hohokus is gonna know real from what I'm givin' em? . . . Listen, I got dancers. They're dark but they're a hundred per cent from New York. And the dances—it's the Lindy Hop with feathers. Don't worry, just write." (181)

Her second assignment, this time for radio, involved writing and announcing a script for Consolidated Edison Company, giving recipes for Christmas cookies in Yiddish:

> A Christmas cookie in Yiddish for a public utility in America seemed a little odd, but it gave me my second lesson in radio: Be surprised at nothing. . . . I got my cue and the words from "Our sponsor" issued forth from my lips like a news bulletin from the Tower of Babel . . . "Eire freindliche gas and electrische company brengen alle menschen fun New York eine speciele reciepe far cookies far dem Yontevdiken seison." (182)

Inspired by this success, she offered her script to NBC; after a tense two-week silence, she was summoned to the NBC offices at 711 Fifth Avenue and told to be ready to go on the air, five days a week, beginning November 20, 1929. At first a sustaining program, within the year the Pepsodent Company—also sponsoring *Amos 'n' Andy* at the time—picked it up and the Goldbergs began their rise to a thirty-year tenure on radio and television and, if we are to believe the words of their creator, in the hearts and minds of the American public.

Early scripts of *The Rise of the Goldbergs* concerned themselves explicitly and intimately with an immigrant Jewish family's assimilation into American life. Just as Berg chose to begin her 1961 autobiography with the story of her grandfather, Mordecai Edelstein from Lublin, Poland, and his worship of America, Christopher Columbus, and assimilation into this new world, so these elements are emphasized in the lives of the Goldbergs: Molly, Jake, Sammy, and Rosie.

> Molly became a person who lived in the world of today but kept many of the values of yesterday. She could change with the times, as did my grandmother and my mother, but she had some basic ideas that she wanted to pass on to her children. Not only were all men created equal, they also had to honor their mother and their father. Abraham, Isaac, and Jacob interchanged easily with Washington, Lincoln, and Jefferson, and the Philistines had nothing on a person who didn't vote. . . . Sammy and Rosie were important to *The Goldbergs* because they helped to teach their immigrant parents how to become Americans. At the same time, the parents tried to teach them some of the rich traditions of the Old World, thus combining the best elements of two dissimilar worlds. (191-92)

Accordingly, the parents in Berg's scripts spoke with heavy Yiddish accents, whereas the children's accents favored standard American with a goodly dash of the Bronx. Much was made of Molly's malapropisms, mostly based on linguistic confusions, and her Old World turns of phrase. The very first program, aired November 20, 1929, contained these lines:

> "Where is Sammy so late? Maybe he got himself runned over by a cabsitac," she worried. "Dey run around so fast like cackroachers."
>
> "Hello, Mum!"
>
> "Vat's de matter so late, Sammy? Let me look at your hends. Playing marbles, ha? For vat is your fadder slaving for vate I'm esking you? A marble shooter you'll gonna be? A beautiful business for a Jewish boy!"
>
> "What's the matter with the marble business?" demanded Sammy. "Didn't Uncle Morantz pay five thousand dollars just to get his name on a piece of marble?"
>
> "Don't enswer me back! If not I'll tell your papa so soon he'll come home! Go vash yourself and take de wiolin! No vonder is a saying dat in America de parends obey de children!"[4]

The first season's scripts, later published in book form, deal with issues such as the difficulties of raising children in an American environment that sometimes clashes with Old World traditions and the immigrant family's striving for economic success and security. Molly's conversations up the air shaft with her neighbor—"Yoo hoo, Mrs. Bloo-oom"—and frequent visitors in their small apartment vividly evoke New York tenement life. The success of this slice of specifically ethnic, but far from atypical, American life resulted in more than thirty-seven thousand letters pouring into NBC's office when Berg became ill and the show was forced off the air for a week—despite frequently changed time periods that required some ingenuity and persistence on the part of the audience to follow.[5]

Something about the representation of ethnic immigrant life and the struggle of the Goldberg family to become "American" both touched the lives of the diverse listening public and proved well suited to the function of radio at this particular juncture in American history. We will see that this theme recurs time and again in early broadcasting programs. Radio drama and explorations of national identity and assimilation went hand in hand. Gertrude Berg's early perception of this phenomenon has been echoed many times; one of the most commonly agreed-upon characteristics of the new medium, as seen by contemporaries and later historians alike, was its ability to promote cultural homogeneity.

In a study done in 1933 by Herbert Hoover's President's Research

Committee on Social Trends, Malcolm M. Willey and Stuart A. Rice concluded:

> Certain it is that the radio tends to promote cultural levelling. Negroes barred from entering universities can receive instruction from the same institutions by radio; residents outside of the large cities who never have seen the inside of an opera house can become familiar with the works of the masters . . . and the fortunes of a Negro [sic] comedy pair can provide social talk throughout the nation. Isolation of backward regions is lessened by the new agency of communication. . . . The radio, like the newspaper, has widened the horizons of the individual, but more vitally, since it makes him an auditory participant in distant events as they transpire and communicates to him some of the emotional values that inhere in them.[6]

Historian Warren Susman echoed these findings fifty years later in an essay titled "The Thirties": "Through their radio sets a unique view of the world and a way of interpreting it came to the American people. . . . Sound helped mold uniform national responses; it helped create or reinforce uniform national values and beliefs in a way that no previous medium ever had before."[7]

More recently, Lizabeth Cohen's detailed study of Chicago workers during the 1920s and 1930s connects the labor movement's success in the 1930s to the "common ground" developed by ethnically diverse factory workers, one important aspect of which was radio: "Radio, probably more than any other medium, contributed to an increasingly universal working class experience," Cohen notes. She says further, "Not only did radio give workers in the same work group, department, and factory more common cultural experiences, but also it made them feel part of a larger, citywide and particularly national culture."[8] Missouri radio listener Edith Krassner, interviewed in 1987, describes her own early experience with radio in similar terms: "At first it was just your own home, your own family and then you would go to church and go to school and those were the only people you came in contact with. . . . [With radio] your whole vision of things, your whole outlook just seemed to expand."[9]

Yet what sort of cultural unity and identity were these programs building? Of what, exactly, did this common experience consist, and what specific ingredients did radio contribute? If radio unified the shop floor, leveled the cultural experiences of diverse races, ethnicities, and regions, and spread a sense of national awareness, what were the lines and parameters, the desired and the excluded, the fiercely contested hierarchies, of this common radio imaginary?

A Medium of Public Definition

It is no coincidence that so many of early radio's most successful programs centered on issues of ethnicity (as with *The Rise of the Goldbergs*), race (as in *Amos 'n' Andy*, another thirty-year success), gender (as in—but not limited to—the denigrated but amazingly prolific daytime "women's" serials), and the twin processes of "Americanization" and "progress" themselves, key terms of both the decade of radio's inception and the century. Broadcasting brought together some of the most powerful agents in the transformation of American culture in the twentieth century—technology, advertising, big business, the federal government, mass audiences, home and family—and combined them in ways that had never before been possible. And unlike other major industrial developments that also combined these factors, such as the automotive industry or consumer products manufacturing, radio's business consisted precisely in the construction and circulation of representations and narratives—symbolic constructions—that not only served a commercial purpose but spoke directly to and about this new society in the making (with, of course, its own agenda firmly in place). In so doing, radio presented opportunities for cultural expression and national self-definition never before available, not only in the United States but in countries around the world. Radio created not only a marketing and distribution system but a system of meanings, a system of transmission of cultural values and mediation of cultural tensions that valorized and "made common" some aspects of everyday experience and marginalized or excluded others, while drawing unprecedented numbers into what Benedict Anderson calls "that remarkable confidence of community in anonymity which is the hallmark of modern nations."[10]

In a society built on the conflict between democratic ideology and a tenuously balanced—but rigorously defended—system of structured social inequity, representations of such powerfully charged social elements as race, ethnicity, gender, and public cultural authority provide far more than entertainment value. The creation of the institution of radio broadcasting as a government-regulated extension of the public sphere gave the experience of "listening in" more weight and influence than going to the movies or reading a popular magazine; its status as a semipublic institution charged with tasks of education and cultural uplift put it on a par with other official institutions, such as schools, churches, and the government itself.

In virtually every nation but the United States, the perceived nationalizing powers of this new medium placed it firmly under the aegis of centralized government, with support from the public and the state, limited private competition, and structures that responded directly or indirectly to government supervision. In Great Britain, for example, the importance of broadcasting in the shaping of national culture and identity was clearly perceived by the founders of the British Broadcasting Company and expressed in the BBC's programs and policies:

> The BBC had founded a tradition of public service and of devotion to the highest interest of community and nation. There was at hand a mighty instrument to instruct and fashion public opinion; to banish ignorance and misery; to contribute richly and in many ways to the sum total of human wellbeing. The present concern of those to whom the stewardship had, by accident, been committed was that those basic ideals should be sealed and safeguarded, so that broadcasting might play its destined part.[11]

Only in the United States was broadcasting allowed to develop commercially, without direct subsidy or state involvement, despite pressures to create a system more like that of the BBC. This had the effect of sending the cultural function of radio "underground." Rather than government-appointed committees, centralized decision making, and public debate over program balance and content, the U.S. system came to rely on negotiations between sponsors and advertising agencies, marketing studies, and network public relations efforts.[12] Lack of direct state control—with its outright acknowledgment of the cultural role of broadcasting, however partisan—contributed to our dominant mythology of "consensus" broadcast history, by which the American system is seen as a foregone conclusion, a natural outgrowth of the "American way," given that it proceeded clearly from the preferences of "the people":

> The culture of the United States must reflect the commercial and democratic populace. . . . [Radio] was an instrument of electrical entertainment aimed at a commercial democracy—a world of independent, average people who preferred an occasional advertising announcement to the implications of a broadcasting system fully regulated by governmental bureaucrats.[13]

Yet a glimpse at contemporary accounts shows no such agreement, neither to the inevitability of commercial broadcasting nor to radio's unproblematic cultural role. To the contrary—writers in the popular press during radio's formative years, representing constituencies as diverse as *QST*, the magazine for radio amateurs, to *Ladies Home Companion*, postulated a number of different possible ways of organizing this new phenomenon in their midst, very few of which included wholly commercial support for broadcasting. Indeed, this was originally seen as one of the least desirable alternatives:[14] "Old Man Difficulty . . . is up and at it again; and in his latest incarnation has assumed what threatens to be the most unpleasant guise in which he has appeared so far. 'Advertising by Radio' is his new name; and a very troublesome pest he is likely to become unless something is done, and that quickly."[15] Other commentators concurred:

> The use of the radio for advertising is wholly undesirable and should be prohibited by legislation if necessary. . . . At least, radio broadcasting should be declared a public utility under strict regulation by the Federal authorities; and it may be necessary to have the Government condemn and buy the whole industry, operating it either nationally or locally on the analogy of the post-office and the public-school system.[16]

Even more common was a "pox on both their houses" attitude that warned against the perils of private monopoly as much as government control: "To put the radio into the hands of the Government would be to give to those in office a dangerous power. To leave such power in the hands of private corporations is to run a danger quite as great as that of bureaucracy."[17]

The vocal and organized forces of radio amateurs threw their support behind the plan proposed by the first Radio Conference in 1922, which made formal and technical allowances for a mixed method of broadcasting in which amateur, government, public, private, and toll stations would be offered reserved spectrum space and differing guidelines.[18] Many envisioned the uses of this kind of mixed service model, by which

> if broadcasting were to be centralized in a group of well distributed stations, it would be possible for each station to include several transmitters each tuned to a different wave length, and each wave length, in turn, devoted to some special form of program. Thus jazz would be 360 meters; educational lectures, 380; classical music, 400 meters, Governmental bulletins, 425 meters, and so on.[19]

To some writers, yet more advanced technology might provide the solution, as in the many proposals for "wired radio." This description comes from an engineer: "Wired wireless looms up as a more alluring possibility. . . . This means that some of our power stations may become broadcasting stations and the wires that heat our toasters and light our lights can bring us the news and music of the world as well. This service can be charged for, and it will be illegal to tap the wires . . . without the payment of a fee." This engineer saw this solution as going hand in hand with a system of government supervision, because even private radio presented opportunities too great for private decision making: "If broadcasting is to grow and prosper, we need a nonpartisan Federal Commission of educators, entertainment and technical experts to govern, regulate, and control broadcasting and to arrange for the collection of a small yearly fee from each owner of a receiving set."[20]

Public subscription was also suggested as a possible means of support. In 1924, the Radio Music Fund Committee was established in New York City; it was envisioned that the committee would collect enough in subscription funds from the listening public to support a program or series of programs over WEAF's toll broadcasting station.[21] These are just a few of the attitudes that were being circulated in mass-market magazines during radio's formative years; though the general public may not have formed such crystallized opinions, it is hard to conclude that any "natural" consensus existed.

In fact, the public was never admitted to the chambers of debate on this issue, as historians such as Robert McChesney demonstrate by illuminating the backstage machinations and bitter battles fought to maintain private ownership and commercial operation in the 1920s and 1930s, in the face of considerable opposition.[22] No clear mandate for unsupervised commercial broadcasting emerged during radio's first decade; the number of radio control bills introduced in Congress during this period testifies to the persistence of the public service/public control model even as commercial networks prospered. Indeed, it was by promising to resolve this dilemma by *combining* the commercial with the public, using the same strategic rhetoric as the BBC but linked to commercial competition, that the Radio Corporation of America was able to clear the way for network broadcasting in 1926 and after. The National Broadcasting Company in its opening declaration promised the same kind of promotion of the culturally desirable and exclusion of the culturally suspect that systems such as the BBC made overtly, behind a facade of freedom of consumer choice:

> Announcing the NATIONAL BROADCASTING COMPANY, Inc. *National radio broadcasting* with better programs permanently assured by this important action of the *Radio Corporation of America* in the interests of the listening public. . . . *The purpose of that company will be to provide the best program available for broadcasting in the United States.* . . . The Radio Corporation of America is not in any sense seeking a monopoly of the air. . . . It is seeking, however, to provide machinery which will insure a national distribution of national programs, and a wider distribution of programs of the highest quality.[23]

Thus our first and dominant National Broadcasting Company took its name not only from its intended scope but even more as an assertion of its centralizing cultural function—and as an indicator of those social and industry elements that it promised to hold in check. *National* commercial broadcasting could both fulfill the technical and cultural promise of radio and set restraints on its potential dangers if left in the hands of scattered, unsupervised small stations; yet, by refusing that official acknowledgment of its national function that would have mandated centralized state control, privately owned commercial broadcasting would de facto provide the same kind of cultural definition *without* the kind of public debate and supervision necessitated by a more openly governmental structure.[24] Debate would be thus displaced from the public sphere of politics to the private sphere of business and consumer choice.

In the United States, then, despite a significant body of opposition, the public interest had become defined as the commercial interest as early as the late 1920s. Regulators continued to see no conflict between them, to the extent of defining commercial broadcasting as inherently "more democratic" than "special interest" educational and public stations—especially when those stations might include such troublesome interests as WCFL, the "Voice of Labor," or WLWL, run by the Paulist Fathers, or the disruptive and diverse amateurs. In displacing outright state definition of national priorities and values onto a presumably transparent system of commercial entertainment driven by advertising dollars, American radio created an extraordinarily effective way of masking its public function behind the discourse of private choice.[25]

The Imagined Community

Lulled by the notion that radio programming resulted from a simple and direct process of consumer choice, exercised primarily in the private sphere over trivial entertainment and leisure decisions, we lose sight of the fact that radio's public impact possessed the power to exceed by far both its makers' intentions and the momentary pleasures of the audience. Whether intentionally or not, radio really did create the voice heard round the nation; no matter what process led to the creation of its unique and oft-disparaged representations, they possessed the power to create a phenomenon greater than themselves. Perhaps the Pepsodent Company's sole intent was to sell a certain amount of toothpaste when it sponsored *Amos 'n' Andy* in 1929—and perhaps a nation tuned in solely to laugh a little and unwind after a long day—and perhaps WMAQ and NBC desired only to bring these two profitable phenomena together; nevertheless, the creation of this particular set of representations within the racial and ethnic context of the 1920s both built on and confirmed a certain set of cultural norms and values that had implications far beyond the isolated experience.

At the very least, listeners' tuning in by the tens of thousands to one specific program airing at a specific time created that shared simultaneity of experience crucial to Benedict Anderson's concept of the modern "imagined community" of nationhood. His description of the modern print-influenced citizen, the newspaper reader, even more accurately evokes the radio listener:

> [The newspaper reader] is well aware that the ceremony he performs is being replicated simultaneously by thousands (or millions) of others of whose existence he is confident, yet of whose identity he has not the slightest notion. Furthermore, this ceremony is incessantly repeated at daily or half-daily intervals throughout the calendar. What more vivid figure for the secular, historically clocked, imagined community can be envisioned? At the same time, the newspaper reader, observing exact replicas of his own paper being consumed by his subway, barbershop, or residential neighbours, is continually reassured that the imagined world is visibly rooted in everyday life.[26]

Yet despite the rise of chains, newspapers remained a primarily local medium in the United States. Radio, more than any other other agency, possessed the power not only to assert actively the unifying power of simultaneous experience but to communicate meanings about the nature of that unifying experience. Radio not only responded to the dominant social tensions of its era but, by addressing its audience's situation directly in music, comedy, and narrative drama, made those tensions the subject of its constructed symbolic universe.

Events in the last decade of the twentieth century have given us pressing new reasons to think about notions of nation and identity, and the roles that race, ethnicity, and communication play in creating them. Anderson locates the beginning of the modern sense of nation and nationality in the profit-driven spread of the medium of print—"print-capitalism, which made it possible for rapidly growing numbers of people to think about themselves, and to relate themselves to others, in profoundly new ways."[27] The spread of print, driven by commercial motives, overthrew the dominance of restrictive official languages, allowed circulation of vernaculars to a wider audience, and eventually led to the overturning of traditional authority and to a whole new concept of the relation of citizen to state, of citizen to citizen, that characterizes the modern age. This "imagined" relationship resulted from the "half fortuitous, but explosive, interaction between a system of production and productive relations (capitalism), a technology of communications (print), and the fatality of human linguistic diversity."[28] And in such an imagined relationship, based on nothing so tangible as concrete geographic boundaries, common ethnic heritage, or linguistic homogenization, but instead on assumptions, images, feelings, consciousness, it is not only the technical means of communication, but the central narratives, representations, and "memories"—and strategic forgetfulness—that they circulate that tie the nation together. "All profound changes in consciousness, by their very nature, bring with them characteristic amnesias. Out of such oblivions, in specific historical circumstances, spring narratives."[29]

The processes Anderson identifies as key resonate significantly throughout the development of radio broadcasting: a system of productive relations driven by that hallmark of twentieth-century capitalism, advertising; a technology of communications significantly different from print, yet even more capable of negotiating not only the linguistic but the ethnic and cultural diversity brought about by the transformations of the modern age; and, like film, a machine for the circulation of narratives and representations that rehearse and justify the structures of order underlying national identity.[30] We can see an awareness of these possibilities in the popular rhetoric that greeted radio from its earliest appearances.

Foremost among prevailing expectations for this new medium of "radio broadcasting" was that of unity, of connection, of "communication" in its purest sense: "Repeatedly, the achievement of cultural unity and homogeneity was held up, implicitly and explicitly, as a goal of the highest importance."[31] Radio would unite a far-flung and disparate nation, doing "more than any other agency in spreading mutual understanding to all sections of the country, to unifying our thoughts, ideals, and purposes, to making us a strong and well-knit people."[32] Echoing Anderson's description of the effects of print culture, several kinds of unity were envisioned as inherent in the spread of this new medium: physical, cultural, linguistic, and finally institutional. Radio technology, though adaptable to many uses that were not pursued, promised at the very least the same bridging of physical distance over time as other modern media of communication. This physical connection, now addressed not to individual recipients but to a vast, invisible audience at large, would most assuredly, it was felt, provide cultural unity as well. As the English language spread into every corner of the nation, "homogenization of the American mind" would follow. And even before 1926, the recognized necessity of setting up well-regulated institutional controls over this kind of power led to the formation of network broadcasting as we know it. As the nation found a voice through radio, the "imagined community" of the twentieth-century United States began to take shape.

Yet it would be a mistake to assume that it spoke univocally. The history of broadcasting is marked by struggles over appropriate use of the medium, from the amateurs and commercial interests in the early 1920s to the conflict between educational interests and networks throughout the 1930s, and this is not to mention the various internal conflicts and pressures within the institution of radio itself: between advertising agencies and networks, Chicago and New York, censors and performers, regulators and businessmen. These well-worn avenues of dispute are tied to broader areas of social controversy, and the choices made by early stations, networks, sponsors, and agencies as they invented themselves and the "business" of radio reflect the tensions of a diverse and divided society. Who would speak to whom, saying what, on whose behalf—and, conversely, who would not be allowed to speak, whose speech would be carefully limited and contained, and who would not be addressed at all—these were questions rarely asked and answered on purely economic grounds, despite broadcasting's basic commercialism. Rather, decisions on matters such as these reflected and reified structures of power and sites of resistance to the social order being created and reproduced over the invisible airwaves. We can see the first indications of these fundamental tensions in the utopian predictions of radio's unifying power, held in tension with the dystopian possibilities that radio had to be kept from unleashing.

First of all, it seemed most obvious that the basic technical qualities of radio would unite the nation physically, across geographic space, connecting remote regions with centers of civilization and culture, tying the country together over the invisible waves of ether much as the telegraph and telephone lines had stitched America together, pole by pole, in the preceding century. Yet this new medium could also bring the public into remote private spaces, as to the housebound, the ill, and the infirm:

> The miner in his lonely mountain hut, the sailor at sea, the explorer in the frozen Arctic or Antarctic where he is completely isolated from civilization, the citizen in his home, all enjoy the best music, listen to addresses delivered by distinguished statesmen and captains of industry, reports of news events and sermons by the world's greatest preachers, no matter where they are delivered. The fact that all these forms of information or entertainment come to him through the air is so miraculous that he never ceases to marvel at the superhuman ability of those who wrested from Nature one of her greatest secrets.[33]

Here the diminishment of physical distance and penetration into private spaces is linked explicitly to the spread of culture—and cultural hierarchies. Radio promised simultaneity of experience without direct contact, exposure to the public in the privacy of one's home. It would be twenty years before this privatized experience would begin to seem itself something of a threat; for radio's early decades, isolation was the condition that broadcasting promised to alleviate, not create, and many a paean was composed (and preserved) to celebrate this anticipated aspect of the brave new radio world.

One of the most poignant descriptions of radio's miraculous physical qualities in the popular press of the early 1920s (and there are many) comes from an account written by a mining engineer stationed in the remote Temagami Forest Reserve in Canada and appearing in *Colliers* in April 1920:

> I am in a log shack in Canada's northland. . . . Three bosom friends are here in the shack with me—my ax, my dog, and my wireless receiving set.

These are vital possessions. If I lose my ax, a frozen death awaits me when the wood fire dies. If I lose my dog—well, you who love your dogs in places where human friends abound just remember where I am. If I lose my wireless set, then I am again cut off from the great outside world which I have so recently regained. . . .

I reach over and touch a switch and the music of an orchestra playing at Newark, N.J., fills the room. . . . A slight turn of the magic knob and I am at Pittsburgh, Pa., listening to a man telling stories to thousands of America's listening children. With that magic knob I can command the musical programs and press news sent out from a dozen radio broadcasting stations. At will I amuse myself or garner the details of a busy world where things are happening. . . .

Only yesterday to be out here was to be out of the world. But no longer. The radiophone has changed all that. Remember where I am and then you can realize how "homy"[sic] it is to hear a motherly voice carefully describing in detail just how to make the pie crust more flaky. No, I may be at "the back of beyond," but the whole world has marched right up to the edge of the little copper switch at my elbow.[34]

Just a few years later, RCA and AT&T were able to mobilize these expectations of physical unity to justify and promote their wired network system—despite the fact that radio's most unique and celebrated property consisted precisely of its "wireless"-ness.

However, this rhetoric of physical connection had some formidable obstacles to overcome. The erasure of distance and separation held a threat as well as a promise. In a society built on structured segmentation and social division as much as on its rhetoric of democratic equality, connectedness posed a danger to the preservation of those physical and geographic divisions supporting social distinctions, such as the separation of racial and ethnic neighborhoods, preferred leisure and cultural sites for different classes and social groups, the insulation of traditional rural society from "corrupting" city influences, and the home as private, feminine domain distinct from the masculinized public sphere.[35] Radio's "immateriality" allowed it to cross these boundaries: allowed "race" music to invade the white middle-class home, vaudeville to compete with opera in the living room, risqué city humor to raise rural eyebrows, salesmen and entertainers to find a place in the family circle. Bruce Bliven touches on this capacity and its dangers in his 1924 article, "The Legion Family and Radio":

Ten-year-old Elizabeth is a more serious problem. Whenever she can, she gets control of the instrument, and she moves the dials until (it is usually not a difficult task) she finds a station where a jazz orchestra is playing.

Then she sinks back to listen in complete contentment, nodding in rhythmic accord with the music. Her eyes seem far away, and a somewhat precocious flush comes gradually upon her cheeks. . . . Mother Legion abominates jazz.[36]

Radio's early period as a "local" medium, with stations owned and operated within a city or community, both preserved certain forms of social separation and threatened, by virtue of its diversity, pervasiveness, and escape from the usual physical mechanisms of control, many of those separations that maintained local social order. Little Elizabeth would never be allowed to go to a local jazz club, but the radio could bring the club into her living room. The creation of national networks superseded local or more random organization in a potentially invasive way, yet established a centralizing structure that could work to control the most immediately threatening aspects of local diversity and maintain local separations. Sanctioned national culture glossed over the rough edges of local or regional difference: how nice to know that Elizabeth's jazz might emanate from the respectable studios of NBC rather than that disreputable station from Chicago's South Side, playing God knows what.

Thus, radio's position in the home, while potentially importing exotic influences, could also reduce some dangers represented by exposure to the outside world. Bliven's "Legion family" acknowledged this usage too:

Bill and Mary spend just about five times as many evenings at home as they used to; Mother Legion rejoices over this especially because of Bill, who was getting in with a rather fast crowd, which used automobiles, pocket-flasks, and road-house dance orchestras for its principal media of amusement. [Now] [t]he older children not only stay home, but they frequently bring in their friends for a radio dance.[37]

Thus, radio's space-transcending qualities, combined with its location in the family circle, held out both promise and threat. Clearly, the *what* of broadcasting would become the next pressing issue—what would come out of that miraculous set and into the living room: abominable jazz, transporting one's children away into exotic and dangerous cultural spaces? Or the strengthening of family unity through shared and culturally sanctioned experiences?

Proceeding "logically," then, from radio's physical function was its power to unify the nation culturally—for better or worse. Usually this goal was elided with the physical—as something radio would "naturally" accomplish, by the inherent character of its technology—yet this naturalizing discourse often masked implicit assumptions about exactly which aspects of the "national culture" were inherently more worthy of universal acceptance than others. Established religion (largely Christian), accepted educational offerings, official "high" culture and art—symphonic music as opposed to low jazz, "legitimate" drama, poetry readings and lectures by "experts"—this was the stuff of radio as envisioned by accounts in the press, and indeed as promoted particularly by official organs of broadcasting: the "best," the "distinguished," the "greatest." NBC announced its arrival in November 1926 by promising "quality" in broadcasting, and its definitions of exactly what this quality would consist of followed closely the myriad articles and speeches that preceded it.[38] Radio's official social role would be one of uplift, of cultural improvement, very much echoing a similar rhetoric developing out of the British Broadcasting Company at the time—yet with very different results.

For never was there a time in the development of broadcasting in the United States when commercialism, and its avenue of access to the popular, did not form a central core of the listening experience. Despite Roland Marchand's characterization of radio as "the last genteel hope," describing the initial "opposition" of networks and advertising agencies to descend to the level of hucksterism on radio that would later characterize it, in fact this reluctance existed more on the level of rhetoric than of practice.[39] Many accounts testify to the pervasiveness of commercial announcements on the air from the very earliest days, whether as plugs for the music stores that provided the records broadcast or as readings of bedtime stories for children from the newspapers that published them, or outright ownership of stations by newspapers or department stores whose chief purpose was the promotion of the parent business. Even by 1922 this was obvious to observers:

> Driblets of advertising, most of it indirect so far, to be sure, but still unmistakable, are floating through the ether every day. Concerts are seasoned here and there with a dash of advertising paprika. You can't miss it: every little classic number has a slogan all its own, if it's only the mere mention of the name—*and* the address, *and* the phone number—of the music house which arranged the programme. More of this sort of thing may be expected. And once the avalanche gets a good start, nothing short of an Act of Congress or a repetition of Noah's excitement will suffice to stop it.[40]

These broadcasters, while often paying heed to "public service" responsibilities, nevertheless had good reason to follow those tastes and desires of their publics most conducive to attracting business—as found, often, in other forms of popular entertainment—and much less reason to be concerned with public image in the eyes of official bodies than the corporate giants.

Commercialism created a popular "pull" in early radio, as it had for the penny press, vaudeville, popular music, and movies, so that alongside radio's utopian discourse of uplift and education there existed for those concerned with cultural control a continuous dystopian fear of the popular, of those diverse and suspect cultural traditions and social groups whose access to the airwaves had begun with the amateurs and extended across the nation. Radio's commercial base gave an automatic entrée to just such elements, it was feared, and therefore the establishment of centralized institutions of control and responsibility became paramount. Occupying a central position in this set of tensions was the vast audience of women—always forming the majority of the radio and television audience—whose identification with disturbing concepts of the "mass" and vulgar popularism threatened to undermine radio's high-culture image, yet whose purchasing power provided the sine qua non of broadcasting economics.[41] Of course, commercialism retained its own objectives and exclusions, and the following chapters will trace not only the tension between official/high culture and commercial/popular pull, but also those tensions within radio's commercial discourse itself that promoted some aspects of popular culture and excluded others in the interests of advertising.

As part and parcel of this physical and cultural unification, it went almost without saying that linguistic unity would be one of broadcasting's main effects. Not only English, but proper, uninflected English, would become the national standard and norm—not a goal to be taken lightly amid the ethnic and regional diversity of the 1920s. Across many parts of the country, even among second- and third-generation immigrants, languages of the native countries continued to be spoken, at home and in church if not in school. The sudden access of the English language into the kitchens and living rooms of several-generation native but only marginally acculturated U.S. citizens would achieve a homogenizing effect rarely discussed but readily apparent.

However, if standard "announcers'" English provided a national ideal, it also worked to cast into cultural disrepute the colorful variety

not only of languages, but of accents and regional dialects whose pos-
sessors now found themselves to be "different"—and not only different, but not as good.[42] It could be argued that such a standard had always existed, in the universities, boardrooms, and country clubs of the
nation's cultural elite, and that radio's homogenization of accent simply made de facto norms more readily "knowable" by the public at
large—an exclusive knowledge becoming more widely available—yet
with expanded access came expanded expectations. Soon even widely
accepted accents, such as the elite southern, became unacceptable on
national network broadcasts. Speaking not only grammatically "correct" but also "nonaccented" English became a ticket into the middle
class for the sons and daughters (and even great-grandsons and great-
granddaughters) of immigrants; radio reinforced what local classroom
education could not.

Yet radio's unprecedented verbal flood did not leave the English language unscathed by the experience. A breezy, slang-filled style of speech
soon became the preferred radio mode, and networks and other bas-
tions of "correct English" fought a losing battle to preserve the finer
points of diction and pronunciation.[43] Local announcers and hosts
brought regional and personal variations to the mike; indeed, many
listeners spoke out strongly against attempts to install "pussy willow
English" as the official dialect:

> If a friend should talk to you in the stilted, unnatural sing-song of the
> broadcaster telling the folks where to go for somebody's soap you would
> end by throwing the nearest cake at him. There is a smug and utterly un-
> sincere familiarity, a servile condescension to the listener, which must be
> maddening to an American public that will not endure such talking in the
> family or in the shop.[44]

NBC might have been presumed to have learned its lesson as early as
1925, when the popular showman "Roxy," told by WEAF management to modify his casual, vernacular delivery to a more "dignified,"
"formal" style consistent with station image, received a deluge of mail
from fans objecting to his sudden stiffness and demanding their old
friend back. Hundreds of newspapers across the country carried the
story, even those much too distant to receive WEAF's signal. This clash
between the high-culture aspirations of many of broadcasting's early
outlets (even to the point of mandating that the unseen announcers
wear formal dress) and the informal, popular tendency preferred by

many in the audience would be repeated often as radio practices took shape. Not so stuffy as the highbrow written word, yet hewing to a standard well above and more unitary than the everyday, broadcast English helped to set a new popular norm across the country.

One broadcaster, later to become NBC's head of program production on the West Coast, addressing an audience of San Francisco police officers, explicitly linked radio's linguistic, cultural, and physical functions not only to Americanization but to restoration of social order:

> Curiously, little is said about the problems offered by the mixture of races included in the word "American." . . . In America no . . . homogeneity exists, or can be obtained, until the entire population has been taught to speak the same language, adopt the same customs, yield to the same laws, from childhood. Now, thanks to radio, the whole country is flooded with the English language spoken by master-elocutionists. American history, American laws, American social customs are the theme of countless radio broadcasters whose words are reaching millions of our people, shaping their lives toward common understanding of American principles, American standards of living. . . . Wholesale broadcasting coupled with restricted immigration can not fail eventually to unite the entire American people into closer communion than anything yet achieved in the history of our development.[45]

Another contemporary article predicted that "those groups which still cling to alien tongues will have English forced upon them, the more they listen to broadcasting; with the result that radio proves to be an important if unconscious Americanizing influence."[46]

Yet radio's efforts toward linguistic control masked a basic transgressive quality of the medium itself, one that posed a less obvious but even more dangerous threat to social hierarchy and order: its ability to transcend the visual. In a society based on visual cues, where appearance superseded almost every other social indicator,[47] radio's ability to escape visual overdetermination had the potential to set off a virtual riot of social signifiers—indeed, this is one of radio's most fascinating attributes. Adults played the roles of children and animals, two-hundred-pound women played romantic ingenues, and ninety-pound men played superheroes; whites frequently impersonated blacks, though rarely vice versa; and one of America's most popular entertainers was a wooden dummy. Women could masquerade as men and, much more often, men as women—and further, men could enter the home to entertain the woman of the house seductively over her morning coffee; women had the potential to enter the public sphere and assume the voice of authority, evading the customary physical and social barriers. How could one be sure a person belonged to his or her purported racial or ethnic group over the radio? How could class distinction be maintained without its usual context of visual cues?

Radio responded by obsessively rehearsing these distinctions, endlessly circulating and performing structured representations of ethnicity, race, gender, and other concentrated sites of social and cultural norms—all through language, dialect, and carefully selected aural context. Early radio seemed absorbed with the portrayal of "difference," of the exotic, from the *Cliquot Club Eskimoes* and the *A&P Gypsies* to the narrative development of *Amos 'n' Andy* and *The Goldbergs*. This was frequently accomplished by the use of distinct and stereotypical dialects and accents, carried over from the realm of vaudeville and the minstrel show. The prevalence of minstrel routines, characters, and dialect on early radio is frequently overlooked, and their use points to central sites of tension within U.S. culture, as the culturally undesirable was projected onto an easily identifiable, culturally devalued minority group.

Variety programs developed elaborate frameworks for incorporating "other" characters into their regularly repeating nucleus of performers, perhaps brought to their fullest flower by Fred Allen in "Allen's Alley"—populated by the likes of Mrs. Nussbaum, Ajax Cassidy, Senator Beauregard Claghorn, and Titus Moody. The flip side of this otherness was the rehearsing of the "norm," the typical American family, in such precursors of the television domestic sitcom as *Vic and Sade, One Man's Family*, and *The Aldrich Family*. In place of traditional class attributes, radio created its own caste of celebrities, drawing as well on the visually familiar ranks of Hollywood stars. The problem of "anchoring" the slippery and potentially trangressive signification of radio's aural signifiers to the set of intended and authorized meanings of networks and producers became increasingly central to network functions, giving rise to "continuity acceptance" and later "standards and practices" departments that helped to legitimate the networks' existence and functions.[48]

Institutional unity, it soon became apparent, had to be established if radio's dystopian potential—physical, cultural, linguistic—were to be held in check so that its utopian "nature" could be fulfilled. Until a comprehensive institutional structure could be developed, a state of experimentation and regional difference existed that allowed for competing definitions of radio's business and concerns, some of which were clearly perceived as transgressive. The importance of Chicago as a center of broadcast innovation points up the culturally homogenizing power of networks as structures stabilized in the late 1920s and early 1930s. Most of the program forms and many of the programs themselves soon to become the most popular on NBC and CBS originated not with the official broadcasting outlets of the major radio companies, usually located in New York, but in the newspaper- and department store-owned stations of Chicago's hectic commercial environment. As these programs found national sponsorship and a national audience over the networks, they were adapted to fit "higher," more stringent network standards, and standard formats emerged on which imitations and early forms of "spin-offs" could build. However, continuing sources of organizational tension, such as the rapidly developing dominance of advertising agencies in program production—in particular over daytime serial production, throughout broadcasting's history—also resisted network control and containment.

The institution of NBC in 1926 and CBS two years later effectively provided the technical, economic, and cultural unification envisioned in Anderson's model of the imagined nation, on which future legislation would rest—and further consolidate. It could be argued that the decisive factor leading to the defeat of educational or public control of radio occurred not in 1934, after the great Communications Act debates, but in the years from 1922 to 1926, as wired interconnection of stations gradually undermined radio's local base and made advertising support nearly inevitable. Certainly by 1934, as one active participant admitted, the "rugged individualism" of commercial competition had set the structures of private dominance past the point of alteration: "What individualism really means in matters of this sort is the practice of proceeding helter-skelter without any plan until an impossible situation has developed, and all sorts of vested interests have been created, and then trying to impose a plan retrospectively in face of innumerable technical and legal obstacles."[49] This is certainly true of the "American system" of commercial network broadcasting by 1934: a de facto and never officially agreed-upon industrial and cultural standard appeared firmly in place, where it would work to centralize and unify American cultural experience and identity as no other medium had ever attempted.

Physically, culturally, in a common language and through national semipublic institutions, radio spoke to, and about, a nation. Like Gertrude Berg—and with uncanny echoes of Benedict Anderson—one 1924 writer clearly envisioned the "Social Destiny of Radio":

> Look at a map of the United States, of Canada, of any country, and try to conjure up a picture of what radio broadcasting will eventually mean to the hundreds of little towns that are set down in type so small that it can hardly be read. How unrelated they seem! Then picture the tens of thousands of homes in the cities, the valleys, along the rivers, homes not noted at all on the map. These little towns, these unmarked homes in vast countries seem disconnected. It is only an idea that holds them together,—the idea that they form part of a territory called "our country." One home in Chicago might as well be in Zanzibar so far as another in Massachusets is concerned, were it not for this binding sense of nationality. If these little towns and villages so remote from one another, so nationally related and yet physically so unrelated, could be made to acquire a sense of intimacy, if they could be brought into direct contact with each other! . . . This is exactly what radio is bringing about.[50]

Yet the "idea" of America extended far beyond geography, as we have seen. What were the social conditions prompting this concern with unity and cohesion?

Creating Americans

Pierre Bourdieu demonstrates that cultural distinctions—such as those prompted by efforts to define early radio—result from a need to contain and moderate sites of social tension, establishing a hierarchy that promises to hold chaotic forces of difference and instability at bay. New social conditions always result from a complex interaction of forces, but occasionally a climactic or overwhelming historical event prompts change in a way that had not been envisioned or planned for, and that provokes a crisis in the capacity of existing power groups to manage.[51] One such phenomenon in early-twentieth-century American life was the sheer volume of the so-called new immigration that brought new bodies, new lives, and a new mix of old cultures to U.S. shores. This influx posed a severe challenge to the sense of national identity the young nation had struggled to develop, and in it can be found the roots of the concept of the "mass"—of the faceless, overwhelmingly numerous "other"—as it would be understood in U.S. culture. And from the beginning, it was in the sphere of mass *culture*, the problems and possibilities associated with the spread of new popular media directed at a mass audience, that Americans would find both the source and the possible solution to this socially troubling phenomenon.[52]

Though immigration and assimilation of primarily European cultures had been a fundamental fact of American life since the very beginning, there still existed until the early 1900s a concept of the "true" or ideal citizen that was in most respects modeled after the Anglo-Saxon:

> With the appearance of a democratic faith there also emerged the ideal American type figure in whom the faith would receive expression. The ideal American was imagined as being of British stock and English-speaking. He tended to be equalitarian in his social and political thinking and even more so in his immediate social relations. He was an individualist; ambitious in a material sense; optimistically devoted to *laissez faire* in economics and politics; fairly scrupulous in business but not possessed of a strong social conscience outside of his group. In private life he was Puritanical, idealizing his women and imposing fairly close social restraints upon them. . . . These were the qualities most prized by Americans. In professing allegiance to them they were forging another important social common denominator.[53]

Adherence to this ideal surely varied tremendously by group affiliation—African and Asian Americans, women, and political progressives may not have agreed on this standard—yet its prevalence in national thinking points to the limits of the assimilatory ideal conceived of as a two-way process. The mythicized American melting pot was expected to consume some types of ethnic and cultural dross completely, leaving the basic Anglo-Saxon metal burnished brighter.

The continued influx of Irish, especially the starved, illiterate, and desperate masses of potato famine Irish who packed ships' holds from 1840 through the 1880s, severely tested the much-vaunted ability of the United States to accommodate diverse backgrounds under its "democratic" system and philosophy. On top of this, the overturning of the country's most egregious contradiction of democratic principles, the enslavement of African Americans, after the Civil War rubbed philosophy against practice even harder, and brought these two most highly denigrated populations into direct conflict with each other, stimulating, among other effects, the minstrel tradition that would find such heavy representation on early radio.[54] Despite the problem that the Irish posed, the strategy of eliding the Anglo-Saxon ideal into its lowest common denominator of "white" or northwestern European worked to keep other, even more "different" groups, in particular newly freed African Americans, firmly at bay.

This definition of American identity at its most fundamental— American = "white"—was written into laws and clearly outlined in practices throughout the nineteenth century; indeed, it was marginal groups such as the Irish who found it necessary to fight the hardest for the supremacy of white European identity, as otherwise their own case for social equity would have appeared precarious.[55] Throughout U.S. history, the strategy of racial distinction has been used quite explicitly to contain unrest and minimize class, ethnic, and gender antagonisms.[56] As Michael R. Winston writes:

> A "foreign substance"—although one embedded in American life since 1619—that could "neither be assimilated nor thrown out," the Negro was nonetheless useful as a foil to the white "new Americans" in the making. As the new American nationality was forged after the Civil War from disparate immigrant groups, "whiteness" became a badge of "true Americanism." Obviously, Negroes, Indians, Chinese, Japanese, and other non-whites could not qualify, regardless of their legal status, length of residence, or cultural assimilation.[57]

This definition of "Americanness" had political and economic utility. David Brion Davis expands on this function, noting the displacement of class division onto race in the period before the Civil War: "During the colonial period, when black slaves worked alongside white indentured servants in Virginia's tobacco fields, lawmakers countered the threat of biracial rebellion by fostering a sense of white solidarity . . . [that] helped sustain the illusion of equality for American whites and immigrants."[58] A similar strategy proved effective in the labor disputes of the late nineteenth and early twentieth centuries, in which white immigrant workers' anger was directed away from management toward the even more desperate black strikebreakers imported to cross picket lines—a position the Irish had occupied just a few decades earlier. As American identity continued to define itself into the twentieth century, it was clearly and explicitly a white northern European identity, with the Irish ironically providing the test case that proved the rule and Asian, African, and Native Americans consigned to the realm of the unassimilable.

However, the tidal wave of "otherness" sweeping onto American shores between 1890 and 1921 threatened to swamp what tenuous social balance had been achieved. More than thirty million immigrants, mostly from southern and eastern Europe, left their homes for the new country during this thirty-year period, reaching a peak in 1907, when 1,285,349 new Americans disembarked. In some U.S. cities, notably Chicago, New York, and Cleveland, the proportion of first- and second-generation "new" immigrants alone—not counting those of northern European descent—amounted to more than a third of the population by 1920. In New York the percentage was almost half. The sheer volume of the new immigration, from countries thought to be backward and resistant to the American "northern European" democratic tradition, created increasing tension. Italians were particularly suspect, believed by some to be "just as bad as the Negroes"[59]—replacing the previously suspect group, the Irish. Earlier tolerance for continued ethnic traditions was felt to be no longer viable; the very definition of what it was to be an American seemed threatened and weakened.[60] Assimilation of this large and resistant lump in the body politic became a matter of some urgency. As one "liberal clergyman" put it: "If we are to have an American civilization we must assimilate the stream of newcomers. If we do not assimilate them they will adulterate us with an admixture of old-world morals."[61] Add to the foreign-born the number of Americans of foreign-born or mixed foreign and native parentage, and the proportion of the "white" population for whom the problems of assimilation were a personal as well as a social concern mounted to almost 35 percent by 1930 nationally, 50 percent in some major urban areas.[62]

World War I turned the fires of the melting pot up until, it was hoped, it would consume itself. The outbreak of ethnic suspicion and hatred directed against eastern European immigrants and any sign of German extraction worked to produce a rhetoric and demonstration of national unity unprecedented up to that point. As Frances Kellor writes, "Until the war, immigrants had not been called upon in a public manner to choose between the old and new countries," and indeed many had maintained close ties with relatives, business, and political connections overseas.[63] Historian Robert Wiebe describes the prewar United States as a "segmented society," whose social contract was based not on cultural unity but on the agreement to live separately, tolerating difference (within limits) as long as it did not interfere with individual enterprise or cross too-dangerous boundaries (such as race).[64] The war asserted American identity in a forceful and unified way, defining the lines of distinction that would be drawn and closing the door on the tolerance of diversity. The new immigrants would be admitted to the fight on America's behalf—enlisting in the army was one way, in fact, of attaining U.S. citizenship[65]—but on the condition that they abandon their separate ethnic identities and ties to the old country. No longer would segmented separatism be tolerated; a patriotic unity, common but strictly hierarchized, would be imposed. IQ tests were developed and administered to the U.S. army's mixed ranks specifically to support theories of racial hierarchy. Their results "proved" the deficiencies and weaker abilities of non-Nordic immigrants and those permanent "aliens," African Americans, in a new scientific institutionalization of America's segmented system of structured inequality.[66]

However, the very need for such tests demonstrated that the easy hegemony enjoyed in the previous century by the dominant upper-middle-class Anglo-Saxon moral universe was beginning to erode under pressure. Many historians have described the feelings of loss and imbalance that American upper middle classes (primarily Anglo-Saxon) suffered during the period of transition to modernity. T. J. Jackson Lears speaks of the sense of disorientation and loss of certainty in religious faith that led to the embrace of the therapeutic discourse of health and physical vigor.[67] Lynd and Lynd's *Middletown* shows a stable small-town society on the verge of change, and by the time of their second study, *Middletown Revisited*, this society was seriously demoralized by the cultural transition brought on by the community's industrialization and exposure to "other" elements from the wider world.[68] The 1920s, the decade during which radio received definition as a medium and a cultural force, showed an exacerbation of conflict that cut across class levels but adhered around the growing tension between "us" and "other"—what did "true" American identity consist of, and which groups held the "true" values? "The old Americans are getting a little panicky, and no wonder . . . America, Americans, and Americanism are being crowded out of America. It is inevitable that there should be silly forms of protest and rebellion. But the Ku Klux Klan and the hundred percenters are fundamentally right from the standpoint of an American unity and destiny."[69] Across the country, an upsurge in violent nativism sparked lynchings, house burnings, and an anti-Catholic drive of previously unheard-of proportions—"silly forms of protest" that killed hundreds and ruined the livelihoods of countless others as America faced up to the contradiction at its heart.

But what gave these teeming masses their ability to make old-time Americans "panicky" was not just their numbers but the new power conferred on them by the culture of consumption. Fueled by the rise of consumer product manufacturing and the enormous increase in advertising, the 1920s promised prosperity for everyone and a new American culture based on rising standards of material consumption. This emergent "culture of abundance" was tied closely to technologies of communication. According to Warren Susman:

> Any study of the culture of abundance begins with the obvious cultural consequences of the new communications. It is not simply that these inventions made abundance available to many and made possible increasingly effective distribution. Consciousness itself was altered. . . . New cultural forms previously unknown developed; those that continued were reshaped repeatedly. At the same time, no other culture expended so much of its energy and resources discussing and analyzing communication and its problems. That became a characteristic of the culture itself.[70]

In particular, these new technologies of communication reached out to the masses in a way that methods of earlier generations could not. Through mass distribution and advertising support, the new media oriented themselves to a broader segment of the U.S. public than ever before, evoking, as we have seen, both utopian visions of cultural community and fears of the erosion of cultural standards. A new industry, advertising, sprang up to recruit the newly arrived—whether physically or economically—into the burgeoning culture of consumption. Suddenly the empire of mass culture blossomed forth: an enormous outpouring of information and representations addressed explicitly to the mass, based on quantity distribution, seeking to cater to the "common" tastes and interests, exceeding previous systems of control based on education and possession of cultural resources. Tabloid newspapers, cheap novels, magazines such as Bernarr Macfadden's *True Confessions*, motion pictures, amusement parks, and vaudeville spoke both to and for a previously dispossessed group, which for all its diversity had one element in common: a lack of exposure to the system of cultural distinctions and shared values that had previously served a primarily white, Anglo-Saxon segment of society.[71]

The results of the IQ tests developed during the war were used to support the oft-quoted notion among advertisers and cultural critics that the "average American" has the mental level of a twelve- (or ten-, or thirteen-) year-old.[72] Roland Marchand charts advertising agencies' discovery of "the tabloid mind" in the early 1920s through the success of such advertising precepts as "Tell it to Sweeney . . . the Stuyvesants will understand." The masses had arrived, and whether the captains of consciousness recognized it or not, they were largely foreign-born or second-generation immigrants for whom advertising and the new mass media became their first and primary introduction to "mainstream" American culture and mores.[73]

Many historians have commented on the role that the burgeoning movie industry played in the lives of immigrants, and in turn the impact this initial audience had on the movies themselves (not least in the origins of most of its influential early figures).[74] Much less attention has been given to radio's similar function in the next two decades, no doubt influenced by the middle-class representations of the radio amateur that dominated the press. However, Lizabeth Cohen provides ample evidence that working-class immigrants in Chicago participated actively in the radio craze of the 1920s, building sets and listening in, often in clubs or groups.[75] Daniel Czitrom points out the interesting statistic that by 1930, "children of immigrants, particularly in cities, were more likely to own radios than any other group."[76] According to figures from the 1930 census, radio ownership among children from foreign-born or mixed-parentage families ranked at 57.3 percent nationwide, with the figure rising to 62.8 percent in the cities (compared to 39.9 and 53.2 percent, respectively, for native-born families). As Czitrom concludes, "These entertainments, and radio in general, seem to have played a significant mediating role for certain audiences. . . . The historical relation between 'media mindedness' and 'cultural otherness' is still largely unexplored, beyond a facile notion of 'Americanization.'"[77]

One key area in which "cultural otherness" and popular media intersected was in the minstrel or "blackface" tradition. From its roots in antebellum street entertainment to its growing popularity in road shows and vaudeville, to its amazing persistence on radio into the 1940s, blackface "humor" in many ways serves as the archetypal example of popular culture's mediations of cultural difference in a divided and ethnically stratified society. It is as characteristic of popular entertainment in the 1920s and 1930s as was the western in the 1950s and 1960s, and probably for many of the same reasons.

David Roediger traces the function of the minstrel tradition in the formation of the American working class as a primary mechanism for defining and enforcing "whiteness," both before and after the Civil War. If "whiteness" was the basic requirement for American identity, those most desperately in need of the inclusion this identity offered were those for whom it was most uncertain. And as Roediger points out, drawing on nineteenth-century descriptions of Irish attributes, "It was by no means clear that the Irish were white"[78]—a fate also awaiting the coming waves of Italians and eastern Europeans in the twentieth century. In order to challenge notions of Anglo-Saxon superiority that explicitly excluded those of the Celtic "race," the Irish in the United States very quickly found it expedient to substitute the concept of "a new and improved 'American race' of white men" in its place. This strategy both reinforced the validity of racial division and redrew its boundaries; as Roediger quotes Dale T. Knobel, "Irish Americans were sure to be enthusiastic about any treatment of American nationality that stressed the relevance of 'race' while putting the Irish safely within the Anglo-Celtic racial majority," despite the symbolic alliance that this forged with the despised British.[79]

The conventions of the minstrel show provided the ideal format for such reinforcement of racial thinking while enumerating and projecting all the undesirable traits associated with nonwhiteness (and therefore non-Americanness) onto an even less powerful—but highly visible—group. "Blacking up"—literally, smearing on burnt cork or other makeup, taking on a dialect and certain characterizations, such as "Jim Crow" and "Zip Coon," that purported to depict "black" traits, and combining music and comic "patter" that often commented on events of the day—allowed performers and audiences alike a freedom to behave excessively, to break the bonds of restrictive definitions of self, to violate norms and American customs while attributing those traits to "blacks," to the "nonwhite other." This opportunity was particularly attractive to those on the bottom of the "white" racial hierarchy. Even before the Civil War, but especially after, the minstrel tradition shows heavy Irish influence, from the high number of Irish performers to the carryover of Irish folk music and the influence of "Irish low-comedy types from the British stage" in the formation of minstrel characters.[80] By the turn of the century the popularity of minstrel shows, within a vaudeville tradition of ethnic humor of other types, would extend to the new immigrants equally in need of its mediating uses. But the primary function of blackface minstrelsy in conjunction with vaudeville's ethnic humor seems to have been the confirmation of a transethnic white identity at the expense of those defined as America's main "other," and by implication any group not "racially" white.

The minstrel figure thus could be used to represent a set of values not associated with, or devalued by, progressive white Americanism. According to Toni Morrison, racial discourse has been central to the project of American literature since its beginning. In her recent critical work *Playing in the Dark*, Morrison offers a re-vision of American literary endeavor in which the "Africanist presence"—that is, the presence of the racial "other," of characters and motifs designated as "black" in the works of white writers—acts as "one of the most furtively impinging forces on the country's literature."[81] In a literature whose primary task was the definition of "a new white man," the impinging force of a nonwhite, nonfree, nondemocratically equal presence provided at once the essential contradiction and the necessary contrast:

> Black slavery enriched the country's creative possibilities. For in that construction of blackness *and* enslavement could be found not only the not-free but also, with the dramatic polarity created by skin color, *the projection of the not-me* [emphasis added]. The result was a playground for the imagination. What rose up out of collective needs to allay internal fears and to rationalize external exploitation was an American Africanism—a fabricated brew of darkness, otherness, alarm, and desire that is uniquely American.[82]

Writers from Cather to Twain to Hemingway took on this deep social and discursive disjunction as a central theme, employing the Africanist persona "to articulate and act out the forbidden in American culture."[83] The fact that literary criticism has ignored this presence so resoundingly is, according to Morrison, a mark of its profound disquieting force. George Lipsitz traces the connection of the minstrel figure with "the natural self at odds with the normative self of industrial culture";[84] others stress its highly derogatory use of "black" "female" characters (always performed by white males) to assert the masculinity of working-class culture.[85] It is not surprising, then, that advertising and the commercial media relied so frequently on "black" images drawn from minstrelsy, usually in settings that associated "mammy" and blackface figures with tradition and nostalgia for a bygone way of life in which "others" labored to provide those things that modern "white" consumers could now purchase in a box. Marchand notes that in magazine advertising of the 1920s and 1930s, "Blacks never appeared as consumers, or as fellow workers with whites, or as skilled workers. Primarily, they functioned as symbols of the capacity of the leading lady and leading man to command a variety of personal services."[86] Like Aunt Jemima, Rastus the Cream of Wheat chef, and eventually Amos and Andy, these figures mediated the conflict between traditional and consumer society through the realignment and reinforcement of racial definitions. Racial discriminations sold products—perhaps particularly well to those with the most immediate stake in maintaining them.[87]

And, fittingly, it was radio that brought the minstrel show and advertising most firmly into conjunction. In the 1920s and 1930s radio employed the figure of the blackface minstrel more consistently than any other one ethnic character, in a multiplicity of settings, from variety shows to daytime cooking programs, to children's shows, and of course the most prominent comedy serial of radio's first two decades, Amos 'n' Andy. Clearly, radio's role as an easily accessible mass medium, tied from the beginning to definitions of national identity, made it a "natural" place for mediations of values through racial distinctions to play themselves out—especially when those distinctions so well served the interests of advertisers.

But there was one more set of key discriminations necessary in this mix of mass consumption and national identity. As advertisers discovered in the years before World War I, the primary consumers, the "household purchasing agents" for up to 85 percent of the new consumer goods on the market, were members of that other underclass, women. With the attainment of suffrage in 1920, women took a giant step toward full inclusion in the definition of public citizen—though outright discrimination in hiring, wages, and treatment under the law continued to be enforced until the passage of civil rights legislation in the 1960s. It is fascinating to note, then, that the next ten years saw the development of the medium that would do more than any other to move public life into the private sphere—as radio moved into the living room, so too did many aspects of politics, leisure, and civic participation. Increasingly, radio provided substitutes for venues that remained closed to women, such as barrooms, political halls, juries, educational institutions, most occupations, clubs, labor unions, professional organizations, and the playing fields of sports.

As the public sphere became privatized, it did so through a medium that would take on the sale of consumer goods to women as its main economic function. This conflict, between radio's role in the "masculine" public sphere and its feminized commercial base, would provide a fundamental underlying tension that program forms, audiences, and appropriate uses of the new medium in general would have to negotiate. Would women be allowed on the air? In what capacity? What would they be allowed to say, or to hear? And what to do with the fact that this immense semipublic institution, embodying so many of the the utopian hopes and fears of a changing society, would be addressing primarily . . . housewives?

Within the context of these expectations, fears, and assumptions, the dynamic evolution of the forms and structures of radio broadcasting from 1922 through the 1940s, culminating in the highly self-conscious nation formation of the Second World War, becomes central to an understanding of our cultural definitions of norm and difference, of "us" and "other," of ourselves as "Americans," particularly as these definitions affect our understanding of race, ethnicity, gender, and public cultural authority—some of the major fronts on which the conflict for national unity played itself out. As the following chapters will show, the primarily female audience and address of radio—along with the many female radio innovators whose accomplishments are usually left out of standard histories—created a medium tailored to feminine concerns (as defined by broadcasters), reflecting and working to define the gender role conflicts facing women and men during these highly formative postsuffrage decades. Within this overall tension, racial and ethnic representation played a particularly crucial role across radio genres, reshaping and erasing some lines of cultural identity even as they reinforced others. The function of representations of African Americans in particular, serving as our nation's primary "projection of the not-me" (to use Toni Morrison's phrase), will be analyzed as far more central to the overall discourse created by broadcasting than standard histories, through omission, have implied. And underlying all of these distinctions was radio's conflicting dual function of upholding cultural standards while selling goods to the public, creating the tension between official and popular culture still endemic to our current debates over television.

► TWO

How Far Can You Hear?

In 1920, radio broadcasting did not even have a name. By 1922, the following forecast could be made:

> So we may begin to picture for ourselves what radio will mean in our homes in the years to come. We shall all have receiving sets—there is little doubt of that. We shall come down in the morning to hear the newspaper headlines read while we eat. A little later, perhaps, a department store will have bargains of interest to announce—sugar-coating the advertisement with some good entertainment, so that we will not be tempted to turn our machines off. At lunch time, the chef of a famous hotel may suggest a tasty and economical menu. In the afternoon there may be a matinee; and at six or seven, when the boys and girls have had their supper and are ready for bed, someone like Thornton Burgess may lift the transmitter in his home and broadcast a Bed-Time Story to a million youngsters all over the land.[1]

These predictions, made by soon-to-be-legendary advertising man Bruce Barton in the *American Magazine* ("more than 1,750,000 circulation"), drew on some established precedents and imagined others. Even before the Wartime Communications Act had removed them from the air in 1917, a rapidly growing community of radio telegraphy amateurs had begun to venture into voice transmission. Once wartime restrictions were lifted in September 1919, amateurs returned to the air with a vengeance, now reinforced with both training and improved technology provided by (and sometimes pilfered from) the military. In 1920 the first regularly broadcasting stations went on the air, ready-built sets became available and expanded radio's audience, and a standard of popular entertainment began to emerge. During the period from 1920 to 1924, patterns and practices were set that would dominate early broadcasting—the same period that saw the American publication of the spurious anti-Semitic *Protocols of the Elders of Zion*, the spread of the Ku Klux Klan into the Midwest, and the passage of the Immigration Act of 1924, which one writer has termed "the Nordic victory."[2] To assume that these two sets of phenomena were hermetically sealed off from each other requires a greater effort at explanation than the opposite assumption. This chapter will explore the relationship of developing broadcasting practices to efforts to control America's rising tide of "difference."

The first attempts at broadcasting arose from a milieu that purported to view the social tensions discussed in chapter 1 as very distant indeed—the rarefied atmosphere of scientific experimentation. Many accounts describe the efforts of pioneers such as Reginald Fessenden, Lee DeForest, and Frank Conrad in developing the transmission of voice and music through the air—referred to as "wireless telephony," as opposed to "wireless telegraphy," the transmission of information through the Morse code of dots and dashes.[3] However, this early phase shows some interesting precedents for radio use. As early as 1913, James Gordon Bennett, publisher of the *New York Herald*, installed a wireless station on New York's Battery in order to provide a news and weather service to ships in the harbor—and, not incidentally, to promote his paper:

> James Gordon Bennett, always seeking publicity for his *New York Herald*, had a wireless station of his own at the Battery in New York City. At 4:15 every morning it would broadcast for the benefit of ships a digest of the day's news, as well as weather reports and probabilities for Sandy Hook and thereabouts. Ship captains came to depend on this feature, and if their Marconi operators did not receive it, gave them orders to do it. This was a point scored for the *Herald*.[4]

Broadcasting weather and news bulletins to midwestern farmers developed as another viable use for radio telegraphy. Both the University of North Dakota and Nebraska Wesleyan University began farm services in 1914, at first to a very limited number of trained Morse code receivers who would circulate the information through other means in their communities. At the University of Wisconsin, Professor Earle M. Terry and his assistants began in 1915 to provide daily news, weather, and crop reports to those in their area.[5] One large group of participants, the amateur wireless operators whose important role will be discussed below, also sent out the occasional "program" from their club meetings, which "usually consisted of an article of some electrical or telegraphic interest," as much to test their members' code-receiving abilities as for the information itself.[6] But the primary use of wireless telegraphy for person-to-person or point-to-point communications made these examples of "broadcasting" rare. Highly restricted as to audience, and limited to coded information, wireless telegraphy led ir-resistibly to the refinements that would allow real voices and music to find a place in the "ether." Early decisions regarding whose voices, saying what, and even what kind of music would make up these initial broadcasts form the first platform on which definitions of radio's cultural role would be built.

These definitions can be seen in the event that has been billed as the "first radio broadcast in the world," an experiment conducted by Reginald Fessenden from Brant Rock in Marshfield, Massachusetts, on Christmas Eve 1906. Fessenden, a former chemist in Thomas A. Edison's laboratories, and subsequently a professor of electrical engineering at Purdue and the University of Pennsylvania, built "two experimental radiophone stations" for the National Electrical Signaling Company, one in Scotland, the other on the coast of Massachusetts. Having tested the system with telegraphic communication, by late December Fessenden was ready to try voice transmission. Staging the event in a way that would become typical of radio entrepreneurship, Fessenden instructed his operators to notify "all ships at sea" by wireless about the planned broadcast on Christmas Eve. Radio's first audience, shipboard "Marconi" operators, stood by. His choice of material—at this point completely unprecedented, though limited by circumstance—remains eerily reminiscent of what would come to dominate radio in the 1920s:

> The program on Christmas Eve was as follows: first a short speech by me saying what we were going to do, then some phonograph music—the music on the phonograph being Handel's "Largo." Then came a violin solo by me, being a composition of Gounod called "O, Holy Night" and ending with the words, "Adore and be still," of which I sang the verse, in addition to playing on the violin, though the singing of course was not very good. Then came the Bible text, "Glory to God in the highest and on earth peace to men of good will." Finally we wound up by wishing them a Merry Christmas and then saying that we proposed to broadcast again New Year's Eve.[7]

An announcer, "quality" music, amateur performance, the Christian religion, and a little self-promotion—a foretaste of things to come, though perhaps it remains one of the few examples of the vocalist accompanying himself on the violin.

Other very early broadcasters included Charles Herrold, known as "Doc," who used radio to further his electrical experimentation and also to promote his San Jose electrical trade school. According to one report, Herrold tapped into the streetcar overhead lines to power his transmitter, and broadcast a mixture of music and advertising to amateurs in the area.[8] His wife later recalled that one of their earliest experiments consisted of transmitting the cries of their newborn son to the community of amateurs as a new kind of birth announcement.[9] Another, far more important innovator, Lee DeForest, with his electrical engineering-trained wife, Nora Stanton Blatch (granddaughter of Elizabeth Cady Stanton), developed the concept of radio as entertainment in his tests beginning in 1907. DeForest in his public statements envisioned radio as a means of bringing culture and entertainment to a broad audience, though the audience his experiments were immediately concerned with addressing consisted of potential investors—thus providing an early example of radio's "uplift" potential being used to attract an elite decision-making group, through established avenues of publicity, while evoking a mass audience in need of "improvement" further down the road.

Though frequently in financial difficulties, DeForest belonged to the educated middle class. His father was president of Talledega College, a segregated Alabama school for African Americans, and thus both "high-culture" values and immediate experience with social distinctions based on race played a large role in his conceptual background. The transmission of opera particularly interested DeForest, and he featured opera recordings in his 1908 transmission from the Eiffel Tower in Paris, designed to attract publicity and investors. In 1910 he experimented with what surely must have been the first live broadcast of opera, from the roof of the Metropolitan in New York—although with disappointing results. Though DeForest also predicted other uses for radio, such as news, advertising, and different types of musical entertainment, his decision to focus on opera in his initial fund-raising demonstrations points to the utility of "high-culture" values in radio's early development—and the willingness of entrepreneurs to exploit them for all they were worth. Interestingly, a forecast of the contested status of women in early broadcasting can be seen in the experience of Nora Blatch DeForest, a trained electrical engineer who assisted DeForest in his early work. Though DeForest supported female suffrage (and used his wife's connections and a 1908 speech that she broadcast on the topic to attract suffragist investment), his insistence on the birth of their child in 1909 that his wife give up her work and devote herself solely to motherhood caused the end of their productive association—and their marriage. Nora Blatch became the first—but not the last—woman to meet resistance in attempting to take an active role in broadcasting.[10]

"Little Boys in Short Trousers"

Despite many setbacks in achieving financial stability and recognition for his broadcasting plans (including frequent charges of fraud), De-Forest's vision of the future of radio remains one of the clearest and most prescient. This may well have stemmed from his close involvement with the most active and aware group of early radio users in the United States, the amateurs—an alliance he shared with another key innovator, Frank Conrad. The importance of amateurs in the development of American radio can hardly be overstated, though most accounts dismiss the 1910s and early 1920s, a period of primarily amateur activity, as irrelevant to radio's eventual uses. It is true that the amateurs—by 1915 highly organized into several nationwide leagues or clubs—proposed a very different scheme for radio from that eventually adopted, but as Susan Douglas amply demonstrates, they had considerable influence on the "social construction" of radio, including such concrete elements as technology and regulation. In the years preceding and immediately following World War I, theirs were the dominant voices on the air, and theirs the dominant role in developing uses and applications for this new medium.

Of course, the amateurs themselves were also subject to social construction. Douglas discusses their discursive positioning as mediators of masculinity in the age of technology. In a society redefining manhood less in terms of physical strength and more in terms of scientific "know-how" and manipulation of technology, the amateurs became America's "boy heroes," rescuing ships at sea, supporting America's war effort, demonstrating scientific ingenuity and skill. However, at other times their activities could be cast in a more negative light; like today's computer hackers, these "boys" could also disrupt official transmissions, spread false information, and create havoc and disharmony in the airwaves. These constructions could be used to support different agendas, but perhaps one that needs to be examined is the one that is most taken for granted: that these were "young, white middle class boys and men."[11] Though no doubt this group constituted the single largest segment, evidence exists to show that both female and working-class amateurs existed (frequently immigrant and/or black, thus shading even the "white" into gray areas), the latter in large numbers.[12] Their exclusion from the dominant representation points to the need to "control" this phenomenon discursively in a way that least threatened established social hierarchies. Radio communication, by means of this construction and not by accurate reflection of real conditions, became understood as "naturally" the province of white middle-class boys.

Even the concept "boys" could be used strategically: reflecting on a period in which amateur organizations, run by men of mature years, represented a highly vocal and organized group heavily involved in lobbying for their interests at radio regulation conferences (and opposed to the dominant commercial interests), Herbert Hoover recollected the activities of "the small boys in radio" who "had established an association of radio amateurs with whom we dealt constantly":

> One day I asked them how they were going to deal with enforcing the assignments of their wave band to prevent interference. The president of the association said, "Well, I don't think you'd like to know what we do."
> "Oh yes," I said, "I would."
> He said, "Well, we just take the fellow out and beat him up."[13]

Hoover must have been referring here either to Hugo Gernsback, head of the Radio League of America, or to Hiram Percy Maxim, founder and longtime president of the American Radio Relay League (ARRL), both men well into middle age and hardly apt to behave in the "boyish" manner described. Casting the legitimate demands of the amateurs in terms of the disorderly actions of "small boys" helped to make the "mature" supervision of radio by responsible corporations seem all the more desirable.[14]

These discursive positionings would play a forceful role in the development of radio regulation, casting into rhetorical disrepute the efforts of amateurs to preserve a model of broadcasting that allowed relatively free access to the spectrum and a much more even balance of power between those who would transmit—actually possess the power to speak over this new medium—and those who would receive. Consensus history points to the "chaos" caused in the limited bandwidths available to the amateurs, as hundreds crowded on and signals overlapped, as the primary argument for the establishment of a frequency assignment structure that favored larger institutional and commercial broadcasters. Actually, the amateurs lobbied hard for an organized assignment system that still would have preserved a more "democratic" model of access to the air. It was the emergent commercial interests themselves that complained the most, violated existing arrangements the most frequently, and stood to benefit the most from a system that would regularize the frequency situation. The history of commercial broadcasting is replete with stories of stations that refused to comply with shared time and restricted frequency guidelines, mainly because they, unlike the amateurs, could not afford to: in order to make their sometimes sizable investments in broadcasting pay off, they had to obtain, through federal intervention, a regular, constant presence with suitable power in the air to attract audiences of sufficient size and consistency. Band jumping, power blasting, and outright frequency grabbing were far more characteristic of early commercial broadcasting in the United States than of amateur broadcasting (though sometimes the distinction between the two groups was not altogether clear). Amateurs, less concerned with profit than with communication and access, attempted to impress regulators and the public with their cooperation and discipline. Finding their efforts constructed as the back-alley fistfights of "small boys" proved dispiriting indeed, and led to the eventual defeat of the participatory amateur model of radio use.

The amateurs were aware of the danger of this nomenclature, and of the fact that they were being blamed for spectrum conditions not of their making. QST, the journal of the ARRL, editorialized in 1921: "Honestly, this business of inaccurate newspaper reports of radio matters is getting to be more than a joke—it's now amounting to a crime."[15] Particularly offensive were reports that portrayed the amateurs as "a flock of little boys in short trousers."[16] By April 1922 this trend had become alarming enough that Paul Godley, head of an ARRL delegation to the first radio conference, "called the attention of the Secretary [of Commerce, Herbert Hoover] to the publicity that in recent months has appeared in the press characterizing the amateur repeatedly as 'The American small boy' and saying that he must be curbed because he was interfering with everything, etc."[17] Though ARRL members might refute these claims of irresponsible interference in the pages of their own journal—complaining that the public, led by the press, was "laying the blame for everything that interfered with their concerts on the heads of us poor amateurs"[18] and stating with exasperated emphasis, "The trouble lies with the *commercial traffic . . .* we *know* that the interference we amateurs are causing during quiet hours is practically zero"[19]—the wireless organizations could not make much headway against the publicity efforts mounted by commercial interests. By 1924, leaders of the ARRL had become cynically resigned to their disempowerment in the ether:

> But say, isn't it funny how the cupidity of commercial interests is always being attracted by amateur development? The history of amateur radio in this country has largely been one of guarding our cherished right to existence from the designs of somebody who would like to have something of ours, generally because they think they can make some money out of it. Ho, hum.[20]

As we shall see, radio amateurs established most of the pioneering uses of this new medium, which commercial organizations would later exploit to the extent of pushing the amateurs to the margins of the field they had once dominated.

Voices in the Ether

Between 1913 and 1915, the reception of voice and music on the air became more and more common. Interrupted by the war, during which time the government actively recruited and trained young men and women in radio communications, the amateurs returned as soon as restrictions were eased in 1919, with much-improved technology. Membership in the amateur organizations soared, and the publications serving them—*QST*, established in 1915 by the ARRL, later joined by *Radio Broadcast, Wireless World,* and others—increasingly reported on "programs" sent out by their members with the intention of entertaining fellow enthusiasts. In October 1920, the Union College Radio Club of Schenectady, New York, wrote the editor of *QST* to request publicity for its "radio concert every Thursday evening from 8:00–8:30 and from 9:00–9:30," open to all, on "350 meters, signing 2ADD." In September 1921, the magazine reported on the recent broadcast of the returns of the Carpentier-Dempsey fight by the National Amateur Wireless Association, a group supported by "Radio Corporation interests," reported by Major J. Andrew White from ringside via telephone and rebroadcast to a relay network of amateurs across the country.[21]

Though the majority of articles in these journals focused on technical matters for the set builder, a recurring column in *QST* called "With the Radiophone Folks" began in December 1921 to report on broadcasts picked up from around the country. The debut article dedicated itself to "that constantly increasing army of Citizen Wireless amateurs who are primarily interested in the reception of radiophone broadcasts" and reported on activities at station 6XG of San Francisco, owned by the Leo J. Meybert Co. This performance of operatic selections sung by "stars of the Scotti company" created quite a stir: "The entire Pacific slope was hushed for this performance. In many cities there were parties of up to fifty listening at a single station, and it is conservatively estimated that at least eight thousand people heard it."[22] Other programs consisted of political speeches put out by the Westinghouse station in Pittsburgh, a piano recital from the American Radio and Research Corporation station in Medford Hillside, Massachusetts, and a program guide showing "concerts," recitals, sermons, and various informational reports from a total of seven stations. Later columns profiled the Westinghouse stations, especially WJZ, and reported on experimental broadcasts from the Marconi Company, General Electric's new station WGY in Schenectady, and most of the other novice "radio telephone" stations beginning to broadcast regularly.[23] These reports demonstrate that by early 1922 purely amateur programs had begun to compete with those of commercial interests. Though *QST* continued to give these commercial efforts polite attention, by 1923 relations between commercial interests and amateurs had soured to the extent that the magazine discontinued taking notice of station broadcasts and renewed its focus on purely amateur activity. This distancing had regulatory roots, as we shall see.

What was broadcast by these amateur "impressarios"? Unfortunately, few records exist because few were kept. Not until 1922 did the mainstream press turn its attention to radio, and by then precedents set by early stations such as KDKA and WJZ had come to dominate public perceptions. However, the practices of Frank Conrad, until 1921 just another amateur transmitting from a garage with the call letters 8XK (though also employed as an electrical engineer at Westinghouse), combined with reflections of these broadcasts in the stated concerns of regulators, may be representative.

The primary focus of amateur transmission and reception had all along been on reception of distant stations, often referred to as "DXing" and compared to "fishing" in the ether. One of the most popular columns in *QST* was called "How Far Can You Hear?" and was devoted to reports of distant station reception. Amateurs were encouraged to keep logs of distant reception that could be verified later, with details of weather conditions, equipment configurations, and geographic coordinates. Therefore, most transmitter operators simply talked—repeating their call letters, locations, and other relevant information, often about the type of apparatus they were using and how they had it configured, then sitting back and waiting for others to acknowledge their transmissions. This could get tiresome, and before long many operators were drawing on components of Fessenden's first broadcast, of their own accord: playing instruments or inviting friends in to do so, airing phonograph recordings, and indulging in "chatter" with various guests on the air, often members of a club. Frank Conrad meantime was doing the same from his garage at East End and Penn Avenues in Wilkinsburg, a suburb of Pittsburgh, attended by an increasing number of amateurs who would frequently call Conrad wanting to know when the next broadcast would be. According to S. M. Kintner, later head of Westinghouse and one of Conrad's early colleagues:

> Finally these amateurs called up Conrad on the telephone so frequently and at such inconvenient times that he established regular times when he would operate his station. This generally was Wednesday and Saturday nights. The information regarding these concerts of Conrad's was gradually passed by word of mouth until quite a number knew of it.[24]

These regular broadcasts, which apparently began in the late spring or early summer of 1920, were two hours long and consisted mainly of the playing of phonograph records, leading to the second major innovation that would prove a lasting one for radio:

> These broadcasts soon exhausted Dr. Conrad's supply of records, and the Hamilton Music Store in Wilkinsburg offered a continuing supply of records if he would announce that the records could be purchased at the Hamilton store. Dr. Conrad agreed and thus gave the world its first radio advertiser—who promptly found that records played on the air sold better than others.[25]

But the commercial interests of a record store owner in Wilkinsburg, Pennsylvania, were not yet sufficient motivation to launch an industry. That necessary step, according to well-known legend, occurred when a Pittsburgh department store, the Joseph Horne Company, hypothesizing that Conrad's broadcasts could be used to promote the sale of radio receivers and components, began to advertise in the Pittsburgh *Sun*. These ads were spotted by Westinghouse Vice President H. P. Davis—Kintner gives us a date, September 29, 1920—who the next day called a meeting of his "radio cabinet," consisting of Conrad, Kintner, and two others:

> He told of reading the Horne advertisement and made the suggestion that the Westinghouse Electric and Manufacturing Company erect a station at East Pittsburgh and operate it every night on an advertised program, so that people would acquire the habit of listening to it just as they do of reading a newspaper. He said, "If there is sufficient interest to justify a department store in advertising radio sets for sale on an uncertain plan of permanence, I believe there would be a sufficient interest to justify the expense of rendering a regular service—looking to the sale of sets and the advertising of the Westinghouse Company for our returns."[26]

A new transmitting facility was built at the Westinghouse plant in East Pittsburgh, with the call letters 8ZZ; this would eventually receive the eighth official broadcasting license issued in the United States on November 7, 1921, to become KDKA. Westinghouse embarked on something of a station-building binge in 1920–21, opening up 1XAE in Springfield, Massachusetts (where the receiving sets would be built), later licensed as WBZ; 2XAI, later WJZ, in Newark, New Jersey; and 9XY, later KYW, in Chicago as well as the Pittsburgh site.

Categories and Distinctions

KDKA, along with the twenty-five stations licensed in 1921 and the more than six hundred stations that followed them in 1922, fit into only one category of those on the air during this period, described by the U.S. Department of Commerce as "authorized to transmit programming consisting of market or weather reports, music, concerts and lectures for direct reception by the general public."[27] These stations existed alongside the hundreds of amateur and experimental stations, many still transmitting in code at least part of the time, and it was by no means clear that the general entertainment stations would dominate broadcasting at this point. The earliest stations on the air showed a mixture of owners and purposes, with the largest number by 1923 being owned by "radio and electric manufacturers and dealers," the next largest in the hands of newspapers and other publishers, followed by educational institutions, department stores, and other retail operations.[28] At least one station was operated by a commercial laundry—to what end, it is hard to say from existing records—and a satisfying, though apparently short-lived, success was enjoyed by the Nushawg Poultry Farm in New Lebanon, Ohio, which combined "information on hog feeding, dairy feeding, and poultry culture" along with "talks on education, art, religion, and commerce." Testifying to the success of this program, W. N. Nushawg, poultry farmer and station operator, enthused: "Prior to the time we installed our outfit our farm was just about unknown. . . . Within the first three months we had over 4,000 inquiries about our products. . . . The farmer has been put in touch with cultural forces which he appreciates, but seldom encounters. And he is grateful for our service."[29]

However, despite somewhat diverse ownership and unclear purposes, already by 1922 some emerging practices can be seen, reminiscent not only of Fessenden's 1906 broadcast but of Bruce Barton's predictions. First of all, an important discrimination was made—significantly, on January 1, 1922, the very dawn of the broadcasting age—disbarring amateurs from the practice they had pioneered, providing recorded entertainments:

> A number of amateur stations and other stations were beginning to broadcast phonograph records which had no real value as entertainment or instruction and which threatened to so seriously interfere with the higher classes of service that it was considered necessary to stop broadcasting by amateur stations until some plan can be arranged which will allow amateurs to do work of this kind, if it can be shown to be of value, on a wavelength just below or just above 200 meters (1499 kHz).[30]

We can see in the use of such terms as "real value," "higher classes," and "threatened" that a hierarchy was being established, in this instance by David B. Carson, commissioner of navigation for the Department of Commerce, under whose aegis radio at that time fell. Certain uses had come to be seen as "higher" than others, as possessed of more intrinsic "value," and a "threat" to their hegemony was perceived as coming from the amateurs, here constructed as an "other." Later this restriction was confined to the playing of "phonograph records, which are not enjoyed by the public but at times becomes [sic] annoying." Given that in fact the public avidly enjoyed phonograph records, as witnessed by the very healthy phonograph and recording industry, this description must be attributed either to distinctions made about the nature of the public (those who were annoyed constituting a different and superior class to those who played and enjoyed recordings) and/or to the nature of the content of these records (some contents being more equal than others). Evidence exists to show that it was the suspicious nature of "jazz" that contributed to this definition. Not only "Mother Legion" abominated jazz.

Voodoo and Delirium Tremens

As Susan Douglas points out, underlying much of the discussion of radio's content was "a set of basic, class-bound assumptions about who should be allowed to exert cultural authority in the ether."[31] These assumptions—not just class but also race bound—directly conflicted with conditions prevalent in the burgeoning recording industry, in which "because of the nature of records and the ways in which they were distributed, record-makers could still cater profitably to minority tastes,"[32] with far less pressure to conform to uniform cultural standards than other media experienced. The rise of "race records," in particular, brought a fomerly isolated and culturally suspect form of music out of the jazz clubs and night spots of St. Louis, Chicago's South Side, Harlem, and the nation's segregated "Darktowns" to a wider public in the privacy of their homes. Neil Leonard reports that "in 1921 over 100,000,000 records were manufactured and Americans spent more money for them than for any other form of recreation. . . . The vast majority of these were popular records (mostly jazz and commercial jazz)."[33] Though by the late 1920s what Leonard refers to as "commercial jazz" dominated the airwaves—big-band jazz performed by white musicians and bandleaders playing a "cleaned up," tame, and popularized version of the original—in the early 1920s jazz was still new and strange to many, and close to its roots in African American culture.

Jazz was greeted with disdain and dark suspicion by the guardians of culture, who objected especially to its connection with the racial "other." "Mezz" Mezzrow, an early Chicago jazzman, put it bluntly, "Our music was called 'nigger music' and 'whorehouse music' and 'nice' people turned up their noses at it."[34] As early as 1917, the *Literary Digest* condensed a report from the New York *Sun* by vaudeville writer Walter Kingley, on this "strange" new word that had entered the American vocabulary:

> In the old plantation days, when the slaves were having one of their rare holidays and the fun languished, some West-Coast African would cry

out, "Jaz her up," and this would be the cue for fast and furious fun. No doubt the witch-doctors and medicine-men on the Kongo used the same term at those jungle "parties" when the tomtoms throbbed and the sturdy warriors gave their pep an added kick with rich brew of Yohimbin bark. . . . Jazz music is the delerium tremens of syncopation.[35]

The writer goes on to link the "discovery" (by white America) of jazz specifically to recording technology. According to his story, a few "dolly girls" who had been touring in a stage show in Cuba told Ziegfeld about this new kind of "funny . . . daffy-dinge music" they had heard there, which had "put little dancing devils in their legs, made their bodies swing and sway, set their lips to humming and their fingers to snapping." Ziegfeld sent someone from the Victor company "down there" to make a recording, which he used in his latest "Folly" on Broadway.[36] By 1920 the word had become familiar, if highly suspect, to Americans of all types, and began to provoke commentary in the press of an increasingly disapproving variety, linked closely to its roots in African American culture.

The editor of the *Musical Courier* described one jazz band's performance as "a kind of savage rite" with "all the players jolting up and down and writhing about in simulated ecstasy, in the manner of Negroes at a Southern camp-meeting afflicted with religious frenzy."[37] In a 1921 article titled "Does Jazz Put the Sin in Syncopation?" Anne Shaw Faulkner, national music chairman of the General Federation of Women's Clubs, wrote that "jazz originally was the accompaniment of the voodoo dancer, stimulating the half-crazed barbarian to the vilest deeds"; tying the phenomenon even closer to its local roots, she claimed that syncopated music (though distinct in her analysis from the more debased "jazz") was "the natural expression of the American Negroes and was used by them as the accompaniment for their bizarre dances and cakewalks." Jazz itself, she asserted, "has also been employed by other barbaric people to stimulate brutality and sensuality. That it has a demoralizing effect upon the human brain has been demonstrated by many scientists." In 1923 her organization launched a campaign two million women strong to "annihilate jazz" by driving it out of public taste and public places, for reasons that Faulkner took pains to spell out clearly:

Jazz disorganizes all regular laws and order; it stimulates to extreme deeds, to a breaking away from all rules and conventions; it is harmful and dangerous, and its influence is wholly bad. A number of scientific men who have been working on experiment in musio-therapy with the insane, declare that while regular rhythms and simple tones produce a quieting effect on the brain of even a violent patient, the effect of jazz on the normal brain produces an atrophied condition on the brain cells of conception, until very frequently those under the demoralizing influence of the persistent use of syncopation, combined with inharmonic partial tones, are actually incapable of distinguishing between good and evil, between right and wrong.[38]

Here "science" and rationality are posed against the dangers of chaotic, irregular, and racialized jazz, which normal rules and conventions should vehemently exclude.[39]

Faulkner was not alone in her endeavors. Just a few months later, in December 1921, Fenton T. Bott, "director of dance reform" of the American National Association of Masters of Dancing, spoke up in another *Ladies' Home Journal* article titled "Unspeakable Jazz Must Go!" He asserted that young people were particularly vulnerable to the corruption of jazz, which was "degrading" and "lowers all the moral standards":

> Those moaning saxophones and the rest of the instruments with their broken, jerky rhythm make a purely sensual appeal. They call out the low and rowdy instinct. All of us dancing teachers know this to be a fact. We have seen the effect of jazz music on our young pupils. It makes them act in a restless and rowdy manner. A class of children will behave that way as long as such music is played. They can be calmed down and restored to normal conduct only by playing good, legitimate music.[40]

The nature of this concern for young people, especially young women, is explicitly tied to matters of ethnic and racial hierarchy in the summarizing comments of the article's author, John McMahon: "Rub the bloom off American womanhood and what is left? The status of the Eastern European female of the species, a barefooted working animal—something a little lower than man." Interestingly, the threat of the illicit is constructed as coming not only from "below," in the "natural" expressions of debased minorities and ethnic groups, but also from above. This article condemns those "fashionable mothers" and the "high society" crowd for whom jazz had become the rage in the early 1920s (giving the Jazz Age its name). As McMahon concludes: "High society would better sign on the dotted line of the popular reform pledge. This civilization will not permit itself to be ditched by any minority, high or low."[41]

In July 1922, the New York State Legislature passed a bill empowering the commissioner of licenses of New York City to regulate jazz, and the music and jazz dancing were banned from Broadway after midnight.[42] Another organization, the Ninth Recreational Congress, convened in October 1922 to declare a "war" on jazz, led by Professor Peter Dykeman of the University of Wisconsin and critic Sigmund Spaeth, among many other luminaries of the high-culture scene. To eight hundred delegates from the Playground and Recreation Association and Community Service held in Atlantic City, Dykeman defended some aspects of jazz but claimed that its danger lay in its undisciplined, racialized performers: "Jazz is the victim of its wild, modern devotees, who are as bad as the voodoo worshipers of darkest Africa." He made the connection to radio and other mechanized means of musical reproduction that are able to evade the usual channels of cultural control: "We are in danger of becoming a nation of piano-pumpers, radio-rounders and grafonola-grinders. Those mechanical instruments, if unwisely used, are dangerous to the musical life of America."[43] Clearly the dangerous cultural form of radio as it emerged in the early 1920s could not be left in the hands of unsupervised amateurs who might play whatever records they chose over the public airwaves into respectable middle-class homes.

Regulated Taste

The end result of this clash of cultures was the 1922 relegation of the amateurs into a definitional and regulatory category that did not include the broadcasting of "entertainments," accomplished through the insertion of this clause into all amateur radio licenses: "This station is not licensed to broadcast weather reports, market reports, music, concerts, speeches, news, or similar information or entertainment."[44] Now anyone who wished to broadcast such information or entertainments had to be licensed as a station; "amateurs" and "broadcasters" were now different groups, much to the chagrin of many. Some of the more organized and highly technical former amateurs applied for licenses and became broadcasters (already, one of Bruce Barton's predictions—that a writer such as Thornton Burgess would be able to pick up a transmitter in his home and read a bedtime story—was now illegal).

But early commercial operators proved not much more mindful of their cultural responsibility—and some would argue less so—than the amateurs. Soon it became necessary to provide yet a further distinction. As these early "entertainment" stations proliferated and filled up the single frequency assigned to them at 360 meters, a new category of license was created. The new "Class B" stations occupied the 400 meter band and were required to meet more "stringent" technical and programming requirements:

> Under that class of license we would not permit the station owner—and he agreed to it—to use mechanical music, phonographs, and things of that kind. The reason we did that was because at the beginning all the stations were turning to entertainments, and at the beginning the people were appreciating it. But later they were tiring of it, and if we had not checked it, it would have had an effect on broadcasting. So we created the special license, and they had to have talent.[45]

"Talent" here refers to live performers, as opposed to records or mechanical means of reproduction, a requirement that would up the ante in radio broadcasting and eventually enforce a move to commercial sponsor support—though, as we shall see, even the biggest, most urban Class B stations kept phonographs and player pianos in their studios for "emergencies."

Class B stations received their licenses in late 1922, and a list of B stations from January 1923 shows many that have survived into the 1990s: WWJ Detroit, WSB Atlanta, WOR and WEAF (now WNBC) New York, WIP Philadelphia, and KHJ Los Angeles, among others.[46] Certainly the emergent legislative refinements had an "effect" on broadcasting: by creating an increasingly finer sieve of social distinctions—live is better than recorded, some audiences are preferable to others, some broadcasters are "boys" whereas others are responsible adults—government representatives of "the people" made broadcasting safe for large commercial concerns. Those "tiring" of recordings included especially the corporate owners of such stations as those mentioned above and their equipment suppliers. However, though these influential lobbyists may have supplied the Commerce Department with impetus to institute such requirements, they also began to create a whole new audience for radio, who could soon purchase the sets they never would have built themselves and find consistent entertainment to enjoy on them. Interestingly, by the early 1930s, when the networks had managed to consolidate their dominant position through favorable frequency assignments and power allocations, the ban on recordings was dropped to facilitate advertising and production—though not without some controversy.[47]

Big Broadcasting Begins

Thus, when we begin to look for the "what" of radio, we are faced even by 1922 with categorical problems. Amateurs no longer broadcast, putting an end to the impromptu programs of people like Frank Conrad. Class A stations on the 360 meter band come and go at random; though carefully parceled out by days and hours, especially in urban areas, there are frequent violations and complaints to Washington. Most of the historical records that still exist come from those stations that jumped quickly into the Class B category, marked by owners with deep pockets and almost always related commercial interests: radio set or transmitter sales (RCA, Westinghouse, General Electric, and AT&T), newspapers (by 1923, the *Detroit News*, the *Detroit Free Press*, the *Kansas City Star*, the *Atlanta Journal*, the *St. Louis Post Dispatch*, the *Rochester Democrat and Chronicle*, the *Louisville Courier Journal*, the *Fort Worth Star Telegram*, the *Chicago Daily News*, and the *Los Angeles Times Mirror*, among others), and major department stores (Bamberger, Shepard Stores, John Wanamaker, Gimbel Bros.).

The company most eagerly poised to enter broadcasting in a big way, and best organized to do it, was the Westinghouse Corporation. While other companies held back, or dabbled in radio at one location, Westinghouse received its four licenses immediately; indeed, it was Westinghouse representatives who had initially suggested that all broadcasting (at that time thinking only about their own stations and a few scattered others) be assigned to one wavelength, 360 meters.[48] And, because Westinghouse's profits depended on the sale of receiver sets and parts to a more widely defined public than the highly motivated amateurs, they immediately took steps to publicize their efforts by disseminating station program schedules to anyone who would write in. We should not discount the simple revolution that a publicized schedule of regular weekly or daily performances represents; not until the late 1920s would such an innovation be tried by the BBC. By December 1921, Westinghouse was circulating a weekly flyer of WJZ's schedule to all who requested it.

Though this schedule covered most of the day, it was not continuous; phonograph records, announcer chatter, and other impromptu events filled up many blank spaces. Sometimes the station simply went off the air. The featured element was the "Daily Concert," from 8:20

to 9:25 p.m. It is interesting to note that the rigidity of time periods to which we have become accustomed did not bother early broadcasters as much. The concert shows a distinct "high-culture" bias: WJZ was out to make a good impression and set high standards, though a little dance music on a Saturday night did not come amiss. Not apparent on this schedule, but clearly noted in program logs starting in 1924, was that most performers came courtesy of a booking agency or concert hall, thus providing a commercial motivation for what was rapidly becoming a sticky issue—nonpayment of artists and music publishers. News service was provided by the *Newark Sunday Call*, with whom WJZ had a cooperative arrangement, every hour from 11:00 to 7:00, and a special general report at 7:55, as well as the "Children's Hour" stories (most likely from 6:00 to 7:00).

By December 1922, WJZ's daily schedule would be supplemented by "talks" at various times on a variety of subjects and a more complete broadcast day running from 8:00 a.m. to 10:00 p.m. There seems to have been little notion up to that time of daytime programming for women, except for a talk on "Women's Fashion, by the Women's Wear Daily Newspaper" at 3:00 daily. Early evenings were dominated by "Children's Hour" and talks on such topics as "Review of the Iron and Steel Industry and Their Relation to General Business Conditions," presented by *Iron Age* magazine; "Work among the Blind Children," by Mary D. Beatty, International Sunshine Society; "How to Select a Motor Car," by Alex F. Johnson; "The Experience of a Cartoonist," by Claire Briggs, courtesy of *Popular Radio* magazine; "Some Facts That Everybody Should Know about Tea," by C. F. Hutchinson, U.S. Department of Agriculture; "Tennis," by Paul B. Williams, secretary of the National Tennis Association; and "Victualling a Big Ship," by the Cunard Company back-to-back with "Your Daily Bottle of Milk," by Mary S. Rose, associate professor, Department of Nutrition, Columbia University. These are merely the selections from one randomly chosen week;[49] it must have been hard for early audiences to contain their excitement. Sports results, market reports, "literary evenings," advice on etiquette, and the Arlington time signals rounded out the schedule.

Despite the resolutely informative and serious nature of much (though, as we shall see, not all) of early broadcasting, audiences tuned in by the thousands, and Westinghouse's gamble on a market for home receivers began to pay off. In the fall of 1922 the company began to circulate a magazine devoted to publicizing its stations' radio schedules, "published weekly to increase interest and enjoyment in Radio Broadcasting"—under these circumstances, could the first "radio wedding" be far behind? In fact, the November 18, 1922, issue of *Radio Broadcasting News* featured the nuptials of George Albert Carver and Bertha Annie McMunn at the Pittsburgh Electrical Show, with a KDKA representative standing by. Wrote one listener:

> So Bertha and George, in the name of the thousands of listeners in, let me extend congratulations and best wishes. Also let me add, that it was the most impressive wedding ceremony I ever heard, not excepting my own. For you know how it is, if you're doing it yourself, well, you are just not accountable. If your own sis, or big brother, or only daughter are getting married, you are busily engaged in seeing that they look all right, and in shedding a few loose tears, and wondering how it will turn out. Or if it is one of those swell church affairs, you are there to see the styles and criticise your neighbor, so there it goes. But over the Radio you have none of these distracting circumstances. And—"If not, hereafter and forever behold [*sic*] your peace"—. Well, when I heard that, with tears brimming in my eyes, just like in dear, old Dad's, I says to myself all quiet and still inside, "Yes dear Bertha and George, if you'll just do that, if you just obey that injunction, you'll trot double and keep in pretty good step all along the matrimonial road. I know, I've been there and am still traveling double.[50]

As Lynn Spigel notes in regard to television, here the receiver in the home functioned even better than "reality," providing experiences that listeners could make their own, respond to emotionally, frequently feeling enough of a direct personal connection that a reciprocal communication followed.[51]

The relationship with their radio sets that these very earliest audiences created, and that broadcasters encouraged, will be discussed below; probably at no other time did an industry take more seriously the responses of its public than in radio's early years, for reasons that span the technical, regulatory, and social. However, other equally or more important factors also worked to determine the nature of early broadcasting programs. Contrary to the dominant "consensus" model, though listeners' comments and perceived interests certainly influenced early broadcasters, specific institutional interests often played a larger role in influencing decisions made on a daily basis. Some stations reflected the interests and predispositions of important investors; some reflected those of station managers working within the limits and restrictions of their settings and corporate directives; some were modeled after the primary businesses of their owners, such as newspapers and department stores—each of which brought a certain preconceived notion of appropriate and functional material to the studio even before the very first listeners could begin to determine what they preferred to have coming in over the headphones, or out of the speaker horn.

We have seen how territorial disputes with amateurs were working during the period 1922 to 1924 to define the nature of what would be broadcast. Even without an official regulatory mechanism in place, distinctions were being made that had immediate and material effects not only on who would be licensed to broadcast, on what channel and at what power, but also on *what* would be broadcast—for reasons that had little to do with a determined effort to ascertain public sentiment objectively. In fact, certain early radio practices *contradicted* purely popular preferences, and indeed that contradiction formed their primary motivation. Early radio regulation exhibited a tendency to *exclude* more than to include—to set up barriers to popular expression in favor of larger, controlling bodies whose own self-interests could then serve to "police" the airwaves. Those who made the daily decisions about radio content—station managers, program directors, announcers—worked within a structural framework as early as 1922 that promoted some uses of the medium and discouraged others. Their negotiations of radio's peculiar situation—working within pressures from above and below, the official and the popular, tradition and innovation—form the basis for televisual practice even today.[52]

Radio Broadcast Central: WJZ

Westinghouse stations hewed closely to the respectable, "high-culture" line, even though their sets (contrary to Roland Marchand's assertion) were manufactured to fit a variety of budgets, not just the elite.[53] Station KYW in Chicago, in fact, specialized almost entirely in opera, broadcasting entire productions directly from the Chicago Civic Opera and also featuring a variety of operatic performers from its studio in the Commonwealth Edison Building. Sponsored heavily by utilities magnate Samuel Insull, whose musical preferences the station reflected, KYW also broadcast local high school bands and orchestras, programs put together by local artists' bureaus (booking agents), and church services on Sunday mornings.

WJZ provides a good case study of high-end commercial broadcasting, not least because its early logs and records have been preserved in the NBC archives, but also because several of its original station staff went on to leading executive positions with the network. WJZ's organization and evolving program practices obtained a higher profile than any other station operating at the time, and provided a crucial early model for station organization and function as well as cultural definition of radio in the United States. In an era in which radio's technical properties were still being explored, most stations began with an engineering-based staff. WJZ appointed Charles B. Popenoe, a Westinghouse "mechanical engineer and efficiency expert" to manage the installation and development of this new enterprise. Unlike Frank Conrad of Pittsburgh, Popenoe had no previous background in amateur radio, nor in any form of entertainment, news, or communication. This necessitated a kind of division of labor soon to become standard in early broadcasting. Assisted by a technical engineer—in this case George Blitziotis, identified in one account as a Belgian former Marconi man who "spoke no English"[54]—Popenoe first hired Thomas H. Cowan from Westinghouse's Testing Department and appointed him announcer, a duty that included "arrang[ing] the program of recordings and mak[ing] himself generally useful."[55]

This staff sufficed for the first few months of operation in 1921, but once the Department of Commerce's licensing standard shifted and live talent became necessary, the station found itself obliged not only to move to a location more convenient to New York-based talent—opening a new studio in the Waldorf Astoria Hotel, linked by telephone wire to the Newark transmitter—but also to expand its staff to include Bertha Brainard as a part-time "booker of talent."[56] Brainard provided early radio with its first tie to the theatrical world, offering a twice-weekly review titled, alliteratively, *Bertha Brainard Broadcasting Broadway*; in August 1922 she assumed the newly conceived role of program manager. That same summer, Milton J. Cross joined the WJZ staff, beginning a long career as one of early radio's preeminent announcers, whose role in early programming will be discussed below.

Westinghouse gave over the operation of WJZ to RCA in 1923, following a period during which the two companies operated it jointly. Also at this time WJZ moved, with its newly opened sister station WJY, to specially constructed headquarters in New York's Aeolian Hall near Times Square, much closer than any other station to the heart of the entertainment district. According to Popenoe, this was part of an established plan:

> It had always been the understanding in the Westinghouse organization that as soon as the Radio Corporation of America would erect a super-station in New York City, that the original WJZ would close down and that the broadcasting responsibility would be taken over from Westinghouse, and all broadcasting by the affiliated companies, Radio Corporation, Westinghouse, and General Electric in the New York City district would be done by the Radio Corporation [RCA].[57]

Claiming the title "Radio Broadcast Central," RCA began to position WJZ and WJY as the dominant force in the nascent industry, ready to extend a unifying voice across much of the nation—a model very similar to the one being developed in Great Britain by the members of the early British Broadcasting Company. "The plan was to have WJZ operate on 455 meters, broadcasting music and entertainment of the lighter vein, whereas WJY was to operate on 405 meters and was intended to specialize in what might be termed 'highbrow' broadcasting. Opera, classical music, lectures and the like were to be the offerings of the new station."[58] This plan gave RCA an advantage in programming over any other stations in the country, and also worked to determine the nature of broadcast entertainment standards across the United States. Ironically, this placement of "highbrow" material in a category separate from the "commercial" would eventually have the effect of all but squeezing the former out; despite attempts to integrate the "serious" with the needs of sponsors, as advertisers discovered the "tabloid mind" and market in the late 1920s, "vaudeville culture" took over the airwaves.

Yet this disparaged access of the popular to the national ether did not by any means reflect an opening to all the diverse strands of American culture equally. A limited and carefully screened version of popular tastes and interests began to define U.S. broadcasting practices. Even before a clear picture of the actual listening audience began to develop, early broadcasters made distinctions and decisions based on an emerging sense of radio's role in maintaining dominant cultural values as well as on immediate economic interests.

The road to vaudeville culture was paved by those with something to sell. A look through the handwritten logs of WJZ and WJY from 1923 to 1927, kept in the NBC papers at the State Historical Society of Wisconsin, reveals three major sources for the bulk of early programming on both stations (and indeed, the stated differentiation of "highbrow" and popular material is hard to discern—the logs show more similar than different material): publishers, including newspapers and magazines; music publishing houses and "song pluggers"; and live remotes of dance orchestras from the dining rooms of New York's prestige hotels.[59] For instance, the WJY schedule for May 17, 1923, shows a "Talk on Good Housekeeping" sponsored by *Harper's Bazaar* magazine at 7:45 p.m., followed by piano pieces by Allen Gleason, from the Pingree School of Music. He is succeeded by Jean Herbert at 8:15, playing music supplied by the B.A. Music Publishing Company. The broadcast day closes with an "Inspirational Talk" by George H. Grebe of the American Trading Company. The next evening, Friday, opens with a concert from the Waldorf Orchestra from 4:00 to 6:00, live from the hotel of that name. Jean Herbert returns, followed by a regular 8:15 sports feature from the *New York Tribune*. A little later, at 9:30, speaker Joe Taylor is sponsored by *Field and Stream*. On Thursday, May 24, Bertha Brainard brings a Broadway play, *Sally, Irene and Mary*, to WJY listeners, sponsored by the Schubert Producers. In June, the American Music Publishing Company begins to present a "Radio Review" from 9:00 to 10:00, followed by a feature called "R. H. Macy Presents." By April 1925 on WJZ the schedule flows from one popular feature to another, as the Hotel Vanderbilt Orchestra is succeeded by a *Wall Street Journal* "review," then a program from the New York Band Instrument Company, the *Brunswick Hour of Music* (sponsored by the Brunswick radio manufacturing company), and the Meyer Davis Park Lane Orchestra from that hotel.

As time went on, informational "talks" such as those presented in 1922 declined as a proportion of the stations' schedules, and music played an increasingly heavy role. Experimentation with networking on a limited basis brought such events as live adaptations of theatrical drama from Schenectady station WGY and sports remotes from Madison Square Garden. "Light classical" music dominated, mixed with a healthy dose of popular songs and the respectable big-band "jazz" of such orchestras as Vincent Lopez's and Paul Whiteman's. Tying this mix of disparate elements together were the early station announcers, whose often combined role of on-air speaker, programmer, disc jockey, and fill-in performer created a distinctively new American cultural figure: the radio personality.

Radiating Personality

Warren Susman has described the twentieth century as a period of transformation from a "culture of character," based on a notion of the moral individual rooted within social values and public obligations, to the culture of personality, "another vision of self, another vision of self-development, another method of the presentation of self in society."[60] Personality consisted less of inner qualities in harmony with an intrinsic moral order than of self-realization and presentation aimed at impressing others, emphasizing qualities such as "charm," "fascination," and "poise." The development of a successful personality paradoxically combined elements of self-realization with the desire to "fit in," to be well liked, essentially demanding that individuals internalize and display those attributes that were most desired by the culture around them—what Susman calls the "performing self." For an assimilatory culture just beginning to develop nationally circulated representations of "normal" middle-class standards through advertising—to which "everyone" might aspire though some were doomed a priori to failure—the culture of personality most frequently displayed itself in the mass-produced celebrity. Susman focuses on the film industry and its star system as the first national mechanism for the production of "a new profession—that of being a movie star or a celebrity."[61]

Radio took the culture of personality one step further, bringing nationalized celebrities into the private sphere. With their place in the family circle, their voices speaking intimately to the individuals listening, their repeated presence every Sunday or Tuesday or Friday night to take up the pleasant acquaintance forged over time, early radio announcers and performers entered into an unprecedented relationship with the vast numbers of people who began to make up a new listening public. During radio's earliest years, from 1922 into the early 1930s, each station's announcers made up its most recognizable public face. After an early insistence on anonymity—similiar to the early years of film—during which on-air personnel were known by their initials only, station announcers played an increasingly important role. Not only did their often ad-libbed monologues provide continuity between varied acts, but their voices became the factor that physically linked listeners in this invisible medium to the identities of stations themselves.

In a speech delivered at a conference of radio representatives of AT&T Associated Companies in February 1923, William E. Harkness, broadcasting manager for AT&T, articulated the importance of the announcer:

> The announcer at a broadcasting station is its principal point of contact with the public. The public know his voice and try to picture him to fit it. If he is not married or not well-balanced he is apt to become light-headed from the mash notes sent to the station by ladies of the audience or by the humorous notes sent in by men whose wives have fallen in love with the announcer's voice and have neglected their household duties to listen to the radio.[62]

Listing the necessary qualities of a good announcer, Harkness emphasized good education, a voice trained for singing or speaking, knowledge of music and foreign languages, ability to hold interest and vary tone, and, finally, "a voice with personality."[63] That this personality be male, and that it was the women of the audience who were characterized as particularly susceptible to his charms, was not so much an accurate description of actual practice but a construction important to defining both radio's appropriate function in society and its new "passive" audience. As radio participation shifted from the active transmitting efforts of amateurs to a more general receiving audience catered to by "professional" broadcasting concerns—and, eventually, as selling products to women became radio's central economic goal—the idea of this new mass audience as feminized and easily led began to figure large in both industry discourse and the concerns of its critics. The announcer "personality" became a significant point of debate and control, as well as a personification of emerging national culture. As George H. Douglas puts it, "When commercial broadcasting began, the radio announcer *was* radio."[64] Though by the 1930s, as both stations and networks ceded production of programs to advertising agencies, announcing became more anonymous and standardized, several personalities from the early years continued to have national recognition. Most of them would later segue into the newly specialized areas of news and sports, two arenas where announcers continued to rule the day.[65] From their early roles as the voices of individual stations, to general network announcing, to later specialization, these men became the national voices of U.S. radio—during its nighttime and more "public"-directed programming hours. The history of women's voices on the air and the equally popular, though now obscure, personalities of the daytime makes another story, which will be told in chapter 5.

In many ways these personalities replaced the earlier figure of the amateur radio operator as the new American hero. Much publicity and adulation from fans surrounds their reputations. Several polls in the 1920s and 1930s served to rank their popularity and establish the terms of their celebrity. As their letters attest, many of the members of radio's earliest public addressed emergent radio celebrities as friends, sent them birthday gifts, advised on remedies for their minor ailments, even baked cookies—and gratefully purchased the products they recommended.[66] Yet already by 1924 a new figure had arisen, soon to take over the role of national celebrity established by the general-purpose announcers. This was the figure of the radio showman, who drew on the same dynamics of relationship with the audience as the announcers, but this time in a slightly different context. It took a peculiar combination of regulatory decisions, industry conditions, and commercially motivated bricolage from diverse cultural traditions to set this relationship in place. One of the first of the early showmen to rise to the surface of radio's new cultural melange was Samuel A. Rothafel, known familiarly as "Roxy," a theatrical entrepreneur who found a new national audience via WEAF and its move toward commercial sponsorship.

WEAF: Adventures in Sponsorship

Historically, the highest profile of any early station has been awarded AT&T's WEAF, credited with the inception of "toll broadcasting," the forerunner of the later dominant radio (and television) practice of selling time for money to advertisers. This historical prominence is in part due to the publication of William Peck Banning's *Commercial Broadcasting Pioneer* in 1946, which still remains one of the most in-depth studies of radio broadcasting practice during the early period available to researchers.[67] However, besides its heavy reliance on AT&T sources—and subsequent laudatory tone—Banning's book unduly emphasizes the significance of WEAF's efforts. In fact, as other early observers pointed out, WEAF's main innovation was that it required payment for what other stations of the time were offering for free—a concept more significant in its eventual discursive uses than in the difference it made for early practices. William Harkness, in charge of AT&T's broadcasting activities, himself admitted in a 1923 speech, "The fact that stations WJZ and WOR both put on free features which are similar to those for which we charge is at present a serious obstacle to the rapid development of the paid business."[68]

WEAF's schedule resembled closely those of WJY, WJZ, and other New York stations, with one eventual significant difference that may, indeed, have stemmed from its overtly commercial purpose and structure: the development of regularly scheduled, sponsored variety programs that mixed the standards of elite and "vaudeville" culture to provide early radio with its most characteristic prenetwork form. Two programs deserve special attention, for both their popularity with audiences and their influence within the radio industry: *Roxy and His Gang*, carried live from the Capitol Theater and hosted by radio's first major "personality," Samuel L. Rothafel; and *The Eveready Hour*, sponsored by the National Carbon Company beginning in 1923.

Rothafel was the manager of the Capitol Theater in New York City, which was owned by the Loews Corporation. During this heyday of the silent film, Roxy presided over not only feature film presentation but a host of other entertainments that included a full vaudeville program (directed by Rothafel himself), orchestra recitals, and master of ceremonies activities that made his presence indeed a performative one. Rothafel took to the air on November 19, 1922, over WEAF. Banning attributes this venture to technological experimentation by AT&T engineers who wanted to test their newly developed public address system and suggested that the director's traditional megaphone could be replaced by the new microphones and speakers. This experimentation expanded to trial amplification and transmission of stage performances, and soon broadcasts of the Capitol Theater's stage show were a regular Sunday-night feature of WEAF's schedule—at a time when not too many other programs occupied it. The following year, the stage show was combined with an additional radio-only segment, broadcast from a specially constructed studio "upstairs at the Capitol," with Roxy presiding.[69] For WEAF, the program provided necessary nonrecorded entertainment material with which to attract sponsors to the air—and for which no payment need be made; for the Capitol Theater, the show served to promote the theater's basic business and establish goodwill in the most direct and representative way possible, free of normal advertising expense.

The shift in the title of the program, from *The Capitol Theater Gang*, as it was first known, to *Roxy and His Gang*, reflects both the initial uncertainty as to just what this new form should consist of and be called and a subsequent emphasis on the role of the central "personality" as its focus. Combining traditional vaudeville comic routines

with songs and instrumental performances from the concert hall, supplemented by short "sketches" or humorous dramatic segments, the
new variety form relied heavily on the ability of the announcer to tie
the diverse parts together, especially as all of the theater and vaudeville
hall's visual cues and audience guidelines were missing in this new
aural medium. The radio "host" spoke directly to his audience, in an
intimate tone and familiar style, guiding them through the unfamiliar
listening experience, organizing and making sense of a potpourri of
entertainment. The diverse elements were united within the ambiance
created around the central personality, who in effect provided neophyte radio listeners with a framework for this new knowledge, a
guide for interpretation. Roxy's Gang became a kind of radio family
for many listeners, who enjoyed the host's updates on the activities of
members of the cast, other family members, and acquaintances as
much as the musical portions of the show.[70]

In a May 1925 article in *Radio Broadcast*, James C. Young described the furor created when "the men higher up at WEAF undertook to edit Roxie's [*sic*] little monologues . . . about the old folk back
home and the condition of Aunt Matilda's health":

> On one eventful Sunday night several months ago, "Roxie" out-did the
> most stilted introduction known to radio. A host of followers listened
> and wondered and became amazed. What was the matter with "Roxie"?
> Next day the papers told them. He had been edited. Immediately an al-
> most unanimous protest poured in upon WEAF, the greatest expression
> of opinion ever drawn from a radio audience. . . . And WEAF relented,
> without even putting an ear to the ground.[71]

WEAF's action apparently stemmed from the in-house opinion that
Roxy had exceeded the bounds of respectable, professional speech by
adopting a "folksy," sentimental style ill-befitting WEAF's image as a
business advertisers' station.[72] The enormous number of local papers
that carried the story attests probably as much to good publicity on
Roxy's part as to his popularity—but the questions of "taste" and ap-
propriateness raised by the incident remain. Even though WEAF re-
lented at this point, when Rothafel attempted to negotiate broadcasting from his newly built theater after leaving the Capitol later that
year, station executives expressed an unwillingness to allow him time
at no charge, as they had previously. At the root of this decision seems
to have been a feeling that Roxy's personal popularity, although useful
in drawing an audience to WEAF's nascent network efforts, had in-

creased to such a degree—while representing certain less-desirable qualities—that Rothafel threatened to overwhelm WEAF's identity with his own. Furthermore, that identity was antithetical in some way to the one desired by AT&T as a broadcasting enterprise. An editorial in *Radio Broadcast* in October 1925, reporting on Roxy's departure from the Capitol, expressed distaste for the unmitigated popular:

> The musical quality of this very popular feature we have never questioned, but it must be admitted that the drooling sentimentality of the presentation spoils what would otherwise be an almost perfect program of its type. Mr. Rothafel deserves much credit for devising a genuinely new type of radio presentation, but why that presentation had to be constantly weighted with expressions of almost tearful sentiment and side remarks which somehow are invariably weightily saccharine—we could never understand.[73]

Roxy would never again achieve the radio prominence that his program on WEAF had enjoyed from 1922 through July 1925, though the show would continue under the direction of Major Edward Bowes, assistant manager of the Capitol, eventually becoming the *Major Bowes Amateur Hour.*

"Eveready Red"

The other star in WEAF's firmament was the National Carbon Company's *Eveready Hour.* Like *The Capitol Theater Gang, The Eveready Hour* featured an integrated presentation of music, drama, and dialogue, but instead of the framework of the vaudeville stage, *The Eveready Hour* used dramatic narrative organized around a "theme" to accomplish the purpose of unity and cohesion. Unlike the Capitol Theater show, *The Eveready Hour* promoted a product—radio related, to be sure—and went to increasing lengths to attach the entertainment to its Eveready batteries. Under the direction of George C. Furness, manager of the National Carbon Company's radio division, each week's program, aired Tuesday nights at 9:00 on WEAF (and eventually ten other East Coast stations), employed an announcer, singers, musicians, and actors to establish a fictional setting or idea around which the dialogue and music revolved.

This format evolved slowly. *The Eveready Hour*'s debut program on December 4, 1923, contained little to distinguish it from the ordinary run of station-based entertainment: an announcer, a collection of songs and musical pieces, with the most typical continuity being the familiar, "The number you have just heard was So-and-So. The next number will be Such-and-Such."[74] Even so, as 1924 went on it became one of the first regularly scheduled self-contained and sponsored programs of this type, gradually conditioning audiences to expect weekly recurrence of identifiable programs. Not until the fall of 1924 did the idea of a unifying theme emerge, following the decision to hire a permanent ensemble of singers and instrumentalists.

It is interesting to note the topics selected for the experiment with this technique, for they represent not only a unifying strategy for an hour of entertainment, but build on and recruit a sense of national unity. The first show depicted "Armistice Day" and employed patriotic songs and narratives about national sacrifice during the recent war to evoke familiar and compelling memories of a nation united around a common purpose. The second, significantly, presented the theme "The Golden Wedding Program" and was organized around "old-time songs" from Stephen Foster to the 1890s, with a fictional setting of "a blizzard-blown farmhouse where, despite the drifts and zero air, neighbors made their way in sleighs to help John and Mary Bishop celebrate their 50th wedding anniversary."[75] This program, prominently celebrating the rural agrarian tradition, happy darkies, and sentiment about a way of life and a personal history shared by very few among the listening audience, was significant in what it represented as the true "American" past.[76]

From these early narrative experiments, punctuated by related musical performances and tied together by Graham MacNamee's narration in character, grew what the program's producers referred to as "the continuity form of radio drama," including original musical comedies and adaptations from the stage. Appealing self-consciously to a newly constituted national audience, The Eveready Hour defined the American experience in relation to "exotic" foreign cultures and in cohesion around slices of American life. Programs such as The Mayor of Hogan's Alley, The Small-Timer, and Local Boy Makes Good celebrated "traditional" American values of individual achievement and assimilation while also introducing listeners to European classical music and concert hall performers.

But for many listeners, the individual programs proved secondary to the attraction of The Eveready Hour's star personalities. First among them was traveling songster Wendell Hall, a vaudeville circuit performer, singer, and songwriter. Hall's original claim to fame consisted of his being the first person in vaudeville to play the xylophone and sing at the same time, and he became known as "The Singing Xylophonist." Failing to attract the widespread attention this feat undoubtedly deserved, Hall also composed and performed his own songs, turning to the radio as one of the many song pluggers hoping to use the new medium to boost sheet music sales. Westinghouse station KYW's need for talent after the close of the opera season in 1922 brought Hall onto the air for the first time; in March he began performing on KYW three evenings a week, becoming its first paid staff artist later that year. Additionally, "in time the expense and inconvenience of his six-foot xylophone led to substitution of the ukelele."[77] This may have been a crucial breakthrough, given the characteristics of his later career. At KYW, Hall worked out a new presentation suited to radio's capabilities: "He chose songs and a style, worked on jokes and a monologue, and above all, learned the importance of personality and variety. Voice was all. . . . Hall ruled that jokes could be used but once and that a new program was needed every night because a radio entertainer could never have a fresh audience."[78] Wendell Hall became a popular radio personality in Chicago.

In 1923, Hall's fortunes took a definitive turn: he composed his soon-to-be trademark tune, "It Ain't Gonna Rain No Mo,'" which radio would make a national hit. But in the absence as yet of national networks, and with use of recordings still discouraged, radio fame in one market, even Chicago, did not necessarily translate into national renown. Hall devised a strategy to overcome this temporary disability: he embarked in June 1923 on a cross-country tour of radio stations, appearing on "about 35 stations and cover[ing] 5,000 miles in four months."[79] Spending up to a week in each local market, Hall not only performed daily on the air but also appeared onstage; performed behind the counter at music stores, which he stocked with sheet music of his hits; and provided programming advice to fledgling station managers in small towns where big-city talent rarely appeared. "It Ain't Gonna Rain No Mo'" became the first national hit song created by the new medium, radio.

As the National Carbon Company and its agency N. W. Ayer began to look around for a permanent cast of performers, Wendell Hall seemed a noteworthy addition. They signed him on in January 1924. Later that month, Hall accompanied a National Carbon salesman and a representative of the Victor Talking Machine Company—with whom

Hall had signed a recording contract—on another nationwide tour, this time promoting a sponsor and a soon-to-be network radio program along with his own personal reputation. He may count as the first radio personality to cultivate an identity with a product, as many artists such as the Happiness Candy Boys (Jones and Hare), the Cliquot Club Eskimoes, and the A&P Gypsies would assume later. Here Hall's red hair—invisible, of course, on radio but helping to personalize that voice-developed presence—provided an associative link with the product (Eveready batteries featured a red-painted top). Billed as "Eveready Red" and the "Eveready Red-Headed Music Maker," Hall began to attract hundreds of letters weekly from all over the country, attesting to the ability of radio audiences to make family friends of—and even form romantic attachments with—its disembodied but intimately present personalities.[80] Wrote one couple from New York:

> My Dear Wendell—for such you must be called—anyone whom can "radiate" such a genial personality as you, at once becomes a friend. Each night you have entertained us, we have just grinned, until it hurt and when A.J.N. [the announcer from WJZ Newark] mentioned to write—why we obeyed that impulse.

Others adopted Hall's breezy colloquial style to sing his praises. A Rhode Island listener wrote, "If there is any grouch around that you couldn't pull a laugh out of he must be dead from the neck up." From Washington, D.C., came the demand, "Please, oh please give us more of the Red Headed Music Maker, everytime we hear him we like him better, he sure is funny as a crutch. After you hear him two or three times and you pick up the paper and find he is going to perform you feel just like you are going to a nice big party and someone you know is going to be there." Another fan decorated his letter with a sketch of Hall, complete with flaming red hair, as the light on a locomotive train running down some tracks. He wrote, "I want this to show my appreciation for the 'Red Headed Music Maker'—you old brick head. You are as much of a crackerjack as any I have heard," and signed off with "Shake—*you are good.*"

Two postcards written to Hall care of station WOC, Davenport, Iowa, on March 19 and 21, 1924, attest to radio's ability to cross lines of distance, age, and social category in an intimate affinity:

> *Grandma* was *aroused* from *"dreamland"* last night at *midnight* by *the* "Radio" which is at head of my bed—sounded like a *voice* in my room. . . .

I am so anxious to hear *"red head"* again I *fell* in *love with him*, even if I am 74 years old.

Grandma wrote again two days later to Hall directly:

Dear Sir—Guess I can call you *"dear"* as your "little red headed sweetheart" is too far away to get jealous of "Grandma" who is 74 years old, but *"fell* in love" with *you* and your "red head." Wish I could see you and tell you how much I have enjoyed your *music* on *"Yuku"* and *your songs* etc. I could see your *smiling face* and *snapping* eyes *in imagination.* Now I want your *picture* and I hope I am not to [*sic*] late to get one amid the *many* others who want one also. . . . I am a lover of the "Radio."

Another letter is interesting in light of Hall's early mode of performance. As might be deduced from the title of his popular song "It Ain't Gonna Rain No Mo,'" Hall adopted a "southern" accent and minstrel style from the very popular vaudeville strain of the time (to be discussed in chapter 3), telling "southern jokes and stories" and speaking in dialect.[81] Given that Hall was born in Kansas and grew up in Chicago, his listeners' presumption of a "natural" regionality was unfounded. A 1924 listener inadvertently raised one of the questions surrounding radio's elision of certain social markers when she exclaimed:

The very idea of that lady wanting to know if you were white or colored. What's the difference as long as she was being entertained and enjoyed it? We all have paid good money to hear and see colored entertainers while she was getting her concert free. I suppose your southern drawl threw her completely off the track, and she could only picture you with a dark face when she heard you speak. Quite different with me . . . won't you please send me a photo of yourself, regardless of color?

The ability of radio to blur racial categories and confuse identities could be as pleasurable as it was troubling to some. Hall's association with *The Eveready Hour* loosened as the unified continuity format took over; by the late 1920s he found it more profitable to specialize in guest appearances on the many variety shows in place by then, as well as continue to do theatrical tours both domestic and abroad. In 1929 Hall assumed directorship of *The Majestic Theater Hour* for the Grigsby-Grunow Company, then produced the Gillette Company's *Community Sing* program in the 1930s. By the mid-1930s, as drama and big-name variety came to dominate the network airwaves, Hall's fame faded.

Wendell Hall, Roxy, and the programs they made memorable provided the American public with a new and unifying experience. The mixture of music, drama, promotion, and personality in these early variety forms prefigured most of what would later develop as a distinctive American popular form, influential across the globe. Yet one more innovation awaited the emerging field of radio practice; it is not surprising that it came out of Chicago.

Chicago: Culture Broker to the World

Newspapers, as noted above, formed one of the larger groups of corporate interests to see the potential and connection to their basic business in radio from the beginning. Newspaper-owned stations contributed significantly to the development of radio broadcasting practices, both in terms of the relationship of advertising to program content and in the origination of specific program forms closely related to newspaper practices. This included not only news coverage on the air—in fact a fairly insignificant part of the typical broadcast schedule until the late 1930s—but, far more important, the development of serial narrative forms closely related to the comic strips and serialized fiction then common to major daily newspapers. This aspect of program development will be discussed in chapter 3, in relation to early radio's single most popular and influential program, *Amos 'n' Andy*. For now, the impetus behind the first newspaper-owned stations and their conceptualization of the business of radio broadcasting provides an important piece of the radio broadcasting picture.

Probably the earliest major urban newspaper to start up a broadcasting service was WWJ Detroit, operated by the *Detroit News*; it competes for the title of "first station in the nation" with KDKA and WHA (University of Wisconsin-Madison). Though both of the latter have received more historical attention, WWJ's claims—and contributions to the commercial field—may in fact take precedence over the other two. WWJ's list of "firsts" (compiled by the station itself) is impressive: from "first radio station in the world to broadcast regularly scheduled daily programs" beginning on August 20, 1920, through "first radio newscast," "first radio sportscast," and "first complete symphony orchestra concert on radio" to first regularly scheduled religious broadcasts and university extension courses, WWJ pioneered in uses soon to become ubiquitous. Fanny Brice, Will Rogers, and D. W. Griffith, accompanied by both Dorothy and Lillian Gish, made their radio debuts on WWJ; and, yes, Wendell Hall passed through on his

1924 barnstorming tour.[82] Early radio stations are fond of making such claims, so perhaps not every one should be taken too literally. Nonetheless, there is no doubt that WWJ saw the potential in radio very early on. For a period in 1921 and 1922 the station shared its frequency with the *Detroit Free Press* and with the Ford Company, programming different time blocks each day, but by late 1922 the *Detroit News* dominated the schedule. Aided by its ability to publicize its program schedule in the *News* daily, WWJ wasted no opportunity to capitalize on each nuance of this fortuitous synergy from day one:

> The sending of the election returns by the "Detroit News" radiophone Tuesday night was fraught with romance and must go down in the history of man's conquest of the elements as a gigantic step in his progress. In the four hours that the apparatus, set up in an out-of-the-way corner of The News Building, was hissing and whirring its message into space, few realized that a dream and a prediction had come true. The news of the world was being given forth through this invisible trumpet to the waiting crowds in the unseen market place.[83]

Beginning with news broadcasts, time signals, and the playing of phonograph records, the *News* began to branch out in late 1921 by hiring permanent musicians and booking talent from Detroit theaters. Gradually adding managerial, programming, and reporting staff, WWJ developed what it saw as a promotion service to the public; in February 1924, C. W. Kirby, the *Detroit News* radio manager, claimed, "Good will is about the only return we expect from our station. The circulation department tells us positively that they list no increases in circulation due to our efforts in radio. The advertising department is of the same opinion."[84] In the early 1920s, most newspapers remained far more interested in promoting their image of public service than in turning their radio stations into advertising-based profit centers. First of all, as William Hedges of the *Chicago Daily News* pointed out in 1924, radio was one effective way for a newspaper to advertise itself, otherwise a difficult task to accomplish other than through billboards: "The radio broadcasting station of the newspaper pours inoffensively its name into the willing ears of thousands of listeners. The various departments of the paper become known to great numbers who had never given a thought to the variety of newspaper service before."[85] So perhaps the value of radio to a newpaper lay less in increasing circulation than in maintaining a viable presence before the public, at a time when many daily newspapers competed in most cities.

Depite Detroit's pioneering efforts, the city in which newspaper-owned stations soon came to dominate broadcasting was Chicago. Both the *Chicago Daily News*'s WMAQ and the *Chicago Tribune*'s WGN would become key stations nationally, as both chain affiliates and originators of programming. Their early operations deserve scrutiny, though only later would they contribute in decisively different ways.

Both the *Tribune* and the *Daily News* first evinced interest in broadcasting in the boom year of 1922. The *Tribune* began by experimenting with a cooperative arrangement with the Westinghouse station KYW, supplying an hour of news daily. When no positive benefit was seen to result from the test, and when advertisers complained about audiences' attention being drawn from the printed page, the *Tribune* withdrew from the scene for two years. However, in 1923 the *Tribune* appeared to rethink this decision, giving prominent position to a series of articles by Robert M. Lee that speculated on the future of radio. After summarizing the nascent medium's history and delineating the lines of power poised for control, Lee concluded that radio would prove an exceptionally influential medium, for good or ill, and that the most pressing issue at hand was that of editorial responsibility:

> Who is to make speeches? Who is to sing songs? Who tells jokes? Who decides on the kind of speech? Shall it be Senator Lodge or Emma Goldman? Shall it be orthodox Republican or reformed socialists? Shall it be stout conservative or unregenerate bolshevism? . . . There is nothing to prevent the most ardent bolshevist from setting up a station and soliciting the multitudes with Utopian invitations. . . . Radio has started full blown. It has no traditions.[86]

Lee evoked a picture of rampant commercialism run amok, with no standards of editorial control outside of those of the large radio companies—in contrast to the "experience in judgement" and "standards imposed by a long tradition" possessed by the newspaper industry. By March 1924, WGN had prepared itself to step into the gap, heroically filling the responsible role of policer of the dangerous social tendencies that it had identified as crucial for its readers. A full-page advertisement that ran on March 28, 1924, read, "The Chicago Tribune intends to maintain in its broadcasting standards of entertainment and instruction worthy of the call letters WGN [World's Greatest Newspaper]."[87]

Actual broadcasting practice, however, had already been developed at the two preexisting stations the *Tribune* would merge to form WGN. WDAP, founded in 1922 by two "socially prominent young Chicagoans," provided most of the key staff of the *Tribune*'s new station. Myrtle E. Stahl had been hired in October 1922 "to take care of the mail, programming, public relations and publicity." She began to put together a schedule and staff, herself originating one of radio's first amateur hours. One of the station's most popular features was the Drake Hotel Concert Ensemble, which played in the dining room downstairs from the station (perched in two old handball courts on the hotel's roof) under the direction of Henry Selinger. Selinger would become music director of WGN and for a time its program manager, as Stahl was directed into secretarial work.[88] Meantime, the *Tribune* had been leasing time from Eugene MacDonald of Zenith, owner of station WJAZ (formerly WEBH) atop the Edgewater Beach Hotel. By mid-March, the *Tribune* dominated the WJAZ schedule, and on March 24, 1924, it assumed control of the station, merging it with WDAP's operations.[89] The call letters WGN were coaxed away from their previously assigned owner, a Great Lakes freighter, and full-scale broadcasting began. In August of that year the editor of the *Tribune* in-house newsletter, Quin Ryan, was added to the staff, becoming a de facto program manager. He would provide several of the key program innovations that would lead to WGN's later well-deserved reputation as the birthplace of the serial narrative drama.

But the predominant emphasis at WGN during its early years was on high culture and education for promotion of public image and public service. Classical and "serious" music prevailed, despite at least one audience poll that indicated a preference for popular music and jazz by 49.4 percent to 26.7 percent.[90] In keeping with its concerns for editorial responsibility, WGN maintained standards perhaps higher than those of the public itself and resisted any moves toward commercialization. Nearby, rival paper *Chicago Daily News* had embarked on a similar project.

The *Daily News* plunged into broadcasting slightly more headlong than the *Tribune*. In a partnership with the Fair Store, one of Chicago's glittering downtown emporiums, which possessed a transmitter and studio space, the *News* determined to venture into radio. Its first decision, in February 1922, was to hire Judith C. Waller, a Chicago native with no radio experience but with a background in advertising. Waller had worked first for the J. Walter Thompson Chicago office, where

she was put in charge of a newly established "woman's department."
(J. Walter Thompson and its important contributions to radio will be
discussed in chapter 4.) She was transferred for a time to the New
York headquarters, but because of family demands returned to
Chicago, where Walter Strong, managing editor of the *Daily News*,
approached her to "run a radio station." William S. Hedges, formerly
radio editor, had already been appointed station manager. Waller
served primarily as program director, announcer, and talent agent.
Two of her initial decisions would affect WMAQ programming for
several years to come: first, that because of a quantity of popular and
jazz music on the air, WMAQ would focus on more serious fare; and
second, that the programming should reflect the structure of the newspaper. As she later related in an interview:

> I think that in the first month or two I gave little or no thought to types
> of programs we would put on. It was a question of getting what you
> could get, except that KYW [the only station on the air at that point] was
> spending most of its time broadcasting jazz, and I felt that there should
> be something else besides jazz on a radio station. However, the Chicago
> Daily News was a family newspaper and as we got underway I became
> interested, and I think the paper was interested too, in publicizing the
> various departments of the paper. When I thought of a women's pro-
> gram, I would think of it emanating from the women's department of the
> paper, or a children's program coming from the children's department....
> We tried to tie the paper and the station together.[91]

Another important aspect of newspaper-related programming was that
it avoided payment for music held by the American Society of Composers, Authors, and Publishers (ASCAP). In 1923, ASCAP first began
to agitate for payment to its rights holders for musical performances
broadcast over the radio. In reponse, the National Association of
Broadcasters (NAB) was formed, with William Hedges of WMAQ at
its head. The fledgling broadcasters' association managed to work out
an initial agreement with ASCAP and continued broadcasting music,
now paying fees based on station size and schedule, but the writing was
on the wall. In order to avoid a permanent state of thrall to the powerful music rights organization, radio stations would have to develop
new approaches to broadcast programming. Adaptations of newspaper-
owned material provided one solution, as we shall see. Another popular option was coverage of remote live events, particularly sports.
Waller later claimed to have initiated broadcasts of the Cubs games:

Back in 1924, or maybe 1925, I went to see Mr. William Wrigley, Jr. The fall before that the World Series had been broadcast, but never had there been a play by play baseball broadcast from a home park. I wanted to ask Mr. Wrigley if he would consent to our broadcasting the home games of the Chicago Cubs. Whether he was intrigued by the fact that a woman was asking him for this privilege, or just because the whole venture was so new, I don't know . . . and so the first broadcast of play-by-play baseball out of the home park was done by WMAQ. . . . At the end of the first year the Cubs finished in fourth place, but their financial receipts were the highest of any club in the National League. . . . it had so stimulated interest, especially among women, that before another year had passed they had established a Women's Day at the park.[92]

The following year the White Sox games and football from North-western University and the University of Chicago were added to the schedule. Drama, live music remotes, and household features modeled on the *Daily News* women's pages filled up most of the day and evening hours. During this period, too, stations lobbied in Washington for favorable frequency assignments as pressure built for passage of the Radio Act of 1927. Trying to anticipate the mood of regulators, keeping standards up for comparative frequency evaluations, and building a favorable impression in the rapidly growing radio audience continued to factor high in early broadcasters' practices.

The year 1926 marks a turning point for radio in many ways, but two events stand out in their significance. Both have much to do with the increasing sense that radio could and should take on a more truly *national* role, and that not only economic but also cultural pressures were being brought to bear on the new medium. The first is the formation of the National Broadcasting Company by RCA in 1926. The second is the origination of the single most popular and influential program of radio's early years, *Amos 'n' Andy*. As the voice of radio extended across the country, it spoke to a nation increasingly in the grip of social change, anxious to define itself as one unified culture even as it marked out and ferociously excluded that which threatened the unified front.

Both network practices and narrative representations set in place an imagined community of the air whose personalities and experiences became more real than those of the neighbors down the block, more real, perhaps, than the listener's own. As an "audience," as "con-sumers" and as a "listening public," Americans shifted among newly constructed identities in some ways unified, and in some ways carefully differentiated, by radio's intimate public address. Just as early personalities such as Roxy and Wendell Hall led neophyte listeners through the proper experience of radio entertainment, so the programs devised by networks, especially those derived from *Amos 'n' Andy*'s serialized representations, would lead Americans through an understanding of themselves as a culture, guided by the alluring voice of their most immediate mass medium.

THREE

Who We Are, Who We Are Not:
The Emergence of National Narratives

The two previous chapters have traced some of the initial negotiations among newly formed broadcasting enterprises, popular taste, and an emerging hierarchy of cultural distinctions. Whether because of commercial necessities, federal regulations, or existing cultural and aesthetic traditions, broadcasters of the mid-1920s began to build up a standard repertoire of representational structures in their increasingly formalized forays into the ether. Even in 1927, when the fledgling National Broadcasting Company embarked on the somewhat daunting task of formulating a standard schedule of nationally distributed programming, few could have predicted the program forms that would eventually come to dominate the airwaves. Yet several strains of cultural representation had already emerged that would soon sweep the nation.

It is hardly surprising that radio would find itself compelled to speak first and foremost on the subject of race and ethnic identity, given the social pressures of the 1920s as described in chapter 1; nor does it seem inappropriate that those voices would come from Chicago, center of a lively, newspaper-influenced approach to broadcasting in a city marked by thriving—and often clashing—immigrant ethnic communities, including the rapidly growing black neighborhoods of the South Side. This chapter and the next examine the emergence of radio's most popular programming form, the serial comedy and its offshoots, tracing them to the seminal and controversial Chicago-originated program *Amos 'n' Andy*. Out of a mixture of commercial exigencies, widespread cultural tensions surrounding race and its relationship to ethnic assimilation and national identity, and the selective adaptation of preexisting cultural forms such as the minstrel show and serial narratives, a new narrative form began to address the American public—a newly conceived version of the American public

75

that placed individuals in a new relationship both to others in their community and to the broadcasting institution itself. This relationship involved careful exclusions as well as assiduously developed ties, and both sides of the process contributed to that phenomenon soon known globally as "American broadcasting."

Race Music and Minstrel Shows

Any discussion of radio's representations of race in the 1920s and 1930s must focus on two things: first, the relative *absence* of black-produced cultural forms and of African Americans themselves in radio's resolutely white public address, and second, the ubiquitous *presence* of one particular form of representation deeply rooted in the divisive race and class hierarchies of American culture, the minstrel show. Homi Bhabha describes the double-edged representational position of marginalized groups as "both 'overlooked'—in the double sense of social surveillance and psychic disavowal—and, at the same time, overdetermined—psychically projected, made stereotypical and symptomatic."[1] This condition applies in varying degrees to a number of ethnic representations on radio, including those in the process of being assimilated into an overarching "white" identity during these crucial years of the 1920s and 1930s. Yet racial hierarchy forms the underlying problematic for the cultural negotiation of ethnicity in the United States generally during this period, and the treatment of African American cultural identity as expressed through radio representations constitutes a crucial, and neglected, aspect of radio's unifying and nationalizing discourse.

As Ann Douglas demonstrates in her recent *Terrible Honesty: Mongrel Manhattan in the 1920s*, racial distinctions, negotiations, and collaborations permeated these vital decades of U.S. popular culture but have too frequently been omitted from social accounts that see only the "whiteface" results of intense struggles over cultural authenticity and meaning.[2] Radio provided both a means of access to the general public for African American voices, sounds, and meanings previously suppressed, but it also set limits and restrictions on their expression through emerging dominant conventions of practice and portrayal, as America struggled with its "mongrel" heritage. Through radio, elements of African American experience became part of the common culture, and African Americans moved into full participation as audiences in this barrier-reducing slice of social life as in few others, yet at a price: the "disavowal" of black Americans themselves in the public sphere created by radio.

Douglas writes, "Black artists and the new sound media met in mutual enthusiam."[3] Though restrictions on the playing of recordings limited the influence of the burgeoning race and jazz record industry in broadcasting practice, live performances of black artists formed an early, if contained, part of radio's emerging voice. KDKA featured jazz pianist Earl Hines in 1921, playing as a duo with Lois Deppe. Burton Peretti quotes Deppe as recalling, "The broadcast created a lot of excitement . . . especially in the colored neighborhoods. . . . there was a radio buff on Wylie Avenue who had loudspeakers sticking out his window" for the crowd that had assembled in the street.[4] That same year, Ethel Waters broadcast with the Fletcher Henderson Jazz Masters in New Orleans. These were occasional broadcasts, as were most musical performances at this early period, but by 1924 Duke Ellington could be heard regularly from the Cotton Club in Harlem on New York station WHN, picked up by CBS in 1929, just as Fats Waller's "Rhythm Club" reached Cincinnati audiences over WWL. Chicago station WBBM, owned by brothers Ralph and Leslie Atlass, specialized in jazz in its early years.[5] As Ann Douglas writes, "If, for the New Negro, culture was politics, even suffrage, the sound media represented something like election to national office."[6] Importantly, radio and recordings allowed direct transmission in aural form of frequently improvised and rhythmically complex black musical performance, preserving blues and jazz in a condition unmediated by Western notation systems and translations by white musicians.

However, the vast bulk of jazz on radio throughout its history featured white musicians and orchestras, and in fact the term was often used misleadingly to designate any kind of mainstream popular music with a "twist" or swing beat. The most popular jazz musicians on the air at that time, such as Paul Whiteman, Bix Beiderbecke, and Tommy Dorsey, borrowed heavily from black jazz traditions to synthesize a more mainstream sound of their own. Such white jazzmen were greeted with seeming relief and celebration by those cultural forces whose distrust of jazz's African American roots had created the atmosphere of censure around this music in the early 1920s. Gilbert Seldes, one of the first critics to take up and defend jazz as an art form, patronizingly dismissed "negro" players and composers in 1923:

So far in their music the negros have given their response to the world with an exceptional naiveté, a directness of expression which has interested *our* minds as well as touched our emotions; they have shown comparatively little evidence of the function of *their* intelligence. . . . Nowhere is the failure of the negro to exploit his gifts more obvious than in the use he has made of the jazz orchestra; for although nearly every negro jazz band is better than nearly every white band, no negro band has yet come up to the level of the best white ones, and the leader of the best of all, by a little joke, is called Whiteman.[7]

In this article Seldes attempts to create a hierarchy around jazz, with very little self-conscious awareness that the very standards he applies are themselves expressly designed to produce the conclusion he seemingly regrets—and with complete assurance of the racial purity of the audience he addresses. Paul Whiteman's name may have been a coincidence, but it was no joke. American composer Virgil Thomson made these distinctions clearer: "Paul Whiteman has transformed [jazz] into something utterly different from its earlier implications. He has refined it, smoothed its harshness, taught elegance to its rhythms, blended its jarring polyphonies into an ensemble of mellow harmonic unity. He has suppressed what was striking and original in it and taught it the manners of Vienna."[8]

This kind of discursive positioning worked to remove actual black musicians from the airwaves. Even though, to quote one historian, "it is literally true that there was more good jazz broadcast in the United States in the 1920s than there is today, virtually all of it live,"[9] much of this popularization was done at the expense of black artists, who remained excluded from regular presence in network broadcasts and studio work through most of radio's history.[10] Peretti quotes white jazz musician Jimmy Maxwell as remembering CBS's practices in the 1920s and 1930s: "The studio worked just like everybody else, they had categories. . . . if you were a black musician you were a jazz player and you didn't get too [many] calls to be a lead player."[11] White musicians and sponsors contributed to the limitations of radio work for black performers. According to Perreti, white studio musicians derided their black counterparts for following "'CPT,' 'colored people's time,' which allegedly made black players undependable for live broadcasting," and sponsors considered black orchestra members to be "illiterate" and "troublemakers."[12]

Even when black musicians were permitted to broadcast directly to the public, their performances were usually contained within program conventions and formats dominated by white culture that presented them as "exotic" or explicitly marginal to normative practices. In 1937, when J. Walter Thompson produced what was billed as the first *All Colored Program* for Fleischmann's Yeast, starring jazz superstar Louis Armstrong, then at the height of his popularity, it was within the confines of a script that insisted on Armstrong's use of minstrel dialect and incorporated a weekly "sketch" by two comic characters, Eddie Green and Gee Gee James, firmly within the demeaning stereotypes of minstrel characterization. When Armstrong refused to speak this dialogue, changing lines into Standard English as he read them over the air, he gained a reputation for being "difficult" to work with; the show was canceled after only six weeks.[13]

This example illustrates the pervasive containment of black presence on the airwaves through the American tradition of the minstrel show. Just as the touring minstrel show itself was becoming a thing of the past, and as vaudeville moved into ethnic comedy and "yokel" humor in its place, radio provided a venue for mintrelsy's survival well into the 1940s. Broadcasts of local amateur minstrel performances found their way onto airwaves across the country in the 1920s; Pittsburgh station KQV in December 1922 presented the fascinating spectacle of the "Ladies of Ruth Chapter No. 89, Order of the Eastern Star of Dormont, PA. Broadcasting for the benefit of the large Radio Audience the 'Minstrel Show,' staged on December 6, at Dormont School auditorium, by this chapter, given with all features of 'minstrelsy,' a high class snappy 'show.'"[14] A picture of the ladies of the chapter accompanied the article in which this announcement appeared, under the heading "Principals in Minstrel at Station KQV"—perhaps to dispell any lingering suspicions that these ladies might actually be black. This kind of amateur minstrel theatrical had a long history in small-town American culture and provided Freeman Gosden and Charles Correll, later to create radio's *Amos 'n' Andy*, with their training.

Vaudeville blackface teams made a smooth transition onto radio in the mid-1920s. George Moran and Charlie Mack stepped off the stage and in front of the microphones as "The Two Black Crows" on local stations, appearing regularly on *The Majestic Theater Hour* on CBS in 1928. WEAF featured "The Gold Dust Twins," Harvey Hindermeyer and Earl Tuckerman, on Tuesday nights in 1924, followed by the *Silver Masked Tenor*. Many network programs featured either "exotic natives" or minstrel teams within their overall continuity. These included "Watermelon and Canteloupe," appearing on WEAF in the early 1930s, and "Molasses and January" on NBC's *Maxwell House Showboat*, the latter played by two African American performers, Ernest Whitman and Eddie Green. As William Barlow points out, many black vaudeville performers found themselves obliged to "black up" and play minstrel roles, on stage and radio. Bert Williams appeared over WHN during his appearances with the Ziegfeld Follies. Jack L. Cooper, who was to become one of the founders of black format radio in the 1940s, sometimes claimed to represent "the first four Negroes on radio" in a 1922 variety show on Washington, D.C., station WCAP, in which he played four different roles, all minstrel inflected. Minstrel routines were frequently included in variety show formats, and programs such as the *Dutch Masters Minstrels* ran on NBC Blue from 1929 to 1932; *The Sinclair Minstrel Show* (NBC Blue, 1932–35) and *Pick and Pat* (NBC Red, 1934) were considered particularly appealing to the older (white) male audience.[15]

Yet figures from the minstrel tradition could also be used in other broadcasting forms, reinforcing caricatured representations out of the burlesqued vaudeville tradition from which they derived. These representations show up especially strongly in daytime shows for women and children as developed by the J. Walter Thompson Company in the late 1920s and early 1930s. Quaker Oats sponsored a kind of soap opera based around its Aunt Jemima trademark character on NBC in 1929. Set on the "old Higbee plantation in Dixie—famous for miles around because of Aunt Jemima's cooking," the show harked back to "those care-free old plantation days" and combined "spirituals" and other music with a serial narrative involving Aunt Jemima and her family, all done in heavily reinforced minstrel dialect and performed by white actors. The script called for much emphasis on cooking and eating, working its commercial plugs for the pancake mix into the plot.[16] Also in 1929, the Cream of Wheat company determined to capitalize on its trademark, the black chef known as Rastus, by creating a children's program around it. Called *The Cream of Wheat Menagerie*, the program featured musical selections performed by the chef's imaginary animal friends, with minstrel dialect introductions between the numbers. This format lasted for one season, from January to September 1929, when it was replaced with the long-running *Jolly Bill and Jane*.[17] Early the next year, Ida Bailey Allen, host and president of

CBS's Radio Homemakers Club, presented a series of talks on "plantation cooking" sponsored by Brer Rabbit Molasses. The first broadcast began with a brief introduction of its characters: "The personnel includes Ida Bailey Allen, president of the [Radio Homemakers Club], author, lecturer, and authority on home economics; Mammy, [an] old colored woman from New Orleans; and the Ginger Bread Man— [word omitted] and brown—just the color of his namesake."[18]

This program relied on the "mammy" figure of the minstrel tradition to contrast the "scientific," modern approach to cooking with the old-fashioned, traditional methods embodied by both the "mammy" character and the "gingerbread man" played by white actor Jessie Gaynor. Very much along the lines described by George Lipsitz in his analysis of early television's working-class and ethnic comedies, the unwanted characteristics of an older cultural tradition were displaced for white audiences onto a racial "other," while the desired associations with warm memory and "old-fashioned cooking" were decontextualized and attached to a new, improved, more "American" product.[19] As the mammy figure exclaims, "Humph. Ah never reads recipes," the scientific homemaker demonstrates, "But, Mammy, in order to cook accurately most people must follow a recipe and measure level," and so on.[20] The timing of these particular representations in 1929 and 1930 must be at least partially attributed to the ongoing success of *Amos 'n' Andy*, whose nationally broadcast blackface comedy spoke to the racial and ethnic tensions of 1920s culture, as we shall see. The emphasis that radio placed on the minstrel tradition, and the corresponding absence of authentic and uncontained black voices on the air, demonstrates the structuring role played by the increasingly nationalized voice of U.S. commercial radio in maintaining social hierarchies and distinctions, and in providing audiences with a way of understanding themselves and their role in this new, modernized American culture of assimilation and consumption.

Learning Whiteness: *Amos 'n' Andy*

Other historians have recognized the importance of *Amos 'n' Andy* in the development of radio programming, yet its subject matter—its central involvement in the question of race—has been treated as an unfortunate irrelevancy, a lapse of taste on the part of its creators, an unfortunate historical remnant whose impact can best be treated by passing over it quickly.[21] But just as the centrality of *Amos 'n' Andy* to the development of broadcast discourse cannot be overlooked, so its subject matter cannot be treated as other than essential to its formal structures and reception. That it was effective in somehow reaching unprecedented numbers of radio listeners and in touching their common experience in some way is attested to by its remarkable popularity over a thirty-year span. That it was influential in the evolving forms of the new medium is also indisputable. Its initial format, providing a daily serialized, open-ended narrative with low-key humor based on a returning cast of characters, resembles soap opera as much as situation comedy, and in fact led to the development of both forms. Followed in 1930 on NBC by several short-lived comedy serials based on comic strips—*Buster Brown and Tige, Mr. and Mrs., Penrod*—*Amos 'n' Andy* also inspired serial drama that would soon move to daytime, such as *The Rise of the Goldbergs, Clara, Lu and Em*, and *Myrt and Marge*. *Amos 'n' Andy* proved to the emergent radio industry that serialized narrative drama, whether comedy, adventure, or romance, could be the basic building block of a new medium.[22]

The role of newspapers, the *Chicago Tribune* in particular, as important innovators in comic, film, and radio serials is an overlooked topic in media history and helps to explain radio's development of and reliance on the serial format. The newspaper is the original serial form: appearing daily, open-ended, with many recurring features. From an initial concentration on factual information and opinion, newspapers expanded in the late 1800s into various forms of fictional serials, patterned after the illustrated serial novels and popular magazine fiction of the day. For the newspapers, serialized fictional forms attracted readers to particular newspapers and retained a loyal readership in a way that straight news reporting could not: though each day's news might be the same from paper to paper and discrete from day to day, its comics and fictional features were unique and continuous. The *Chicago Tribune* had been an early innovator in this area, particularly in the development of comic strips. Lyonel Feininger debuted his pioneering strip, "Kin-der-Kids," in the pages of the *Tribune* in 1906; by the 1930s the paper was one of the biggest syndicators of comic strips nationally, including such titles as "The Gumps," "Gasoline Alley," "Little Orphan Annie," "Moon Mullins," and "Dick Tracy."[23]

In 1913, the *Tribune* expanded its interest in serialization to another medium, sparked by a circulation war among Chicago newspapers. *The Adventures of Kathlyn*, one of the very earliest of the film serials, arose as a joint venture between the *Tribune* and the Selig Polyscope Company. This undertaking was patterned after an earlier collaboration between the journal *Ladies World* and the Edison Kinetoscope Company in 1912, resulting in *What Happened to Mary?*, the first film serial.[24] Both ventures made full use of the self-supporting publicity such a collaboration could provide: the movie reinforced the audience for the printed serial, and the newspaper publicized the movie.

Radio served a similar purpose for newspapers in the 1920s and 1930s. As interest in the new medium rose to ever-greater heights, a radio outlet could be used to draw readers to the newspaper for schedules, promotions, scripts, comics, advertising tied to popular radio features, and promotion for the newspaper in general. In turn, radio programs on newspaper-owned stations enjoyed an immediate and crucial advantage over those with different ownership: free, motivated, and frequent publicity. This could both entice artists of renown onto the air, in the days before radio performers were paid, and ensure a show's continued presence in the public mind.

At the same time, the American Society of Composers, Authors, and Publishers (ASCAP) had begun to agitate for payment for radio performances, thus threatening the economic mainstay of most radio stations of the period: unpaid talent whose reward was perceived to result from just the kind of publicity that a newspaper could provide. It became imperative for broadcasters to look around for a new economic base. In *The Classical Hollywood Cinema*, Bordwell, Staiger, and Thompson document the movie industry's early turn to fictionalized narratives as a response to the demand for regular, inexpensive product.[25] A similar situation was beginning to develop in radio broadcasting in 1926, and broadcasters responded in two ways: first, by forming commercial networks, whose larger listener bases could justify higher fees to offset programming costs; and second, by developing the serial narrative form, which could both regularize product output and assure a consistent, steady flow of material. Musical programs could be, and were, similarly stabilized, and forms of anthology drama were initiated; children's "story hours" brought readings from fictional narratives onto the air from the very earliest years. Yet drama developed specifically for the radio medium, in a recurring format, remained just beyond the imagination of radio's busy program directors.

Meantime, two "song and patter" entertainers had made their debut on nearby station WEBH. Known as "the harmony boys" or sometimes as "the two songbirds," Charles Correll played piano to Freeman Gosden's ukelele, in between bouts of "happy banter and jesting." The two had met as traveling producers for the Joe Bren organization, a company that provided material and semiprofessional direction for public groups putting on amateur variety shows, usually featuring minstrel acts.[26] Hired by WGN as a "harmony team" in the fall of 1925, they had an act that fell well within the established format of musical variety, with nothing that would distinguish it from the general run of radio programming.

It is unclear exactly whose idea it was to add drama to the variety mix on WGN, but in the context of the *Tribune*'s previous experience with serialization, it was a logical extension. One account attributes the idea to Ben McCanna, an executive in charge of broadcasting at the *Tribune*, who expressed a desire for a "radio theater" incorporating "bits of drama and musically pictured incident" in a station memo.[27] Arthur Wertheim credits Henry Selinger, the manager of WGN, with the idea of developing a radio adaptation of "The Gumps," a popular comic strip run in the *Tribune*.[28] In Correll's own words, from a newspaper interview in 1926: "WGN wanted a radio comic strip—that is, a daily feature that would run along in sequence to hold the interest of the fans. . . . We had been at the station about a month and they suggested that we put on a radio version of the Gumps. But we . . . proposed that we start a colored comedy, instead."[29] The reason given for this change was that Gosden and Correll felt uncomfortable with the Gump characters and preferred to establish their own; they chose blackface characters because of their previous experience with minstrel shows and also, as Gosden stated in a much later interview, "because blackface could tell funnier stories than whiteface comics."[30]

Sam 'n' Henry debuted on WGN on January 12, 1926, without any trace of the "musically pictured incident" or anything other than two voices, speaking in a version of traditional minstrel "dialect."[31] Like a comic strip, and unlike any other evening program of this period, the show ran regularly and repetitively, six nights a week, from 10:00 until 10:10 p.m. This, and the serial nature of its story line, allowed it to build up a loyal listening audience in the Midwest and as far as WGN's clear-channel signal would carry. In addition, the *Tribune* served as a ready-made publicity medium for the program, urging readers to tune in to Sam and Henry's latest adventures and publicizing Gosden and Correll's live performances. During 1927, the paper ran an illustrated *Sam 'n' Henry* script in its Sunday Metropolitan section and syndicated it to other newspapers across the country.[32]

By early 1928, *Sam 'n' Henry* had become so popular nationwide through personal appearances, recordings, books, toys, and other ancillary products (such as the "Sam 'n' Henry" candy bar) that demand for the program exceeded the reach of WGN's signal. Though NBC had been in operation for more than a year, WGN was not a network station, and indeed NBC had not yet deigned to interest itself in the somewhat lowbrow popular programs that many local stations might have provided. The alternative was to record the program on disk and then distribute copies to other stations across the country. This was an innovative and somewhat subversive idea; recording on disk was difficult and untested, and as yet no radio program of any reputation had elected to bypass the network distribution system in favor of syndication. However, WGN, for reasons that are unclear considering the *Tribune*'s highly developed comic strip syndication business, refused Gosden and Correll permission for this pioneering attempt at radio syndication.

Judith Waller, program director at rival *Chicago Daily News* station WMAQ, recognized the value of *Sam 'n' Henry*'s growing popularity and offered Gosden and Correll a contract that included syndication rights. Because the *Tribune* held copyright ownership of the name *Sam 'n' Henry*, a new name had to be devised. After a brief period of uncertainty—trying out "Jim 'n' Charlie" and "Tom 'n' Harry" as new possibilities—the names "Amos 'n' Andy" were agreed upon. [33] The first episode of the new show aired on March 19, 1928.

The syndicated *Amos 'n' Andy* retained—in fact repeated, with some variations—the story line from *Sam 'n' Henry*. We first meet the two main characters as they head to the train station, this time in Atlanta. Arriving in Chicago, they are confused and disoriented, taken advantage of by several city slicker types, and finally directed to a place "where two colored boys can get a room"—South State Street, in real life the heart of Chicago's growing African American district. They find a room, take on and leave various jobs, and are introduced to a men's social club (in *Sam 'n' Henry* known as the "Jewels of the Crown," in *Amos 'n' Andy* changed to the now famous "Mystic Knights of the Sea") presided over by the Kingfish, whose character was to become the focus of the television show. Later the two buy a broken-down car and found the "Fresh Air Taxicab Company"—named for their car's lack of any sort of top covering.

Due to the wider scope made possible by the new "chainless chain," stations all over the country could now air *Amos 'n' Andy*. Gosden and Correll would record the programs six weeks in advance and ship records out to subscribing stations. In addition, every night at 7:11 p.m., *Amos 'n' Andy* went out live from WMAQ in Chicago. The *Daily News* backed up the program's popularity with a comic strip with dialogue written by Gosden and Correll, recapping the pair's nightly adventures. In 1929, Waller attempted to interest a network in national sponsorship of the program.[34] This was done in conjunction with William Benton of the Lord and Thomas advertising agency, who convinced the Pepsodent toothpaste company that *Amos 'n' Andy* would make an appropriate vehicle for their advertising. Again, it was unusual for a sponsored radio program at this time not to incorporate its sponsor's product more directly into the program, if only in the title. Pepsodent's sponsorship of *Amos 'n' Andy* worked to clear the way for a new style of radio advertising, the separate "spot" appearing at breaks in the program.

The show made its NBC network debut on August 19, 1929. This further escalated its popularity: between 1929 and 1931, at its height, it is estimated that *Amos 'n' Andy* attracted an audience of forty million nightly. Wertheim describes some of the effects of its phenomenal success:

> The telephone company claimed that calls declined during the show's fifteen minutes on the air. . . . Motion picture theaters installed loud speakers in lobbies so that fans could hear the program over a radio placed on the stage. . . . "There are three things I shall never forget about America—the Rocky Mountains, Niagara Falls, and *Amos 'n' Andy*," said the playwright George Bernard Shaw.[35]

Obviously the program was touching a chord of some kind in, and about, the American psyche.

Though an examination of institutions and economics can delineate the necessary conditions for an innovation to occur—in this case, the utility of serialized drama in the type of radio-newspaper collaboration conducted by the *Tribune* and the *Daily News*—it cannot account for a text's meaning or reception, both in terms of the audience and as an influence on future radio texts. A text must draw on its social and cultural context both to find its means of expression and to reach an audience that will understand it—though understandings will vary. *Amos 'n' Andy* grew from cultural roots in the serial narrative and social satire of the comic strip,[36] the racial humor and characterizations of the minstrel show, and the American vaudeville tradition of ethnic humor, already featured on radio. These influences manifested themselves in an intricately and precisely constructed text, producing a discourse that touched on many topics but whose fundamental, and essential, focus remained on race and the definition of racial identity.[37] I am concerned in the following discussion with two issues: the signification of "blackness" in *Amos 'n' Andy*, or how the program defined its characters as "black" and the significance of that definition; and the program's secondary discourse on enculturation, or how the encoding of "blackness" was embedded in a larger discourse on enculturation of diverse groups into a loosely unified society, and the role played in this process by the "Africanist presence."[38]

Cultural Projections

Radio does indeed seem a strange medium when one considers that two of its most popular shows—*Amos 'n' Andy* and the later program starring Charlie McCarthy/Edgar Bergen—were predicated on purely visual elements, skin color and ventriloquism, that could not be transmitted over the air. It is as if one of film's greatest stars were invisible. Thus, the first question that must be asked is, How did first *Sam 'n' Henry* and then *Amos 'n' Andy* position characters as "black"? Clearly, it was not through the visual cue of skin color, nor was it through introductory narration. According to WGN's account, announcer Bill Hay opened the broadcast with the simple words "10:10. WGN. *Sam 'n' Henry*." The show went directly into these lines of dialogue:

Sam: Henry, did you ever see a mule as slow as dis one?
Henry: Oh, dis mule is fast enough. We gonna get to de depot alright.
Sam: You know dat Chicago train don't wait for nobody—it just goes on—just stops and goes right on.
Henry: Well, we ain't got but two more blocks to go—don't be so patient, don't be so patient.
Sam: I hope they got faster mules dan dis up in Chicago.

Most obviously, Gosden and Correll's initial and continued characterization of Sam Smith and Henry Johnson as "black" relied heavily on minstrel show conventions with which radio audiences were already familiar. This was done through use of a certain kind of dialect and accent accepted as "black"; however, separating this accent from that of a white southerner required additional cues. One of these was use of ungrammatical and confused English, another the definition of the two characters solidly in the tradition of the "Zip Coon" and "Jim Crow" minstrel types. The first episodes establish the character of Amos as Jim Crow—hardworking, sincere, yet superstitious and none too bright, constantly fooled by the machinations of his friend Andy, patterned after Zip Coon—lazy, devious, and manipulative, yet more frequently outsmarting himself, given to womanizing and dubious financial schemes. Also, early episodes offhandedly, but effectively, establish the characters' designated race through their interactions with others and through self-description ("where two colored boys can get a room").

Though both Ely and Wertheim emphasize that Gosden and Correll avoided the most vicious kind of racial humor and characterization in wide circulation at the time, there are many references to elements and activities whose significance lies in racial stereotypes. For example, the show appeared at 7:11 p.m. on WMAQ—a clear reference to crap games, frequently associated in the white imagination with blacks; in episodes 10–12 of the earlier show, Sam and Henry are arrested for shooting craps. Other episodes focus on superstitiousness, as when Sam and Henry give up a job rather than encounter "ghosts" or refuse to work in a funeral parlor, and make frequent reference to drinking and gambling.[39] Through these cultural "cues," Gosden and Correll reminded their audience that these invisible characters should be regarded as "black," and also, of course, reinforced the definition of just what this designation meant.[40]

Yet, though insisting on racial identity in comic characterization, the social consequences of racial identity are resolutely ignored in the program's narrative. Amos and Andy and their associates appear to live in an all-black world, complete at all levels of the social strata. White characters rarely, if ever, appear, and if they do, seem completely free of any kind of racial prejudice or discrimination.[41] The black community is presented as entirely self-sufficient and prosperous, with its own professional and business class, heirs and heiresses, millionaires, bankers, police, and so on, never encountering any kind of racial barriers, never encountering the white world of strict segregation and racial discrimination in any form. Usually, supporting characters do not speak in dialect; their race is rarely identified, leaving open the possibility that blacks and whites could interact far more freely and equally than in fact was the case at the time. Certainly the black characters never seem to encounter any injustice or even unfriendliness; indeed, references to whites or to the system of racial segregation are almost never made.[42] Though Gosden and Correll, and their various publicity outlets, always emphasized the "true-to-life" characteristics of the show—claiming that their characters and settings were based on careful "research" in Harlem and other black communities—it becomes obvious that *Amos 'n' Andy* bore very little relation to anything authentically African American, owing its surface "blackness" only to the imposed racial identity of its characters. In this light, what was the program about?

The dominant preoccupation and source of humor in *Amos 'n' Andy*—which, because it is central to minstrel show characterization as well, is implicated as essentially "black"—is the theme of cultural incompetence. This was not a new idea, having been a staple of vaudeville "ethnic" humor for a century before *Sam 'n' Henry* appeared. One signification of cultural incompetence involves language use and "funny accents," a device milked by "Dutch" acts, Irish acts, Jewish caricatures, and the stage Italian since the dawn of vaudeville. Other "ethnic" traits involved the common situation of the immigrant: "humorous" native customs that clashed with American norms, strange dress, exaggerated speech, odd superstitions, misunderstandings in communication, money troubles, being taken in because of cultural ignorance.[43]

In the 1890s, the "rube" act became popular in vaudeville, shifting the problem from the amusing accent and habits of the immigrant to the ignorance of the country boy in the big city. Through this device the ethnic status of the naïf gradually lost importance—perhaps reflecting the increased tension surrounding the new waves of immigration—blending into a country/city distinction without ethnic markers. This evolution was eventually repeated in radio, though in the 1920s many of vaudeville's ethnic acts carried over onto the new medium: Jack Pearl's character Baron von Munchausen and his famous line, "Vas you dere, Sharlie?"; Sam Hearn, who played the Jewish storyteller Schlepperman on Jack Benny's show; Mel Blanc's Mexican caricatures on Jack Benny's show and others; and Fibber McGee's Greek neighbor Nick Depopolous, played by Bill Thompson. Other shows, such as

The Life of Riley and the serial *The O'Neils*, made use of ethnic "types" within a well-acculturated framework.

Albert McLean, in his book *American Vaudeville as Ritual*, states that a primary function of this kind of humor was "to encourage a sense of community among the diverse groups constituting the American city." Therefore ethnic humor always existed in careful balance with the sensibilities of the performers—who often belonged to the groups they were satirizing—and the audiences themselves. In his words, "The jokes had to leave off at the point at which members of the audience could no longer laugh at themselves."[44] The problem with minstrel and blackface routines, which satirized African Americans, is that for the most part neither the performers themselves nor the audiences who laughed at their antics belonged to the satirized group. Most vaudeville theaters were segregated, with blacks making up either an excluded or highly restricted part of the audience; almost all of the popular blackface acts were performed by white men.[45]

Therefore, one function of the blackface figure in American vaudeville—and in *Amos 'n' Andy*—was as the ultimate outsider, the extreme case against which all other ethnic groups could feel themselves superior—"the projection of the not-me." Toni Morrison puts it even more bluntly: "It is no accident and no mistake that immigrant populations (and much immigrant literature) understood their 'Americanness' as an opposition to the resident black population."[46]

But *Amos 'n' Andy* takes this projection one necessary step further. By posing their two main characters as "native immigrants"—part of the black migration from South to North, farm to city—Gosden and Correll both reflected historical reality and made it mean something beyond simple historical reflection.[47] Amos and Andy's move from Alabama/Georgia to Chicago objectified the status of African Americans in 1920s society as a permanently unassimilable underclass, repressing their outsider status based on race beneath a "cover story" of physical dislocation. Had the two characters remained in Alabama, yet still exhibited such cultural incompetence, questions might be raised about a society that had refused to enculturate such people as these more fully after so many American-born generations. By posing Amos and Andy as rural immigrants to the big city, the show displaced racial otherness onto the comic figure of the "country bumpkin," itself a stand-in for the ethnic immigrant. Combining conventions of ethnic humor with the "country bumpkin" mythos, and tying both to established "black" minstrel characters, *Amos 'n' Andy* created a powerful vehicle of displacement for the society of immigrants to whom it appealed.

Indeed, it is as a "foil" to problems of cultural assimilation that *Amos 'n' Andy* achieves some of its most typical humor. Its use of dialect reinforces the idea of a kind of permanent cultural "accent," emphasizing the unassimilability of African Americans as a group.[48] Amos's confusion over the simplest words and Andy's invariably mistaken explanations take cultural ignorance to an extreme, as in this excerpt from a segment on the 1928 election:

> *Amos*: I don't know either to be a Democrat or a Republican.
> *Andy*: Well, where wha' your ancestors?
> *Amos*: My aun' didn' have no sisters.
> *Andy*: No, no, your ancestor, your . . . never min'. . . . Listen, Coolidge is a Republican an' fo' de' las' fo' years or so he's done had Hoover locked up waitin to put him in office.
> *Amos*: What you mean he done had Hoover locked up?
> *Andy*: Well, I was readin' in de paper right after Hoover was nomulated dat Coolidge was gettin' ready to take Hoover out of de cabinet.[49]

However humorous the lines in themselves might be, their context—performed in dialect recognized as "black," demonstrating an extreme form of cultural and political naïveté—positioned the characters of *Amos 'n' Andy* as our nation's "permanent immigrants," always arriving, never arrived.

Within this context, *Amos 'n' Andy*'s central theme of cultural incompetence linked to race provided a nation of assimilators with comic relief in a "worst possible case" scenario. During the chaotic years of the booming Jazz Age, the onset of the Great Depression, and the tensions of the prewar era, *Amos 'n' Andy* showed an uprooted nation, in James Baldwin's words, "where the bottom is":

> *Because he* [the Negro] *is there*, and *where* he is, beneath us, we know where the limits are and how far we must not fall. We must not fall beneath him. We must not fall that low. . . . In a way, if the Negro were not there, we might be forced to deal within ourselves and our own personalities, with all those vices, all those conundrums and all those mysteries with which we have invested the Negro race.[50]

Amos 'n' Andy's wholly artificial discourse at once identified problems experienced by the outsider attempting to assimilate and projected a representation of nonassimilation in its extreme form onto a small and easily identified minority, African Americans. This combination of identification and projection allowed for a wide range of responses, from those struggling with similar situations to those racist sensibilities who saw in Amos and Andy all their most cherished prejudices objectified.[51] The ambivalence of African American audiences becomes understandable: at once experiencing the same displacements as the rest of the audience, yet asked to respond to a representation that identified them as the "other," black listeners responded to the program in ways that differed across class and regional lines to a greater degree than did white responses.[52]

Other analyses of *Amos 'n' Andy* proceed from the assumption that the show presented a portrait of African Americans at a certain point in time and have concentrated on describing the similarities and dissimilarities of real African American lives to their blackface representations. This misses the point: *Amos 'n' Andy* was not intended to speak to, or about, real American people of color any more than, to use Morrison's comparison, *Uncle Tom's Cabin* was meant to be read by Uncle Tom. Instead, "the subject of the dream is the dreamer":

> The fabrication of an Africanist persona is reflexive; an extraordinary meditation on the self; a powerful exploration of the fears and desires that reside in the writerly conscious. It is an astonishing revelation of longing, of terror, of perplexity, of shame, or magnanimity. It requires hard work *not* to see this.[53]

Substitute "social" for "writerly" conscience—as befits a medium produced institutionally and distributed to millions—and this statement describes *Amos 'n' Andy's* role in exploring and defusing one of the central tensions of U.S. culture, particularly in the context of the 1920s and 1930s.

By 1935 the *Amos 'n' Andy* craze had eased. Though the show was still popular, other situation comedies and serial narratives had eclipsed its ratings. Gosden and Correll, understandably exhausted by the effort of sole writing and acting responsibility since 1926, introduced other actors and writers and in 1943 adapted the show to the half hour, once a week sitcom format, developed by others and by now so familiar to us all. The program had ceased to be innovative, and its own narrative changed as Amos became less important, Andy and Kingfish became the main characters, and new characters such as Lightnin', Sapphire, and Algonquin J. Calhoun took prominence.[54] By the 1960s, after the television controversy, the show was regarded as an out-of-date embarrassment (though it received wide play in syndication), and by 1972 one writer could conclude, "There probably isn't much point in trying to read some deep sociological significance into *Amos 'n' Andy*."[55] Yet *Amos 'n' Andy* did not arise in a cultural vacuum; as a key text in broadcast development—which involves construction of an audience as much as of a text—the terms of its discourse live with us still.

Blackness on Radio

In thinking of radio's construction of an audience, the medium offered unique possibilities for the redrawing of racial lines. As an aural medium, freed from the use of visual representations that dominated other popular culture forms—from theater to vaudeville to photography to movies—it offered reading positions in which race, defined as skin color,[56] disappeared. Radio might have developed as a medium in which race was simply absent—allowing performers to play any type of character, to avoid stipulating a racial identity at all, and permitting listeners to supply their own descriptive characterizations based on whatever representational traditions their experience supplied. Here we can see the limitations of mere technology to influence practice; as demonstrated above, tradition and convention defied technology in the earliest days of radio's dispersal to return with a vengeance, insisting over and over upon the racial and ethnic markers that the technology itself might have erased. In order to contain the danger that removal of America's primary method of making racial and social distinction threatened, early radio worked hard to confine representations of African Americans and other "nonwhites" within the narrow and derogatory categories set up by the minstrel tradition—saying, in effect, *Here* is blackness on radio: marked by minstrel dialect, second-class citizen traits, cultural incompetence. In effect, then, by setting up only this category of representation as "black," radio engineered its freedom to categorize *all other* representations as white. White became the default mode of radio representation, not simply by habit or common agreement or convenience, but deliberately and forcefully through a system of representation that carefully overdetermined this distinction and assigned greater cultural value to all that was defined as nonblack. Minstrel representations such as *Amos 'n' Andy* made radio safe for whiteness, carefully delimiting the possibility of race-indeterminate readings for all members of the newly constituted radio audience.

For white audiences, this reified bifurcation of characterization into an easily identifiable "black" and an all-else-encompassing "white" elided otherwise significant ethnic differences into a "whiteface" whole. Even programs such as *The Goldbergs* and *I Remember Mama*, while marking out some degree of white ethnicity, carefully placed their characters in the assimilatory trajectory. White audiences were invited to see themselves in the vast majority of representations on radio, to read out the dissimilarities between their own ethnic experience and that of the vast undifferentiated "America" constructed on the air, and to pose this identity in strict and stark contrast to those defined as "black." Black audiences found themselves forced out of this easy identification with the mainstream of radio, specifically assigned to "another" place marked by traits designated from the outset as the "not-me." In a discursive universe that assigned "black" racial identity *only* to characterizations that fit with minstrel stereotypes, that defined whiteness as the norm and therefore consigned any demonstration of nonwhiteness to the nonnormal—and yet that insisted on the delineation of nonwhiteness as the sole avenue of representation for certain groups—black audiences were consigned to that state of "double consciousness" described by W. E. B. Du Bois:

> It is a peculiar sensation this double consciousness, this sense of always looking at one's self through the eyes of others, of measuring one's soul by the tape of a world that looks on in amused contempt and pity. One ever feels his twoness, an American, A Negro; two souls, two thoughts, two unreconciled strivings, two warring ideals in one dark body, whose dogged strength alone keeps it from being torn asunder.[57]

Thus, even though the presence of a set of representations specifically redeemed from the overbearing whiteness of radio and identified as "black" could hold some empowering elements, the passing of these representations through the filter of white consciousness created a double bind for black audiences.

Although many African Americans spoke out against *Amos 'n' Andy*'s derogatory narrative, others enjoyed the show, found some validation in the acknowledgment of their experience, praised the background portrayal of a self-sufficient black world, and—particularly for the urban middle-class audience—participated in the "projection of the not-me" onto the rural bumpkin figure of displacement. Yet, when confronted with the role that these representations played in the white imagination, their articulation is complicated and made contradictory. This situation has not altered with time. Henry Louis Gates Jr. writes of his enjoyment of the series on television as a boy:

> What really captivated me was that in the all-black world of Amos 'n' Andy's Harlem, there was an all-black department store, owned and operated by black attendants for a black clientele, whose children could sit on the lap of a black Santa Claus. . . . and then I saw it . . . there in the heart of Santa Claus Land, perched high on the display shelf, was Arbadella's talking doll. She was wearing a starched, white fluffy dress, made all the brighter by contrast with the doll baby's gleaming black skin. A black doll! The first I'd ever seen. How fortunate those people in Harlem are, I thought. Not only do they have their own department stores; those department stores sell black dolls![58]

Critic Margo Jefferson relates a similar experience, yet contextualized differently:

> Belonging to the type of the educated Negro, I found Lightning provocatively unlike me (which let me laugh at him) and yet oddly like me (which let me laugh with him). For one thing, we were both cross-eyed. For another thing, which had precious little to do with race, I was a child, and his was the comedy of regression. . . . One day at school I was chatting with a classmate, and we started recounting the last episode of "Amos 'n' Andy." Nothing seemed more natural than that he would slip into a rendition of one of Kingfish's famous exclamations. . . . as soon as the words came out of his mouth, I stopped enjoying myself. I smiled weakly and hurried the conversation on. But because he was white and I was black, all sorts of other things had suddenly attached themselves to Amos, Andy, Lightning and Kingfish: charged talk about "equality" and "prejudice," and what holds "us" back and how "they" like to think we behave.[59]

This contradiction can be seen in the reception in the black press of a later comic figure, Eddie Anderson's "Rochester" on *The Jack Benny Program* (discussed in chapter 7). The *Chicago Defender* lists the program as "Eddie Anderson—with Jack Benny," in a radio listing that ignores most of the networks' offerings to concentrate on those few that include the rare appearance of an African American performer. The *Negro Year Book 1941–46* prefaces its description of "The Negro on Radio Programs," "Standing out as the most popular of all Negro actors appearing regularly on the radio is the comedian, 'Rochester' (Eddie Anderson), valet, friend and general adviser to Jack Benny,"

but devotes the next several pages to those programs that permit appearances of African Americans either outside of or in direct opposition to the reigning minstrel category.[60] That even in 1946, after five
years of concentrated war-effort-inspired attempts to "improve" representations of blackness on the radio (discussed in chapter 8), these
attempts could be enumerated in their singularity points to the dogged
persistence of limitations on black representation, and the effectiveness of institutional restrictions on nonminstrel black appearances and
performance, that formed the very essence of radio's national identity-
building discourse. The centrality of these distinctions to radio's most
cherished functions and purposes can be seen in such seemingly dispersed details as Arturo Toscanini's stipulation that no black performers be allowed in his much-celebrated NBC Symphony Orchestra—
marking off the network's high-culture efforts from the taint of
blackness—and Estelle Edmerson's inadvertent intervention in Los
Angeles union practices in the 1950s: even in 1954, separate and unequal local chapters of the American Federation of Musicians (AFM)
worked to keep black musicians off the air.[61] Thus, even in a medium
that possessed the potential to defy racial categorization and segregated audience experience, the importance of the dynamic of ethnic
assimilation into "whiteness" and the marking off of the nonwhite remained too central to radio's construction of identity to be left to the
perceptions of the audience alone. And though race and racial representations form a key area of radio's narrative operations, another important social distinction—never separate from racial issues but bound
up in the same cultural hierarchies—worked to define audience experience and expectations in another way: the subversive realm of gender, the delineation of a separate "women's sphere" within the once-
undifferentiated flow of radio broadcasting. This issue will be taken
up in chapters 5 and 6. But radio's negotiation of race and gender, of
the unacceptable and the transgressive, took place in a framework of
commercial development and evolving institutional practices that
shaped the narrative and voices dominating radio practice for the next
thirty years. Sometimes agreeing, sometimes conflicting, the emergent
networks and their advertisers created the system known as American
broadcasting.

► FOUR

Eavesdropping on America: Kitchen Table Conversations

If in the early 1920s each station developed "its own homemade sound,"[1] usually linked to the central business of its owner and relying on local and promotionally motivated talent, by the late 1920s most stations and the emerging network programming departments viewed themselves as program originators looking for sponsors. Programs initiated on a sustaining basis attracted audiences and advertisers to the idea of radio, and the sooner an outside sponsor could be found, usually through an advertising agency, the better.

One of the innovations of the fledgling NBC Program Department in 1926 was to reverse that equation, placing sponsor interest first in the program creation process. Bertha Brainard, formerly station manager of WJZ, who had won out over Phillips Carlin, program manager at WEAF, to become NBC's first director of commercial programming, described her department's functions in a 1926 letter to a potential client: "This department secures suitable talent of known reputation and popularity, creates your program and surrounds it with announcements and atmosphere closely allied with your selling thought."[2] A chapter for a book on "careers in advertising" written in 1932 by John F. Royal, vice president for programming at NBC, indicates clearly that the purpose of network sustaining programs was first and foremost to attract sponsors, despite representations made to the FRC that these programs fulfilled public service responsibilities.[3] Their role, then, as first NBC, then CBS, saw it in the late 1920s and early 1930s, was to act as corporate impressarios, rounding up talent, devising program ideas, and putting on a continuous series of shows, then brokering them to a sponsor, usually through an agency. This role was about to change.

The Legacy of Amos 'n' Andy

The popularity of Amos 'n' Andy, particularly after its network success, hit the radio industry like a bolt of lightning and pointed the way to the development of a whole new narrative form. Drawing on the serial comic strip, the vaudeville skit, and the fledgling genre of radio drama, the "dialogue sketch" became the most frequent addition to station and network schedules in the early 1930s. Harrison Summers lists a total of five narrative-format shows—characterized as "Informative Drama" or "Light, Homey or 'Love Interest' Drama"—on network schedules of the 1927–28 season. By 1932, these categories had expanded to seven others—adding "Comedy Drama," "Thriller Drama," and "Women's Serial Drama" at night and repeating these and several others for the daytime—with a total of forty programs listed.[4] Some of these were very short-lived; others persisted throughout the history of radio and continued onto television. While radio programming expanded generally, and the musical variety and "light music" format remained the most popular overall, the dramatic narrative program evolving out of the dialogue sketch showed the most striking growth and represented a truly new form unique to radio. In 1935, the number of drama programs had expanded to more than sixty, not including the nighttime music/comedy/variety programs, such as *The Jack Benny Program*, in which the comedy dialogue segment had slowly begun to take over much of the action. By the 1946–47 season, the total of drama programs amounted to 133, including more than forty women's daytime serials alone. And these were only the network programs; many local stations and program syndicators specialized in drama programs as well, which they aired at various times of the day.

In the following section I will concentrate on the evolution of the serial/series dramatic narrative form, looking first at a few of the pioneering shows in this genre and then discussing their eventual differentiation into subgenres, such as family drama, thriller drama, the daytime serial, and the comedy sketch on the variety show. This can in no way be a comprehensive study of this very popular form; I will focus on those shows whose popularity indicates a high level of success in negotiating that narrow and contested terrain within which the interests of the U.S. radio industry and the listening public converged, as well as those programs that were significant in influencing the genre in less obvious ways. Analysis of the daytime serial will be carried over into chapters 5 and 6, within the context of the development of separate genres for women in the daytime; some of the best-known comedy/variety programs, such as those starring Jack Benny and Fred Allen, will be discussed in chapter 7, along with other high-profile nighttime offerings, such as *The Lux Radio Theatre* and Orson Welles's *Mercury Theater of the Air*.

Finally, one very important aspect of these genres' development must be discussed: the role played in radio production by the major advertising agencies, under whose aegis and impetus most of the more popular program formats originated. The increasing "popularization" of radio (always with a certain privileged audience and purpose in mind) found itself often at odds with the more highly controlled vision of the major networks, particularly NBC, and resulted in frequent clashes and ever more vitriolic criticism of the shows' "low" cultural standards. The networks' struggle for control over popular tastes and values rose to a peak during the 1930s as radio became a highly profitable and stable national institution.

The Rise of Radio Narrative

While *Amos 'n' Andy*'s racially fraught comedy made the biggest splash in serial drama development, many other innovators in the late 1920s experimented with the new form. Some achieved only local popularity; others went on to become network staples. Whereas a few, like *The Rise of the Goldbergs* and, to a lesser extent, *Fibber McGee and Molly*, included representations of ethnicity directly, others consciously eschewed America's mixed heritage by creating the classless, raceless, rigidly gendered world that existed nowhere but on radio and later television, under the heading of "the typical American family"— an irony from which we still cannot seem to break quite free. Yet one of the early innovators in dramatized serial narratives took quite a different approach. Bernarr Macfadden's *True Story* magazine, and the radio show that he initiated in 1928, specialized in the revelation of the shocking, the scandalous, the tragic and unusual, under the exculpating cover so useful to many a broadcaster or journalist before and since: the stories were all *true*. Radio's ability to bring the exotic into the American home here generated a narrative impulse similar to, but along a slightly different track from, *Amos 'n' Andy*.

Bernarr Macfadden must surely rank as one of the most bizarre and flamboyant figures of the early part of the century, and also one of its most prolific publishers.[5] Building on his *Physical Culture* empire of lectures, pamphlets, and books—with titles such as *Brain Energy Building and Nerve-Vitalizing Force, Be Married and Like It!*, and *The Virile Powers of Superb Manhood: How Developed, How Lost,*

How Regained—by the early 1920s Macfadden published a series of tabloid-style magazines (as well as the notorious *New York Graphic*, the ur-tabloid newspaper), among the most popular of which were *True Story, True Experiences,* and *True Romances.* In 1924 he expanded into *True Detective Stories;* these would form the basis for the Macfadden entry into radio broadcasting. Beginning with morning setting-up exercises along *Physical Culture* lines, which aired on WOR in 1923 and later featured John Gambling, the Macfadden formula expanded into radio serials in 1928. *Physical Culture Prince* debuted in 1927 on NBC as a fifteen-minute program Monday nights at 7:45, modifying into the *Physical Culture Hour,* a thirty-minute program, aired on CBS, at 9:00 on Monday nights from 1928 to 1929. Simultaneously, *True Story Hour* went on the air in 1927 for an entire sixty minutes on CBS, Friday nights at 9:00. *True Romances* (Tuesday 8:30) and *True Detective Mysteries* (Thursday 9:00) began in 1929, all on CBS; both of these were half-hour dramas airing at prime mid-evening weeknight times and formed a not-inconsiderable part of the fledgling CBS schedule.

Perhaps Macfadden's increasingly controversial reputation as owner of the *New York Graphic* as well as sundry court cases challenging his medical ideas and morals made this heavy emphasis on the *True* trademark less desirable, but by 1931 only one Macfadden serial remained, inconspicuously titled *Mary and Bob,* now on NBC on Tuesday nights.[6] Later radio ventures included *The Court of Human Relations* (NBC, 1933), which dramatized "human interest" stories in a courtroom format, and *The Good Will Hour* (Mutual, 1936), an advice-column show starring John J. Anthony. Each of these program types spawned multiple imitators; truly Bernarr Macfadden represents one of radio's overlooked innovators and deserves more attention from broadcast historians than he has received.

All of these productions were supervised out of Macfadden Publications headquarters. The person most immediately responsible for these radio enterprises was William Jourdan Rapp, editor of *True Story* since 1926, who also oversaw the magazine's transformation from its early amateur-contributor days to something approaching "respectability." Originally, *True Story* may have provided the closest thing to an untrammeled venue for young urban women's voices in the public media. Stories were selected from submissions from readers; once received, they went to a "manuscript department" under the direction of Susie Wood, formerly Macfadden's secretary, which consisted of

> numerous girl readers, including stenographers, dancing teachers, and even wrestlers, who were instructed to read not for style or good taste, but "for interest," and to rate a manuscript on a scale of 90 to 100, depending upon how they felt while reading it. Stories rated 95 and better were read by Macfadden himself and his wife, and later by others in the editorial hierarchy.[7]

Macfadden's wife, Mary, later claimed during divorce proceedings that *True Story* had in fact been her idea originally, dreamed up at a point when the Macfaddens faced financial difficulties and needed a change of direction. Whether or not that was true, the "woman's angle" definitely prevailed at the magazine, and it opened up a segment of the changing, younger working woman market that previous homemaker-oriented publications had not touched.

Of course, this unmediated catering to previously unrecognized aspects of modern urban life, particularly its "scandalous" and sexual aspects, horrified those concerned with upholding traditional ideas of morality and feminine sexual modesty. To move the private lives of women into the public sphere was to challenge accepted norms of social behavior and gender roles. George Gerbner, analyzing confession magazines three decades later, remarks on the brutality of the woman's tabloid world and its insistence on the inevitability of sin and punishment. He cites a study by Wilbur Schramm that counted, in a survey of one hundred stories, twenty-five accidents (seventeen fatal), sixteen fistfights, fourteen murders, twelve violent quarrels, eight rapes, and four suicides, all of this "savagery" taking place in a family setting, with characters "dominated by some inner, and preferably innate and uncontrollable, urge that drives them inexorably to violate some code of conduct."[8] Typically, this drive is sex. Besides violence, the one hundred stories also contained "40 cases of adultery, 32 of premarital relations, and 4 of prostitution . . . usually described with gusto, even though covered over with later shame."[9] Even though the stories might condemn the sexual motivation of actions in the end, they dwelled repeatedly on sexual deceits and misconduct in stories with such titles as "I Killed My Child," "I Want You," "Side Door to Hell," and "How Can I Face Myself? I Let Him Cheapen Me."

However, William Jourdan Rapp had another perspective on his market's concerns. Denying that his magazines and radio programs overemphasized sex, Rapp linked romance, marriage, and relationships to women's dependent economic condition and the domestic consequences of such "scandalous" behaviors as adulterous husbands, drinking, and other threats to women's lives: "Security. . . . That's their chief concern, not sex."[10] Rapp brought in established writers, added articles on social issues, developed an emphasis on advice and instruction, and generally attempted to curb some of the magazines' more excessive qualities as the 1920s progressed. Though such publications as *True Romances* and *Dream World* picked up in the torrid romance department where *True Story* left off, Macfadden also extended his empire into real-life crime stories in *True Detective*, whose eponymous radio program started another radio genre tradition.

Memory Lane

Alongside *True Story*'s revelation of the abject and *Amos 'n' Andy*'s projection of it onto race, however, other dramas took up settings in "small-town America" and provided a vision of family and community life untroubled by such disturbing elements—often going to great narrative lengths to make sure these elements remained marginal and contained. One of the earliest of these was *Memory Lane*, which debuted in April 1927 from station KPO San Francisco over the NBC West Coast network.[11] Created by Arthur S. Garbett, later to become West Coast educational director for NBC, it started out as "just old songs, the dear melodies of the 'seventies, 'eighties and early 'nineties." In November of that year, Garbett handed over production to H. C. Connette, a transplanted Indiana native who decided to create a fictionalized setting for the songs by introducing "a little dialogue between two Hoosiers. So 'Pa' Smithers and his wife, Rosemary—she that was a Jenkins—came into being." Set in the small village of "Goshen Center, Indiana," at the turn of the century, *Memory Lane* went to a half-hour dramatic format, with just a short musical introduction and close, in 1928. More characters were added in the form of neighbors, relatives, and short- and long-term visitors to the fictional town; in anticipation of later serial dramas, in three years more than seventy characters performed before the microphone. Writing in 1931, Connette debated over what to call this format he had created:

No, "Memory Lane" is not drama. It might be comedy but there is not enough plot to call it that. My idea of it is expressed in my coined word "homeolog." Each week the audience gets glimpses of the home life of the Goshen Center folks, their simple pleasures, their squabbles, quickly made up, the "box socials" of the Ladies Aid, the annual church fair, the picnics and all the rest of those things that made life full and pleasant back in the days of my boyhood.[12]

This comfortable existence may have seemed exotic to the majority of its listeners, but in the California of the 1920s and early 1930s quite a few migrant midwesterners could relate to the kind of life they had left behind. As one "lady listener" wrote, "It is an oasis—where we can forget the scramble of the working world and go back for thirty minutes a week to the old 'Home Town.'"[13] In March 1931, after three years as a sustaining program on the West Coast network, the program found commercial sponsorship by the General Petroleum Corporation, makers of Violet Ray gasoline and Socony Motor Oil. The way was prepared for such a decision by the similar half-hour program that GP had sponsored on the national NBC network since 1928, *Socony-land Sketches*, continued until 1935, by which time it ran six days a week.

For on-air promotion, like *Amos 'n' Andy* and unlike many other programs of the time whose products were tightly tied to the action of the shows, General Petroleum would have found it hard to work mention of such recently invented products as gasoline and motor oil into its plots. Rather, the show confined itself to less-than-subtle association in opening and closing monologues: "Friends, the products of General Petroleum are just as dependable as the good, honest, home folks whom you have just heard in Memory Lane."[14] To test the effectiveness of its venture into radio, General Petroleum printed a promotional newspaper called the *Goshen Center Bugle* and announced that it would be available at GP stations. The response, added to the gasoline purchased by those listeners who stopped by to pick up their free copies, convinced the company to continue to sponsor the program.

Real Folks

Another early dramatic serial in this same vein was *The Real Folks of Thompkins Corners*, but with one significant difference: this time sponsorship came first. Chesebrough Manufacturing Company approached NBC in early 1928 with an idea that, despite the success of print advertising with sales of Vaseline, there was "still more juice in the sales orange." NBC responded by producing "a fitting background of homely associations for 'Vaseline' products," imparting "a quaint, simple personality to them, much in keeping with their plain old-fashioned effectiveness."[15] *Real Folks*, set in the fictional town of Thompkins Corners, location unspecified, debuted on the NBC Blue network on August 6, 1928. Revolving around the main character of Matt Thompkins, mayor and leading citizen, whose many roles included editor of the town paper, general store manager, postmaster, and leader of the town band, and his wife, Martha, the show also featured "typical" small-town inhabitants such as Charlie Kehoe, garage owner; Judge Whipple; Grandpa and Grandma Overbrook; Mrs. Templeton Jones, wealthy widow and social arbiter; Fred Tibbett, the barber; and assorted children. As this program was set in "the present," unlike *Memory Lane*, some acknowledgment of the changing nature of most American towns and cities received a nod; as the program brochure goes on to describe: "Gus Oleson, Tony, and Ah Sing Wong make up the 'foreign element.' Mrs. Templeton Jones says they 'lend a continental touch.'" In Thompkins Corners, black citizens did not exist, and the town's immigrant population was carefully demarcated from its "normal" inhabitants. Also in keeping with the representations of *Amos 'n' Andy*, but strikingly different from *The Goldbergs*, the "foreign element" consisted of unmarried men, again setting them apart from "normal" family life.

NBC worked hard to produce the same attribution of reality so important to *True Stories*:

> This program is real! it touches analogous sympathies, drawing an almost universal response from all classes in sophisticated cities and rural villages alike. . . . You are not conscious of "listening in" on this program. You "overhear" it! with the half-guilty feeling of being an eavesdropper. For the "Real Folks" never seem to be aware of your silent presence. They never speak to you directly. They go about their business with an unsuspecting innocence that tends to heighten the sense of reality. You find yourself right in their midst![16]

Because the program was built to order for the product, Vaseline could be worked into the everyday plots. "For example, Matt will tell how he spreads a little 'Vaseline' jelly over his face before shaving, or Martha will advise Elmer to put some 'Vaseline' on that sore toe of his."[17] NBC argued that this "interweaving" technique gave the advertising message added force and credibility, and avoided the potential "offense" in more direct selling messages: listeners would scarcely be aware they were being sold. Chesebrough renewed the program for two more fifty-two week seasons. In 1932, sponsorship of *Real Folks* switched to the Log Cabin Company, and the show moved to an early-evening position on CBS; this would be its last season.

In the Backwoods of Modernity

Shows such as *Memory Lane* and *Real Folks* remained a staple form on radio, perhaps culminating in the long-running "hillbilly" comedy *Lum and Abner*—in turn the inspiration for such television classics as *The Beverly Hillbillies* and *Gomer Pyle*. Comedians Arthur Allen and Parker Fennelly deserve a mention here, because they probably created more shows in this genre than anyone else before or since. Specializing in New England settings, Allen and Fennelly created *Snow Village* in 1930, followed by *Uncle Abe and David* for Goodrich Tires in June of that year on NBC as well as *The Stebbins Boys* in 1931, and eventually five others. *Uncle Abe and David* may have been particularly influential. Uncle Abe and David, operators of a small-town country store, "Everybody's Equiperies," quickly abandoned it to make a visit to New York, and the program revolved around the "two rubes in the big city" theme, very similar in its way to *Amos 'n' Andy*'s basic premise. Fennelly would go on to play Allen's Alley inhabitant Titus Moody, cut from the same mold, on *The Fred Allen Show* in the 1940s.

However, the general store idea proved catching. Few may recall the show created by Jim and Marian Jordan for WMAQ in March 1931, preceding their 1935 long-running hit *Fibber McGee and Molly*. Originally titled *Smackout—The Crossroads of the Air*, the program centered on the character of Luke Gray, played by Jim Jordan, proprietor of a general store frequently "smack out" of items requested. Jordan also played a number of other characters, as did Marian, with roles ranging from Teeney (a small girl she would carry over to *Fibber McGee and Molly*), Mrs. Bedelia Thomas, Geraldine, Mrs. High-Hat Upson, and even Bertha Boop, a Hollywood film star recuperating from the pressures of the glamorous life. Full of homey phrases—such as "Cross my heart and spit on the sidewalk" and "Well, wouldn't that jest paint ye purple, cut ye in two, and plow ye under"—and tall tales, Jordan developed the role of small-town general store proprietor into a radio classic.[18] The scripts were written by Don Quinn, whose efforts seem to have been the essential ingredient that transformed the occasional skits the Jordans had been performing on various Chicago radio stations into a regularly occurring serial drama. Marian Jordan had for a time performed the role of an Irish housewife, Nora Smith, on a Chicago serial drama called *The Smith Family* from 1929 to 1932, forecasting the plot line of a popular 1940s serial when she ran for political office on a Progressive ticket against her husband, and won. (Later, *The Story of Mary Marlin* would feature Mary as a U.S. senator who became engaged to the president!) All of these talents culminated in the series that made the Jordans famous.

Smackout was one of that first generation of Chicago shows picked up by NBC in the early 1930s, contributing to the trend toward Chicago-based programming on which NBC would capitalize for some of its most enduring genres. It ran on a sustaining basis for its entire four-year life span. In 1935 the Johnson Wax Company expressed interest in sponsoring the show, inspired by the recommendation of Henrietta Johnson Louis, a loyal listener who happened to be the daughter of H. F. Johnson, head of the Johnson Wax Company.[19] By this time, the general store format had been widely imitated, so a change of some kind seemed to be desirable. Drawing on Luke Gray's "tall tales" tradition, but this time with a husband and wife as main characters, the show began in a peculiarly transient setting: a cross-country automobile tour. *Variety* described the duo as "a hen-pecked husband and wise-cracking wife," and another review called Fibber McGee "a sort of 'Irish Baron Munchausen.'"[20] *Fibber McGee and Molly* aired for the first time on April 16, 1935, written by Don Quinn and introducing a new character, Harlow Wilcox, the spokesman for Johson's Wax whose encomiums for the product found their way into the script in inventive forms, much to Fibber's chagrin. After a brief touring period, the McGees settled down at 79 Wistful Vista, where they remained until 1952. The show originated from Chicago until 1939, when it switched production location to Hollywood, still over NBC.

The traditions of ethnic comedy and minstrel representations were never far from the central action in *Fibber McGee and Molly*. Molly's brogue modulated as the seasons passed, and Fibber became less of a rube and more of the scheming but bumbling husband so closely associated with the sitcom form. Yet one of the earliest regularly appearing supporting characters was the McGees' "houseboy" Silly Watson, introduced in 1935 and becoming a regular during Marian's extended illness and absence from the show in 1937. Clearly modeled on the Jim Crow stereotype, Silly Watson has been described by one historian as a "stereotyped, ignorant, and foolish handyman."[21] The role was played by Hugh Studebaker, a white actor later known for his soap opera roles and as the star of *Bachelor's Children*. Another minstrel character, Beulah, the McGees' "black" maid, was introduced in 1944, played by white male actor Marlin Hurt, who spun the character off into its own half-hour show the next year. In many ways Beulah represented a culmination of the many ethnic regular and incidental characters popularized on *Fibber McGee*, most played by versatile "dialectician" Bill Thompson. Thompson's characterizations included the Greek restaurant owner Nick Depopolous, Molly's drunken Irish Uncle Dennis, other Irish, Scottish, Greek, and Russian characters, as well as the regularly appearing "Old Timer." By the mid-1940s, Thompson's and other ethnic characterizations had come under fire as demeaning the groups they represented; only minstrel characters continued significantly into the 1950s. These representations provided not only humor but contrast to the increasing "normalcy"—carefully constructed as nonethnic "white," middle-class and proud of it—projected by the McGees as the show modulated into something much more closely resembling the humorous family dramas—such as *Vic and Sade*, *The Aldrich Family*, and the serial *One Man's Family*—so popular in the late 1930s and 1940s.

However, another extremely popular and long-running program would take not only the general store setting abandoned by *Fibber McGee* but also its emphasis on the "rube" character to new heights: *Lum and Abner*, a series created by Chester Lauck and Norris Goff. The two had backgrounds very similar to Gosden and Correll's, having grown up in rural Arkansas and gotten their start in show business doing blackface skits. Legend has it that the Lum and Abner characters resulted when Lauck and Goff auditioned for a benefit performance in 1930 in Meena, Arkansas. Discovering that everyone else was planning on blackface (again, most likely influenced by *Amos 'n' Andy*'s success) they switched to hillbilly characters on the spot.[22] This led to radio performances over KTHS in Hot Springs, Arkansas, beginning on April 24, 1931. That summer they moved to Chicago as a summer replacement over WMAQ, thus coming into contact with the

Jordans; Marian Jordan made a few appearances as Teeny on *Lum and Abner*.²³ The show was picked up by NBC in 1935, sponsored by the Horlick Malted Milk Company.

Set in the fictional backwoods town of Pine Ridge, Arkansas (later, the real Arkansas town of Waters changed its name to Pine Ridge), *Lum and Abner* completed the transition away from ethnic comedy to the "rube" format. Pine Ridge's location did not allow for the intrusion of many "foreigners," and most of the show's action and humor derived from the comic misunderstandings and scrapes of its naive "hillbilly" characters. However, *Lum and Abner* continued the populism of most of radio's comic series: valorizing the common, everyday values of simple folk, with "big-city" ideas and people who think themselves superior to others providing the villains of the piece and common sense triumphing over all. Everybody was basically the same in Pine Ridge, and woe to those who thought otherwise.

The Serial Drama

This populism would take an interesting twist as radio schedules began to differentiate between daytime and nighttime programming in the mid-1930s. What would later become indelibly associated with the daytime women's audience—the soap opera—started out as nighttime general-audience serials, again from Chicago. On the East Coast, Gertrude Berg's *The Rise of the Goldbergs* and, slightly later, Paul Rhymer's *Vic and Sade* would contribute to the tradition that Chicago had started. I have already noted that elements of *Amos 'n' Andy's* story line followed the serial format, and certainly its scheduling five days a week would soon be found only in the daytime. But until 1935, most of these comedy/drama serials aired at night, where they found enthusiastic audiences. The shift to daytime and the development of the soap opera form will be discussed in chapter 5, but a few pioneering serials deserve recognition as important components of the Chicago radio drama movement.

Two of the earliest dialogue serials were *Clara, Lu and Em* and *Myrt and Marge. Clara, Lu and Em* resulted from the efforts of three sorority sisters at Northwestern University who developed a comic skit that they performed at various university functions. In 1930, after their graduation, Louise Starkey (Clara), Isobel Carothers (Lu), and Helen King (Em) took their sketch to WGN. Described by Judith Waller as "a back fence gossip skit," the show featured two neighbors in a Chicago double, Em and Lu, and their housekeeper, Clara.[24] In the beginning the show was improvised from brief notes, and the three actors played off each other in a way that later became reflected in scripts. Their dialogue—naturalistic, frequently overlapping and repetitious, full of back-and-forth—provided a form of narrative construction that was unique to radio and contrasted with the more tightly scripted variety and dramatic shows. Most plots involved the trials and tribulations of Em, whose five children and "unreliable" husband gave Lu, a widow, and Clara frequent cause to dispense advice and commiserate, as did Lu's eventual courtship and marriage. The humor was subtle and often ironic, and required habituated listeners to pick up on its lightly murmured sardonic twists.

In 1931 *Clara, Lu and Em* joined the NBC Blue lineup at 10:30 each weeknight, sponsored by Super Suds detergent—indeed the first soap opera. In 1932 it moved to daytime, sponsored by Colgate, thus representing the first daytime serial drama now understood to be specifically for women audiences. By 1935 Palmolive Peet had taken over as sponsor, and the subject of one day's conversation (January 6, 1936) was a recent report by the Mayo Clinic that men are in fact the weaker sex—or, as Clara says, "They ain't got the stamina." The ensuing dialogue gives an indication of the kind of low-key social satire the three performers worked into their scripts:

Lu: Do you mean in their mentality?
Em: On no, no goodness, men ain't giving up their mentality. Oh no, they're keeping their mentality.
Clara: Well, that's good. I don't approve in taking away their mentality. That'd be an awful blow to men.
Em: There has been news come out in the past, of course, that men's mentality wasn't much different than women's, but men never paid much attention to it. Didn't bother them—but this business of them being weaker on the physical side they seem very interested in it. . . . From the very time men is born they just can't handle life—just can't grapple with it a t'all like a big strong woman. . . . Now that they have found out I'm afraid everything is going to be so different.[25]

Later episodes had the three friends traveling to New York City, where elements of the "rube" comedy crept in. In 1936 Isobel Carothers died suddenly, and the program went off the air. Its remaining two creators tried a comeback six years later, but by this time they found themselves in a daytime schedule dominated by a much-changed serial format.

The CBS nighttime serial *Myrt and Marge*, created, written, produced, and performed by the mother-daughter team of Myrtle Vail and Donna Damerel, debuted in 1931. Its setting was the stage: Myrt played a veteran dance director in charge of a Broadway chorus line; Marge turned up in the first day's script as a nearly starving "gypsy" whom Myrt soon took under her wing. More drama than comedy, the show drew on its stage environment to work music, tap dancing, and theatrical intrigue into the plots. Though its large cast of characters, and plots that focused on travel and adventure as much as romance, made it popular with evening audiences of both sexes (despite its position opposite *Amos 'n' Andy*), in 1937 CBS moved the show to daytime, the new ghetto for women's serials. Retooled by its creator, Myrtle Vail, who succumbed to the multiple-writer system by then established, its daytime ratings never equaled its former numbers. The show remained on the air even after the death of Donna Damerel in 1941, with Helen Mack replacing her for a few seasons, but the program ended its eleven-year run in 1942.[26]

Clara, Lu and Em, *Myrt and Marge*, and *The Rise of the Goldbergs* represent a high-water mark for the contributions of female writers and producers addressing a nighttime radio audience. Though many highly creative talents, such as Irna Phillips, Jane Crusinberry, Elaine Carrington, and Anne Ashenhurst Hummert, would continue to build the daytime serial form, the consignment of woman-produced shows to the feminine preserve of daytime largely removed women as creators from the nighttime airwaves, where they could address a more general public. This "ghettoization" will be discussed in chapter 5. However, as serial drama faded from the evening air, a new genre rose to take its place.

Adventure in the Evening

Swelling in numbers from five in 1931 to forty-one in 1946, the "thriller" or adventure series increasingly dominated the course of series narrative addressed to a mixed-gender audience. Though overshadowed in ratings and in publicity by the big-time comedy/variety programs, these long-running series rose to increasing popularity and still retain large fan followings even fifty years later. One of the most popular in the early years was *Gangbusters*, what would now be called a "reality-based" program and a forerunner of *Dragnet* and its current offshoots (such as *America's Most Wanted*).

Itself growing out of the Macfadden *True Detective* model, *Gang-busters* promised "*facts* in the relentless war of the police on the underworld . . . *authentic case histories* that show the never-ending activity of the police in their work of protecting our citizens."[27] The show opened with a loud aural barrage of machine-gun fire and sirens (hence the popular expression "coming on like gangbusters") and ended with a description of real-life wanted criminals, reportedly leading to many arrests over the show's twenty-year life span. As the 1930s drew to a close, however, the highest-rated evening thriller dramas adhered to a fairly set formula. Usually featuring a (white male) law enforcement-related character—detective, district attorney, police officer—or frequently a journalist (or photographer), the hero was assisted by a female sidekick of some kind—secretary, reporter, or vaguely employed girlfriend or fiancée. The programs relied on fast-moving action and rapid plot resolution, often involving rescue of the heroine by the stalwart hero at the very last possible minute—or if not her rescue, then the rescue of civilization in general. The art of the sound effect was developed to new heights in this genre, and many of its characteristics were translated into the prestige drama of the 1940s. The most popular programs of the 1940s, such as *Big Town, Mr. District Attorney*, and *Casey, Crime Photographer*, brought forward their female characters and romance-related plotlines in the interests of the majority female audience. However, the more cartoonlike children's programs of the 1940s are the ones that seem to be remembered best in published histories today—perhaps because their writers made up the boy audience sought after by the programs. Shows such as *The Green Hornet, Jack Armstrong, All American Boy, The Shadow*, and *The Lone Ranger* were frequently criticized for their formulaic aspects, emphasis on violence and mayhem, and ability to excite and upset young listeners, but were never as thoroughly disparaged as their daytime counterparts, the soap operas.

J. Fred MacDonald, one of the writers to emphasize the thriller drama, explains the attraction of this genre for late 1930s and 1940s radio in terms of value definition: though week after week criminals and villainous gangs violated the law in subversion of shared social standards, the heroic investigator at once set about restoring law and order and bringing criminals to justice, in a kind of secular "passion play" that demonstrated and strengthened American norms and values:

As these champions of justice acted out their formulaic lives, they actually provided a paradigm for effective social existence. . . . Detective programs, therefore, supplied millions of Americans with understandable stories of achievement within a competitive, mass society. . . . radio detective programs performed a strategic role in strengthening the tenor of existence within the American commonwealth.[28]

Of course, such stories also allowed for the introduction each week of violations of American values, supplying paradigms of subversive social existence and patterns of criminal "achievement." This may account for some of the fascination of the thriller genre—a safe and culturally endorsed way to experience a challenge to the social order, within a narrative of containment.

It is interesting to note that in criticism of the soap opera form, the narratives' introduction of socially troubling phenomena such as divorce, adultery, and various types of criminal behavior was emphasized as disruptive and socially undesirable in itself, with little acknowledgment of the moral solutions usually supplied in the end. This surely has something to do with the serial form, as opposed to the series, as the former required a more extended reading to arrive at resolution than did the simplistic crime-chase-arrest plot of the detective series. It may also have to do with the revelation of "private" (feminine) as opposed to "public" (masculine) types of social disorder. MacDonald seems curiously untroubled by the fact that the detective social paradigm was supplied quite explicitly for white, "nonethnic" men only, showing women and those of other racial and ethnic categories as existing outside its models for achievement and social effectivity. He explains this omission on the part of the series writers as reflecting the mores of their time, but his own (and others') omission of consideration of such aspects in discussion of their purported meaning for audiences cannot be so easily dismissed. If indeed we can read the detective genre as policing the boundaries of social order in a way that provided a model for individual audience members, the specific way in which these models were embodied and presented must factor into such a reading. This becomes particularly relevant when we remember that the majority of the evening audience consisted of women, who were the main selling targets of the companies that sponsored the shows. This argument also, of course, applies to race. Although MacDonald remains one of the few radio historians to devote a significant discussion to African Americans in broadcasting, he ignores the implications of exclusion and selective representation in those program forms, such as the thriller/detective genre, that never specifically mention race and thereby speak volumes about it.

The Big Time: Comedy/Variety Shows

By the mid-1930s, with women's serial drama consigned to the daylight hours and thriller/detective programs building up audiences, especially in the early fringe time periods, the most prominent and highly rated programs on the air were the prime-time comedy variety programs, such as *The Jack Benny Program*, the new *Fibber McGee and Molly*, Fred Allen's *Town Hall Tonight*, *The Eddie Cantor Show*, *Kraft Music Hall* with Al Jolson, and *Burns and Allen*. *The Edgar Bergen and Charlie McCarthy Show*, and *The Bob Hope Show* also drew in large audiences by the late 1930s, with *The Baby Snooks Show* with Fanny Brice and *The Kate Smith Show* by 1940 providing female voices on the nighttime airwaves once again. All of these programs had incorporated significant amounts of comedy narrative by the mid-1930s, interspersed with musical numbers and repartee between the host and the guests; for some programs, such as *Jack Benny*, *Burns and Allen*, and *Fibber McGee and Molly*, the ongoing series narrative took up most of the show's airtime. Kate Smith introduced *The Aldrich Family* and *The Abbott and Costello Program*. Bob Hope and Bing Crosby, and to a lesser extent Fred Allen and Edgar Bergen, drew heavily on Hollywood stars and film dramatizations and skits.

How do we account for the amazing transformation of network radio over a ten-year period from a medium heavily dominated by music to one that emphasized comedy/dramatic narratives for ever-larger portions of its expanding schedule? The activities of two closely related industries contributed heavily to this process: the advertising agencies, who by the mid-1930s had taken over the bulk of radio production, and their allies the Hollywood film studios, whose initial efforts to move into network radio had been rebuffed, but whose potential for bringing large audiences to the medium was quickly recognized by sponsors and agencies—to the networks' frequent chagrin. The ensuing struggle for control over programming and the negotiation of standards for "appropriate" radio behavior would leave an indelible mark on the forms of radio and television to follow—and on the nature and substance of radio's national voice.

By the mid-1930s, prime day and night hours were dominated by agency-produced programs over which the networks often had little control, despite their official function as trustees of the public interest. One of the largest and most "radio active" advertising agencies in the United States during this period was the J. Walter Thompson Company. The story of this agency's entry into broadcasting, and its relationship to the dominant network at the time, NBC, provides a glimpse into the machinations behind the stars and programs soon to become so familiar to the American public, and reveals some of the terms on which the negotiation of cultural standards and traditions took place.

JWT and the Philosophy of "Showmanship"

Though, according to Roland Marchand, advertising agencies were slow to see the possibilities in radio for product promotion, this attitude varied greatly from agency to agency.[29] There did indeed exist opposition to radio in agencies in the early 1920s—hardly surprising, considering the tight connection between ad agencies and the print media, who did indeed have something to fear from competition with radio. Marchand and many other writers cite articles that appeared in the print trade publication *Printers' Ink* from 1922 through 1926, objecting to the use of radio as an advertising medium. These, however, hardly represent the interests of the entire advertising field, many members of which may have been cognizant of a need not to offend the print media but demonstrated a growing awareness of the possibilities the new medium presented.

The full chronology of advertising agency involvement in radio does indeed deserve a history in itself, not least because it is virtually coterminous with commercial radio broadcasting. One or two examples of programs and experimental broadcasts made by advertising agencies in the 1920s may be helpful. As already noted, the N. W. Ayer agency was responsible for what was arguably the most influential show on radio in the early 1920s, *The Eveready Hour*, sponsored by the National Carbon Company, a maker of batteries (a product of obvious relevance to radio listeners). Having organized a radio department as early as 1923 and participated in the earliest experimentation in network broadcasting through AT&T's limited distribution of *The Eveready Hour*, N. W. Ayer continued to experiment actively during the mid-1920s, turning to dramatic fictional programs, literary adaptations, and variety show formats.[30] Another example is the William H. Rankin Agency, one of the heaviest early users of station WEAF's toll service beginning in 1922, which provided one of the earliest examples of Hollywood-agency-radio interaction by inviting actress Marion Davies to give a talk on "How I Make Up for Movies" for its client Mineralava.[31] By most accounts this was the first time a premium was offered—an autographed picture of the actress herself—to all those who would write in to say they heard the broadcast, and the "thousands" of requests that poured in helped to establish radio as an effective medium for reaching a consuming public.[32]

At J. Walter Thompson, it appears, the agency was led into radio by a few of its more adventurous clients. Though obviously interested in the medium—and refusing to join in a 1924 protest by a print-dominated committee opposed to radio advertising—a rather wistfully titled article in the J. Walter Thompson *Newletter* from February 1925 sums up activity to date: "Why Don't We Use the Radio?" The article summarized activity by radio stations and WEAF advertisers but still concluded, "This is a questionable medium for us to use at present." Primary objections concerned the "unsettled state" of broadcasting in 1925, the possibilities for misinterpretation of the spoken word, the impossibility of ascertaining circulation, and a concern that radio's more "indirect" selling might not be as effective as print.[33] But another article two weeks later acknowledged that two JWT clients had gone on the air regionally, both broadcasting "household talks" for women, both written in connection with JWT's "women's division" of the Chicago office.[34] One of them, Mary Hale Martin, previously the featured print service columnist for the Libby canned goods company, would continue with her Friday-morning *Mary Hale Martin's Household Hour* well into the 1930s.

Not until 1927, however, would JWT form its first official Radio Department, under the direction of William H. Ensign—formerly of N. W. Ayer and musical director for *Roxy and His Gang*. By May 1928, according to Ensign's departmental progress report, two new employees had been added, and by July JWT's radio clients included Goodrich Tire Company, Shell Oil, the Isuan Corporation, Certo Gelatin, and Maxwell House Coffee, with proposals out to six other clients, most of whom would go on the air that year. Also in Ensign's report were the number of agencies that had organized radio departments in the preceding year—fifteen major firms, including Young & Rubicam; Barton, Durstine and Osborne; Lord, Thomas and Logan; and Lennan and Mitchell. It is interesting to note that talk of television's imminent arrival occurred at this early date.[35] Over the next year, use and acceptance of radio continued to build at JWT, and by 1929 the department was ripe for a takeover.

Chapter 5 will detail the struggle for power between JWT's men's and women's groups that occurred in 1929, during the course of which Aminta Casseres of the New York Women's Division lost her bid to be head of the Radio Department to John U. Reber, previously an account executive and head of new business. "The Grim Reber," as he was known around the JWT offices, became director of the Radio Department in May 1929, and he very quickly grew disenchanted with the limited role envisioned for agencies by the radio networks, particularly NBC. A longtime colleague, Calvin Kuhl, who worked closely with Reber during most of his career at JWT, recalled him to be "the first to dismiss the 'radio experts' (producers, writers, directors) furnished by NBC, and use agency people to direct and write the show." Kuhl goes on to describe Reber's programming philosophy as it developed in the late 1920s and early 1930s:

> At the beginning NBC naturally turned to Broadway and Vaudeville for writing and directing experience. . . . These people were hidebound in their thinking and techniques. . . . They thought of the audience as so many tuxedo clad and evening gowned bodies in rows of seats before a stage. . . . In the late 20s and early 30s an advertising agency on behalf of a client might approach NBC with a tentative interest in "buying" a show, and NBC would then dream up a show via its culls from Broadway and Vaudeville. . . . Well, almost immediately after persuading a J. W. Thompson client to buy a half hour of such NBC produced twaddle, John, complaining to NBC of the mediocrity and unimaginativeness of their fare, said "Hell, if that's the best you can do, we can do better, with our own writers and directors," which he then proceeded to do.[36]

Reber himself began sounding this note soon after his ascendancy as chief of radio. In a representatives' meeting in April 1930, by which time JWT had more than thirty-three shows on the air amounting to sixty hours a week, Reber claimed bluntly, "Our Radio Department can do a better radio program than the National Broadcasting Company," citing client testimonials.[37]

The term most frequently used to explain JWT's proficiency was "showmanship": JWT had it, NBC didn't. Most specifically, "showmanship" resulted from knowledge of the audience and its tastes.[38] Unlike NBC, with its dual agenda of at once profiting from commer-

cial programs and upholding and maintaining cultural standards before the public, advertising agencies such as JWT had realized some
time previously that it was mass sales that produced advertising profit,
and mass sales resulted from attention to the "tabloid mind."

As early as 1923, the *JWT News Bulletin,* an in-house newletter of
campaigns and ideas, reveals a concern with the habits and emotions
of the "common" reader. In "Mrs. Wilkins Reads the Ladies Home
Journal," JWT copywriter Dorothy Dwight Townsend evokes the
world of those recently arrived in the middle class, looking to the mass
media for ways to assimilate and "improve" themselves:

> She looked in at homes she would never dare to enter; studied the get-up
> of women she never dared stare at in the city. Such smart women—in
> such beautiful homes—they did things with such an air! She studied the
> woman showing her friend the waists washed in Lux. The next morning
> when she washed out Helen's party stockings she would think of them.
> Unconsciously she had found herself holding up dainty things with two
> fingers—her other fingers crooked and outstretched as the Lux women
> always did it. . . . She would have told you her mother taught her all she
> knew about housekeeping but she had learned more from this magazine
> than her mother ever knew.[39]

By 1927, JWT had recognized not only the existence but the value of
"these vast new layers of people who have money to spend and who
have very few media to reach them excepting the tabloids and confession magazines" and had begun to advocate a new "lowbrow" approach to advertising.[40] Here we see not only the acknowledgment and
market empowerment of a previously unrecognized social group, but
the beginnings of the identification of the media's role in reaching
them—particularly radio, in which the terms *mass* and *culture* would
come together in a powerful new combination.

This approach culminated in JWT's famous Lux Hollywood star
endorsement campaign, not surprisingly spearheaded for the company
by the eastern advertising manager of *Photoplay* magazine, acting as
an intermediary in signing up stars for endorsements. By 1928, JWT
claimed that "it was impossible to wash your hands in Hollywood
unless you used Lux Toilet Soap," and numerous effusive—but never
paid—endorsements began to appear in mass-circulation magazines.[41]
These efforts were much aided by the flamboyant personality of JWT's
Los Angeles agent, Danny Danker, who by all accounts succeeded in
ingratiating himself with the upper levels of Hollywood stardom by

living the Hollywood life, to the chagrin of stuffier New York JWT personnel, including John Reber. According to one anonymous "ex-employee (female)" on record in the JWT files (and marked "obviously unquotable"): "Danny Danker was THE POWER in Hollywood and was said to operate very much like dear Louella, getting any talent he wanted through blackmail. He also ran a procuring service for visiting executives and had a stable of starlets handy at all times."[42] It is generally agreed that John Reber "was perhaps the first to realize that the star system, the lifeblood of motion pictures, could revolutionize radio,"[43] and he is widely credited with leading the movement of radio production to Hollywood. To accomplish this he had to rely on the network of contacts and endorsements that Danker had established, though it was not a comfortable relationship. According to longtime JWT Hollywood writer Carroll Carroll:

> Mr. Reber did not want Danny to have anything to do with "his" department. But Danny's power was such in Hollywood that—as our needs for guest stars grew—Danny became more and more essential to the operation. . . . Naturally as Danny's power grew the seething feud between him and Reber boiled harder. Who would have won is anybody's guess. Danny died first.[44]

Reber sent a young and inexperienced Calvin Kuhl out to Los Angeles in March 1934 to serve as the nominal head of JWT radio operations there, but it seems mostly to keep an eye on Danker and report back. However strained their relations, the combined efforts of Reber and Danker ushered in what has been called "the Hollywood era of radio," which was also the era of agency dominance. By the mid-1930s, JWT was producing at least five shows in each year's top ten, all from Hollywood, using its unparalleled access to Hollywood talent procured, by whatever means, by Danker and his associates. Soon other agencies rushed to start Los Angeles offices as well. By 1942, JWT could claim to have developed more radio stars than any other organization, including Rudy Vallee, Burns and Allen, Al Jolson, Walter Winchell, Eddie Cantor, Major Bowes, Fanny Brice, and Edgar Bergen and Charlie McCarthy. In pioneering both the big-name variety show and the film adaptation program, most notably *The Lux Radio Theatre*, JWT also brought established Hollywood stars to the radio in increasing numbers.

By the mid-1930s, not only prime time but most of the daytime schedule as well was occupied by programs supplied by agencies on behalf of sponsors, especially the extremely popular daytime serials. Though the networks continued in their program-building efforts, establishing talent bureaus in New York, Chicago, and eventually Los Angeles, in an effort to stabilize the situation, and often coming up with successful formats, their main objective remained to sell these programs to clients. These clients' agencies would then take over the programs' production, contracting with the NBC Talent Bureau for writers, stars, and so on, and using NBC facilities only for rehearsal space and actual broadcast. Many agencies declined even this small amount of dependence on the networks—and CBS never attempted to initiate programming or control talent to NBC's extent—so that the daytime hours in particular became sponsor franchises.

Large companies such as Procter & Gamble bought time in one- to two-hour blocks and programmed them with shows produced either in-house or by agencies hired for the purpose. Blackett-Sample-Hummert, home of Frank and Anne Hummert's "soap opera factory," operated almost totally outside of the networks' supervision, as will be seen in the controversy over "tasteless and inappropriate" content discussed below. Indeed, the late 1920s move away from musical variety programs toward fictional drama and serial narrative was driven almost entirely by the agencies, displacing the more educational, "tasteful," and derivative forms encouraged by early network practices. Production sites such as Chicago, further away from network headquarter operations and historically more amenable to the interests of their commercial clients, led the way in network adoption of these forms, often resisted at first by NBC and CBS as disreputable and lax in their standards. In addition, it was agencies that first began to push for the use of recorded programs, called transcriptions, for clients who wished to avoid network costs and reach regional audiences for more effective advertising. This early form of syndication was much resisted by the networks, because it cut them directly out of the business in favor of the other main opposing interest in radio, powerful stations, who could program transcriptions at their own discretion and retain all profits.[45]

Network Woes

It did not take long for this kind of challenge to network authority, and the disdainful attitude that went with it, to have an effect on NBC operations. Though sale of as much time as possible to sponsors remained from the beginning the primary goal of both networks, the control exercised by the increasingly powerful agencies began to undermine the networks' control over their own business. When sponsors or agencies created and owned their own programs, they could jump from network to network when more favorable time slots opened, leaving a network without the property its distribution system had helped to build up. Even more saliently, networks were placed in the awkward position of having to defend themselves to the FCC, to their affiliated stations, and to the public when criticism of programming practices arose, in order to sustain the idea that they were in fact operating as trustees of the public interest, without being able to wield much actual power over what went on during those programs. Despite such controlling policies as required submission of scripts before broadcast to the Continuity Acceptance Department, the presence on each set of an NBC director, and the continuing existence of commercial program departments and talent bureaus, agency productions increasingly eluded network control. A plaintive note crept into NBC interdepartmental correspondence.

In June 1932, John F. Royal complained to Roy Witmer, head of sales at NBC, about the agencies' failure to submit their scripts, called continuities, in sufficient time before broadcast:

> In my opinion the agencies take advantage of us, not only in the matter of late copy, but in many other things. . . . The clients, through their agencies, talk about cooperation, but they seldom give any. The trouble is that each agency thinks only of its own programs. They are selfish and inconsiderate. . . . If the agencies found that it was necessary that their continuities be a part of their general merchandising plan, they would have them ready, but inasmuch as it only means cooperating with the broadcasting company, that is the last thing on their minds.[46]

NBC attempted to crack down on this procedure, but by May 1933, the agencies had devised another way around network censors. Bertha Brainard, head of commercial programming, described a new problem:

> Agencies and clients have been in the habit of sending to Continuity a skeletonized script which they do not believe will be used on the air. This is read carefully by the Continuity Department, stamped as the master, and sent through to the Production Department. Not infrequently on the day of the rehearsal an entirely new script is brought to the Production man for his use. He then endeavors, if the material seems to be objectionable, to reach anyone in authority for approval on

the script. This is an entirely unsatisfactory method, particularly on the week-ends.[47]

Brainard outlined a new policy, by which only a script stamped "master" and so approved would be allowed to be broadcast, under any circumstances. Unfortunately, even this process could not contain the danger seemingly inherent in commercial production. The infamous Mae West episode of 1937 demonstrated that even a preapproved script could be *read* differently over the air from how it might be read in a continuity office, undermining the power of the written word.[48] Even worse, some entire genres of programming in their essence seemed to subvert institutional and social control. Three types of programs were especially problematic: the stand-up comedian on nighttime variety, children's adventure programs, and women's daytime serials. All of these genres had been developed by advertising agencies.

The big-name variety shows pioneered by JWT, including *The Fleischmann's Yeast Hour* (Rudy Vallee), *The Chase and Sanborn Hour* (Eddie Cantor/Bergen and McCarthy), *The Shell Chateau* (Al Jolson), and *The Kraft Music Hall* (Al Jolson/Bing Crosby), provided high-profile entertainment on NBC, attracted large audiences, and generally boosted the reputation of the network—but at a cost. Though anchored by recurring casts of hosts and orchestras, and a few established cast members who supported the hosts, most functioned by inviting stars from the movies, vaudeville, and other venues to perform on a nightly or multinight basis. This provided ample opportunity for surprises, as witnessed by an October 1935 memo from Roy Witmer to a member of the production department, D. S. Shaw:

> The Program Department complains that on Fleischmann-Rudy Vallee programs, Shell, and Kraft, they are often not informed concerning guest artists, and that the only way they know what's on the show is when they hear about it on the next day. It seems that the same is true on A&P, Lucky Strike, and Vicks. . . . Won't you please see that a particular effort is made to keep the Program Department informed well in advance about all guest appearances?[49]

This problem was exacerbated when the so inconsiderately invited guests resorted to humor unacceptable to the network. Despite the policy of preclearance of scripts by the Continuity Acceptance Department, comedians in particular were notorious for changing their routines on the air, or inflecting even previously approved material with different meanings.

Sometimes these routines affected not just network proprieties, but those of other organizations connected with the network, whose interests also had to be taken into account. One interesting exchange involved the Disney Company, always sensitive to public image. First, on May 12, 1933, the network was required to censor a Bert Lahr appearance on *The Chase and Sanborn Hour* that involved a character called "Mickey the Louse." The following lines were cut:

> *Woman*: Now Mickey. Is that nice? Kicking Mr. Lahr in the shins?
> *Mickey*: Well, that's as high as I can kick.[50]

Other lines that were cut for different reasons filled a full typewritten page.

This incident was followed just a few months later by a Fanny Brice routine on the same program, referred to as "a burlesque on 'Mickey and Minnie Mouse,'" which prompted a letter from William C. Erskine of United Artists, in charge of publicity for Disney: "I regret exceedingly that the program prepared by Chase and Sanborn was contrary to the policy of Walt Disney Productions. . . . the material contained in this script was so contrary to Mr. Disney's expressed wishes with regard to radio broadcasts that . . . their New York representatives requested me to telephone you in this regard."[51] In an attached note, John Royal asked, "Do you want to show this to Reber's office?" Evidence that he did just that exists in Reber's terse scrawled note at the bottom, "Mr. Royal: Many thanks." The battles continued.

On May 27, Bert Lahr again offended with another fairly innocuous joke, again prompting the red pencil from the Program Department: "What's the difference between a snake and a flea? A snake crawls on its own stomach but a flea ain't so particular."[52] However, a handwritten note at the bottom of the page reads, "Mr. Royal: Lahr said this anyway. I heard it," signed "Mac." Just a week or so later, Fanny Brice was the offender, due to the following exchange:

> *Fanny*: Abe, why do you spank the boy like that?
> *Abe*: I spanked him to impress it on his mind.
> *Fanny*: Where do you think his mind is?[53]

The following week brought a whole page of problems. Two of the jokes seem suggestive enough of NBC policies to quote:

> *Man*: I don't speak such good English so I have to feel for my words.
> *Fanny*: Well, they ain't tatooed on me!

Another indicates the special problems radio posed for its censors.

> *Brice* (answering the telephone): Hello Mrs. Greenberg—this is Mrs. Cohen—oy am I sick. I was in bed all day with three doctors and two nurses.

In parentheses after this it reads: "We suggested this cut because of the possible double meaning Miss Brice might have given it."[54] A hand-written note at the bottom of one of these complaints suggests overall network sentiment: "Just another case of NBC B damned."[55]

By October 1933 the issue had become one of more generalized concern. In a letter from Burke Boyce, then head of what would become continuity acceptance, to John Royal, head of programming, a note of despair is sounded:

> It is getting to the place where it is almost impossible to have any uniformity or certainty on the question of reading for policy. It is merely a question of how hard a client or agency fights to keep a questionable gag or situation in a continuity—or whether or not we can sell the idea to the salesman on the account that the gag is bad in the first place. . . . Chicago doesn't help matters, being much less strict in the matter of taste than we are. It would not be impossible for an agency to take a gag which we have rejected here in New York, and get it put on a Chicago program. . . . Certainly the agencies and clients have not reached the point where they agree with us on what is acceptable in the average American home. And certainly our programs are of a lower standard of taste and humor than they were a year or two ago.[56]

The difficulties experienced by New York headquarters in their dealings with the less stringent Chicago office helps to explain the reluctance of NBC to open up a Hollywood studio, which, being even further removed, promised to bring similar problems. However, the movement of agencies to the West Coast soon gave the network no choice. Though NBC set up makeshift facilities in 1935 in "an old barn" on the RKO lot, problems developed almost immediately.[57]

In September 1936, Sidney Strotz, head of production in Chicago, sent a deputy, Clarence Menser, to observe conditions in Hollywood and report back, under the guise of overseeing the first West Coast production of NBC's *First Nighter* program. Menser sent in an extremely critical twelve-page assessment of the many weaknesses of both the NBC Hollywood production studio and the talent bureau. He concluded, in part:

Most of the programs are produced by agencies . . . so that the NBC program directors in Hollywood have little to do, except observe. . . . In general, the agencies have moved in and taken over our Hollywood studios for the production of their own programs. They buy little or no talent from NBC there. They have no respect whatever for our producing ability on the West Coast, and they are inclined to tolerate us only because we have the physical setup there which can be used for their purposes.[58]

Correction of these problems led to the creation of NBC's West Coast studios. But Hollywood variety programs were not the only troubling aspect of network-agency relations.

Daytime Dirt

By 1936, daytime hours were dominated by two types of continually worrisome programming: daytime serials for "housewives" and action/adventure serials for children. With the creation of the New York Continuity Acceptance Department in 1934 and the appointment of Janet MacRorie as head, the many complaints circling around these two genres—again, created, entirely produced, and sustained by agencies—now had someone whose job it was to take heed of them. The opening salvo in this newly institutionalized skirmish was fired by MacRorie in October 1936. In a memo to Bertha Brainard, head of commercial programming, she describes her objections to several of NBC's daytime offerings:

Back Stage Wife: Script filled with heart-break and misunderstanding between husband and wife. Scheming theatrical managers, sneering newspaper columnists, a leading lady who is a dope fiend.
Just Plain Bill and Nancy: Full of confinement cases and unsolved disappearances.
Five Star Jones: Highlights of story are the expectant motherhood of Sally and all the discomfort it entails; the avowed hatred for fatherhood of her husband; his utter neglect of his wife for another woman.
True Story Court of Human Relations: Dramatizations presented before a "judge." Immorality is usually sugar-coated but intimation of it is always strong. Titles of stories are frequently a deliberate appeal to the sensational and morbidly curious-minded.

She concludes: "It seems to me that all of this material is beyond cure through censorship. Amputation is the only remedy and I think you will agree it is a little too late for that."[59]

But despite this conclusion, by February 1937 MacRorie brings another offensive program to the attention of John Royal and Roy Witmer, not so coincidentally a JWT-produced program called *Husbands and Wives*, sponsored by Pond's:

> This program has been a border-line case in respect to good taste ever since it came to NBC. The problems almost always have to do with beds, bedrooms, and the habits of their occupants. The program is cheap and suggestive. Each week there is a long battle to have deleted the more objectionable material. . . . I believe it is a mistake to accept a program such as "Husbands and Wives" unless it is agreed by this Company and the Agency that the intimacies of marriage be avoided. In this sort of thing, the implication that can be brought out in the playing is worse than the written lines. Reviewing "Husbands and Wives" for policy violations is not enough. I believe that this program warrants your investigation.[60]

Whether as a result of the ensuing investigation or not, the program was not continued beyond the 1937 season. One month later, however, the problem resurfaced, this time in the form of "57 letters of criticism from [the] audience" attached to a report by MacRorie, directed to Brainard and forwarded from her to Witmer. (Unfortunately, the original memo and the letters do not seem to exist in the NBC files.) Brainard summarizes:

> We have been receiving so many letters about the tragedy and misery of the daytime scripts that something should be done by the Vice President in charge of Sales to call to the attention of the agencies controlling these daytime scripts that the women of America have enough troubles of their own. If they are to enjoy listening to radio the programs should bring them to a land of make-believe where good things happen. . . . Isn't there something you can do to help?[61]

Witmer's response is measured; as director of sales, whose position depends on allowing agencies a fairly free hand, he sketches out what could reasonably be described as the overall network position on the matter. Walking a delicate line between abandonment of standards and the need to attract audiences, Witmer points out:

> I must call your attention to the fact that the mail response to these programs is without doubt greater than any other programs reponse that we know of. When you get a million and a half people writing in for Ma Perkins' seeds, and a couple of million for something else, there is hardly any conclusion to reach except that they *listen* at least. . . . If we are so keen about keeping tragic dramatizations away from the radio audience, why do we put on a program sustaining such as we did Monday night . . . "We Are Not Alone"? The fact that James Hilton wrote the book detracts nothing from the tragedy of the story.[62]

Here the nature of this conflict begins to reveal itself in all its complexity. Tragedy and morbidity on daytime, controlled by agencies, differs from highbrow drama and morbidity on sustaining by NBC; the network must negotiate between the two. One popular strategy for rebuffing criticism is indicated by the use of ratings and numbers; the other is indicated by Witmer's separate response to MacRorie:

> I hold no grief [*sic*] for these particular programs. I too think they are morbid. But are we to give the radio audience what they apparently like to listen to or what we think they ought to have? The advertisers pursue the former course. The British Broadcasting company the latter.[63]

The mere presence of a Continuity Acceptance Department, and later Standards and Practices, appears to have satisfied the networks' need to maintain some valid claim to the moral high ground, even if the department's recommendations were largely impossible to implement, given agency domination of production. One result of this exchange was a codification of network continuity acceptance policy that year, resulting in a policy manual put togther by MacRorie's office and adopted for network use. Yet its effect on the worst offenders, in MacRorie's view, was negligible. One year later, in February 1938, she again issued a list of particularly offensive programs—all daytime, all agency produced—this time bypassing the complacent director of sales and going straight to the top, to Lenox R. Lohr, president of NBC networks:

> With criticism mounting against the merit of radio programs in general and the question of public interest stressed so strongly, I believe we should ask for change in type of material used on the following programs broadcast from New York.
> (a) "John's Other Wife"—a daytime show. Quite bad; story poor—an endless conflict between the wife and her husband's business associates. . . .
> (b) "Just Plain Bill and Nancy"—a daytime show of no merit whatever—tragedy is paramount—babies arriving, babies dying, adults going out of their minds—oxygen tents, hospitals, murders, robberies, etc. . . .
> (f) "Dick Tracy"—the moral of right coming out on top is greatly overshadowed by colorful deeds and skill of the miscreants. Plenty of gun play and screams. . . .
> (h) "Mrs. Wiggs of the Cabbage Patch"—a succession of calamities—never a happy moment—robberies, murders, deaths by natural causes, gangsters, ex-convicts—no relation between radio script and book of same title.[64]

The addition of children's programming here reflects the beginning of one of the first "moral panics" to hit radio, later to be continued for television.

Yet this tension had its beneficial aspects for both parties. For the agencies, the networks presented a convenient and efficient way to reach a nationwide mass audience without the trouble of researching and purchasing individual markets. With the power to determine pretty effectively the nature of their programs, agencies chafed under network restrictions but appreciated some aspects of centralized control, such as network supervision of other agency and clients' activities—to preserve a "high-class" selling environment overall and to prevent clashes between advertisers. NBC also had an interest in the success of sponsors' shows, especially as it affected the profitability of their owned and operated stations, and served as a central publicity source, promoting agency programs in the same breath as it promoted its own identity. For most listeners, agency programs *were* the network; the networks had a vested interest in their quality and profitability, which paid off for the sponsors. Also, through this system the agencies assured themselves of a double source of commission: typically, an agency received not only a 15 percent commission on time purchased from the network on which a program was placed, but also 15 percent from the sponsor for building and producing the program.

For the networks, the advantages of this sytem had been stronger in the early days, when undercapitalized and unprepared radio programming departments found themselves overwhelmed by the task at hand and accepted welcome help from agency producers. This ready source of quality material helped to build the networks up and establish strong affiliate relations, fending off threats of superpower independent stations and transcription services and keeping live network transmission the dominant radio form in the United States. As the 1930s progressed, and complaints about the commercialization of radio arose cyclically from the public and from the FCC, networks could point the finger of blame at sponsors and their agencies while holding up their own blameless behavior in off-prime sustaining cultural and educational programming; the FCC bought this very effective line for thirty years.

With the advent of television, this same structuring tension would be put to new uses, culminating in the changes brought about ostensibly by the quiz show scandals but, as several historians have pointed out, actually arising out of the networks' increasing impatience with dependence on sponsors and agencies.[65] This rising friction could take on strange and petty forms, as perhaps best exemplified in one of Fred Allen's better-known scrapes in 1947. Allen had already gained a reputation as radio's bad boy, and he was frequently censored for taking on the network itself as the butt of his jokes. On April 20, 1947, his show included a routine that referred to the previous week's show being cut off abruptly by NBC, having run over its time limit. The next week, Allen's script included the following lines:

> *Portland*: What happens to all the time they save cutting off the ends of programs?
> *Allen*: Well, there is a big executive in radio. He sits in a little glass closet with his mother of pearl gong. When your program runs overtime he thumps his gong—Bong!—you're off the air. Then he marks down how much time he's saved.
> *Portland*: What does he do with all this time?
> *Allen*: He adds it all up—ten seconds here—twenty seconds there—when the big executive has saved up enough seconds, minutes and hours to make two weeks, he uses the two weeks of *your* time for *his* vacation.

NBC found this characterization of the "big radio executive" offensive and threatened to fade out the exchange if the script was not revised. Their suggested alternative: change it to "There is an advertising agency executive who sits over there. . . ." When Allen refused this change, his program was faded to a hush for twenty-five seconds.[66] NBC had clearly had enough. Though it would take the networks until the late 1950s to vanquish their longtime rivals and take back the dominant position they had lost in the 1930s, it is no coincidence that the networks' most influential early president, Pat Weaver, began immediately to undercut the power of the agencies with shared sponsorship and network-produced spectaculars.

But until that happy day, radio networks of the 1930s responded to the pressures of social negotiation in two ways: first, by creating a separate daytime sphere in which the worst offenders of official taste could be contained, as I will discuss in chapter 5; and second, by encouraging a type of domestic drama that avoided the pitfalls of race, ethnicity, and troublesome gender-related and sexual material, along with overstimulating adventure, by focusing on the "average American family." Carefully white, middle-class, and small-town, confining its interests to the everyday doings of noncontroversial folks in America's heartland, such programs often achieved very high standards of writing, acting, and empathy with a popular way of life and were faithfully followed by large audiences. Among the best known and most loved of these were *Vic and Sade*, Paul Rhymer's paen to simple family life; *One Man's Family*, written by Carlton E. Morse, really a serial but adhering to nighttime standards; and *The Aldrich Family*, a show that developed into more what we would now call the domestic sitcom, combining drama and comedy. Another strand of this emergent format consists of the husband-and-wife comedy, exemplified by *Fibber McGee and Molly* but also by such shows as *Easy Aces*, written by Goodman Ace and starring himself and his wife, Jane; *The George Burns and Gracie Allen Show*, which started out on the JWT-produced *Fleischmann's Yeast Hour* (Rudy Vallee); and many more.

Though not particularly prevalent until the late 1940s, this format led to many of the sitcoms carried over onto early television, such as those starring Joan Davis, Lucille Ball, and Burns and Allen, as well as *Life with Luigi*, *The Life of Riley*, *The Honeymooners*—the list goes on. Though sitcoms of the 1950s have received an increasing amount of critical attention, few scholars have made use of the story of their roots in radio, to the detriment of many very revealing sources of social and cultural context. However, other forms and controversies dominated the decades of radio. The story of women in the daytime, prestige drama in the nighttime, and the transformation of both during the war years must be added to our history.

► FIVE

The Disembodied Woman

In September 1925 an article titled, "A Girl Reporter-Announcer Speaks Up: Radio in Days of Yore" appeared in the newly minted fan journal *Radio Age*. It describes the experience of Gwen Wagner at station WPO, Memphis, Tennessee, a full four years previously, in 1921:

> Our staff in those days consisted of two. My only assistant was a young chap by the name of Percy Root, who took care of the mechanical end of the station at night and, during the day, worked at something else. . . . For myself, I worked during the day as reporter on the newspaper which sponsored the station. In addition to my general assignments, I wrote all the material for the radio column, engaged the radio artists and arranged the programs. At night I went out to the studio and broadcast.[1]

There are two interesting aspects to this account: first, the fast pace of radio development in the 1920s indicated by the phrase "days of yore" applied to a period only four years earlier; second, the fact that the writer is a young woman, writing not as a member of the audience or as a performer, but as an active participant in the production of radio—a category of person we are led by our history books to believe did not exist.[2] Serving as combination station manager, talent agent, program director, announcer, writer, and publicist, Wagner was not unusual for this period in radio's development. Broadcasting only from 7:00 to 9:00 p.m., she presided over a schedule that featured "news brevities," baseball results, a bedtime story for children, and one or two musical features, often centered on phonograph records or the mechanical piano.[3]

The experiences of Gwen Wagner and others like her—and the denial of their existence by received history—points to the problematic but central role played by gender in the definition of the appropriate functions of broadcasting. Broadcasting, both radio and television, exhibits a peculiar contradiction that has rarely been remarked upon by

130

historians and commentators. Whereas the majority of its audience is female—ranging from 55-60 percent at night to more than 70 percent in the daytime—and the purchase of products by women provides its most basic economic support, its ranks of writers, producers, directors, actors, executives, critics, and regulators remain predominantly and resolutely male—at least, so we are led to believe. In turn, scholarship and critical study of media have assigned the structural function of gender a nominal role, and this arrangement is accepted as "natural," or merely reflective of prevalent conditions in society at large. Traditional studies of broadcasting institutions, economics, and policy deal with a world in which women, as individuals and as a group, barely seem to exist and in which it is only the discourses and actions of men that have relevance. The audience, though frequently invoked as the basic sine qua non of the entire operation, remains a vague and undifferentiated entity, remote and passive, and nowhere is its predominant constitution as female even noted in most cases, much less addressed openly. However, criticism of television is often based in terms that "feminize" devalued practices and hold high those designated as more "masculine" or serious—so that whereas gender is disregarded in one sense, it permeates the entire system in another.

Recent feminist scholarship, drawing on cultural studies theories of active reading and resistance, has gone a long way toward redressing the effects of this blind spot. In the works of Julie D'Acci, Lynn Spigel, Mary Beth Haralovich, Ellen Seiter, and others in this vein the feminine audience is no longer constructed as a passive nonentity but as active and selective contributors to broadcast meanings and reception. However, a tendency exists to accept as a given the basic dichotomy of production and reception still inherent in this model: women are the audience, men the producers. Assigning a more powerful role to the woman as audience member recognizes an important and long-neglected aspect of television's social role, but in one way tends to obscure a perhaps even more important aspect of broadcasting: women as participants in broadcasting's social address, actively competing for control over their own voices and venues, vying for the right to speak and be heard by the public at large. Here history can illuminate the blind spot of gender in broadcasting by demonstrating that this dichotomy was indeed artificial, created not "naturally" or by automatic reflection of social conditions but actively struggled over, debated, contested by the men and women—on both sides of traditional gender discourses—involved in early radio's definition and construction. Women in fact invented and sustained some of broadcasting's most central innovations and served in key decision-making roles, and furthermore participated in the development of entire genres that spoke to them as a specific group about the interests and concerns of women's lives. It is history writing that has consigned women to the sidelines, not historical events themselves.

From its early days, women recognized the significance of this new medium of radio and seized the opportunities for social negotiation and change that it offered; many men as well wholeheartedly supported (and profited from) this recognition. As in any new field, early flexibility gave way to institutionalized rigidity that worked to contain and repress radio's more potentially disruptive aspects. Yet the history of broadcasting has been only half written if gender and its structuring role are neglected, in light of television's highly feminized forms and uses. In this chapter I can only begin to lay out some of the broadest ways in which gender worked in the formation of broadcasting, but it is my hope that identification of major aspects of this central conflict will point toward many avenues for further investigation.

Bent Hairpin Detectors: The Women of Amateur Wireless

Though some media, like television, come so completely bound up in existing highly developed industrial structures and practices that very little space exists for uses alternative to those that control their development,[4] many technological innovations go through a period of relative indeterminacy. In chapter 2 I have traced some of the ways that wireless amateurs found to employ the new medium of code and voice transmission, and the way that their discursive construction as "small boys," in the press and in the policy debates of the early 1920s, provided a way to contain and curb the "excesses" of amateur practice. Yet one construction that has escaped reflection is the notion that this was a male preserve. Evidence shows that women participated actively in amateur radio, from set building to DXing to occupying professional positions as wireless operators, despite the social obstacles they faced.

Presumably, young women were drawn to the medium by the same qualities that appealed to their male counterparts—the romance of invention, communication over distances, transcending boundaries of space and time, membership in an interesting hobby group, and job training opportunities—yet another possibility that seemed to both intrigue and plague women wireless amateurs was the ability to escape determinations of gender.[5] In a medium at first not even aural but transmitted by an invisible hand tapping out Morse code at a transmitter, identity could remain unfixed by traditional gender and other status distinctions. This persistent and compelling potential, and the anxieties it induced, forms the basic backdrop to women's involvement in radio. Later, as radio became primarily a medium of reception in the home, its domestic situation seemed to suit it particularly to the needs and interests of women. Both radio's capacity to blur the basic distinctions of gender identity and its potential for allowing the private voices of women access to the public airwaves represented threats to established order that had to be contained. This familiar pattern—the challenge of a new technology producing efforts to control and restrict its uses—begins in the days before radio per se, with the wireless amateurs.

In 1923, Abbye White won third place in *Radio Broadcast*'s set-building competition with an original design that allowed reception on five different circuits. The opening remarks of the essay in which she submitted her design reveal some of the hopes and anxieties that women in amateur broadcasting experienced: "Rather fearfully I venture into your contest, for I do not know if we of the fair sex are allowed in or not. But your rules say nothing against it—so here I am."[6] She was not alone as a female set builder, as other reports confirm.[7] Wireless was a field in which many rules had not yet been clearly established, and in its early days it was populated by young men and women with a taste for the adventurous and different, who were less likely than some to insist on the social categories that in many cases their hours spent in garage or bedroom wired into the ether were an attempt to escape.

But the practical matter of employment supplied the most immediate impetus for the participation of women in wireless transmission. Potential job opportunities beckoned even before the First World War, at least in limited areas. *QST*, the journal of the American Radio Relay League (ARRL), one of the largest of the amateur associations, reported in August 1916 that department stores, in particular, preferred female wireless operators and that efforts were being made to train young women in the New York area.[8] Wireless clubs sprang up at women's colleges and as part of Girl Scout activities. Other women participated in wireless as a hobby and a passion. In the 1916 debut of a regular column devoted to profiles of ARRL members, *QST* presented a cameo on Emma Candler of station 8NH in St. Mary's, Ohio, one of the key operators in the ARRL's cross-country relay network and holder of a first-grade commercial license. Candler related her fellow amateurs' frequent surprise in finding out that the colleague they had been addressing as "O.M." (for "old man," a frequently used slang term) was actually an "O.W."[9]

The war years brought an enormous increase in the number of female "hams" on the air, as hundreds of young women were trained by the U.S. Navy to function as wireless instructors for the men who took their skills onto ships and to shore stations overseas. *QST*'s August 1917 issue—its second to the last before publication was suspended during the war years—anticipated postwar changes with an editorial titled "The Ladies Are Coming." The author welcomed in advance members of "the fairer sex" onto the airwaves, but expressed concern with questions of identity and proper etiquette: What should replace the careless use of "O.M."?

> It will not be OW, from what we have heard from various young ladies. They do not take kindly to being referred to semi-affectionately as Old Woman. Some of them will let Old Lady pass, although there are others who object even to this. We would not venture to make a suggestion in such a delicate matter, but just the same, we fully expect to hear DG. This will sound pretty chummy, but in wireless where you cannot see the other person, and where you never expect that you will see them, and where formalities are more of a dead letter than in anything else we know of, it might be that calling an unknown young lady dear girl, might be taken all right.[10]

Overall, the wireless fraternity, at least in print, welcomed women into its ranks, as the above-quoted editorial hastened to "extend the glad hand of fellowship" to female members of the ARRL. Yet anxiety showed in predictions that "language will have to be improved a little because, 'keep out, you big Ham' will not be exactly polite when the ladies are around. . . . we fully expect to see a general uplift throughout the fraternity when the ladies join us." What existing female operators might have thought about this is not recorded.

After the war, women did indeed begin to make their presence known. Though the occasional male amateur might complain about his wife's usurping of the wireless transmitter—"When she and Mrs. 8ER get chewing about Mrs. 2ZZ's new hat, the rest of you might as well quit"[11]—amateur organizations proved more sympathetic to female colleagues than did technical schools, employers, and the U.S. government. An anonymous editorial by "The Old Woman" in September 1920 claimed that the navy had refused to allow women to operate ship-to-shore stations or to attend advanced technical training courses during the war, and although women were free to apply for licenses, their inability to get practical experience on transmitters (controlled by the government and limited to military personnel during the war years) set up a barrier to their passing the operator's exam: "Yes, deary, you're right, it's possible to learn what's in the book, but when your lack of experience costs you twenty points, and you have to make seventy five out of a possible eighty on what you know, it requires considerable application."[12] A sympathetic male writer summarized the obstacles faced by women seeking employment in the field after the war, "The young woman who has taken any interest in wireless and has progressed up to the rank of a Commercial Wireless Operator has absolutely no chance," and proposed that they be trained as "radio stenographers" for technical companies.[13]

Many women, of course, received more advanced training than this, a phenomenon still new enough to cause astonishment in one ARRL member attending a Bureau of Standards workshop on technical issues:

> We were struck by the number of ladies present. . . . We asked if the learned gentlemen members of the staff dictated notes during lectures. The answer was "No." Then we tackled from another slant. Were the ladies the secretaries of some of the distinguished scientists who made up the staff? Again, "No." Well, who were the ladies, anyway? Then we found that they were physicists, electrical engineers, chemical engineers, metallurgists, etc.[14]

During this period of fierce controversy over female suffrage, as the Nineteenth Amendment was debated and ratified state by state, the identity and nature of women became increasingly a topic of considerable social anxiety. Who were these ladies, anyway? If women refused to perform in the gender roles traditionally assigned to them, and insisted on moving into other positions and identities, how to maintain the social—and previously designated "natural"—distinctions that separated women from men? This question became particularly relevant in the invisible realm of the ether.

One way to defuse the threat posed by the disembodied women of wireless was to focus on the physical confirmation of gender identity provided by the visual; another was to "out" women amateurs by openly publishing their gender. The writer of the radio stenographer letter acknowledged this anxiety: "A great majority of radio bugs will no doubt disapprove of my suggestions . . . because they would rather have the fair damsels where they can throw their lamps on em' now and 'en—so to speak. Especially so now-a-days with those low cut 'everythings.'"[15] The woman who could speak without being seen controverted a more traditional feminine role—to be seen and not heard—and any article featuring a woman operator felt obligated to include comment on her physical appearance and/or effect on men, usually including age, attractiveness, and marital status (not normally a feature of profiles of male amateurs).[16] These anxieties continued into broadcast radio as well, particularly in the 1924 debate over women announcers, which will be discussed below. But the coded transmission of wireless radio allowed many women to keep their cover of gender-neutral identity (presumed male) throughout their careers on the air.

Well-meaning efforts to welcome the emergence of a female operator in a district, often by praising her as the "first" and calling for more women in the air, had the unintended side effect of forcing other female amateurs operating under gender-anonymous conditions either to declare their presence or allow the presumption of an all-male fraternity to predominate. A Houston amateur whose letter to *QST* was published in December 1921 asked the editor what he meant "publishing an announcement of 'a' first district O.W.? The Houston Radio Club has *four* of them as members, and I can name at least *ten more* that are actually operating in the fifth district."[17] A few women, such as M. Adaire Garmhausen of the bent hairpin detector, came out publicly to write on women's and general radio issues. Though we can never really know the exact number of women wireless amateurs participating in the early phase of the medium, their numbers are less important than this evidence of the anxiety created by the gender-obscuring properties of radio and the activity of women in this new sphere, which would be repeated again and again as radio became a national medium.

A Woman's Place

But even the more passive, less technical, and public use of radio being promoted by the new category of commercial "radiophone" broad-

casters awoke possibilities for feminine participation in the medium. To many, radio's position in the home made it a "natural" venue for women. Between 1920 and 1924, radio edged its way into the living rooms of America from its previous accommodation in the workshop or garage. Though the techology was not yet terribly well suited for its new family status—battery acid ruined rugs and sideboards, and headphones made family listening difficult[18]—a new audience of men, women, and children began to look to radio for familiar entertainment and information made excitingly new by radio's magic voice, supplied to them by radio's enthusiastic entrepreneurs.

Not wanting to be left behind, or responding to the radio debut of their competitors, early radio stations frequently operated at the margins of established businesses, with low budgets and even lower revenue expectations.[19] It was unclear that radio could ever turn a profit, but equally clear that everybody was doing it, and that someone within the company would have to be assigned radio duties. There was no prestige in this early radio work, and usually it consisted of an additional assignment on top of one's regular duties.

Under these conditions, it was a natural place for women. Gwen Wagner's experience is typical: "Somebody had to be gotten in a hurry and nobody wanted the job. At last the eye of the managing editor fell upon me. I was the only woman on the staff and, I might add, the last resort in this time of trouble."[20] Indeed, once the technical operation of the station was gotten out of the way, many of the ensuing responsibilities seemed to fall well within traditional feminine pursuits: mingling with artistic and cultural groups, issuing invitations for their appearance on the air, acting as a kind of radio "hostess," and, presumably, writing thank-you notes the next day. It began to seem equally clear that much of the radio audience would consist of women. If radio existed primarily as a medium in the home, and given that men occupied the workplace for most of the day, women constituted the audience available. And as the commercial possibilities of radio came to be realized in the mid- to late 1920s, the economic role of women as the primary purchasing agents for the family increased women's appeal as audience members. Advertising studies confirmed that 85 percent of household purchases were made by women, making them the obvious target for radio's increasingly commercialized address.[21] This factor, along with early 1920s experimentation and highly localized production, made radio a marginal, innovative, and often loosely

structured operation into which the brave new women of the 1920s could venture with less resistance than in more conservative, established professions.[22] To illustrate the more flexible gender categories of the 1920s, I will focus for a moment on the careers of two pioneering women broadcasters whose initial involvement in radio typifies the broader-based experience still available to women in the early 1920s, but who are atypical in going on to long-term careers in network broadcasting: Bertha Brainard and Judith Waller.

After serving as an ambulance driver in World War I, Bertha Brainard began announcing for WJZ in 1922 and rose to become the station's first program director, then station manager, and later NBC's director of commercial programming through the 1930s and 1940s. Her work in radio took place in two parts: one actually on the air, announcing and producing programs for WJZ, and later, after WJZ had been acquired by NBC, as one of the few women executives not assigned to women's, children's, or public service departments.[23] As station manager for one of the country's preeminent stations, Brainard articulated a program philosophy directly related to the role played by the female audience in radio's development:

> Since I have been connected with WJZ, I have watched the increase of women's interest in broadcasting, realizing that it was one great factor which was working for the good of radio in general, demanding that the program managers arrange constantly better and more interesting programs. . . . Because most women have the opportunity to listen in more hours every day than most men, I consider that their opinions on broadcasting are very important. Many of them are deep students of broadcasting, steeped in the lore of the microphone. And I have found that most of them are constructive critics.[24]

In 1923 she inaugurated a "broadcast hour devoted especially to the interests of women," one of the first, which became "widely popular."[25] Brainard carried her conviction that women represented radio's primary audience over to her position as NBC's director of commercial programming. She stated her case even more strongly in a memo she issued in 1932, addressed to Roy Witmer, head of NBC's Sales Division, regarding NBC's policy of setting daytime ad rates at one-half those of nighttime:

> On my return from vacation I find your memorandum dated July 30 which advises that the rates prior to 9:00 a.m. are to be equivalent to the regular daytime rate heretofore effective. . . . I am looking forward to the

day when you and the sponsors realize that the daytime hours are our most important selling times and the rates for the daytime hours will be double those of the evening, in view of the fact that all our real selling will be done to the women in the daytime, and the institutional good will programs will be directed to the mixed audiences after 6:00. I am such a confirmed feminist that I thoroughly believe this is going to take place, and in the not too distan[t] future. . . . What do you think?

Witmer scribbled a reponse on the bottom of the memo: "I'll go with you part way: day time rates equal to night time."[26]

Though daytime rates stayed the same, Brainard was able to exert considerable influence on the definition and shape of early commercial network radio. Until radio production moved decisively into the hands of advertising agencies in the mid-1930s, the Commercial Program Department typically developed ideas for programs at the behest of potential sponsors, mediated by the network Sales Department.[27] Brainard's notion of the different functions of day- and nighttime programming, as I will argue below, became partially realized in network practice during the 1930s, leading to a much more firmly marked delineation between men's and women's appropriate spheres in radio discourse—but with a very different power base from the one Brainard had envisioned.

Another woman influential in the development of early broadcasting was Judith Waller, who started in 1922 as station manager of WMAQ, the *Chicago Daily News* station. She later became vice president and manager of WMAQ, Inc., under William S. Hedges, president, and was appointed NBC's director of public service programming, Central Division, after NBC bought WMAQ in 1931.[28] Besides her innovations in sports broadcasting and in the development of *Amos 'n' Andy*, discussed in chapter 3, she founded one of the longest-running experiments in education by radio, the *American School of the Air*. Her involvement with the formation of CBS—then called United Independent Broadcasters under the management of Arthur Judson—led to an offer of resignation when NBC acquired WMAQ, but when it was not accepted, Waller continued as educational director for the network, carrying over many of WMAQ's locally developed programs, including *The University of Chicago Round Table*, the jewel in NBC's public service crown for more than twenty years. As Waller recalled in a 1948 interview, her NBC assignment, though prestigious, represented a narrowing of her previous duties at WMAQ:

While I was interested in educational and cultural types of programs, I also had to be, as manager of the station, very much interested in other types of programs as well. I would not say that my own interests tended more towards the educational side than they did towards any other part of the radio schedule. I had been just as active in selling programs of all types of sponsors and thought of programs and sales together after the station became commercial.[29]

However, despite Waller's experience, upon NBC's purchase of WMAQ she was shifted from the Commercial Program Department, under the direction of Sidney Strotz in Chicago, and into the educational side of radio, where she remained for the next thirty years. Though it was clear by this time that commercial programming would occupy the bulk of the broadcast schedule and provide its economic support, conditions in the regulation of the broadcast industry made a visible commitment to public service and educational programming highly advisable, as I will discuss below. It is interesting to note that by the late 1940s, the directors of educational and public service programs at all four networks were women: Waller and Margaret Cuthbert at NBC, Helen J. Sioussat at CBS, Grace M. Johnson at ABC, and Elsie Dick at Mutual. By contrast, Brainard's untimely death in 1943 removed the only female head of commercial programming at any of the networks; sales departments, where most of the economically profitable work lay by the late 1930s, were always staffed exclusively by men.

What happened to change the early 1920s climate of acceptance, in which women like Gwen Wagner, Bertha Brainard, and Judith Waller could find easy entry and quick promotion with responsibilities that ranged across all aspects of the radio schedule, to the later period of the 1930s, in which women's efforts were confined to public service, educational, and children's concerns and the culturally disparaged forms of daytime "women's" genres? The process was complex and had much to do with the increasing capitalization and prominence of the industry, with all the resistance to social innovation and flexibility such change brings in its wake. Three episodes serve to illuminate the shift that occurred, however, and some of the reasons and traditions behind it. First, a debate over women's voices on the air that received industry attention in the mid-1920s acted to discourage women's on-air employment, building on familiar fears from wireless days; second, as advertising agencies became primary powers in radio production an important definitional transition occurred, as we shall see in

the case of the J. Walter Thompson Company in the late 1920s; and third, the regulatory struggles of the early 1930s led to a differentiation of daytime and nighttime programming that identified women's interests with the disparaged commercialized form of the daytime serial. Within these restrictions and increasingly narrow institutional confines, women continued to employ the radio medium—both as audiences and as producers—for exploration of issues of relevance to women, and to resist network and agency efforts to define their interests too narrowly.

"Are Women Undesirable—Over the Air?"

In 1924 a debate arose in the broadcasting community that threatened the careers of women such as Brainard and Waller, and that was used for two decades to limit women's opportunities to enter the field of broadcasting. The debate began when *Radio Broadcast* magazine ran a commentary on the suitability of women as radio announcers, provoking a controversy that extended over several months and eventually made its way into general public awareness. It should be remembered that in early broadcasting, from the beginnings of standardized operation in 1922 into the early 1930s, the station announcer occupied a key position in broadcast programming. Usually combining the functions of program producer, talent coordinator, and on-air "host"— and often expected to fill in with musical or comedic talent when guest artists failed to appear—the announcer became the most prominent figure in early radio, a celebrity in his or her own right. Though as program forms standardized and became more self-contained the role of announcer as the "glue" in the station schedule decreased, early announcers went on to provide news and sports coverage, introduce programs and "emcee" musical variety shows, and serve as the voice of the sponsor during commercial breaks. During the 1920s, many women played this role on stations around the country,[30] but by 1930 nonperforming women's voices had virtually disappeared from nighttime schedules and could be heard only during daytime hours devoted specifically to "women's" concerns.

The debate was sparked by a letter received by Jennie Irene Mix of *Radio Broadcast*, who had just a few months earlier originated one of the first regular monthly columns of radio criticsm and review, "The Listener's Point of View." Mix reported that one reader, a phonograph record dealer, wrote in to say that the poor sales of recordings featuring women speakers caused him to speculate that the public would not accept female radio announcers, on grounds that "the voice of a woman, when she cannot be seen 'is very undesirable, and to many, both men and women, displeasing.'" Does this mean, asked Mix, that "when a woman is speaking she may be fascinating as long as she remains in sight, and becomes displeasing the moment she cannot be seen although she may go right on talking just as delightfully as the moment before?" To explore this issue, Mix invited the opinions of several station managers, all male, for the September 1924 edition of the magazine.

Though two of the managers dismissed the idea, citing the many women on radio and improvements in the reproduction of higher-pitched sound, most agreed that women announcers and lecturers—though not performers, singers, or household advice columnists—suffered from a variety of handicaps. "Few women have voices with distinct personality. It is my opinion that women depend on everything else but the voice for their appeal," stated W. W. Rogers of the Westinghouse company and KDKA. Corley W. Kirbett, director of station WWJ Detroit, opined bluntly, "I do not believe that women are fitted for radio announcers. They need body to their voices. . . . When women announcers try to be congenial in their announcements, they become affected; and when they attempt to be business like they are stiff." J. M. Barnett, manager of station WOR, concluded, "For certain types of radio work I consider that a woman's voice is very essential; but for announcing, a well modulated male voice is the most pleasing to listen to," because women's voices tend to be "monotonous." Or again, according to M. A. Rigg of WGR in Buffalo: "There are many reasons why, to my mind, it seems advisable to use a man as announcer, especially during the heavier part of the work."

Mix defended women announcers by noting that most of these managers expressed their views as matters of personal opinion; therefore, she concluded, they had not been inundated with complaints from listeners regarding women announcers. She let the matter drop with an additional feature on the many women in fact on the air as announcers, including those at the stations of the managers cited above. Mix died unexpectedly in 1925; her column was taken over by John Wallace, who revived the debate in 1926 by reporting on the results of a survey undertaken by radio station WJZ. Stating that a poll of five thousand listeners showed that men's voices were preferred to women's by a margin of a hundred to one, Charles B. Popenoe, the station manager, speculated:

> It is difficult to say why the public should be so unanimous about it. One reason may be that most receiving sets do not reproduce perfectly the higher notes. A man's voice "takes" better. It has more volume. Then, announcers cover sporting events, shows, concerts, operas, and big public meetings. Men are naturally better fitted for the average assignment of the broadcast announcer. . . . But perhaps the best reason suggested for the unpopularity of the woman's voice over the radio is that it usually has too much personality. A voice that is highly individual and full of character is aggravating to the audience that cannot see the face and expression which go with the voice. We resent a voice that is too intimate on short acquaintance, and the woman announcer has difficulty in repressing her enthusiasm and in maintaining the necessary reserve and objectivity.

It is encouraging, I suppose, that in two short years women had gone from being perceived as having no personality on the air to having too much, but either condition seems to be a liability when the woman cannot be physically viewed.[31] This survey would be cited frequently in radio circles in coming years, as in a 1933 article by Martin Codell discussing the more numerous examples of female radio announcers in Europe. Questioning the lack of women on the U.S. airwaves, he concludes:

> First, there is an apparently unshakeable prejudice among the broadcast impresarios against women announcers; they are convinced that women's voices do not have the proper appealing quality . . . [and] say it is impossible to send a woman out on an assignment like covering a baseball game or football game or political convention or such like news events. They simply are not physically or by experience and temperament suited to the job, we are told.[32]

However, it becomes obvious in these comments that the matter under debate concerns the development of definitions of appropriate radio content and audience as much as the gender of those announcing it. If the proper business of radio is to broadcast "men's" concerns—such as news, sports, and politics—to a male audience, then the exclusion of women is only "natural." If, however, the main business of radio is to cater to the predominantly female audience—as, indeed, the daytime hours did quite effectively by the late 1920s, populated predominantly by female announcers and talent—then a different order of priorities might prevail. This definitional debate played itself out across the many economic and policy-related venues of broadcasting in the late 1920s and early 1930s. One particularly interesting incident occurred at the J. Walter Thompson agency, which I have discussed in chapter 4 as an important contributor to the development of broadcast practices during this period. Though not every agency experienced a similar process, JWT's decision to pursue radio broadcasting not as an adjunct to its women's advertising department but as a more high-profile, public image-oriented endeavor changed the face of accepted standards.

"New Business," Not "Women"

Though initially slow to get involved, the J. Walter Thompson Company by the late 1920s had moved heavily into radio advertising. By 1935, it produced in-house five of the top ten programs on radio; by 1942 it could boast of having produced thirty-five out of the eighty top-ranked shows from 1935 to 1942.[33] In the mid-1940s it occupied second place among the top five major agencies in radio production.[34] With clients including Standard Brands, Lever Brothers, Swift and Company, and Lorillard, JWT produced both nighttime and daytime programs for a variety of different radio audiences, though always heavily oriented to household products.

Until the 1960s, JWT also pioneered a unique corporate structure. Under the leadership of Helen Lansdowne Resor, an early female advertising executive and codirector of the firm with her husband, Stanley Resor, JWT operated separate men's and women's editorial groups, specializing in different kinds of advertising. Employees were segregated strictly by sex—women copywriters, artists, and groups heads working exclusively in the women's group, men in the equivalent men's group. The groups competed for accounts, but special expertise in advertising women's products based on its female advertising staff had been a JWT claim to fame since 1917. Helen Lansdowne Resor recalls:

> The success of the J. Walter Thompson Company has been in a large measure due to the fact that we have concentrated and specialized upon products sold to women. Of all retail purchases, a very large proportion are made by women. . . . The advertising appeal which seeks to increase the sales of products bought by women must be made with knowledge of the habits of women, their methods of reasoning, and their prejudices. My work for the Company has been based on these conditions and principles, and I believe that it is conceded in the advertising industry that our agency is pre-eminent when it comes to advertising articles for women.[35]

Her belief that women advertising executives were best qualified to reach this audience was reflected in the organizational structure of JWT. Ruth Waldo, one of the first female vice presidents of the company, recalled in a later interview:

> When a woman works for a man or in a men's group, she becomes less important, her opinion is worth less, her own progress and advancement less rapid. Then she does not have the excitement and incentive to work as hard as she can, nor, in a men's group, does she get the full credit for what she does. But with the knowledge and confidence of Mrs. Resor's support, a woman at Thompson could advance in her own group without having to compete with *Men* for recognition of her ability. She has greater independence and freedom; a woman's ideas could be judged on their value alone. It was one less handicap.[36]

This system paid off in the relatively high number of female executives at JWT compared with other firms; nine women occupied vice president slots by 1964.[37]

In 1929, the highest-ranking woman at JWT was Aminta Casseres, an editorial group head in the women's division. JWT had established an independent radio department in December 1927, under the direction of William H. Ensign. He was replaced in March 1929 by Henry P. Joslyn, formerly of the music department—not such a surprising selection when one considers the content of much of radio up to this point. But over the next two months, with the perceived value of radio as a potential center of profits increasing, a power struggle ensued among Joslyn, representing a more traditional view of radio as presenting indirectly advertised musical programs; Casseres, who saw radio as a medium for reaching women; and John U. Reber, in the "new business" department (whose predilection for "showmanship" was discussed in chapter 4). One radio department employee described this battle for control somewhat tongue-in-cheek:

> Mr. Joslyn, who had long been head of the radio department, called me in. He liked my continuity, he said. Would I make such and such changes in the script before ten o'clock the next morning? Feeling that my script must have had merit to warrant his attention I gurgled with delight and said yes sir. . . . On returning to my desk, I was summoned by Miss Aminta Casseres, one of the copy executives. She said that as the new head of the radio department, she wanted to thank me for writing my continuity. She asked if I could make certain revisions—a very different set from the ones Joslyn suggested. Would I bring her a revised script back in the morning, say at 10? I said yes ma'am, and returned to my office to

ponder. . . . It was not for long. The phone rang and I was asked to come
to John Reber's office. He said that he had been appointed head of radio
and liked my stuff. Here were the changes to make (all different from the
other two sets). . . . I was not at the meeting when these three worthies,
each armed with one of my scripts, fought out their conflicting ideas. . . .
But after several weeks of intramural shennanigans, during which I had
to write all the Thompson shows three different ways, Reber emerged,
bleeding, as Our Radio Chief.[38]

Elsewhere, Colwell states that Helen Resor had backed Casseres as
radio head, with Stanley Resor preferring Reber. John Reber's ascen-
dance at JWT marks a departure in the address and discourse of commercial radio programming. Reber is frequently credited with the development of high-profile nighttime programming built around star
personalities. His projects included the *Fleischmann's Yeast Hour* with
Rudy Vallee, one of early radio's biggest successes, and *The Lux Radio
Theatre*, one of the first—but far from the last—JWT program based
in Hollywood. Indeed, JWT, under Reber's direction, became the first
major agency to build a studio in Hollywood, and Reber's emphasis
on the Hollywood prestige connection had a profound effect on radio
programming and economics from the 1930s on.[39] It is impossible to
say how different Casseres's programming philosophy may have been,
but based on an article that appeared in the October 1929 *JWT News
Bulletin*, her interests lay in "human drama" programming and radio
as an "emotional medium," as well as the development of daytime
hours—programming strategies that later found application in those
genres designated as "women's" domain.[40]

The Feminine Majority

Before the institution of standardized concepts of audience, programming, and appropriate scheduling, most radio stations provided a
fairly undifferentiated mix of programming addressed to anyone who
might be listening—whether male or female, old or young. Given the
fact, too, that before the structure of frequency allocation adopted
with the Radio Act of 1927, many stations were confined to one or
two hours at different points in the day, and also the absence of reli-
able audience research until the late 1930s, concepts of programming
appropriate to daypart and division of specialized "women's" from
general programming were slow to emerge.[41] Indeed, many early proposals for radio assumed that women would be the main audience for

commercial broadcasting at any time of the day or night, and that programs should be designed accordingly.

One of the early visionaries in this area was Christine Frederick, a well-known marketing expert specializing in the female consumer. Her 1922 article in *Good Housekeeping* titled "Radio for the Housekeeper" was one of the first to argue that radio had particular relevance to women's lives. Frederick proposed a consistent daily schedule of educational and informative material for women in the home, modeled after the Chautauqua circuit programs. This would include not only "household interests," such as housekeeping and cooking, market reports, and care and hygiene of children, but also physical education ("setting-up" excercises); "cultural topics," including correct English, musical programs, and drama and book reviews; and "social interests," including current events, public affairs and politics, sports, finance, and club and organizational activities. She writes:

> The radio telephone, it seems to me, is primarily an invention for the benefit of women. Its greatest achievement is banishing isolation. . . . Isolation, whether mental or geographical, has been the cause of much of woman's restlessness and has done more to retard her progress than any other one factor. . . . I am sure the radiophone will assume a social significance which women will be quick to grasp and employ to their own advantage.[42]

Frederick envisioned broadcasting to women as not just occurring during daytime hours but spread throughout the broadcast schedule.[43]

Building on the position of radio in the home, "home service" programs—usually featuring appealing hostesses who cheerfully dispensed household, child rearing, and health information interspersed with light musical entertainment—became some of the most popular shows on the air during radio's earliest years, attracting audiences of all types. In fact, these programs can be seen as the prototype for the essential characteristics of the broadcasting schedule as it would develop generally: dialogue and music emceed by a congenial host, punctuated by information and selling talks. Though this particular genre of program later fades from the schedule per se, one reason for its disappearance is the absorption of its practices across the broadcast schedule, now broken into separate programs and dayparts.

The precedent for all of these, though noncommercial, may well have been the U.S. Department of Agriculture's *Housekeeper's Chats*, featuring a main hostess called "Aunt Sammy" (Uncle Sam's wife). In the days before networks, scripts were sent to stations all over the country, and each local station cast its own "Aunt Sammy" to host a fifteen-minute daily program featuring household advice, recipes, skits with incidental characters, and a listener write-in question period.[44] Along these same lines, station KYW in Chicago aired a "daily recipe talk" sponsored by the People's Gas Light and Coke Company hosted by Anna J. Peterson, People's director of home service, daily at 11:30 beginning in early 1923. When Peterson, in an effort to gauge the extent of her audience, issued an invitation to a "radio tea" at the gas company on March 10 to all of her unseen "radio pals," almost fifteen hundred people turned up from Chicago and surrounding towns. An article in the *People's Gas Club News* notes that many men and children enjoyed the tea, cookies, and entertainment provided, "for the listeners-in include men, boys and girls as well as women."[45]

Station WJZ had begun a woman's half hour from 4:00 to 4:30 each weekday in 1926, featuring Mrs. Julian Heath, president of the National Housewives League, who provided information on a variety of home-related topics, at this point unsponsored. Heath saw radio as a means of extending the reach of such public organizations focused on women as the National League of Women Voters and local women's clubs, and had earlier proposed the production of weekly programs to be supplied to local stations. These programs would address women specifically as public citizens, "urging them to exercise their right to participate in civic affairs" while at the same time promoting the use of radio to a very appealing demographic group. By emphasizing the latter point, Heath hoped to obtain cooperation and publicity through radio retailing publications and organizations.[46]

In terms of network programs, on CBS Ida Bailey Allen, a journalist who in 1924 became food editor at the *New York Sunday American* and, after a popular series of broadcasts over WOR, formed the National Radio Homemakers Club, began a regular daytime show in September 1928. By the following year she had expanded to a two-hour show (10:00 to noon) five days a week from her own specially equipped studios in New York. Allen was an independent producer; in partnership with two associates, she sold half of the show's fifteen-minute segments to sponsors, retaining the rest of the time for

sustaining programs, featuring interviews with famous authors, actors, women's clubs' presidents; a skit ("The Sewing Circle"); "The Home

Decorating Studio," with listeners invited to simultaneously practice the decorating techniques at home; "The Beauty Boudoir" with a professional beauty specialist, demonstrated beauty care as the broadcaster described the action. There was a Children's Corner; a series of lectures by distinguished physicians; dramatic presentations by Charles Coburn with other stage luminaries. The music, planned by Charles Premmac . . . included live, from the Mrs. Allen's Studios, a mixed quartette of fine voices; a male trio; a piano soloist and accompanist. Two orchestras and a mixed chorus were piped in from CBS. The U.S. Marine Band was piped in from Washington every week; U.S. Senator Capper of Kansas on "What's New in Washington," was a regular featured speaker.[47]

This program ran until 1932, at which point Allen diversified into syndicated cooking shows and, in 1936, live radio shows over Loews' station WHN broadcast from the Ziegfeld Theater, presided over by Louis Sidney, later vice president of MGM. These programs featured "audience interviews by Mrs. Allen, accompanied by a body-guard holding a traveling 'mike' while she tossed off one-minute interviews with members of the audience"—an early version of the daytime audience participation talk show.[48]

In the spring of 1928, NBC's Pacific Coast network had also debuted a daily mixed advice and entertainment program, which it called *The Women's Magazine of the Air*. In 1931 NBC brought this multiple-sponsor magazine format to the Red network, describing its *Woman's Radio Review* as "a program combining the entertainment, news items and information of proved appeal to women . . . available for non-competitive commercial sponsorship in periods of fifteen minutes."[49] This entertainment would include a full twelve-piece orchestra along with three regular female "experts" on various topics. By 1932 there were more than twenty daytime home service programs on the air, but this represents a high point, soon to decline.[50] Already major sponsors were experimenting with women's daytime serials, which by the end of the 1930s would dominate daytime network broadcasting.

The daytime radio homemakers' programs, though never highly emphasized or promoted in network broadcasting schedules, represent a use of radio whose potential for direct, unmediated address to women, used in a way that would allow women to speak for themselves and mobilize around social concerns, was ultimately undermined by the commercial pressures that by the late 1930s filled up the daytime hours with serials, soon to become known as soap operas. In chapter 6 I will address the conflicted cultural status of this unique radio form.

Daytime women's talk programs persisted, however, as I will discuss in the conclusion to this volume in the context of the contested career of Mary Margaret McBride, whose successful combination of the hypercommercial with more serious content for women would provoke both praise and criticism. A different version of radio's daytime potential was presented in 1932, the turning-point year, by Margaret Cuthbert, head of the Women's Division at NBC; though never realized, it shows the potential for organized women's voices that received little encouragement from the network organizations:

> Great possibilities will be opened when the company moves into Rockefeller Center. The daytime division might become a great national headquarters for women. Liaison could be effected with the General Federation of Women's Clubs, the Parent Teachers Association and other groups. Their leaders would use it as a forum and would keep their membership of millions in close contact with all the activities of the NBC women's division. The latter would become a dominating influence in women's club affairs. It would cooperate with university extension courses, schools of fine and applied arts, with the work of the foundations, with the government's projects for social welfare.[51]

Though Cuthbert went on to assure network heads that this program would be profitable as well as socially useful, already the writing was on the wall. Daytime radio would become the staging ground for more continuous dramatic narratives directed specifically toward women than any other medium has offered before or since.

► SIX

Under Cover of Daytime

During the years before network standardization, managers such as Bertha Brainard and Judith Waller presided over station schedules that showed far less program differentiation by daypart than later became the rule. Daytime as well as nighttime schedules show a mix of musical variety, talk, serial drama, and "serious" music programming, demonstrated by the fact that several later staples of the daytime schedule started out in the evenings. Shows such as *The Rise of the Goldbergs, Clara, Lu and Em, Myrt and Marge,* and *Just Plain Bill,* pioneers of the serial drama form, ran for the first five or six years of their lives in the nighttime hours, moving to daytime only in the mid-1930s, when the networks decided to clear the night air of serial drama. One writer for *Variety* discussed the change in daytime in these terms:

> As regards daytime programs—a change has taken place here, too. . . . the daytime programs are now nearly all serials. This development is one of salesmanship, not showmanship. The serial for the housewife, like the serial for the child, is designed to sustain interest in a continued story, day by day, and with it bring sales. Crude, perhaps, as compared to the evening program, it nonetheless has not yet burned itself out.[1]

By 1936, according to *Variety*'s statistics, the network daytime schedule consisted of 55.3 percent serial drama, 16.1 percent "talks," and 11.4 percent juvenile programs. In contrast, more and more of the evening schedule showed domination by the big-name musical/comedy variety and dramatic adaptation program, a program type rarely found on daytime. In *Variety*'s designation of these programs as "crude," equating women's levels of sophistication with those of children and distancing the more "serious" programming of the nighttime hours, can also be seen the subordinate positioning of women's programming so central to emergent broadcasting practices.

151

The Feminine Mass

The growing distinction between daytime programming for women, as opposed to nighttime programming for a more "general" (male-characterized) audience, resulted from a complex network of definitions and decisions more taken for granted than looked at critically, and involving more than simple economics. Much of it had to do with radio's dual mission of public service and profit, and the conflicting ideas of appropriate audience and content that ensued. This tension, between programming for profit and programming for public image, rests on both gender and class distinctions, but I will argue with Roland Marchand that radio and advertising executives shared an image of the "feminine mass"—the lower- to middle-class buying audience considered as feminine—as distinct from that of the nighttime critical audience of public decision makers.

According to Marchand, by the mid-1920s major advertising agencies had arrived at a definition of consumers as "an emotional, feminized mass, characterized by mental lethargy, bad taste, and ignorance":

> The growing consensus about audience emotionality helped fuse the other observed audience traits into a composite conception. Popular convention defined emotion as a particular characteristic of women—and the advertising audience was overwhelmingly female. In fact, nearly every characteristic commonly attributed to the masses was also conventionally a "feminine" trait—capriciousness, irrationality, passivity, and conformism.[2]

Marchand explains that these associations stem partially from the need of educated, upper-middle-class advertising men to distance themselves from the masses they somewhat cynically manipulated:

> As a last resort, in the protection of their self-esteem and as a psychological weapon against cultural engulfment by the tastes of the consumer masses, advertisers could always emphasize the stereotyped gender distinction between advertisers as men and consumers as women. This distinction shielded the advertising elite . . . from being debased by the vulgarity and backwardness of the consumer masses.[3]

Andreas Huyssen theorizes this feminization of mass culture more broadly, exploring "the notion which gained ground during the 19th century that mass culture is somehow associated with women while real, authentic culture remains the prerogative of men." This conceptualization had material consequences: "The universalizing ascription of femininity to mass culture always depended on the very real exclusion of women from high culture and its institutions."[4] Negotiations of high and mass culture played a large role in the development of radio. Broadcasting maintained a deeply conflicted social status as a public institution upholding official "high" culture, yet given over to selling products for private profit to a mass audience. Its mass/private/feminine base constantly threatened to overwhelm its "high"/public/masculine function.

Why did this discursive dilemma come to the fore in the 1930s? Robert McChesney convincingly argues that the period from 1928 to 1936 represents virtually the only window during which serious debate over radio's social and commercial function came close to effecting structural changes in the advertising- and network-based system. Rebutting accounts of broadcasting's origins that portray its commercial base as eagerly accepted by the U.S. populace, or as a result of careful planning and debate, McChesney demonstrates that this was a period of intense lobbying and ideological controversy, with proponents of radio's educational and public service uses eventually outgunned by the commercial radio lobby, through Congress.[5] The effects of this debate on programming have not been seriously studied; it is usually felt sufficient to state that commercial programming developed apace as "serious," sustaining public service programming faded from the schedule.

Broadcasters during this period of contested credibility had two formidable projects to take on. One was exploiting an economic base that clearly rested on the female purchaser of household products. This we recognize because it remains primary in the television and radio programming we observe today. The other, however, has frequently intervened in this primary economic relation, particularly during periods of transition—such as that from radio to television in the 1950s—when the public image of the medium takes on a role as important as that of economics. In the 1930s the radio industry had to convince regulators that their mission consisted as much of public service programming as of sheer commercialism, even in the hours sold to sponsors, in order to rebuff educational broadcasters' claims on the spectrum. According to McChesney:

> The commercial broadcasters had to convince the public and public officials that they were firmly committed to high-grade cultural and educa-

tional programming. . . . establishing a commitment to cultural programming was seen as being of fundamental importance in keeping increased
government regulation or even radical reform at bay. Any and all network
programs along these lines were heavily publicized by the networks.[6]

Another way of achieving this end was to create a differentiation
between daytime and nighttime programming, by which daytime became the venue for a debased kind of commercialized, feminized mass
culture—heavily dominated by advertising agencies—in contrast to
the more sophisticated, respectable, and masculine-characterized arena
of prime time, also dominated by agencies but subject to stricter network controls, as we have seen in chapter 4. Nighttime thus became
the more highly "visible," public part of the broadcast schedule, and
daytime hours increasingly private, less "visible," even obscure—despite
their substantial audiences and important economic function. Only
women were listening, and they were not the ones with access to official corridors of economic or regulatory control.[7]

It is within this tension between the hidden, subversive, and publicly
disparaged space of daytime radio and the public, authorized, and de-
feminized address of nighttime radio that the careers of such popular
radio innovators as Irna Phillips, Jane Crusinberry, Frank and Anne
Hummert, and Mary Margaret McBride were built, in both serial and
magazine-style "talk" programming innovated on daytime radio.
Under cover of daytime, women addressed the issues confronting them
during the conflicted decades of the 1930s and 1940s, especially the
tension between the enforced domesticity of the 1930s and women's
increased frustration with this limited role, in forms developed specifically for this purpose and least likely to be penetrated or understood
by the executives and critics whose discourse dominated mainstream
radio reception.

"Serialized Drool"

As we have seen, the serial form began auspiciously enough on nighttime radio schedules across the country. Neither its open-ended, five-
(or six-) day-a-week narrative form nor its explicit link to commercial
intent up to and including integrated advertising (as in the *Real Folks*
program), nor even its subject matter at first inherently condemned the
serial to a category apart from other forms. Programs such as *Clara,
Lu and Em*, *Myrt and Marge*, *Amos 'n' Andy*, and *Just Plain Bill* displayed all those characteristics later denigrated as uniquely and inher-

ently "feminine," but were in fact enjoyed by large and loyal audiences of both genders and featured in early network prime time lineups. Yet by the mid-1930s, it was precisely these characteristics—their somehow overly loyal (even "neurotic" and "addicted") audiences, the often slow and tortuous open-ended plots, their explicit purpose as selling vehicles, and above all their "morbid" and contested subject matter— that made daytime serials a subject of national concern.

As Robert C. Allen has pointed out, serials and their audiences received a level of condemnation and scrutiny never meted out to nighttime audiences and programs; studies of the daytime audience started out with "the assumption that it constitutes a nonnormative mode of media consumption behavior most likely to be engaged in by a distinctive and 'different' subaudience," despite ample data to the contrary. The daytime audience becomes "that which must be explained," as opposed to "normal," nonneurotic, and unproblematic nighttime audiences.[8]

These same observations were made by Irna Phillips, deservedly credited with innovating the daytime serial format—again, out of Chicago.[9] Although, as we have seen, important models existed by 1930, Phillips's experimental serial *Painted Dreams*, which debuted October 20, 1930, over station WGN, represents one of the first serial narratives expressly designed for women to be aired in the daytime. Though not an original idea—court documents in a subsequent legal dispute credit WGN station manager Henry Selinger with the idea for a daytime serial to be used to sell products to women—the show existed only as an idea until Phillips was hired to write and perform it. *Painted Dreams* ran daily except Sundays until April 1932. With the central characters of "Mother" Moynihan, her daughter, and a young female boarder, Sue Morton (Phillips played both the mother and Sue Morton), the show focused almost exclusively on the experiences of women, and indeed no regular male cast members were introduced until late in the show's run. The conflict most basic to the program's dramatic structure was that between traditional and changing gender roles—Irene Moynihan, the daughter, was characterized as "the aspiring modern girl, with ambitions toward a career," against Mother Moynihan's and Sue Morton's more traditional views.[10]

Though a legal dispute over ownership of this serial would end Phillips's involvement in 1932, by June of that year she was back on the air, this time at rival station WMAQ, with a direct carryover of the basic plot of *Painted Dreams*, now called *Today's Children*. In this program, Mother Moran, her daughters, Eileen and Frances, and their boarder, Kay Norton, continued the familiar debate between marriage and career in between more humble household problems to be solved by judicious use of the sponsor's products. This time, having learned her lesson, Phillips retained ownership of the show, even subsidizing its production herself for the first four months until General Foods picked it up in November, succeeded by Pillsbury in 1933. Audience response was tested first by Phillips herself in August 1932, when she offered a picture of Mother Moran's son's anniversary celebration (featured on the show); more than ten thousand responses were received. When Pillsbury attempted a similar appeal in 1933, more than 250,000 listeners sent in labels to receive copies of a brochure outlining the program's backstory and profiling the characters. This overwhelming response began to receive broadcasters' attention: "The amazing allegiance of hundreds of thousands of women not only to the members of the cast but to Pillsbury products is a constant source of wonderment even among those professional people who for years have been working with radio."[11]

Phillips went on to create some of the most enduring serials in radio and television history, including *Woman in White* (credited with being the first medical serial, 1938–48), *Road of Life* (1937–59), *The Guiding Light* (1937–the present, in its television form), *Lonely Women* (1942–46), *The Right to Happiness* (1939–60), and *The Brighter Day* (1948–56). Both Agnes Nixon, creator of the television soaps *All My Children* and *One Life to Live*, among many others, and William Bell of *The Young and the Restless* were trained as staff writers under Phillips.[12]

Phillips was a fiercely independent entrepreneur who retained ownership rights to all her shows, producing through Carl Wester & Company and allowing agencies, sponsors, and networks little control over her soap opera empire. Despite this—or more likely because of it, along with the impressive audience loyalty and selling results her serials engendered—her relations with such hard-to-please sponsors as Procter & Gamble were, as Ellen Seiter points out, far more amicable than many.[13] Yet even Phillips could be nettled by what she perceived as unfair and unaccountable criticism of the soap opera form—or, at least, of her own serials. In particular, Phillips objected to critics' characterizations of the serial audience as "nonnormative"—neurotic, vulgar, childlike, and stupid. Such charges could come from within the industry itself or from outside critics. One of the most vitriolic assessments not only of Phillips's proposed (but never produced) serial *Rainbow Court*, but of daytime radio in general, appears in a review done by Willis Cooper of NBC's Program Planning Board in 1934, submitted to Sidney Strotz, head of NBC's Chicago Bureau:

> This program . . . is another of the amateurish type of programs that have attained such popularity with a certain class of listeners. . . . it panders to the crude emotions of the shopgirl type of listener, and it trades upon the maudlin sympathies of the neurotic who sits entranced before the radio, clutching a copy of "True Confessions" and (possibly) guzzling gin and ginger ale. Despite the many things that are wrong in a show of this type, it will undoubtedly be successful. . . . It will sell cheap products to vulgar people. . . . But to people who have an I.Q. of something higher than 15 years, it will be another of the dreadful things that the radio brings.[14]

Phillips had no venue in which to reply to this attack, but when *Variety* asked her to write a piece to be called "In Defense of Daytime Serials" for a special review-preview issue in 1947, she asked the pointed questions: "Does the I.Q. of a housewife change after six o'clock, or doesn't she listen? Or does the advertiser, who knows that approximately 98 per cent of all products used in the home is purchased by the home maker, ignore the daytime serial listener after six o'clock?"[15] Thus asserting the normalcy and intelligence of daytime listeners— who, as she points out and as studies by 1945 confirmed, were the same people who made up the greatest proportion of the nighttime audience—Phillips tried to draw the serial back into the mainstream of radio practice and to reveal the falseness of the dichotomy between daytime/female audiences and nighttime/masculine ones so carefully drawn by the industry.

But the criticisms most taken to heart by Irna Phillips and other serial writers were charges that the events and experiences they portrayed were not "realistic," but were in fact "hopelessly melodramatic" or "morbid." In 1943 *Variety* had published a four-part series called "Analyzing the Daytime Serials." In the last installment, Phillips's serials were singled out for disparagement along a number of lines, but most of all for her "morbid slant":

> Thus, over the last few years, Miss Phillips' stories have contained a variety of brutal physical situations, divorces, illegitimate births, suggestions of incest and even murders. Whether that sort of material is emotionally

or mentally upsetting to neurotic listeners is a matter for psychiatrists to decide. Admittedly, however, it is hardly uplifting, or inspiring, or, in the normal sense, even entertaining. Yet there is nothing objectionable in such material if it is used with taste and dramatic skill, as Shakespeare and Eugene O'Neill prove. But in undiscriminating or clumsy hands, it inevitably arouses resentment.[16]

Here it is the nature of the content itself that is under attack, as well as its handling by the author (with the neurotic character of the audience taken completely for granted). Certain kinds of subject matter are disreputable, unless sanitized by "taste" and dramatic skill. The author, Hobe Morrison, gives examples of the tasteless handling of uninspiring materials as presented in Phillips's serials: a painter who goes blind, the "dubious setup" of a "spinster" who decides to adopt a child, a (suspected) illegitimate baby, divorce and remarriage, all presented in a "lurid" and melodramatic way: "There is never the slightest suggestion of lightness or enjoyment, but the emphasis is constantly on emotional contortion and mental anguish. Thus, the general flavor of the serial is depressing, though it may be engrossing to certain listeners." These issues of female sexuality and lack of male control over reproduction often troubled critics, both male and female. In her three-page letter of reply, Phillips defended her subject matter by pointing out that such events do indeed occur; divorce was hardly an unusual experience and she herself, a "spinster," had just adopted two children.

As for illegitimate births and incest, Phillips denied that her scripts ever implied such a situation. Illegitimacy, particularly, was a forbidden area for the serials. In one spate of correspondence in 1940 among Phillips, NBC, and Carl Wester, Phillips was required to provide assurances *in writing*, before further production of the show could proceed, that "the baby which Janet [Munson, of *Woman in White*] announces is on the way is to be the child of John and there is to be no question of the child's paternity nor will there be in any way implications or inferences pointing toward Kirk as the child's father."[17] However, as we shall see, daytime serials lent themselves to a kind of narrative indeterminacy that differed from other radio formats, and even though plots might resolve in morally "uplifting" ways, often many different interpretations and conclusions were encouraged. In general, Phillips insisted on the realism of her subject matter and asserted that airing such subjects proved ultimately inspirational, not depressing, to her listeners.[18]

Here, as Robert Allen demonstrates, Phillips and her critics rehash the same critical battles that raged over the domestic novel in the 1800s and the "women's film" of the 1930s and 1940s. Written generally by women, for women, but critically disparaged as melodramatic, turgid, and frivolous, women's fictions have inspired high-culture critics to condemn the "damned mob of scribbling women" since Nathaniel Hawthorne's time. Addressed, as Allen states, to women as a "distinct group within American society," women's fictions recognize the existence of a "subculture" of women placed in a common oppositional relationship to the dominant male-characterized culture and possessing certain common interests, experiences, and conflicts to which these disparaged feminine forms give voice.[19]

Whether these concerns are "real" or fantasy—Ellen Seiter points out that middle-aged female sexuality was one recurring topic of the soaps that many critics found particularly ludicrous; other widespread themes were marrying "above one's station," supreme maternal self-sacrifice, and glamorous careers[20]—they opened up subjects for discussion, identification, and emotional response that more "respectable" media left out as trivial or sentimental. Here Nancy Fraser's notion of the feminine "subaltern counterpublic" becomes particularly relevant. Fraser analyzes the way in which the liberal bourgeois conception of the public sphere—a definition in which broadcasting institutions were heavily invested—was constituted as essentially masculine, in inherent opposition to the feminine/domestic sphere.[21] This distinction was used to confine women to the private, domestic side of life, while denying them autonomy in either sphere. Because the essence of, and basic requirement for, social agency is masculinity, the feminine becomes precisely that which is devalued in public discourse.

By this same token, Fraser argues, the liberal concept of the unitary public sphere, although seemingly built on inclusion and equality, in fact rests on the exclusion and subordination of women and other subaltern groups. Therefore, assertions of the "public good" or "public interest" must be framed in ways that preserve the "natural" social hierarchies and separation of spheres—and end by disbarring the feminine, defined as "private," from public discourse. Fraser proposes that we should instead recognize the existence of numerous subaltern counterpublics constituted specifically in resistance to this definition of the unitary, but exclusive and gendered, "public" of bourgeois liberal institutions.

Arguably, female writers and producers such as Phillips opened up a space on the public airwaves for a feminine subaltern counterpublic to emerge, who responded to the serials' attempts to open up the restricted sphere of public discussion to topics usually dismissed as "women's issues"—private, personal, and therefore unsuited to public discourse. For the radio industry of the mid-1930s, faced with regulatory challenge to its public service nature (seen as threatened by overcommercialism), the confluence of the feminine/private and the commercial exemplified by serial programs had to be distanced and played down as much as possible—while still retaining that important source of revenue. One way to do this was to emphasize the difference between nighttime and daytime programming by characterizing the latter as "female" and the former as "male"—even though logical analysis showed that the audiences for the two overlapped considerably—and then to direct critics' attention to the advertising agencies and sponsors who dominated daytime broadcasting. This had the dual advantage of automatically elevating the cultural status of nighttime programs most identified with official network practice—the negotiation of which will be discussed in chapter 7—while seeming to isolate the nonnormal and culturally debased to the daytime, the proper sphere of women and children—and sponsors.

In fact, Phillips claims that daytime radio could get away with far less than nighttime when it came to controversial issues, such as politics, race, and sexual matters. When quizzed by reporters in a 1945 NBC press conference concerning the introduction of problematic material—specifically, that of race—Phillips claimed that her efforts to introduce such issues had been censored by the network. When the questioner pointed out that racial issues had been addressed on radio, Phillips asked whether that was on day- or nighttime. When the reporter answered, "Night," Phillips responded, "Well, we do not get the breaks that night time programs get."[22] Given the high level of network censorship seen in chapter 4, this remark should perhaps be understood in terms not so much of subject matter but of its treatment.

As the *Variety* critic mentioned above noted, serials were often criticized for their lack of action and humor and their "tortuous," drawn-out plotlines, emphasis on sentiment and emotion, and "lugubrious" rehashing of action and reaction so that "nothing ever seems to happen" and events unroll at a "torpid" pace. However, as several later scholars have pointed out, this kind of development allows for a far more subtly inflected treatment of subjects than does the quick wrap of the action drama. In a serial narrative, controversial subject matter, once introduced, can be examined slowly from a variety of perspectives, its implications developed across many plotlines, and several different points of view aired in great detail before some kind of resolution finally occurs—and, of course, any resolution can later be reversed, up to and including death. Contrary to some generalizations about serials' content, crime and its resolution played a large role in soap plots. Murder, theft, abductions, and trials stemming from such crimes entered at one time or another into almost every serial on the air. What distinguished the treatment of crime on the serials from its treatment on action/adventure or detective programs at night was, first, the emphasis on the "who" and "why" rather than the "what." Crime often stemmed from dysfunctional relationships, and it was the disruption of family structure and personal relationships caused by criminality that received the most emphasis. Second, the likelihood of false arrest, mistaken identity, and misplaced accusations that often prevailed—with all their implications for juicy, drawn-out plotlines—differentiated the serials from the much quicker and more black-and-white resolution of the nighttime programs. Nearly every serial heroine was falsely accused of crime at some point or another; nearly every serial hero was implicated in criminal activity at some point, though he may have later reformed.

This kind of judicial and moral indeterminacy in daytime soaps so often emphasized by critics and network censors was firmly dismissed by writers such as Phillips, who contended that her programs always resolved along socially acceptable lines—the baby turns out not to be illegitimate, the divorce is justified, the perception of an affair is shown to be a misunderstanding, the implied incest is a case of mistaken identity—and that in fact she worked with the recommendations and endorsement of numerous social agencies when developing socially relevant issues in her plots. However, it is equally true that by the time a subject faded from the scene, ideas and perspectives alternative and sometimes oppositional to the endorsed resolution had usually had ample time to assert themselves.

The following scene from an early episode of *Today's Children* illustrates the serials' ambiguity. An immediate crisis has been provoked by Frances's opportunity to take a job "in the East," which would mean postponing, perhaps permanently, her impending marriage to Bob.

While endorsing, on the whole, the importance of marriage and family through the opinion of visiting family friend Judge McCoy, Frances Moran's desires for individual achievement and a career receive sympathetic and convincing expression. Thus, for every bit of dialogue on the Judge's part that endorses a traditional view, Frances gets an equal opportunity to present her case against that view:

> *Judge*: Look around you, my child, look about you today—go into our courts of domestic relations and what do you find? The result of attempted compromise of careers and marriage—divorce—children whose lives are being ruined—lives of men and women that have been wrecked. Why? Because nature will not compromise. Woman has ever been the maker of homes. The male has ever been the provider and protector—the female has ever been the bearer of the young—and do you women of today think you can suddenly and completely change the natural laws that have gone on since time began? . . . Your dream— ah, no my dear—it should be yours and his—don't you understand?

Frances responds dubiously, "Supposing what you say is true . . ." (a remarkably resistant comeback, given the weight of the Judge's position, age, and authority) and continues to debate his seemingly irrefutable view. She has already had the opportunity to set forth her ideas fairly forcefully:

> *Frances*: Why—why can't a man be satisfied, as much as a woman has been in the past, with a division of interests—is it necessary for a woman to be in the home twenty four hours of the day? Is it necessary for a woman to give up every other outside interest she may have—just because a wedding ceremony has been performed? Must a woman's only reason for living be the raising of a family? Is it fair—is it right— that just because women didn't realize their capabilities and possibilities in the past, should they ignore them—suppress them—now that they have found them?

And later:

> *Frances*: Yes, that's what Bob says—that's what you say—that's what all the men say—they're all alike—selfish, egotistical, vain—either woman must lose herself completely in the personality of a man, in her marriage, or the game is off.

At the end of the episode, as Bob and the Judge leave, the resolution proceeds along the lines endorsed by Judge McCoy and traditionalists everywhere. But stage directions may cast doubt on the wholehearted acceptance of these conventional views:

Frances: Good night, Judge. I think I'll go to bed—I'm kind of tired—but I—I'll be thinking of you, Bob—goodnight. (DOOR SLAMS) (PAUSE) (SOB) My dream—my painted dream—I guess—yes, I guess my place is here—with Bob—(THEME UP AND FADE)[23]

Hardly a ringing endorsement of traditional feminine roles. Of course these roles were central to the plots of daytime serials, but so were, equally, their disruption, questioning, and opposition. To the conventional resolution "and they lived happily ever after," daytime serials showed the long-term consequences.

Further, the resolution of plots often does not take place so much in the program itself but carries over into the lives of its viewers. Research into audience behavior shows that serial viewers and listeners frequently discuss their "stories" with friends and relatives, fiercely debating the morality—and realism—of characters and their actions. The programs become springboards for discussion and even active change in viewers' real lives. High-culture critics, accustomed to the strict separation of the audience and the work of art developed in the late nineteenth and early twentieth centuries, often expressed appalled disdain for serial listeners who would write to their favorite characters as though they were real people, send them gifts, give them advice on what they should do in current plot situations. Obviously, these women were deluded, susceptible, neurotic. But this conception of the preferred, distant relationship of the audience and the text was a carefully cultivated and relatively recent one, as Lawrence Levine demonstrates, and listeners' treatment of the serial as permeable, flexible, and participatory resembles audiences' treatment of such icons of culture as Shakespeare in the popular theaters of the early 1800s.[24] Levine cites many instances of levels of audience participation in popular drama—such as the Kentucky farmer who stopped a stage production by taking up a collection for a family depicted as starving, after delivering a speech reflecting his view on the action[25]—that made serial listeners, by comparison, seem models of rationality and decorum. Added to this confusion over the appropriate relationship of text and audience was the fact that serial producers often paid considerable attention to the letters written in by fans, using them as indicators of characters' or stars' popularity, as gauges of public opinion over controversial plot developments, and as support for inclusion or exclusion of material, even when they represented a fairly negligible source statistically. Thus, listeners who took an active role in writing to their favorite serial characters or commenting on their actions had a reasonable expectation that their opinions could make a difference.

Equally, as Phillips herself pointed out and Allen analyzes in depth, this kind of permeable, open-ended, and long-term narrative and the kind of readership it demands creates difficulty for the critic who wishes to "dip into" a serial to make observations and then leave; accepted critical practices fundamentally falsified the serial reading experience. Phillips objected vehemently to *Variety* writer Hobe Morrison's assertion that listening to a total of twelve episodes of one of her current serials (*The Road of Life*) qualified him to criticize her entire oeuvre. Dr. Louis Berg, in his famous pamphlets attacking serials in the 1940s, was revealed to have been basing his allegation of physical and psychological disturbances caused by serial listening on his own experience only, over a short period of time. Allen convincingly demonstrates that the social science methods developed to study both the serial text and its listeners in the 1940s employed methods of analysis wholly unable to come to grips with the most basic aspects of the form, above all their fundamental and unquestioned singling out of the serials and their listeners as "that which must be explained."[26]

In adopting their contradictory, permeable, tolerant treatment of subjects defined as personal, private, and unacceptable for public discourse, daytime serials reflected and catered to the position held by their primary audience in relation to society in general: ambiguous, resistant, possessing knowledges and competencies denied and derogated by publicly expressed values, always marked as not properly part of the mainstream, acceptable, masculine public society. Yet daytime serials were always constrained by the economic purposes they served; there were limits on the amount and nature of difference that serials could bring to their audiences.

Thus, the culture of consumption as expressed by radio spoke a mixed message to women. It was through the purchasing power conferred by gender-traditional division of labor that women acquired a powerful place in media economics and address, resulting in increasingly prevalent venues of feminine employment, representation, and participation. This new position allowed for the public airing of resistant and hitherto excluded concerns, often challenging those gender distinctions upon which both practices of consumption and radio production were based. Yet the continuance of such a system required that these challenges be contained and defused, through such practices as the "ghettoization" of women's programs, the gradual exclusion of women from non-feminine-designated areas of production and industry managment (especially news, nighttime entertainment, and sports, as well as the key programming and sales positions in networks and agencies), and the denial of the primarily feminine audience of nighttime programming.

Phillips proved adept at manipulating the slippery terms of daytime serials' bargain with public opinion, avoiding excessively controversial topics, bowing to pressure when necessary, emphasizing and publicizing her work with social and government agencies—which included the Office of War Information, the Bureau of Family Relations, and the Child Welfare Division of the American Legion, among many others—and above all maintaining her independence and ability to take her program to another sponsor or network if the need arose. She also kept her name firmly attached to the serials she produced, even though the actual writing required the assistance of a "stable" of largely anonymous subwriters.[27] This kind of mass-production aspect of serial production—the soap opera "mill" or factory, as it came to be known—represents another site for cultural criticism of the form. Within an overarching cultural aesthetic that placed highest value on authorial control, praising the work of art most distinctly the product of a singular artistic vision, unique and personal, the assembly-line characteristics of the daytime serial were singled out for particular criticism. Once again, the fact that most nighttime comedy, drama, and variety programs also employed anonymous sets of gag and dialogue writers escaped critical attention—at least partially because of these programs' careful, though artificial, attribution of "authorship" to a central figure, as I will discuss in the next chapter. The daytime serial innovators most closely associated with the assembly-line approach to soaps were Frank and Anne Hummert.

"Hummerts' Mill"

Though Frank Hummert, in particular, was frequently credited with "invention" of the serial format in the popular press of the 1930s and 1940s, he actually came rather late to the genre. Through his collaboration with advertising executive Anne Ashenhurst (whom he later married), however, he represents one of the first of the established advertising figures to see the possibilities that daytime radio promised and to plunge wholeheartedly into its development. His prominent position no doubt aided the recognition on the part of large sponsoring corporations, especially Procter & Gamble, that daytime radio could be used profitably to sell products, and companies who had dabbled in serial sponsorship now found an incentive to make the serial the dominant form on daytime radio. By the late 1930s, no more prolific source of soaps existed than the radio department of Blackett-Sample-Hummert (BSH). Raymond Stedman asserts that "46% of the daytime serials that were brought to network radio between 1932 and 1937, and 30% of those introduced between 1927 and 1942" came from the (assisted) pens of Anne and Frank Hummert.[28]

Frank Hummert had had a long and distinguished career in advertising before jumping into radio. Known for his work during World War I on bond drive publicity—he coined the famous slogan "Bonds or Bondage"—and serving as chief copywriter at the Lord and Thomas agency, Hummert joined the Chicago firm Blackett and Sample in 1927 to institute and direct a radio production department. In 1930 he hired newspaper reporter Anne Ashenhurst, formerly of the *Paris Herald,* as his assistant. Together with writer Robert Hardy Andrews, the BSH radio department began to experiment with daytime serial production. Once again demonstrating the close connection between newspaper and radio, Andrews had achieved success as the author of *Three Girls Lost,* a serial in the *Chicago Daily News*—later published as a novel and made into a film by Fox.[29] Hired by Frank Hummert to write an experimental radio serial called *The Stolen Husband,* which aired briefly in Chicago in 1931, Andrews moved on to create three of BSH's pioneering serial efforts: *Judy and Jane, Betty and Bob,* and the nighttime drama *Just Plain Bill,* all debuting in the fall of 1932 under the sponsorship of Folger, General Mills, and Kolynos toothpaste, respectively. With the latter two the production team came to realize that this formula could be expanded indefinitely—but Andrews's writing capacity had its limits. As BSH's lineup grew in 1933 to include *Marie, the Little French Princess, Easy Aces* (moved from nighttime), *The Romance of Helen Trent* (to become one of the Hummerts' longest-running and most successful serials), and *Ma Perkins* (another long-running success), all of them on the air for fifteen minutes daily five days a week, clearly a more efficient system of production had to be devised.

Along with sheer demand for material, another economic factor contributed to the formation of the "soap opera factory": the networks' early policies for pricing time to advertisers during the day. As agencies moved to half-hour and hour-length programs at night, the daytime schedule remained carved into fifteen-minute segments priced at one-half the cost of nighttime air. Discounts were given to sponsors buying blocks of time; the more time purchased, the greater the discount (a policy not encouraged at night). Some sponsors might buy time in chunks of an hour or more a day. This created, as Irna Phillips observed in 1942, an inducement for serial programming:

> The trend toward five-a-week programs . . . was being brought about by the practice of giving discounts to buyers of time on the basis of frequency. . . . This uniformity and frequency imposed some very definite conditions on the advertiser's daytime effort. . . . With this realization came the birth of a new "art form" predicated not upon the verities of dramatic construction as they had always been known, but upon the exigencies of the clock and the calendar.[30]

To meet these exigencies, by 1939 the Hummerts—married in 1935 after the death of Frank Hummert's first wife—employed a stable of fourteen to twenty writers, with another dozen or so who could be called in on an ad hoc basis. This aspect of BSH serial production attracted quite a bit of attention in the popular press. The Hummerts encouraged analogy with such practices as the writing studio of Alexandre Dumas *père* and painters of the Italian Renaissance, but more often such terms as *factory, mill,* and *assembly line* crept into print.

Time described the writing process in 1939.[31] The Hummerts themselves either purchased existing properties or devised the basic situations for new serials (often, as we shall see, from proposals by outside authors), then sketched out the major plotlines over the next four- to six-week period. These high-level sessions, conducted at the couple's Greenwich, Connecticut, home, resulted in a set of outlines, each of which covered the action over four to five episodes at a time, dictated to "a battery of stenographers." The article gives an example from *Mary Noble, Backstage Wife:*

> Suspecting that Cynthia Valcourt murdered Candy Dolan with Ward Ellman's gun, after Tess left the flat, Mary, Larry and Ward rush to Tony Valcourt's penthouse to have a talk with Tony and Cynthia, having sent Tess Morgan to her apartment. Arriving at the penthouse, they are refused admittance by the butler. . . . If Cynthia gets away, Tess may take the rap for the crime. Can they save her? What will Tess do?

The outlines were sent to the Hummert "assembly line" of "ghost" writers, as the article puts it—usually no more than two or three writers were assigned to a single soap, though each might work on more than one concurrently—who fleshed out the action with dialogue and stage directions. Six "script readers" were employed to coordinate efforts among dialogue writers and actors, directors, and producers as a show progressed. In a serial's initial phase, each script required approval from Frank or Anne Hummert before proceeding to the Hummerts' independently owned production company, Air Features, Inc., kept strictly separate from the writing operations. According to *Time*, "No Hummert ghost may even stick his nose inside Air Features' production studios." Most of the Hummert serials went out live, often twice a day—once for the East Coast and Midwest, a second time for the West Coast time zones—and some ran at two different times on the two NBC networks, requiring two more live production sessions a week. Some were produced for transcription only, and after the adoption of magnetic tape reproduction in the mid-1940s they could be taped during the first live broadcast, which would then be played back for later time zones.

Despite this fairly rigid division of labor, the assertion that serials were entirely mass-produced is contradicted somewhat by an examination of the Hummerts' actual output. Several of their long-running shows had originated not out of the Hummerts' fertile brains but as adaptations of novels, such as Mrs. *Wiggs of the Cabbage Patch* (on CBS for American Home Products beginning in 1935), from a book by Alice Caldwell Rice; *David Harum* (NBC Blue for Babbitt in 1936), based on a best-selling novel that had already been made into a film starring Will Rogers (1934); and of course *Stella Dallas* (NBC Red for Phillips in 1938), from the book by Olive Higgins Prouty and the highly successful 1937 film starring Barbara Stanwyck—not to mention the 1940 public image-building *Light of the World* (NBC Red for General Mills), featuring stories from the Bible. Of course, with the possible exception of the last example, the source stories were substantially exceeded as the serials went on.

Others, including the radio versions of some of the above, were either adapted from serials already introduced on regional stations, which retained the efforts of their original creators, or showed close identification with one writer or writing team. *Easy Aces* remained the brainchild of Goodman and Jane Ace, on nighttime and daytime radio.

Helen Walpole and Jean Carroll served as primary writers for the popular *Our Gal Sunday* (CBS for American Home Products, 1937) for most of its run and also collaborated on *Lora Lawton* (NBC, 1943). Helen Walpole also served as the main writer for *Stella Dallas* and contributed to *Second Husband* (Dr. Lyons products on CBS, 1937, originally an evening serial). Elizabeth Todd is largely associated with *Amanda of Honeymoon Hill* (NBC Blue for Phillips, 1940) and *Young Widder Brown* (NBC Red for Sterling Drugs, 1938), though this prolific and hardworking writer also contributed substantially to *Second Husband*, *Lora Lawton*, and the long-running *Backstage Wife* (Mutual/NBC for Sterling Drugs, 1935) and later wrote for comedian Fred Allen. *Lone Journey* (NBC Red for Procter & Gamble, 1940) was created and written by Sandra Michael with the collaboration of her brother and sister, Peter and Gerda. Michael became one of the most respected writers in the business with her wartime soaps *Against the Storm* (Compton for Procter & Gamble, CBS, 1939) and *The Open Door* (Ted Bates for Standard Brands, NBC, 1943). *Valiant Lady* (NBC Red for General Mills, 1938) stemmed from writing team Addy Richton and Lynn Stone, who also wrote *Hilltop House* (Benton and Bowles for Colgate, CBS, 1938) and *This Life Is Mine* (CBS sustaining, 1943), often writing under the joint pen name Adelaide Marston. Husband-and-wife team Theodore and Matilda Ferro originated and supervised *Lorenzo Jones* (NBC Red for Sterling Drugs, 1937), and the team of Carl Bixby and Don Becker contributed to *The Man I Married* (NBC Red for Procter & Gamble, 1939) and *Beyond These Valleys* (CBS for General Mills, 1939) for BSH, as well as a rival soap, *Life Can Be Beautiful* (NBC Red for Procter & Gamble, 1938), for the Compton Agency.[32] Though all of these programs were supervised by the Hummerts and employed many staff writers, not all traces of authorship were erased by serial production; in fact, many nighttime programs showed less continuity in writing overall than did the serials.

But serial production was unrelenting and labor-intensive, and such practices allowed the payment of relatively low wages to both writers and actors by the same economics operative in sales of the products that supported the serials: volume and consistency. Though individual writers for other radio programs might receive considerably higher rates than the Hummerts' writers—indeed, it is the Hummerts' practices that are often credited with inspiring creation of the Radio Writers Guild in 1937—this was justified by the steadiness of the employment, week in and week out, whereas other writers were employed on a piece-by-piece basis. One magazine writer called the Hummerts "the Fords of the serial industry."[33]

These attributions of characteristics of mass production again worked against favorable critical reception of the serial form. Works of fictional narrative produced under such conditions could hardly aspire to the status of "art." Reflecting a kind of hidden, private feminine version of reality, they could not aspire to the level of documentary, either. As a newly and artificially created form closely attached to overt industrial interests, they could not pass as works of folk art, despite their popularity with a presumed naive and lower-class audience. Further, as many critics pointed out disparagingly, very little humor could be found in the hours of the daytime, so that even the lighter status of comedy did not apply as it could to evening genres. And then there was so much of it—by the time Rudolph Arnheim conducted his 1944 study, his research assistants had more than sixty network and local serials to attempt to follow weekly. What were these daytime serials? The most prevalent temptation was to dismiss them as simply trash, a debased form for deluded minds. Yet, as we have seen, this conclusion taken to its logical extreme ends by condemning as fools an estimated 46 percent of American women (and an unspecified percentage of men), and raises uncomfortable questions about the nighttime audience—constituting the majority of the American people. Perhaps these narrow options obscured another way of understanding daytime serials that critics of the time were not ready to address.

If considerations of audience, commercial function, authorship and popularity were not sufficient to differentiate daytime serials from the unquestioned bulk of radio fare, one difference still existed that truly marked out the serials as a unique form: their insistence on a certain kind of subject matter, handled in a certain way. Similar to the domestic women's novel, the primary subject of the soaps was women's lives, focusing on family relationships and domesticity; matters of sexuality, childbearing, and child rearing; and marriage itself. Within this last focus, two concerns surfaced frequently: the tension between marriage and a career, and the struggle for dominance or dependency between men and women. Overall, perhaps the main characteristic distinguishing daytime serials from nighttime dramas, action/adventure shows, and other more masculinized forms can be summed up in Garrison Keillor's

Gertrude Berg (Courtesy Photofest)

▪▪

WEEKLY PROGRAM
RADIO-PHONE SERVICE
WESTINGHOUSE ELECTRIC & Mfg Co.
STATION W J Z, NEWARK, N. J.

MON., DEC. 12th, TO SUN., DEC. 18th, 1921.

This program can be heard by any one with suitable radio receiving apparatus within a radius of 100 miles of Newark.

The service is absolutely free.

Tune Instruments for 360-meter waves.

REGULAR CONCERT
DAILY, 8:20 to 9:25 P. M.

MONDAY - - - Mme. May Peterson, Prima Donna Soprano, Opera Comique, Paris

TUESDAY - - - Os-Ke-Non-Ton, Indian Baritone: Messrs. Bertram Haigh and Ralph Brown, French horns; Miss Anita Wolf, Pianist

WEDNESDAY-Mme. Gretchen Hood, Prima Donna Soprano, Theatre de la Monnai, Brussels

THURSDAY - - Miss Helen Davis, Soprano; M. Cliff Young, Pianist

FRIDAY - - - Westminister Orchestra

SATURDAY - Dance music

SUNDAY - - Miss Ethel Mackey, Soprano and Miss Mary Emerson, Pianist. Sacred Music

OTHER FEATURES

General News - - Newark Sunday Call News Service, daily, 7:55 P. M.

Children's Hour - - "Man-in-the-Moon" stories, by Miss Josephine Lawrence © Newark Sunday Call Tuesday and Friday, 7:00 P. M.

Hourly News Service - - Newark Sunday Call; weekdays, every hour from 11.00 A. M. to 7:00 P. M. on the hour.

Radio Amateurs' Night - - Thursday 7 P. M. J. B. WALKER editor Scientific American

Weather Forecast (Official Gov't) - - Daily, 11:00 A. M., 5:00 and 10:03 P. M.

Marine News - - Marine Engineering Service, weekdays (except Saturdays), 2:05 P. M.

Official Arlington Time - - Daily, 9:55 P. M.

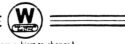

(Program subject to change)

Typical program of a radio-phone broadcasting station, mailed out weekly to interested parties

WEAF's largest studio, 1924. Left to right: Sam Ross, program director; V. A. Randall, chief announcer; Helen Hahn, receptionist, announcer, pianist

Charles Correll and Freeman Gosden perform as Amos and Andy (Courtesy Photofest)

Chester Lauck and Norris Goff as Lum and Abner (Courtesy Photofest)

Marian and Jim Jordan as Fibber McGee and Molly (Courtesy Photofest)

Helen King (Em), Louise Starkey (Clara), and Isobel Carothers (Lu) in *Clara, Lu and Em* (Courtesy Photofest)

Myrtle Vail (*right*) and her daughter, Donna Damerel, broadcasting *Myrt and Marge*
(Courtesy Photofest)

Miss Ham gives permission, via radio, for a nearby amateur to call on her.
She has never seen him and now it looks as if others has been listening in also.

Cartoon from *QST* (February 1921) illustrating the dangers of wireless to both gender and racial boundaries (Courtesy *QST*)

"... a dim idea that you might discover
something about crystals."

Illustration of an article by M. Adaire Garmhausen in *QST*
(May 1921) (Courtesy *QST*)

Bertha Brainard (Courtesy Photofest)

Judith Waller (*right*) with her secretary, Bertha Neuwerth (Courtesy Photofest)

Irna Phillips in 1935
(Courtesy Photofest)

Jane Crusinberry
(State Historical
Society of Wisconsin)

Eddie Anderson and
Jack Benny. The NBC
caption reads, "The
VACS [Volunteer Auxil-
iary Camp Services]
asked Mary Livingstone
to take charge of the
party for the boys at
Birmingham Hospital
on December 22, 1944.
Here we see Rochester
and Jack Benny engag-
ing in a little horseplay
for the boys." (Copy-
right National Broad-
casting Company, Inc.
All rights reserved)

Fred Allen and his
frequent opponent
(State Historical Society
of Wisconsin)

Cecil B. DeMille in
directorial persona
as "producer and
director" of *The Lux
Radio Theatre* in 1942
(State Historical
Society of Wisconsin)

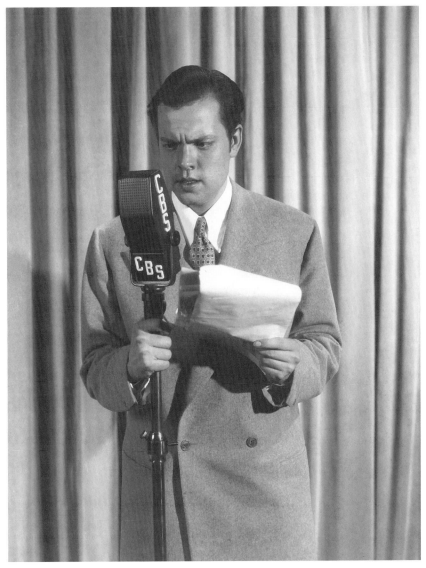

Orson Welles before the *Mercury Theater* mike (State Historical Society of Wisconsin)

A *Command Performance* broadcast, with Bing Crosby, Dinah Shore, Frank Sinatra, and Judy Garland (Courtesy Photofest)

Sylvester "Pat" Weaver at NBC (Copyright National Broadcasting Company, Inc.

Mary Margaret McBride in the 1930s (Courtesy Photofest)

famous phrase describing his fictional radio town of Lake Wobegon: all the women were strong, all the men were good-looking.

In contrast to the action show heroines' constant passive victimization and rescue by strong men and women's role as "dumb Dora" or harebrained wife in nighttime comedy, in serials women provided the strong characters, for good or evil. Men occupied ancillary roles, usually as love interests for the women, and were often "problematic" to some degree: unstable, disabled, or criminal. Using the Hummert serials as representative of the whole, the typical radio serial heroine (if there is such a thing) is either unattached to a man—she is single, widowed, or separated—or, if she is married, her husband represents less a source of strength and narrative control than of problems with which the heroine must deal. In the former category, *The Romance of Helen Trent* (CBS for many sponsors, 1933) stands out. Predicated on the adventures of Helen, "who sets out to prove for herself what so many women long to prove in their own lives, that because a woman is thirty five—or more—romance in life need not be over—that romance can live in life at thirty five—and even beyond," the plotline relied on an endless succession of suitors, never accepted, and often becoming very problematic indeed. Marie, the "little French princess," the three daughters of *Doc Barclay's Daughters* (CBS for Personal Finance, 1939), and Kitty Keene (not to be confused with Kitty Foyle or Pretty Kitty Kelly) of *Kitty Keene Inc.* (NBC Red for Procter & Gamble, 1937) fall into the young and single category. Widows include *Ma Perkins* (NBC Red for Procter & Gamble, 1933—formerly on WGN, 1932), who ran a lumberyard and supervised a large and unruly family; *Young Widder Brown*, who ran a tearoom; and Constance Tremaine, *Arnold Grimm's Daughter* (CBS for General Mills, 1937), who not only ran a lingerie shop, but, upon her father's illness, took over his factory job and invented a new stove that saved the business.

The most famous, of course, was Stella Dallas, one of radio's rare divorcées who went beyond the book and film's self-sacrifice for her upwardly mobile daughter by, in the radio version, becoming an action heroine:

> The new Stella could, while bound, escape entrapment in a skyscraper by dangling darning thread she had extracted from her purse until it attracted the attention of a passer-by far below. This bit of ingenuity preceded a rescue from gangsters of her daughter, Laurel. . . . She could help an injured pilot nurse an airliner to the ground against one-hundred-to-

one odds or escape enchainment to a tree in "darkest Africa" and continue her hunt for rare orchids.[34]

But even more plentiful than the single or widowed (rarely divorced, until many decades later) were those women struggling with difficult marital situations.

A remarkably common serial situation involved class differences, usually a girl from the wrong side of the tracks who married into a wealthy family, resulting in disinheritance and/or a constant struggle for adjustment and acceptance. In *Betty and Bob*, the Hummert ur-soap, humble Betty was married to Bob, son of a millionaire who signaled his displeasure by cutting the young couple off. Their initial experiences resembled the plot of the popular comic strip "Blondie," but later took on a darker note, as Betty struggled with Bob's infidelities and lack of business success. Bill, the homely barber of *Just Plain Bill*, acted as a strong male character and adviser in the town of Hartville, but the main dramatic situation involved his daughter Nancy's marriage to wealthy playboy Kerry Donovan and the troubles that ensued. In *Backstage Wife*, heroine Mary Noble's situation was summed up each week in the show's opening lines: "the story of Mary Noble and what it means to be the wife of a famous Broadway star—dream sweetheart of a million other women." Mary, a former stenographer from Iowa, battled constantly against her husband's temptations to stray as well as her own ample opportunities, though of course she remained faithful despite the additional problem of his jealousy.

In *Our Gal Sunday*, the situation of "an orphan girl named Sunday, from the little mining town of Silver Creek, Colorado," who married "England's richest, most handsome lord, Lord Henry Brinthrope" each week had to address the question, "Can this girl from a mining town in the West find happiness as the wife of a wealthy and titled Englishman?" all the while residing at Black Swan Hall in a very snooty area of Virginia. This situation was echoed without the Britishness but with a different kind of "foreignness" by *Amanda of Honeymoon Hill* (NBC Blue for Phillips, 1940), in which a "humble southern girl" married into the wealthy and aristocratic Leighton family, set in "America's romantic South . . . a world few Americans know." In these shows the possession of wealth or social status seemed to serve as a symbolic substitute for the gender basis of social power; women in the audience, with their limited ability to survive economically outside marriage, occupied the same relation to material wealth and the social mobility it brings as Sunday to Lord Brinthrope or Amanda to Edward Leighton. As for these heroines, it was their domestic virtues that provided them their lives and livelihoods.

Occasionally the situation was reversed, and a formerly wealthy or aristocratic character struggled to adjust to coming down in the world. This was the case with Marie, the French princess, and of course for Bob of *Betty and Bob*, as well as for Adam Waring and his strong wife Vivian of *The Man I Married*, in many ways a rehash of Betty and Bob, involving the disinherited son of a millionaire struggling to resettle in a small town. This class-based clash rendered such husbands difficult, making them resemble the most characteristic premise of the daytime serial, the problematic husband. Of course, all husbands were problematic, as were wives, at some point in these narratives based on relational conflict, but the basic setup of many of the Hummerts' soaps built these difficulties into the plot, sometimes constructed as physical disabilities. Most common were blindness and crippling diseases or accidents that left their male victims in wheelchairs; many suffered bouts of amnesia, brain injury, and other mental dislocations. The first example of this type seems to be the title character in the 1937 humorous serial *Lorenzo Jones*, whose characterization as an Italian American garage mechanic, spending most of his time on useless inventions to the dismay of his more practical wife, resembles the bumbling husband figure of *Fibber McGee and Molly* more than most serials' men. However, Lorenzo's bout with amnesia in 1940 took the show in a more serious direction. His disability—along with a specific ethnicity and class not common to serials—was similar to that of Dan O'Leary, husband of *Houseboat Hannah* (NBC Red for Procter & Gamble, 1938), a former cannery worker who lost his arm in an accident and whose wife struggled for "happiness and security for her family" on their houseboat in San Francisco's "Shanty-Fish Row."[35] That same year saw the debut of *Valiant Lady* (NBC Red for General Mills, 1937), in which the lead character earned that title by coping with a "brilliant but unstable" physician husband suffering from, among other things, brain damage. Other serials featuring disabled husbands were *The Right to Happiness* (Compton Agency on NBC Blue for Procter & Gamble, 1939), *Helpmate* (BSH on NBC for Old Dutch, 1944), and *Life Can Be Beautiful* (NBC Red for Procter & Gamble, 1938, by the Compton Agency). Even when these basic afflictions were not built into the premise, they provided an extremely common plot device as the serials wended their way through the decades: a physical explanation for the serial men's weakness and a leveling of gendered social differences, effective since the time of Charlotte Brontë.

Critics found the serials' "emasculation" of the American man troubling indeed. James Thurber summed up a decade of research in 1948 with the statement, "The man in the wheel chair has come to be the standard Soapland symbol of the American male's subordination to the female and his dependence on her greater strength of heart and soul."[36] Or, in the words of a *Saturday Evening Post* writer, "The male animal is not portrayed in flattering tones in the average serial. Normally, the men are just putty in the hands of designing women. . . . A man, on these serials, can always be talked into doing anything by a sufficiently persuasive woman, and the heroines of the serials are always persuasive."[37]

However each plotline resolved—usually (but not always) along lines that reinforced women's essential domesticity and the idea that their appropriate function of power was within the sphere of home and family—the serials functioned to open up a space on the airwaves in which concerns specific to women and women themselves dominated. Here writers—both men and women, but clearly this was a more welcoming site for women's efforts than most of radio—and their highly participatory audiences defined the scope and treatment of subject matter relevant to women's lives, unhampered by definitions of public discourse, aesthetics, and audience that worked to exclude such topics from other venues. Daytime serials both addressed and helped to create an explicitly feminine subaltern counterpublic, reinforcing and acknowledging the differences between men's and women's lives within the hierarchy of American culture, and providing ways to envision changes, negotiations, and oppositions. Although few serials endorsed a specifically feminist agenda, and indeed most took very conservative positions when called upon to do so, their constant friction against social standards, cultural distinctions, network censors, and high-culture opinion finally may have worked to open up options previously unavailable to their audience—or at least room to assert a range of possibilities.

Ironically, though many serial women were employed outside the home, some with substantial high-level careers or occupations that supported the entire domestic unit, these efforts always remained secondary to their domestic concerns. This offhandedness about professional success created the impression that these women could achieve in the public world with one hand tied behind their back, so to speak. This certainly was the case with radio's most publicly prominent strong woman, Mary Marlin.

Public Women: Jane Crusinberry and Mary Marlin

In many ways, *The Story of Mary Marlin* differs from most other serials on radio. Created in 1934 on WMAQ by Jane Crusinberry, it went to network on NBC Red on January 1, 1935, at an airtime of 5:00 p.m. under the sponsorship of Kleenex, through ad agency Lord and Thomas. This early evening slot represents a hedging between the still uncertain demands of day- and nighttime schedules, as did the basic situational premise of *Mary Marlin*: a young wife with a small son accompanies her newly elected senator husband to Washington. Set in the public world of politics, the character Mary Marlin dealt with public as well as personal intrigue, and is best known for the plot twist that caused Mary herself, upon the disappearance and presumed death of her husband, to assume the senatorship and serve the country in this highly prominent public capacity. Here was a daytime serial with a female U.S. senator as the lead character!

Furthermore, it was popular: *Mary Marlin* remained one of the highest-rated daytime serials from 1937, the first year daytime shows were rated, to 1943. In the 1937 to 1938 season, having been moved to a slightly earlier 4:15 time slot on the NBC Red network, it achieved the highest rating of any serial (10.4) on the air, even with a separate airing on NBC Blue each morning at 11:00, with a 6.1 rating. This was the year in which Mary's husband, Senator Joe Marlin, having had an affair with a socially prominent Washington hostess in the previous season, disappeared in a plane crash over Siberia, prompting the president to appoint Mary to take the senator's place. It was also the year that sponsorship shifted from Kleenex to Procter & Gamble. During Mary's years as senator in her own right, ratings continued to climb, reaching a peak in 1943.[38] Additionally, *The Story of Mary Marlin* refuted the mass-produced attribution of most serials. Author Jane Crusinberry originated the drama and remained its sole writer through 1943; it was her only radio effort, and she defended it from sponsor, network, and agency interference as strongly as she could.

These unusual aspects for a serial prompted difficulties not experienced by producers such as Irna Phillips or the Hummerts. As Ellen Seiter points out, Crusinberry came under constant censorship and criticism for precisely those qualities that marked *Mary Marlin* out as different in its treatment of appropriate feminine and masculine spheres. The show's Washington setting meant that sensitive political issues figured constantly in *Mary Marlin* and caused a degree of sponsor and network discomfort not apparently generated by other day- or nighttime programs—daytime because their domestic settings and preoccupations eschewed the overtly public and political; nighttime because of the greater leeway allowed comedians and commentators in that more public setting. Seiter concludes: "While critics have often attributed the insularity of the soap opera world to its narrative conventions and to the cult of domesticity it inherited from nineteenth century women's fiction, Crusinberry's case suggests that more direct censorship was in force."[39]

Critics and analysts such as Rudolph Arnheim and James Thurber pointed to the selfish individualism of the serials, in which problems in characters' lives were attributed not to overarching social conditions, amenable to solution by community effort, but as matters of either chance or the actions of evil individuals. This kind of problem mandated solution on the level of the personal, not through collective effort or organized community action. However, community action is political and social conditions are often controversial, and Jane Crusinberry's efforts to introduce the minimal kind of political background necessary to her story line—such as the election of a labor union leader as president—met with stiff resistance from sponsor and network alike.

In 1938, in the midst of tensions around the pending Wagner Act, any reference to unions became problematic to the serial's sponsors, who requested that Crusinberry "completely eliminat[e] any reference to any controversial or contentious nationally-legislated labor problem, or, in fact, any of its attributes, adjuncts or tangents"[40]—a considerable limitation when your main character serves as a Senator under a pro-labor president. Later Crusinberry was asked to drop all use of the word "union" from her scripts in favor of the term "labor leaders" and "labor groups," because the word itself was considered inflammatory.[41] Crusinberry was also cautioned that when her election plots followed actual political events too closely, she must make changes to avoid controversial comparisons. Thus, in 1940, in reaction to NBC's attempts "to discourage the election plot entirely," the Compton agency drew up a series of guidelines for handling the upcoming fictional election on the serial. First, the agency demanded a six-month delay between the actual election and its representation on the serial; second, the narrative should "include no contemporary politics as the basis of either campaign"; third, scenes depicting realistic elements such as the presentation of a bill in Congress should be avoided; and neither candidate should be identified as affiliated with either the Democratic or Republican Party.[42] Later that year, any reference to American involvement in the war met with discomfort and disapproval, and Crusinberry was commanded to "do no propagandising whatsoever."[43]

Resistance also ensued when Crusinberry attempted to address real-life social problems too directly. Though a plotline involving juvenile delinquency and child labor laws received the go-ahead, the sponsor warned: "You know, of course, that there are certain religious groups, notably the Catholic Church, which have taken a strong stand against certain child Labor legislation on the grounds that it would interfere with the control by the family of its children. . . . you must be exceedingly careful not to antagonize any religious group."[44]

Even social realism unconnected to pending legislation exceeded network comfort levels. For the broadcast of May 26, 1939, Crusinberry was required to drop the word "brothel" and substitute such terms as "one of the most unsavory and disreputable quarters of Shanghai," where an unspecified type of "neglect and degradation" occurred.[45] Other areas of censorship included references to alcohol, "unmarried love," criticism of the medical profession ("Jane, it is absolutely against P&G's policy to ridicule doctors to any degree at all"),[46] and "subversive activities." The limitations amid which industry executives felt comfortable were clear: problems could not be too private (as in issues of reproduction, sex, birth control, incest, and the like), but neither could they be too public (no labor unions, social criticism, racial line crossing, or feminist agitation). Yet these strictures were constantly challenged and violated.

As soap creators knew and their audiences understood, daytime serials were meant to go too far, to be excessive, to present actions and characters who offended various sensibilities and provoked impassioned audience reaction—because it was in this dynamic relationship to the audience that the serials reached the kind of narrative closure always deferred in the text itself. Often this audience relationship, as I have noted, took the form of active participation, with audience members writing letters to shows' creators or sponsors. Jane Crusinberry employed a staff to keep careful track of the mail she received, and for a period in 1935 a synopsis of each letter and its recipient's identity was kept on file.[47] These lists reveal not only who tended to write in but the ways in which these listeners used the serial as symbolic reinforcement and assertion of their personal identities and values. Women, young and old—and quite a few men—could make public pronouncements and assert control over elements of social and cultural conflict in their characters' lives in a way that actual social position denied them in their own.

One group of letters concerns the marital conflict that got *The Story of Mary Marlin* off the ground: Joe, not yet a senator but a struggling lawyer, seems inclined to cheat on Mary, his wife of fourteen years, by "continued attentions" to his young stenographer, Sally Gibbons. In the first month of the serial he asks Mary for a divorce, and Mary leaves their home in Cedar Springs and eventually takes a job as a journalist in New York City. Indeed, it is Mary's newspaper coverage of a high-profile murder case Joe is trying that helps Joe to win it and achieve the recognition that later leads to his nomination as a senatorial candidate. Though she remains in love with Joe and the divorce is never carried through, two other men, David Post and Peter Fortune, appear on the scene to compete for Mary's affection.[48]

Far from being deluded or lost in fantasy, many listeners demonstrated a clear understanding of the dynamics of the radio industry in lobbying to see their values dominate in the serial narrative. A letter from Dwight, Illinois, is summarized: "The day Sally marries Joe will stop listening to program and using Kleenex." One listener sent verbal "Orchids to Mary and Kleenex," but another threatened, "If Elizabeth is allowed to spoil the Mary-Peter romance, will never use product again." Strong support for the wronged wife was expressed in several letters: "Joe is terribly dumb—program is not long enough" and "Divorce Joe, or if you must go back, make him wait and suffer" (this listener was prescient). Others put it in moral terms, "Joe sinned against the sanctity of the home. Mary will commit the same sin if she returns." Some agreed with this basic position and condemned the actions of home wrecker Sally. Mrs. Annie Cunliffe of Chicopee, Massachusetts, wrote (as synopsized), "Let the *young hussy* clear out of town and let Joe alone. He can never be happy with her. Similar case in town. Hopes program will be good lesson to rising generation." A male listener, Glenn Fenner of New Preston, Connecticut, "advises Joe to get on to himself—'Sally sure knows how to bawl.'"

However, other listeners dissented from this view. "Some Housewife Listeners" from Denver, Colorado, objected, "Mary too sweet to be real—like Sally better because she is real—more of Sally." Others suggested alternate endings: "Group of women discussing story. Joe and Sally should be punished. Mary should marry real man like David or Peter." However, another fan advised, "Drown Peter for keeps." Listening in groups and discussing the story was a common experience. Letter writers included the president of the Mary Marlin Fan Club in La Habra, California; a Mrs. G. S. Hensill, who tuned in with the others in the Yosemite Creek Ranger Station in Yosemite, California; and "a neighborhood club" in "A Little Colorado Town." Several writers mentioned that they sat down to listen with their entire families; schoolgirls wrote in together that they wished the program's time slot could change because at the end of summer their school schedules would interfere with their listening; and mother and daughter fans wrote in a similar fashion, one stating that her "little daughter's heart is 'near broke' because she cannot listen after school starts."

Many demonstrated their knowledge of and expectations for the mechanics of serial production: "Since story is reaching climax, afraid it will be discontinued"; "Ask players to speak louder—can hear announcer"; and "Mary Pauline Callender talks too long. Program not long enough." Another, pathetically, wrote to say she "is dying and hoped the story would be finished soon—[was there a] book?" Others commented on the voice quality of the actors; some praised the fine writing. Letters often included references to the sponsor, Kleenex. Though women made up the bulk of the writers, several men offered their opinions. Thomas M. Robinson Jr. of Berkeley, California, praised the show as the "gem of the air. Salute author. Scene August 16 [of] Whitey dying was very fine." William Washburn of Bridgeport, Connecticut, said tersely, "Good story—excellent cast." Many wrote in to request summaries of episodes they had missed for various reasons or photographs of the cast or background information on the star, Joan Blaine,[49] or to express hope that a book would be published (as was frequently done for soaps) that would cover the narrative for the first season.

At the end of 1943, *The Story of Mary Marlin* had an average rating of 9.5, with a peak of 10.6. But late that year, the producing agency sold Procter & Gamble on a replacement show of its own devising, and sponsorship of *Mary Marlin* switched to Standard Brands. However, not only was this new program, *A Woman of America* (Benton and Bowles for Procter & Gamble, CBS, 1943) scheduled on NBC at the same time as the recast *Mary Marlin* on CBS, it also starred Anne Seymour—so that the long-running serial was now competing directly not only against its own former network time period but its own former star. Crusinberry complained about these changes and about "considerable agency plot interference" that led to her departure from active involvement in the program: "As the best way out of a difficult situation, I allowed them to plot the show and engage their own writer."[50] Upon Crusinberry's retirement from the show the ratings plummeted; as a promotional brochure later claimed, "It's a striking comment on the sensitivity of the daytime listening audience that when Miss Crusinberry left the program—they left too."[51]

Ironically, given the plot changes that producers were urging Crusinberry to make, the program that replaced *Mary Marlin* was a war-inspired drama of historical "public women." One of the few soaps to be set in the western United States, *A Woman of America* featured Anne Seymour playing both Prudence Dane, a pioneer on the Oregon trail, and the narrator, Prudence's great-granddaughter Margaret. When the historical story finished up, the story shifted to the present with another actress, Florence Freeman, as Prudence's descendant and namesake, a modern-day newspaper editor. Not only did the serial's narrative feature "public women," it also declared its emergence from the private, personal world of daytime by bringing a series of special guests to the microphone, often in place of an opening commercial, to address the audience on public service—a device common to wartime soaps. *A Woman of America* did this a total of twenty-seven times, featuring usually "war heroes or women who were devoting their energies to the war effort in some particular capacity."[52] This serial ran only until 1946, with middling to low ratings. As the war ended and attention turned away from the public to the private sphere, especially for women, and television loomed, the daytime serial would undergo significant changes. But *The Story of Mary Marlin* in many ways represents a high point for the depiction of women in a publicly prominent capacity. Its popularity with audiences, combined with its extremely suspect relationship to the broadcasting hierarchy, indicate that the serial form was capable of far more than its critics and producers gave it credit for and that, indeed, it was those critics and producers who most sought to confine it to the circumscribed, specialized world of daytime. Jane Crusinberry later attempted to get her story adapted to television, without success; her career and Mary Marlin's ended simultaneously.

How the Other Half Lives

In a 1942 article written for prospective clients, Irna Phillips addressed herself to the question, "Why Can't We Do Something Besides a Daytime Serial?" After a discussion of the origins of the serial and its suitability to the conditions of daytime audiences and economics, she concluded that any "dark horse" newcomer format would have a difficult time succeeding: "We can be reasonably sure that the daytime serial will prevail unless this dark horse is better able to cope with these forces and conditions inherent in daytime radio. For cope with them it must, or join the vast limbo of other non-dramatic programs that advertisers have tried and abandoned since sponsored daytime radio entertainment first began."[53] While her answer tended to endorse her own area of expertise, by 1942 broadcasting practice certainly bore out her conclusion that the serial form was the one best adapted to the circumstances of daytime. However, two issues remain to be explored behind the incontrovertible fact of serials' daytime dominance.

First, a question not answered by Phillips, or even by astute critics such as Robert Allen, is why the same principles did not apply across the board equally to programming at night. If serials, with their continuing narratives, amenable to inexpensive production, created unprecedented listener loyalty and product sales among precisely that audience most powerful in the marketplace, day and night, then why not feature them on the nighttime schedule? This is a practice that U.S. television would discover and exploit very effectively in the 1970s and continue through the 1990s, as other countries had been doing for far longer—why did it take U.S. broadcasting so long? The answer, as we have seen, has far more to do with public image and the notion of gendered spheres than with economic maximization. Daytime economic conditions themselves were not natural or self-evident, but were created by network and sponsor practices predicated on certain valuations in which gender and gender role assumptions and hierarchies set the terms. For sponsors and their agencies, network daytime policies presented a windfall that they were not anxious to lose. For the networks, considerations beyond the immediate economic, involving regulatory policy and public image, worked to create a separate, and unequal, daytime ghetto for programming designated as "women's"—and for the confinement of female writers, producers, and their topics of concern. But what of nighttime genres? A series of hierarchies operated there, too, creating distinctions between "good" and "bad" programs, designating some as purely popular and others as culturally meritorious, making assumptions about the audience and its interests equally as provisional as daytime's. In the next chapter we will look at some of the evening's most prominent programming, the visible public face of radio, and some of the techniques for negotiating radio's cultural tensions employed by the likes of Jack Benny, Fred Allen, Orson Welles, and *The Lux Radio Theatre.*

Second, by the late 1930s another daytime genre had emerged that, although not threatening the daytime serial, did attract considerable audiences and attention: the daytime talk/interview show. An outgrowth of the women's service programs displaced by the soaps, the format found its apogee in the career of Mary Margaret McBride, although scores of other women and men moved into similar roles both locally and nationally as television loomed on the horizon. By the early 1940s, the morning or "breakfast" show had risen rapidly in popularity. In the conclusion to this volume, I will explore McBride's career within the public/private dynamic developed here and link it to emergent television practices. In between, in history as well as in the complex development of broadcasting, came the significant national identity-building years of World War II.

▶ SEVEN

The Disciplined Audience: Radio by Night

By the late 1930s, most of the programs that would occupy the top slots in the newly installed broadcast ratings for the next ten years had made their debut over the American airwaves. U.S. broadcasting had become a stable, institutionalized system, increasingly profitable and dominating American entertainment habits.[1] Twenty-six million households owned at least one radio and spent an average of five hours daily listening to the offerings of three national networks[2]—NBC's two chains, the Red and the Blue (until 1943, when the Blue became ABC), and CBS—and one lesser competitor, Mutual, founded by a trio of powerful independent stations—WOR (Newark), WLW (Cincinnati), and WGN (Chicago)—along with a host of local stations often playing nationally syndicated programming.[3] Advertising agencies remained in even firmer control of prime evening hours than they did for the daytime, though this fact was downplayed by all involved.[4]

The single most popular genre on the nighttime air was comedy/variety: programs such as *The Jack Benny Program, The Edgar Bergen and Charlie McCarthy Show* (also known as *The Chase and Sanborn Hour*), *Burns and Allen, Fibber McGee and Molly,* Fred Allen's *Town Hall Tonight* (with other titles that included *The Fred Allen Show* and *The Texaco Star Theater*), *The Bing Crosby Show* (actually *The Kraft Music Hall* before 1946), and *The Bob Hope Show*. All employed a format that combined either one male host or a male-female team with an ensemble of supporting characters, music (usually with an in-house orchestra or singing group), guest stars, comic dialogue, and comedy/drama sketches, with varying degrees of emphasis on these components according to the talents of the host(s).

Another genre gaining in popularity was what Harrison Summers characterizes as the "prestige drama" format. Whether featuring adaptations of films, as did *The Lux Radio Theatre, The Screen Guild*

183

Theater, and *The Silver Theatre*, or stage and literary adaptations as did Orson Welles's *Mercury Theater of the Air* and *The Hollywood Playhouse*, this format maintained a solid presence in high-profile network time slots, with *Lux* clearly leading the pack. From 1937 to 1946, radio's heyday, virtually all network programs receiving more than a 25 Hooperrating fell into these two categories. (The few exceptions consisted, for a season or two, of the program featuring Walter Winchell, a news/gossip columnist; *The Aldrich Family* and *Mr. District Attorney*, dramatic series of the domestic comedy and detective adventure type, respectively; and *Kay Kyser's Kollege of Musical Knowledge*, a quiz program.)[5]

It is obvious from their basic structure that these program genres drew on a variety of cultural precedents. The comedy/variety format combined vaudeville humor and skits with concert hall or nightclub performances, along with elements developed primarily in radio such as the ubiquitous announcer, continuing character sketches, and the central "personality." The dramatic program borrowed directly from stage and screen, but filtered its materials through radio techniques such as the host/narrator, rotating guest stars (often drawn from Hollywood), and a recurring cast of supporting actors. Audiences had grown accustomed to these elements, either in their original settings or as developed over the first decade of radio broadcasting, and indeed it is remarkable how little change occurred in radio programs once these few successful formats achieved popularity in the mid- to late 1930s. Other, more innovative forms came (including the series comedy/dramas that would dominate television) and, in some cases, went (where now is the "inspirational talk" form purveyed by such early radio figures as Cheerio and Tony Wons?), but for almost fifteen years these two main formats weathered the tensions raging around this new version of the national culture so accessible to, and so enjoyed by, all but the most determinedly highbrow critics.

Such programs walked a fine line of cultural negotiation. By virtue of their prominence and popularity with a wide cross section of the American public, their commercialism could not entirely condemn them, nor could critics make feminizing attributions about such large mixed-gender audiences (at least not very effectively, though they did try). However, all possessed the capacity to offend some section of this large listening public, and as we have seen in chapter 4, network censors kept close watch on certain problem areas—the same, essentially, as those troubling on the soaps: the too private (sex) and the too public (politics). Yet the lines and parameters of cultural permissiveness were drawn a little differently on the nighttime genres. A bargain had been struck with radio's public and its critics that kept these programs free from the most virulent cultural condemnation while still allowing them to strain against restrictions, to make fun of the very standards that kept them in check, to stretch the boundaries of the culturally acceptable in some directions even while they reinforced and maintained certain other significant distinctions. In fact, it may be the very balancing act performed by these programs that made them so popular. To use Lawrence Levine's term, both their marking out of the "sacralized" areas of this new national culture and their selective violation of these evolving norms provided a newly constituted public group—the national listening audience—with the pleasures of identifying with certain sanctioned values while enjoying popular resistance to others, skillfully delineated by the programs' writers and producers.

Levine charts the process that led to the creation of cultural standards in U.S. society in the late 1800s through the turn of the century, among them the familiar designators *highbrow* and *lowbrow*, and relates them to the need for social order and hierarchy. For a culture threatened by the influx of "foreign elements," not only speaking different languages but holding different values and traditions from those of the threatened Anglo-Saxon elite, the cultivation of knowledge and standards of a particular kind helped to distinguish the "cultured" from the vulgar while at the same time providing a negotiable barrier: keeping some groups out, letting others in. The nineteenth-century "escape into Culture" allowed those whose values were threatened to "identify, distinguish, and order this new universe of strangers."[6] It also provided latecomers to the privileged groups a means of access obtainable by assiduous study and cultivation: "Indeed, the elites had more allies than they were ever comfortable with, for to many of the new industrialists as well as many members of the new middle classes, following the lead of the arbiters of culture promised both relief from impending disorder and an avenue to cultural legitimacy."[7]

Levine identifies several ways in which this hierarchization was accomplished: by creating separate spaces in which "Culture," as opposed to popular entertainments, was performed and enjoyed (hence the building of museums and symphony halls); by encouraging a notion of the sanctity of the text (and with it the primacy of the author and/or interpreter as inviolate artist); establishing a canon of "sacralized," endorsed cultural texts (and purging the vulgar and popular from their ranks); and by disciplining audiences to accept these new standards and behave in a manner appropriate to them (discouraging the more open contestatory and participatory mode of the earlier century).

Thus, symphony halls, the "legitimate" theater, museums and libraries, and the texts and behaviors they celebrated and held uplifted from the crowd acted both to mark out the new field of "high culture" and to preserve it from the degradation of the masses—except for specialized "educational" missions of uplift. And, as Levine states:

> Inevitably, in a heterogeneous nation in which the working classes were more and more composed of recent immigrant groups and migrant blacks, the ideology of culture assumed ethnic and racial dimensions. . . .
> . . . From the time of their formulation, such cultural categories as highbrow and lowbrow were hardly meant to be neutral descriptive terms; they were openly associated with and designed to preserve, nurture, and extend the cultural history and values of a particular group of peoples in a specific historical context."[8]

Broadcasting broke into this process at a highly critical moment, as we have seen, and became a key element in the ordering of the American cultural hierarchy. Early regulatory decisions attempted to mark radio out as a controlled and sanctioned space in which the "vulgar," such as black jazz performers or race records, could find only a tenuous and sanitized foothold.[9]

Further, in many ways the radio listener possessed in an ultimate form the properties desired in a disciplined audience: a space drastically separate not only from that of the performer but from the fellow public as well, a "docile" and passive relationship to the cultural text with limited opportunities for support or disapproval, rendering them "less of a public and more of a group of mute receptors . . . a collection of people reacting *individually* rather than collectively."[10] Thus, radio's more public nighttime listeners were encouraged to see themselves and to behave as a *disciplined* audience, forming a relationship to radio entertainers and programs characterized by intimacy and loyalty that yet maintained the boundaries between performance and listener so frequently violated by the vulgar audiences of the soaps.

Network standards and sponsor interests ensured that the canon of culture's more important values would remain sacrosanct, that control would be invested in the dominant figure of the host (usually, as we shall see, a "front" for the many other contributors to a radio broadcast), and that well-recognized cues would be given for invoking response of a certain measured type (such as purchasing a product). Yet radio's basic commercialism also ensured that elite standards could not entirely predominate; instead, seeking out popular approval for purchase of products, it carefully courted the tastes of the lowbrow, a task made more acceptable and less threatening to social order because of the disciplined position of the listener. Placed in the hands of large, government-endorsed corporations, whose early assurances of quality and high cultural standards conflicted with their need for economic support, radio became a commercialized medium with one foot in the vulgar popular and one foot on the ladder of social hierarchy.

Radio's most successful personalities and programs took note of this central contradiction and responded in an outbreak of satire, parody, and self-consciousness. Not since Shakespeare—the popular bard of American colonial days, not the highbrow deity of the twentieth century—had so much pointed criticism of social standards, institutional interests, and cultural pretentiousness found such a wide forum. This criticism had to stay within certain heavily negotiated social bounds—of class-based "taste," racial and ethnic characterizations, gender distinctions, and sexual and political subject matter. Overall, social hierarchy was not to be directly challenged, and the emergent institutional hierarchy of radio itself, though a fair target for jokes, could not be baited too persistently (as Fred Allen found out).

Yet radio's producers and funnymen employed the same resistant humor as early film comedians such as Charlie Chaplin and the Marx Brothers: "They created a rapport with their audiences that generated a sense of complicity in their common stand against the pretensions of the patrons of high culture."[11] In varying degrees—from the smooth popular showmanship of Cecil B. DeMille on *The Lux Radio Theatre* to the highbrow but disruptive theatricals of Orson Welles, from Jack Benny's self-satire to Fred Allen's pointed barbs—nighttime radio took on American society and its distinctions and institutions and showed them up for what they were—within limits. The job of its sponsors, producers, and networks was to encourage this cultivation of the popular while keeping it not too far out of alignment with the shibboleths of Culture.

Similarly, radio programs played with the disciplined position of the listening public. Some programs created audience substitutes within the shows themselves, such as the laughing and applauding studio audience that became more and more popular for big-time variety shows, or the ensemble of characters who reacted to the central figure's humor. Both Mary Livingstone and Portland Hoffa, Jack Benny's and Fred Allen's wives in real life and ensemble members on the air, began their association with their respective shows in the character of fans who came to praise and stayed on to needle—neat figures of audience displacement and identification. Others addressed themselves directly to their unseen collective public, acknowledging their "presence" despite total physical absence. Orson Welles used this device in his original *Mercury Theater of the Air* series on CBS called *First Person Singular*, telling stories as the invisible "I" to the equally invisible "you" of the listeners. These elements of self-consciousness and satire found on the popular shows of nighttime radio constitute a unique response to the demands of an emerging cultural form and specific historical conditions. They at once encouraged audience response and kept it carefully disciplined and contained. The significant year for the development of the comedy/variety format was 1932; for the "prestige drama" program, 1936.

Walking the Line: Jack Benny and Fred Allen

In the wake of the passage of the Communications Act of 1934, a spate of articles on the future of radio appeared in the press. Having represented themselves as the best possible custodians of broadcast culture's dual mission, to uplift and to sell, radio networks and stations found themselves under some pressure to carry through on that commitment. Criticisms were made of commercial broadcasting's more vulgar side, and predictions advanced in some quarters that the days of unmitigated cultivation of the popular were over. As one journal stated in 1935:

> For the past seven years radio broadcasting has been operated on the vaudeville formula, and even the ex-booking agents of the 10-20-30 cent circuits recognize that the pattern is getting threadbare. In their frantic endeavor to get the ear of the average listener they have shot below their mark and are beginning to suspect that perhaps there is no such person as the average listener. They have witnessed the upset of many theories about this elusive creature with the fourteen year old mentality, and find that he likes highbrow music, editorial chats on economics and politics, and even listens to poetry by the Pulitzer winners. Now the master minds of radio broadcasting would like to mend their ways, and they are mak-

ing strenuous efforts to reflect a conscience sensitive to good taste and culture.[12]

Along these lines—and most directly, to appease reformers and regulators—both NBC and CBS instituted new educational and cultural programming efforts in the early 1930s. NBC established a Public Service Department under the direction of Margaret Cuthbert to oversee "women's" and children's programs, in response to some of the most vocal criticisms of network fare.[13] CBS initiated the American School of the Air, with Alice Keith as director, to provide specifically educational programming, though Keith left in disgust at the network's lack of carry-through in 1932.[14] In addition, NBC organized the NBC Symphony Orchestra in 1936 to entice renowned conductor Arturo Toscanini out of retirement and bring "fine music to the masses"; CBS similarly continued to subsidize the New York Philharmonic broadcasts under the cultural guidance of host/arbiter Deems Taylor. A few of the larger institutional advertisers sponsored "uplift" programs such as the *Ford Sunday Evening Hour* of classical music, which began airing on CBS in 1934.

Evidence suggests, however, that the "average listener" would have noticed these broadcast improvements and efforts at uplift only if they had broken into the middle of *The Jack Benny Program*. The same years—1932 to 1936—that saw the heaviest debate over radio's cultural role and broadcasters' public service responsibilities also witnessed the establishment of vaudeville culture's latest and most successful offshoot, the comedy/variety program. Both Jack Benny and Fred Allen, two of its most acclaimed practitioners, debuted over the airwaves in 1932.[15] Their careers show striking similarities as well as significant differences: emerging from very similar cultural background and experience, both functioned as key figures in radio's new negotiation of high and low culture, but ultimately the two diverged. Benny became America's beloved "fall guy," the first in a still-continuing series of resistant incompetents whose very inability to conform to the "normal" embodied the contradictions of radio as an institution and America's new consumer culture. Allen, directing his satire outward rather than inward, evolved into broadcasting's gadfly, remaining popular for his skewering of the sacrosanct but also attracting mixed critical praise and condemnation for his unrelenting exposure of society's—and radio's own—hypocrisies and shortcomings.

Both started out as performers on the small-time vaudeville circuit. Jack Benny was born Benjamin Kubelsky into a Jewish immigrant family settled as shopkeepers in Waukegan, Illinois. Young Benny received violin lessons and entertained notions of a stage career, first performing with a local children's symphonic orchestra and then, for pay, in the orchestra of the local vaudeville theater. He took his show on the road in 1912, when the orchestra pianist, Cora Salisbury, asked him to join her to form a piano-violin duo that would play a mix of classical and popular numbers on the midwestern small-town vaudeville circuit. The act was billed originally as "Salisbury and Kubelsky— From Grand Opera to Ragtime," but a name change was mandated when a well-known violinist, Jan Kubelik, objected to the similarity. Now as Ben K. Benny, the young performer teamed up with a new partner, pianist Lyman Woods, and began to insert comedy into the act: "Benny often fooled about with his violin and held the fiddle in an amusing manner. He would roll his eyes, pretend that he was having a hard time playing a difficult number, and wave his little finger during an easy passage."[16] The duo also began to satirize popular songs and do comic imitations of concert players. Eventually they succeeded to the point of playing on the major circuits, even as second act at the Palace Theater in New York, vaudeville's major showcase, in 1917. Benny joined the navy in 1918 and continued to perform in navy camp shows, expanding further into comedy, which eventually led to an act called "Izzy There, the Admiral's Disorderly," for a traveling navy production, *The Great Lakes Revue*. After his navy stint, Benny continued to develop the humorous side of his violin playing in a new act billed as "Ben K. Benny—Fiddle Funology, " which began to seem too close to the very similar schtick of another better-known performer on the Orpheum Circuit, Ben Bernie. With a final name change he became Jack Benny, and gradually the comedy proportion of his act increased, developing into a humorous "suave" character whose pretensions— and their destruction—formed the main subject of his act. By 1924 Benny was billed as the star attraction at the Palace, and in 1926 he appeared in the the the Schubert Broadway revue *Great Temptations*.

Meantime, Benny had met his future partner Sadie Marks, who was from an orthodox Jewish family in Vancouver. Benny and the Marx Brothers were performing on the same bill at the Orpheum in Vancouver, and Sadie's family were distant relations of the Marxes—Zeppo Marx introduced Sadie to Benny. They were married in 1927, and in

1928, according to Benny's reminiscences, "I was breaking in a new act and using a 'dumb girl' for about a four-minute routine. I was working the Orpheum Circuit when the girl took sick and had to go to the hospital. So I asked Sadie to help me out for a few weeks till she recovered. . . . Sadie became part of the act in Seattle and was she ever a hit!"[17] Sadie's stage name at first was Marie Marsh, and she served as a "singer and foil" to Jack's violin playing and comic persona, "an innocent 'dumb dame' type who got the last laugh by putting Benny down for his conceit."[18] By late 1928, Benny was offered the position of master of ceremonies at the Palace, which led to a brief stint in films even before his fame as a radio personality. He played a "suave master of ceremonies" in the early MGM sound film *Hollywood Revue of 1929* and in two other unmemorable efforts in 1930, *Medicine Man* and *Chasing Rainbows*.

But Benny's radio career began in early 1932, with a guest spot on Ed Sullivan's interview show on WHN (New York). This five-minute spot, scripted by former Burns and Allen vaudeville writer Al Boasberg, attracted the attention of both NBC and the N. W. Ayer agency. On April 6, 1932, the NBC Commercial Program Department arranged for an audition of Jack Benny for Ayer and its client Canada Dry, after which its head, Bertha Brainard, made an assessment of this new comic: "We think Mr. Benny is excellent for radio, and while the audition was unassisted as far as orchestra was concerned, we believe he would make a great bet for an air program."[19] *The Canada Dry Ginger Ale Program* went on the air May 2, 1932, over NBC twice a week from 9:30 to 10:00; it ran for almost a year.

Two important antecedents existed for the type of show Jack Benny found himself in, and helped to shape, over this formative year. The N. W. Ayer agency, as discussed in chapter 2, produced one of the earliest regularly scheduled shows in radio, *The Eveready Hour*, with its mixture of music, dialogue, and drama. Canada Dry competed in the ginger ale market with rival Cliquot Club, whose primarily musical show *Cliquot Club Eskimoes*, with band leader Harry Reser, had been one of the most popular on radio for three years already. In addition, by the 1931–32 season—that preceding Benny's debut—a program combining comedy/variety and orchestra had broken all previous listener statistics: *The Chase and Sanborn Hour* with Eddie Cantor. In the fall of 1931 it was still a much more common practice to combine music with almost every conceivable type of commentator (what Sum-

mers calls "semi-variety"): impersonators, interviewers, poetry readings, "investment talk," and even "overseas talk" (the *Florscheim
Frolics*). By the fall of 1932, after Eddie Cantor's unprecedented 28.9
Hooperrating, ten new comedy/variety shows debuted. Jack Benny
was swept onto radio in this tide of cultural adaptation, which at first
differed little from its precedents. Less of a comic character and more
of the traditional master of ceremonies, Benny figured in the early
Canada Dry program only in short "gags" between introductions of
musical numbers, performed by George Olsen and his orchestra and
singer Ethel Shutta. By August, Benny had brought his former partner
and wife onto the show, in the initial persona of an enthusiastic but
critical fan named Mary Livingstone.

Benny was not an ad-libber and depended heavily on good writers
throughout his career. Writer Al Boasberg continued to provide most
of Benny's continuity in the early months, but in 1933 Benny replaced
him with brilliant but difficult vaudeville writer Harry Conn, who had
also contributed to George Burns and Gracie Allen's vaudeville acts
and radio program. Some of the commercial dialogue provided by
Conn involved humor at the expense of the sponsor and product—a
popular radio device, and one that Benny and others would continue,
but it may have led to Canada Dry's dropping of the show in January
1933. However, the General Motors Company picked it up to publicize Chevrolet cars in March 1933, and it was in this incarnation that
the Benny program began to take on familiar form.

Now teamed with NBC announcer Alois Havrilla, orchestra leader
Frank Black, and tenor Frank Parker, along with Mary and an occasional "stooge" (often ethnic, such as Sam Hearn, who did Jewish im-
personations), Benny began to develop his "fall guy" character as the
object of his ensemble's jokes. An egotistical, bragging, "Beau Brum-
mel of the air," Jack set himself up so the others could knock him
down with quick cuts and insults, including his trademark stinginess.
Along the way, a sort of "show business family" began to emerge,
with Benny in the character of "himself"—a variety show comedian
and emcee—and the others as his disgruntled, but loyal, employees.
This reflexive persona was, of course, carefully constructed, and one
thing it involved was the casting of Jack Benny as the "author" and director of his fictional (and, by implication, actual) cast and show. By
constantly making Benny the butt of jokes about how little he paid his
"employees," the ensemble members, their actual employment by the

advertising agency (now Young & Rubicam) was masked, along with Benny's similar status. The seemingly natural and spontaneous conversation among a bunch of people putting on a radio show concealed the efforts of writer Harry Conn and others, as well as those of directors, agency producers, network personnel, and so on. Jack Benny's self-conscious persona as precisely the host of the radio show being listened to at once allowed radio itself to figure into many of the jokes and simultaneously concealed the true conditions under which radio production was actually taking place. This positing of authorial control, employed to mask a more complex and collaborative production process, would become a hallmark of radio genres and represents one way that the emerging medium sought to employ the criteria of "high culture" in its presentation—though frequently parodying itself, as we shall see.

Benny's persona marks a middle ground between the unselfconsciously direct "showmen" of early radio, like Roxy or Wendell Hall, who appeared as "themselves" with personal identities congruent with their stage personas, and the fictionalized characters of emerging serial and series drama forms, such as Fibber McGee and Molly, Myrt and Marge, and Amos and Andy. Over the years a complex and detailed "life" was built up around Benny and his cast, involving not only his professional but his "personal" life, with cast members coming over to his house, going shopping or on trips, taking the show on the road, and getting into various scrapes.[20] For instance, Mary might accompany Jack on a shopping expedition in New York to (reluctantly) buy Christmas gifts for the other performers; or Ronald Colman and his wife, regularly appearing as neighbors living next to radio star Jack Benny in Beverly Hills, might stop by to complain about something; or the show might "drop in" on tenor Dennis Day at home with his mother, a well-known Benny foe. Interestingly, all of the cast members except Sadie Marks Benny and, later, Eddie Anderson (as "Rochester Van Jones," Jack's black valet) performed under their own names, thus acknowledging and validating their "real" professional identities as band leader, comic, and so on, underlying the show's fictional diegesis. Only the sole woman and the sole African American were denied this validation: outside of their characters, they did not "exist." However, both eventually assumed their new identities almost completely: Benny claims that both "Mary" and "Rochester" became known as such to their real-life families and close friends, Sadie Marks Benny even going so far as to have her name legally changed to Mary Livingstone.

This mixture of fiction and "reality" percolated over into the other major comedy innovation of the Chevrolet and succeeding General Tire and General Foods programs: satiric sketches that lampooned movies, books, and plays. These could take on the tone of self-satire, as the not-very-good "fictional" comedy team of the fictionalized Jack Benny show—underpaid, overworked, led around by the nose by their stingy, demanding, and self-deceiving boss, "Jack Benny"—gave lame and farcical performances of respectable properties such as *Little Women* or *Uncle Tom's Cabin* or movie westerns. On another level, of course, well appreciated by their "in-the-know" radio audience, the highly skillful team of comedians brilliantly lampooned not only the objects of their satire but radio performance itself.

Throughout these comic changes Benny's persona developed and remained consistent as the transgressive, but seemingly unassailable, authority figure. Jack comically violated all the norms of American masculinity. Obviously wealthy but unable to spend money, thinking himself the pinnacle of masculine attractiveness but unable to interest women, suave and debonair but unable to handle simple situations, the authoritative host of a major radio program but unable to command the respect of his employees (and, later, a white man totally dependent on his black servant, in a relationship with strangely homoerotic implications), Benny's constructed persona embodied the abject even as it relied implicitly on a set of norms personified by the supporting characters. Mary Livingstone's character evolved from the "dumb dame" or "smart-aleck girl" into a kind of efficient assistant, who kept Jack out of the most egregious scrapes and punctured his self-delusions. Benny later characterized her as "a kind of heckler-secretary."[21] Her peculiar "family," from whom she received frequent garbled missives, resembled that of Gracie Allen and provided comic contrast. Every other ensemble character had a specified task on the program—announcer, singer, band leader—but Mary was simply Mary, never positioned as Jack's wife in the show (Jack's character was unmarried), though most listeners would realize that this was their real-life relationship, and never specifically positioned as anything else—simply "there." Her ambiguous position in this confluence of real and fictional narratives, given the fact that she was the only woman on the program aside from occasional guest stars, speaks to the ambiguous position of the professional woman on radio.

When the program moved to General Tire sponsorship in early 1934, Don Wilson joined the cast as announcer. He was a former football player and a rather large man, and his size and weight became frequent targets of Benny's jokes. As the announcer, Wilson was responsible for integrating the sponsor's advertising messages, and perhaps for that reason became another voice of sanity in the fictionalized world of the broadcast, ribbing Jack for his bad violin playing and stinginess. But he could be ribbed himself for the know-it-all qualities that the role of announcer imparted. In this scene, not only Wilson but the kind of knowledge he represents is being spoofed. Wilson is having a conversation with guest singer Dorothy Kirsten:

> *Wilson*: Oh, Miss Kirsten, I wanted to tell you that I saw you in "Madame Butterfly" Wednesday afternoon and I thought your performance was simply magnificent.
> *Kirsten*: Well, that's awfully kind of you, Mr. Wilson, but who could help singing Puccini? It's so expressive—particularly the last act starting with the allegro vivacissimo.
> *Wilson*: Well, that's being very modest, Miss Kirsten, but not every singer has the necessary bel canto and flexibility or the range to cope with the high tessitura of that first act.
> *Kirsten*: Well, Mr. Wilson, didn't you think in the aria "Un Bel Di Vedremo" that the strings played the con molto exceptionally fine, with great sostenendo?
> *Jack*: Well—I thought . . .
> *Mary*: OH SHUT UP![22]

General Foods, to promote its product Jello, picked up sponsorship of Benny's show from October 1934 until 1942, and in this period a new cast brought all these elements together to take the show to its top-rated position. Phil Harris replaced Frank Black as orchestra leader and developed the character of a "conceited Southern playboy," harddrinking and hard-living, as a foil to Jack's moderation and timidity. Kenny Baker replaced Frank Parker as singer, but later moved to Fred Allen's show, at which point Dennis Day took over. Both Baker and Day played the role of the ingenue: innocent, credulous young men, none too bright. Beside them Jack was a pragmatic genius. In 1935, writer Harry Conn, who had virtually created the program as it had developed and remained, demanded a half share in its ownership. When Benny would not agree, Conn left and a new team of writers came aboard, headed by Ed Beloin and Bill Morrow, who were primarily responsible for scripting the new ensemble.

Another major supporting character, first introduced in 1937, was Eddie Anderson playing Rochester, Jack's all-around general factotum, chauffeur, and housekeeper. Here Benny's use of a "black" character, though taken from the minstrel tradition of white projections onto African American characters, also differed from what had gone before. First of all, Rochester was not played in blackface by a white man, but by an accomplished black comic actor. From a start in vaudeville in a comedy act called "Three Black Aces" with his brother and another performer, Anderson moved on to nightclub performances in Los Angeles and at Harlem's Cotton Club. In 1937 he had already appeared in three Hollywood films, including a leading role in *The Green Pastures*. Bill Morrow wrote a script that called for a black Pullman porter for the May 28, 1937, broadcast, and Anderson, with his distinctive voice and comic timing, proved so successful in getting laughs that Rochester was added to the show as a permanent character in June. Rochester's characterization contained many of the prevalent minstrel show stereotypes, but differed from other limited roles for African Americans not only in its position for a black actor on a top-rated show but in the character's relationship to his white employer. Rochester insulted and criticized Jack along with the rest of the cast; some of his lines allowed for a certain amount of awareness of the artificiality of black stereotypes to appear as well. In the initial episode, when Jack asks the porter for a suit that he had requested to be pressed, Rochester replies, "Gee, I'm lazy, don't I remind you of Stepin Fetchit?" When the doorbell rings in a later script and Jack demands that Rochester answer it, Rochester refuses: "Boss, you're nearer to it than I am." As an additional conflicting factor, Rochester's traits in many ways mirrored those of white bandleader Phil Harris, also portrayed as heavy-drinking, womanizing, and uneducated, even to the point of being illiterate (and also "southern"). However, Harris never spoke with the minstrel dialect that Rochester did in the early years, nor did he perform personal services.

Benny recounts an episode that had Rochester helping him prepare for a boxing match with Fred Allen (in the course of their much-publicized "feud"). When Jack dared Rochester to hit him, Rochester responded with a blow that knocked Jack out. According to legend, listeners from the South wrote in to object to this "attack on the white race and the dignity of the South."[23] Whether this is accurate or not, it is certain that black radio audiences objected to the more minstrelized representations of Rochester, including his dialect, purported laziness and ignorance, and stereotyped behavior that involved drinking, gambling, and chasing women. The show was not above watermelon and razor jokes, either. Here the familiar dilemma enters. The presence of a black comedian on a prime-time program was a source of pride for some African American critics. The *Chicago Defender*, for instance, billed the show in its radio listings as "Eddie Anderson—with Jack Benny"; *The Negro Handbook* of 1944 lists it as "Rochester and Jack Benny"; the *Negro Year Book* of 1946 mentions in its section "The Negro in Radio Programs" that "standing out as the most popular of all Negro actors appearing regularly on the radio is the comedian 'Rochester' (Eddie Anderson), valet, friend and general adviser to Jack Benny."[24]

Yet the offensive minstrel elements of the depiction were undeniable. Both Jack Benny himself and writer Milt Josefsberg have noted that during the war years they were required by the prevailing zeitgeist to tone down their ethnic and racial humor, including the more minstrel-like parts of Rochester's character. But in February 1950, for a show in New York hampered by the illness of almost all the writing team, a script that had been aired ten years previously was dusted off and broadcast without such changes. It contained this segment, in which Jack telephoned around "Harlem" to such places as the "Gin Till You Spin Club," looking for Rochester:

Jack: Hello?
Mamie: Hello, Mamie Brown, the sweetest gal in town talking.
Jack: Miss Brown, this is Jack Benny.
Mamie: Oh-oh.
Jack: I'm trying to get in touch with Rochester. Is he there?
Mamie: He *was* here.
Jack: Oh . . . well do you think he'll come back?
Mamie: In all modesty, I can *guarantee* that.
Jack: Hmmmm . . . Well, when he returns, will you please tell him to call my hotel . . . and you can also tell him I'm stopping his salary.
Mamie: Oh, that ain't gonna bother him. He now *owns* the building that houses the Harlem Social, Benevolent, and Spare Ribs Every Thursday Club.
Jack: Oh, yes, I heard about that. He wins from everybody, doesn't he?
Mamie: Yeah, when I opened the door and he came in on one knee, I thought it was a proposal.[25]

The network's switchboards lit up and numerous angry letters and editorials protested the reappearance of depictions thought to have been banished from the air. The NAACP launched a nationwide letter-writing campaign. Benny apologized, and the later radio and television show never returned to this emphasis with the Rochester character.

Still, Rochester served a similar function within the dynamic of *The Jack Benny Program* as did Amos and Andy: as the projection of so-cially undesirable traits onto race, with race thereby reinforced as a meaningful, and debasing, social distinction. However, given the abject role played by Jack, Rochester's traits represent our more familiar por-traits of successful masculinity. Rochester gambled for money and won large sums, which he spent freely and with much enjoyment. Unlike Jack, he was successful with women—to an excessive degree. Though he worked hard and complained about low pay (as did all the cast), he was able to slip away to live his own life whenever he felt like it. Yet, as Margaret McFadden points out, Rochester was peculiarly feminized as well. Serving more and more the place evacuated by Mary Livingstone, as Jack's "wife," Rochester's role is described by Benny:

> Rochester became one of the greatest assets on the show. . . . He became more than a butler. He was my housekeeper. He did the shopping, waxed the floors and made the beds. He did the laundry. Sometimes I made a little money on the side taking in laundry from the Ronald Colmans and other neighbors. Rochester drove the Maxwell. He drew my bath and when I was immersed therein, he handed me my soap, washrag and celluloid duck. Afterwards, he massaged me with baby oil. When I suf-fered a spell of insomnia, Rochester switched on the motor that gently rocked my bed and he sang, "Rock-a-bye, baby, in the treetop," until I fell asleep.[26]

Here Jack becomes infantilized and Rochester takes on the role of mother/wife; this role was often alluded to humorously in the show in a way that, according to McFadden, was "both homoerotic and evocative of slavery":

> [Rochester] wears flowered aprons over his suits in movies with Jack and makes constant reference to the cooking, cleaning, and washing he has to do. Those are tasks not usually done by male servants, again suggesting feminization. Rochester also uses the same kind of illogical logic and "ir-rational" thinking that characterizes female characters in 1930s radio and movies. The experience with slavery is evoked when Rochester re-counts his lawyer's reaction to his contract with Jack. Rochester explains ruefully, "He just shook his head and said 'Lincoln wouldn't like this!'"[27]

Benny employed other types of ethnic characters as well. Sam Hearn played the Jewish storyteller Schlepperman, along with other Jewish dialect parts. Later, Artie Auerbach played the similar role of Mr. Kitzel. Mel Blanc appeared in a number of roles, including his famous Mexican characterizations but also as Jack's music teacher, Professor Le Blanc, and often as animals or inanimate objects. Ethnic characterizations were a common source of humor in radio comedy, using to advantage broadcasting's aural nature, and Fred Allen would take such characterizations to national fame even during the war years on his "Allen's Alley" segment. Though a few objections were registered, overall *The Jack Benny Program* never received the kind of criticism or network and sponsor difficulties as did Fred Allen. Writer Milt Josefsberg recounts some problems over the years with NBC's Continuity Acceptance Department, but these were mostly related to mild sexual double entendres. The show's 7:00 time slot on Sunday nights mandated a "family" format, and the type of self-directed satire developed by the Benny program contained and restricted its social commentary within the limits of character. Critic Gilbert Seldes remarked in 1956 that almost all radio comedy consisted of insults; this was certainly true of comic personas such as Jack Benny's. By turning social satire inward, so that the comic and his ensemble become the symbolic representatives of negative cultural traits, humor becomes personalized, individual, and its larger implications are contained and defused within the parameters set up by the comedy of personality. Though marked by resistance to "high culture" in its many manifestations, through satire, spoofs, and insults, *The Jack Benny Program* retained its creation of an "author," defused its satire through the filter of personality, and encouraged the disciplined participation of the audience by its self-enclosed humor.

At one point the show reached out for the kind of audience response that had become popular in the new audience quiz and participation programs. Its conception is telling: Benny and the show's writers proposed an "I Can't Stand Jack Benny Because . . ." contest, and 277,000 entries were received. The winner, Carroll P. Craig of Pacific Palisades, California, wrote:

> He fills the air with boasts and brags / And obsolete obnoxious gags.
> The way he plays his violin / Is music's most obnoxious sin.
> His cowardice alone, indeed / Is matched by his obnoxious greed.
> In all the things that he portrays / He shows up my own obnoxious
>   ways.[28]

Benny's self-deprecating humor allowed for an individualized response, as well.

One comic who resisted this kind of containment was Benny's real-life and fictional rival, Fred Allen. The Fred Allen/Jack Benny on-air "feud" became a long-running and long-remembered feature of both their acts. Starting in 1936, when Fred Allen spontaneously insulted Benny's violin playing by comparing Benny unfavorably to a ten-year-old amateur who had just performed Dvořák's *The Bee*, the feud continued for more than ten years. Allen made more of it than Benny, for reasons that Benny recognized: "It wasn't in my radio character to attack other people and my humor came out of *my* being the butt of everybody else's jokes. I was at a disadvantage. I couldn't be as nasty as he could be."[29] Another exchange neatly reflects back on the two comics' differing authorial positions: in response to one of Allen's ad-libbed barbs, Benny replied, "You wouldn't dare talk to me like that if my writers were here."[30] Though it mostly served as a publicity stunt, this feud also highlights important components of the contrast between Benny's and Allen's humor—all the more significant for the performers' many similarities.

Fighting Fred Allen

Fred Allen was born John Florence Sullivan to a chronically under-employed and alcoholic father and a mother who died when he was three years old.[31] Raised by his aunt in Boston's Irish immigrant neighborhoods, Allen lacked the musical training of Benny Kubelsky but made up for it by taking up juggling, in imitation of vaudeville acts he had seen. At first performing in local amateur nights, by 1914, at the age of twenty, Allen entered small-time vaudeville with a "juggling monologist" act, combining standard jokes and one-liners with humor directed at his own poor juggling abilities. Using a variety of names, from Paul Huckle to Fred St. James to "Freddy James, the World's Worst Juggler," he eventually borrowed the last name of his agent, Edgar Allen, to become Fred Allen.

After a successful engagement at the Palace in 1919, Allen toured on the big-time vaudeville circuits, and in 1922 appeared in the Schubert's musical revue *The Passing Show of 1922* at the Winter Garden. There he met his future wife, Portland Hoffa, a dancer and chorus performer from Portland, Oregon (hence her name). They married in 1927 and Hoffa joined Allen's act, doing "bit parts, 'dumb dame' jokes, and dancing."[32] Their new team act found them a place in the popular music revue *Three's a Crowd*, which ran from 1930 through 1932. By 1932, when the show closed, the Depression had exacerbated vaudeville's slow demise. Looking around for alternatives, Allen and Hoffa came up with a format that they thought might succeed on radio, rounded up a cast, and made an audition recording. Allen describes his idea:

> Since the radio comedian really had to depend on the ears of the home audience for his purpose, I thought that a complete story told each week or a series of episodes and comedy situations might be a welcome change. It would enable the listener to flex his imagination, and perhaps make him want to follow the experiences of the characters involved. This, if it worked, would insure the radio comedian a longer life. Hoping for longevity in the new medium, I planned a series of programs using a different business background each week—a newspaper office, a department store, a bank, a detective agency, etc. The comedy would involve the characters employed in, or indigenous to, the assorted locales.[33]

Allen submitted the recording to the head of Corn Products Inc., whose product Linit Bath Oil had been featured on the *Linit Bath Club*, which had aired a combination of celebrity interviews and orchestral music for fifteen minutes five times a week on CBS since 1931. Linit must not have been happy with its relatively low Hooperrating of 4.9. No doubt swept onto the air by the comedian wave started by Eddie Cantor the year before, Allen debuted as the "Knight of Bath" in the *Linit Bath Club Revue* on CBS on Sunday, October 23, 1932, from 9:00 to 9:30—five months after the first Jack Benny program for Canada Dry went on the air.

Like Benny's first program, the Linit show featured a heavy dose of music but also began to introduce comic sketches, written by Allen and "an assistant," in which Allen, Hoffa, and a supporting group of "stooges" played a variety of roles. Most of these relied on standard vaudeville humor, with some social and political satire thrown in. In 1933 the show switched sponsorship to Best Foods, makers of Hellmann's Mayonnaise, under the direction of the Benton and Bowles agency. This new *Salad Bowl Revue*, now on NBC on Friday nights at 9:00, ran only from August to December. In January 1934, Allen changed sponsorship again, this time to Bristol Meyers, touting the laxative Sal Hepatica. This show became the *Hour of Smiles* in March after the company, disappointed with the ratings of its two separate

Wednesday-night shows—a musical program from 9:00 to 9:30 advertising Ipana toothpaste, followed by Allen for Sal Hepatica at 9:30—combined them into an hour-length program promoting both products, "Sal Hepatica for the smile of health . . . Ipana for the smile of beauty." For the *Hour of Smiles*, Allen and his cast created the fictional New England town of Bedlam and based their comedy skits around the doings of its inhabitants. In recognition of this setting, the show's name was changed in July 1934 to *Town Hall Tonight*, set fictionally in Bedlam's town hall.

In late 1935, agency production shifted to Young & Rubicam, and neophyte advertising man Sylvester "Pat" Weaver was placed in charge of Fred Allen, who had already begun to earn the reputation for being "difficult" that would mark his career. Weaver claims little influence over the content of the shows; he was mostly responsible for troubleshooting between Allen and those in charge, including sponsor, agency, and network, and the writing of the commercial continuities. Though Allen employed writers—notably Harry Tugend, Arnold Auerbach, and Herman Wouk (of later literary fame)—he obsessively rewrote each script and often, especially during the early years, ended up using virtually none of the writers' work. Allen's humor also relied heavily on ad-libbing, which led to many of his troubles with network censors. Ad-libs not only evaded the script-based control process but caused difficulties with the timing of the show, causing abrupt cutoffs and fades that formed another bone of contention with the network.

The show was organized into four parts. First, after an orchestral piece followed by Allen's introduction and commercial plug, came the "Town Hall News" segment, relating the events in Bedlam and using them to comment on current topics and issues. Then Portland Hoffa came on with the evening's guest, in a spot later called "People You Didn't Expect to Meet." Eschewing the standard celebrity interview, Allen's show was unique in featuring ordinary men and women with unusual professions or hobbies. In Alan Havig's words, Allen "developed comedy from the lives of average people, the 'little men' and women from the world beyond the RCA building who were 'average' only in their noncelebrity status. Their odd occupation or unique abilities brought a panorama of interesting human diversity to Allen's microphone; there was nothing like it on any other comedy-variety show."[34] Hoffa and Allen then exchanged lines, with Hoffa in the role of a scatterbrained woman with a peculiar family, similar to Mary

Livingstone's. This was followed by a skit by the Mighty Allen Art Players, kept anonymous during these early shows but consisting of Roy Atwell, Jack Smart, Eileen Douglas, Alan Reed, Walter Tetley, Minerva Pious, Charlie Cantor, John Brown, and various others.[35] Here Allen's satirical sketches were performed, lampooning topical issues and, frequently, show business itself. Allen took on politicians, social programs, news events, sponsors, network vice presidents, Hollywood, radio programs, advertising agencies, intellectuals, and many other topics, some of which cut too close to the heart of those involved. Finally, this hour-length show included an amateur segment, featuring performances by various talented nobodies who had been screened by Allen's staff. This unscripted segment allowed Allen to ad-lib freely, a feature he particularly enjoyed.

Many of Allen's skits took on the pretensions of high culture. This sketch poked mild fun at intellectuals and Ivy League circles, a favorite target:

Allen: You *are* a Harvard man, Mr. Higginbottom.
John: Yes. At Harvard we speak Latin practically all of the time. Pro bono publicum.
Allen: Pro bono.
John: Publicum. It means don't pick your bones in public.
Allen: I rarely do. But thank you for this little etiquette hint. Now, Mr. Higginbottom, you were voted the smartest student in the class of '38.
John: Yes. I've got a B.A., an A.B., a Ph.D., an M.A., an L.L.D., and an M.D.
Allen: What are you going to do now that you're out of Harvard?
John: I'm going right home, the town is giving me another degree.
Allen: Another degree?
John: Yes, it's a W.P.A. Whatever that is.
Allen: You wouldn't know at Harvard, naturally.[36]

Weaver recalls that he himself was drafted into Allen's skits three or four times a year, in his real-life persona as an advertising agency executive.[37] Alan Havig summarizes one of these sketches:

After the removal of half his brain in a medical experiment at Quinceton College, Mopey escapes from his locked room. "Gad!" the college president (Allen) exclaims. "A man with half a brain loose on the campus. He's going to be difficult to find." But Mopey has spent the six months since his escape on Madison Avenue becoming Sylvester P. Weaver, a successful ad agency vice-president. The grateful half-wit endows his college with a fortune. Inspired, President Allen rushes to the laboratory to undergo total brain removal. "With no brain at all I'll make a million dollars in the movie industry and Quinceton will be saved."[38]

This sketch neatly combines Allen's contempt for the overly highbrow and the new elite of popular culture: mixed targets that often pitted his opponents against each other. A satire of the daytime serials prompted indignant objections from John McMillin of the Compton Advertising Agency, producer of several of Procter & Gamble's biggest soaps. Referring to the broadcast of May 29, 1940, which included a ten-minute skit by "a couple of stooges who apparently insisted on telling what they thought was wrong with daytime radio," he complained:

> They first poked fun at the summaries of action which tease the succeeding day's episode. Then they decried the excess of sorrow in daytime serials. They suggested that each episode should be complete in itself, and this could be done by having a succession of murders or fatal accidents until every member of the cast was done away with. . . . The unflattering remarks about daytime radio are exactly the kind that we and Procter & Gamble complained so bitterly about a couple of months ago. . . . we must ask you to give us positive and definite assurance that this kind of backhanded slapping at daytime radio will be discontinued.[39]

Niles Trammel, one of the network vice presidents so often the butt of Allen's scorn, defended the broadcast and took full responsibility, stating that he had gone over the script carefully with Janet MacRorie, head of continuity acceptance:

> It seemed to me it poked fun at radio in general and, while it did refer to serial programs as well as contests, it did not specify daytime serials. You will also remember it brought in Jack Benny and several other types of programs. I am certain it could not be considered as being harmful to the Procter & Gamble interests. As I advised you, I am personally watching any references that might be made to daytime shows which might be considered derogatory or harmful and after very careful consideration I did not feel the Allen broadcast centered attention on any specified type of broadcast. . . . It took in the whole field and as I listened to it I thought it was very amusing. I will continue to do my utmost to see that your interests are amply protected.[40]

These are the kinds of disputes that network executives would have preferred to avoid, and Allen was skilled at provoking them.

In October 1939, upon returning from summer hiatus, the program's title was changed to *The Fred Allen Show*, still retaining the same sponsor and agency and still on NBC Wednesday nights. Allen later claimed that the agency forced him to abandon the town hall format in order to imitate the now successful Jack Benny show:

> I claimed that radio was like the pickle business. Let Jack Benny go along selling his big dill. I would take the other side of the street and peddle my little gherkins. It was as futile as trying to convince a Russian delegate at the U.N. Nothing helped. The Town Hall title disappeared. We became just another group of actors gathered around a microphone in a radio studio. The colorful illusion had been completely stripped from the program.[41]

However, sponsorship switched to the Texaco Oil Company in October 1940 and the show became *The Texaco Star Theatre* under direction of the Buchanan Agency. It moved to Sunday nights on CBS in February 1942, and in June returned to its original half-hour format. This came as both a relief and a burden to Allen. He had grown weary of the demands of writing an hour-long show and looked forward to working just with the regular cast in tightly scripted comic sketches in the new format. But thirty minutes did not give much leeway, and with Allen's ad-lib style, timing the show to suit network and sponsor became more difficult than ever. The show remained at this time until June 1944, when Allen went on summer hiatus and remained off the air for more than a year due to the problems with high blood pressure that also kept him from taking his show overseas during the war years. When he returned to the air, in October 1945, it was as part of NBC's stellar Sunday-night lineup: Jack Benny at 7:00, Bergen and McCarthy at 8:00, followed by Fred Allen at 8:30. J. Walter Thompson took over the show, now for Standard Brands.

During these later incarnations, from 1942 until Allen's departure from the air in 1949, one of the most popular features of his program was the "Allen's Alley" skit, occupying most of the first half of the program. The Alley grew out of Allen's satires of news interview and movie newsreels on the *Town Hall Tonight* broadcasts. The Alley was less a real neighborhood than a gallery of regional, ethnic, and class-based "types" who responded to Allen's questions related to topics from the current news. Original inhabitants included Fallstaff Openshaw, the "Bard of the Bowery," played by Alan Reed; John Brown as John Doe, the "average American citizen"; Minerva Pious playing Mrs. Nussbaum, Jewish housewife; Charlie Cantor as Socrates Mulligan, an Irish ignoramus; and Jack Smart as Senator Bloat, precursor to the more famous Senator Beauregard Claghorn, a pompous politician.

After Allen's hiatus in 1944 and 1945, he returned with only Mrs. Nussbaum remaining from the previous Alley, and three new members: Senator Claghorn, "from the South, that is," played by Kenny Delmar (the model for Warner Bros. cartoon character Colonel Foghorn Leghorn); Parker Fennelly as Titus Moody, dry New England farmer; and, added a year later, Ajax Cassidy, a drunken, loutish Irishman. Though they varied by region and personality, and employed many of the oldest chestnuts of ethnic humor, all remained consistently working-class, relatively uneducated, and "of the people," in continuation of Allen's basic populist resistance to "bigness" and self-importance of any sort. A whole new stable of writers assisted Allen with these skits, including Nat Hiken, Vick Knight, Roland Kibbee, Sidney Fields, Bob Weiskopf, Elizabeth Todd, Al Lewis, Larry Marks, and Aaron Ruben.[42]

These recurring characters, along with the more standard celebrity interview format of the second half of the post-1942 show, led Allen in a direction more similar to other programs on the air and less in line with his earlier iconoclastic insistence on the "little man" and resistance to showbiz standards. Most of the characterizations fell firmly within the lines of stock vaudeville humor. As Allen knocked on their separate doors and asked a question of topical interest, each character responded according to a type well established by the conventions of radio. Mrs. Nussbaum's stock malaprop response to Allen's knock was something like, "You vas expectin' maybe Cecil B. Schlemiel?" Titus Moody aswered with a laconic, "Howdy, Bub." Ajax Cassidy might bluster, "Who's there lookin' for a brawl? Oh, it's you, Allen." Senator Claghorn's response became a national tag line, "Somebody, Ah say somebody, is knockin on mah door."

Minerva Pious, who played Mrs. Nussbaum, claimed that the figure of Ajax Cassidy received the most complaints, because there was very little other than negative aspects to his stereotyped Irishman: loud, bullying, frequently drunk, and ignorant.[43] Possibly Allen found it difficult to satirize the ethnic group to which he belonged; other critics found Cassidy the least well developed of the Alley inhabitants. Mrs. Nussbaum was the longest-running ethnic character on the Allen show. Her malapropisms and dialect placed her squarely in the tradition of countless other Jewish acts, and during and after the war various objections to this depiction were made, such as this one directed at NBC: "Mrs. Nussbaum is no longer funny—she is merely a grievous racial stereotype in an age where too many graves attest to the evils of racial stereotypes. Ajax Cassidy is a buffoon who must cast a dubious reflection in the minds of those who know how dissimilar he is to modern-day Irish-Americans."[44] Titus Moody raised few eyebrows; indeed, he possessed no personally disturbing traits except eccentricity and a deprecating wit similar to Allen's.

The most colorful and popular character of the later Alley was Senator Beauregard Claghorn, who very nearly continued in his own show on NBC in the early 1950s and inspired Claghorn dolls, Claghorn hats, and Claghorn compasses (which pointed only south).[45] In this figure Allen had two juicy objects for ridicule: politicians and the South. As historians of the South have pointed out, in the postwar years the American southern states took on by projection many of the negative traits characteristic of the country as a whole, including racism, cultural backwardness, resistance to change, and corrupt politics.[46] Claghorn took these aspects to the extreme in his Yankee-baiting insistence on the superiority of everything southern, to which nonsoutherners could feel easily superior themselves. From "so far down south that mah family is treadin' water in the Gulf Stream," Claghorn called "people from Alabama Yankees." He went to school at CCNY—Charleston, Chattanooga, Natchez, and Yazoo. He belonged to Ah Smelta Delta fraternity and graduated "magnolia cum laude"; his class voted him most likely to secede.[47] His famous line, "That's a joke, son," came from his second appearance:

> *Allen*: Tell me, Senator Claghorn. How do you feel about the employment outlook down there in Washington?
> *Claghorn*: We're investigatin' it, son. . . . Senator Pepper is red hot on the subject. (dead silence) Pepper's red hot, I say.
> *Allen*: I—I know, I know.
> *Claghorn*: That's a joke, son! It's witty! Pay attention!

A few lines later, he claimed to "represent the Solid South. . . . Ah loaned Mason and Dixon the chalk the day they drew up the line."[48]

Another time, Claghorn described a performance by the Mobile Philharmonic. The orchestra's conductor is Arturo Tuscaloosa, who conducts with a hoe handle instead of a baton, and it is the only orchestra in the world with a hound-dog choir: "Son, when the Mobile Philharmonic does the Barcarolle, you kin hear the barkin' 20 miles away." What does the Mobile Philharmonic play? "All the classics, son. Everythin' by Rimsky Culpepper. The Georgia Cracker Suite. The

Flight of the Boll Weevil. Poet and Sharecropper. Moonshine Sonata. Rhapsody in Grey."[49] Claghorn claimed, "No man livin' can make me wear a Union suit!" At Thanksgiving, he ate only the part of the turkey that was facing south, in bed he ate only Georgia crackers, and he never ate applesauce in case there might be a northern spy among the apples. Compelled to travel to New York, he claimed, "When Ah pass Grant's Tomb, Ah shut both eyes. . . . Ah never go to the Yankee Stadium! Ah won't even go to the Polo Grounds unless a southpaw's pitchin'."[50] Unlike the other characters in the Alley, audiences were encouraged to laugh as much *at* Claghorn as with him. This allowed Allen to mix outward-directed social satire with the cherished though irritable populism that marked the two poles of his humor.

Although, according to an article written for Allen's comeback in 1945, he "shun[ned] synthetic humor, as he does the current radio fad of situation comedy,"[51] in many ways reliance on the Alley figures marked a move in that direction. Havig states that the Alley segments "neutralized potentially threatening or divisive subjects when they directed Allen's public questions inward, transforming world dilemmas or national headlines into idiosyncratic anecdotes."[52] This might seem to imitate Jack Benny's use of the ensemble to contain social criticism and commentary within the bounds of the radio family circle, but, unlike Benny's turned-inward, self-deprecating comedy, Allen's humor was turned outward, directed at shibboleths of both high and mass culture as Allen saw them, earning enemies on both sides.

In Allen's eyes, the networks occupied the same position as the more traditional keepers of morality, enforcing cultural standards to which Allen could not subscribe and at which he directed the bulk of his humor. In his own work on the radio business, Allen designated advertising agency and radio vice presidents as "molehill men": "A molehill man is a pseudo-busy executive who comes to work at 9 a.m. and finds a molehill on his desk. He has until 5 p.m. to make this molehill into a mountain. An accomplished molehill man will often have his mountain finished even before lunch."[53]

In a 1945 interview, Allen publicized his difficulties with the networks: "Allen feels that these network censors abrogate his constitutional rights and force on him the limits of what he considers the censors' non-existent imagination and sense of humor. . . . His life is made miserable by censors and vice-presidents who quash his pet ideas." One verse of his satiric skit "The Radio Mikado" contained the lines:

If you want to know who we are
We're the hucksters of radio . . .
We're vice-presidents and clerks;
Confidentially we're all jerks.

Allen was ordered to delete the word "hucksters" by one of the "jerks" involved. He described the relationship of program producer to network: "It's like going into a pool hall. You rent a table. Then the guy hides the cue from you."[54]

As early as 1938, a flurry of NBC interoffice memos detailed the difficulties of exerting control over Allen's scripts, culminating in Janet MacRorie's exasperated summary:

> The first draft of the continuity usually reaches us about one o'clock on Monday and from then until Wednesday at nine, post meridian, Continuity Acceptance presents politely, begs and cajoles Agency representatives to persuade their talent, namely Fred Allen, to refrain from such examples of libel, derogatory reference, vulgarity, cross-reference, and other irregularities as may have been encountered in the script before us. No representative of Continuity Acceptance has approached said Fred Allen on the matter of producing the script earlier. Our heart-felt sympathy is extended to the unfortunate person who did.[55]

This difficult three-way relationship—Allen, the agency, and the network—was to reach a peak in 1947. Television loomed on the horizon, and network continuity acceptance departments were determined to improve public image and affiliate relations by cracking down on dubious material. The controversy was sparked by the rejection of some lines in a Titus Moody routine that Allen claimed had previously been approved; J. Walter Thompson (via *Variety*) leaped to Allen's defense by claiming, "The script had been in NBC's hands since Friday afternoon; the last of the bluepenciled lines was 'the brainstorm . . . of the night guy in charge of censorship' and was thrown back at Allen 7:45 Sunday evening just as he got back from dinner."[56] Allen intimated that he was considering leaving NBC for the more liberal milieu of CBS. One of the show's writers claimed that "there are now eight guys at NBC [headquarters] who are having a field day with the script and that, since it's the only top NBC comedy show originating in New York, the web's continuity acceptance boys in Manhattan are making a super-production out of it."[57] But NBC reserved special vengeance for material that criticized its own controlling practices. In the wake of Allen's April 20 cut from the air, the network took a new militant stance toward Allen's brand of satire; as *Variety* reported: "The programming boss [Clarence Menser, who had replaced Janet MacRorie] maintains that it's bad enough for critics outside the industry to throw barbs at radio ('only I don't call them critics, they're just complainers'), but it's a black eye to radio when those from within persist in fouling up the air. 'We're just not going to take it.'"[58] This kind of publicity inspired the American Civil Liberties Union to weigh in, asking for an accounting of NBC's high-handed actions. Their letter of response to NBC President Niles Trammel's explanatory letter indicates the high stakes at risk in the networks' careful balancing act at this delicate time:

> You will undoubtedly recognize the dangers in the precedent that might have been established had the ban on unfavorable comments on the networks been further enforced. Radio, operating on a federal franchise, the ultimate ownership of which rests not with the stations but with the public, should be open to criticism. We are glad to note that the National Broadcasting Company will not hinder any criticism in the future.[59]

Ironically, it was Allen's very attitude toward the networks, among other things, that won him praise in terms normally associated with highbrow standards not familiar to popular radio. Allen became known as a "comedian's comedian," an intellectual as well as a funnyman. In tones reminiscent of the early 1930s, the *Saturday Evening Post* commented cynically:

> And since it is generally conceded that the Allen program is one of the most intelligent comedy shows on the air, some observers—those who'll still be hanging up their Christmas stockings when they're eighty—deduce that radio audiences may be growing up, that they no longer demand that their favorite programs be tailored to serve the emotional and intellectual requirements of an ape.[60]

He was compared to Mark Twain and Will Rogers, and such respected literary humorists as James Thurber and Robert Benchley admired him.[61] One "radio executive," when asked to explain why a sponsor might be willing to pay Allen's expensive program costs, stated, "Fred's stuff has a quality sign on it. Of course, he has listeners at all levels. But you would be surprised how many professors, publishers, surgeons, bishops, mathematicians are Fred Allen fans."[62] Allen was also popular among the professions he so trenchantly satirized. "Few people in the entertainment world miss his program," the same article alleged, and quoted Abel Green, editor of *Variety*: "The other comedians are Fred Allen's Bobby Sox Brigade. They swoon at Allen." Allen received a Peabody Award, for "comedy unexcelled over a period of 12 years" in 1945, his year of broadcast hiatus.[63] Its timing provoked him to wonder if this wasn't official encouragement to remain off the air: "Next year, if I keep away from Hollywood, I will probably win the Academy Award."[64]

Despite this skepticism and irreverence, Allen won praise specifically from those whose values he denigrated, largely through participation in some of the recognizable attributes of sacralized culture. He cultivated his reputation as sole author of his program. Despite one writer's assertion that, after working with his team for a while, Allen would accept material with "only minor tinkering,"[65] most accounts emphasize that Allen wrote the bulk of each program, drawing on ideas booted around by his writing team in sessions that took up Tuesday through Thursday of each week. This became a highly publicized part of the Allen persona, emphasizing his heavy involvment in each program and the grueling demands of such a schedule. Here was comedy with an intellectualized author behind it, not the work of nameless, faceless radio hacks or feminized soap opera assembly lines. Allen also participated in such widely accepted and traditionally sanctioned practices as using ethnic humor to mark out the limits of the permissible and joining in the highbrow condemnation of the popular through his scathing satires of serials and movies, and the people who enjoy them.

Despite his populist bent, Allen was not above sniping at his fans. Of the "class of people" who came to his midnight rebroadcast for Pacific Coast audiences, Allen said, "most of them look as though somebody had turned over a pool table and they crept out of the pockets." Others, he claimed, noting the number of tourists filling the New York studio, must have resulted from "a slow leak in Iowa."[66] On the other hand, his contempt for network hypocrisy in defending the cultural high ground out of the basest self-interest won him admirers from groups who looked on radio itself as overly populist. Allen's show, like Benny's, resulted in a carefully negotiated cultural balancing act that directly reflected and commented on the position of radio itself. Listeners were asked to recognize the contradictions and inconsistencies in radio's role and laugh at them. At the same time, Allen became a kind of totemic figure of resistance, a comedian agonistes standing in for the "artist" struggling with the system, positing a place outside that system for all of those who understood and appreciated him—even as they themselves worked within it, passively added to the Nielsen numbers, purchased the products that kept it going. Other key figures in radio embodied its contradictions in similar ways.

Illegitimate Theater: Lux and Mercury

As we have seen, the question of authorship, basic to cultural legitimacy, posed a problem for broadcasting. The complex and diffuse conditions of broadcasting production conflicted directly with the fundamental tenet of cultural hierarchy: that a work of art possess a sole creative author from whose individual genius the work stems. Indeed, this authorial diffusion seemed the fundamental characteristic of radio, with its production process that required the collaboration and cross-purposes of sponsors and their marketing interests, networks with their commercial purposes, agency "creative" personnel with equally suspect aesthetic ends, anonymous stables of writers, a cast of various talents, a host whose name usually led the program but whose authorial status was not entirely clear, directors, technicians, sound effects men, station managers, and on and on. Given this tossed salad of efforts, how could artistry survive? And without artistry, what was the relationship of this medium to Culture? One option was to dismiss it as "trash" not worth even bothering with (except as a sociological problem), as demonstrated in the emphasis on daytime serials' vulgar conditions of production (and reception). However, the dismissal of an entire medium out of hand flew in the face of common sense. Even the staunchest highbrow could concede that when works already possessed of artistic merit were translated into the air some genuine "Cultural" good could come out of it—witness opera and symphony orchestra broadcasts and perhaps even quality productions of legitimate drama.

Networks, as discussed above, were anxious to play along with the notion that radio could provide authentically "Cultural" experiences. Yet given the basic economic and structural conditions of the medium, how could such a quality effect be achieved? One tactic that seemed feasible in the mid-1930s was the development of the hour-length dramatic program—not a serial, not comedy, not a manifestation of vaudeville culture, but serious drama dominated by a presiding genius. Whether this genius was drawn from the ranks of Hollywood nobility (somewhat spurious, but possessed of an attractive glitter) or from the ranks of the artistically legitimate theater (but with an edge, to keep it from seeming too stuffy), it was this genius persona that provided the key to prestige status. Just such a presiding genius could be found at the heart of each of the two most successful "prestige drama" formats, *The Lux Radio Theatre* and the *Mercury Theater of the Air*.

The Lux Radio Theatre evolved from the tradition invented by Bertha Brainard in radio's first years with her *Broadcasting Broadway* feature. Later carried over into a popular and long-running series, *The First Nighter*, which debuted on NBC in 1929, the radio adaptation of Broadway plays always maintained a presence on network schedules, despite the problems of translating the stage's visual elements into a solely aural medium. Actual real-time broadcast of stage drama from the theater had been dropped early on in favor of dramatic re-creation of the theatergoing event. "The genial First Nighter," the fictional characterization of a Broadway theatergoer, strolled down Broadway and entered the "the little theater off Times Square," where an usher showed him to his seat as the curtain prepared to rise. "At intermission, between the acts, an usher would call out, 'Smoking in the downstairs and outer lobby only, please!' After the commercial a buzzer would sound and the usher would call out, 'Curtain going up!'"[67] *First Nighter* remained on the air until 1945, presenting not only theatrical adaptations but original radio dramas, some by Arch Oboler of *Lights Out!* fame. Though long-running, it never achieved the ratings of *Lux*, perhaps partially because of its relatively loose framework and lack of a central figure of identity.

Other precedents for *Lux* existed within the advertising and radio practices of its primary producer, the J. Walter Thompson Company. An innovator in the use of testimonial advertising, JWT's presence in Hollywood in connection with its celebrity campaign for Lux Toilet Soap led to its strategy of showmanship discussed in chapter 4. In particular, the groundbreaking and popular *Fleischmann's Yeast Hour* with Rudy Vallee built on the "showman" tradition pioneered by Roxy and Wendell Hall, but in this case the persona was a smoke screen. Despite Vallee's characterization as a kind of nightclub host in the show's exposition, discovering talent and inviting guests to appear, emceeing the weekly hour of entertainment from a fictional club and conversing with patrons, conducting the music, and directing the performance, the true nature of his contributions was revealed rather gleefully in a JWT internal meeting: "The facts are that Vallee doesn't know now what is going to be rehearsed this afternoon. He doesn't write one word of the script. All of the things about how he first met these people, etc., we make up for him. . . . This was done so successfully that all the theatrical publications are now hailing Vallee as the greatest showman in radio, not second even to Roxy."[68]

When asked whether this widespread credit to Vallee had been actively encouraged by JWT press releases and publicity (Helen Lansdowne Resor asked, "Was that inspired by us?"), John U. Reber, JWT's Radio Department head, replied, "I don't think so. They fell for it." The in-house reason given for the development of this technique was to extend the benefit of Vallee's name and reputation over the course of the entire hour-long program, lending his seal of approval and mark of personal genuis (though this time of a strictly popular variety) to all of the various acts that appeared on the Vallee show—specifically so that people would not switch their dials to other programs during the times that Vallee himself was not on the air. Thus, the notion of "authorship" had a commercial utility as well.

Though JWT had originated *The Lux Radio Theatre* for Lever Brothers in 1934 as a direct competitor to *First Nighter*, produced in New York and based on Broadway theatricals, the agency soon realized that, in quantity and in entertainment standards, New York theatrical material was not suited to the radio audience. Too much of it depended on the sheerly visual, as in the craze for musical and dance-based productions; material considered acceptable in New York could not always find approval in living rooms across the country; and the number of plays available for adaptation could not meet radio's heavy production demands. Hollywood began to look like a more promising source for mass-appeal entertainment properties, and with a strong base of star and studio contacts already in place through Danny Danker and the JWT Los Angeles Bureau, production of the show shifted to Hollywood in 1936 with Danker at its helm. As *Variety* later explained it, "The New York Thompsonites decided to reward Danker [for his success with Vallee and Lux soap] by moving Lux into his bailiwick and give him complete charge."[69] Along the lines of their strategy with Rudy Vallee, JWT sought a strong central personality around whom to base the program, one who could serve as the "author" and dominant associative influence to guarantee the show's "Hollywoodness" and entertainment value in much the same way that Vallee's imprint marked the program of popular music. Few other directors possessed the flair for self-publicity that Cecil B. DeMille did;

his reputation for showmanship in film matched the image that JWT encouraged for itself in the field of radio.

Though *Lux* did not possess the pretensions to high culture that Orson Welles's debut would, the agency and its producers worked hard to maintain a first-class, glamorous image. The reasons for this have to do not only with selling products but with attracting Hollywood studios to participate. For *Lux* to retain value as a promotional medium for studio properties and stars, the actual selling of soap needed to be kept at a distance from the program's Hollywood elements, lest too direct an association with commercialism tarnish the product that Hollywood had to sell. DeMille played a crucial role in this important mediation. First of all, introductory and closing material was used by JWT to emphasize his persona as producer/director (often seeming to include elements of writer and agent as well), thus reinforcing DeMille's authorial presence and obscuring the actual functions of the agency. One introduction serves as an example:

> If there's a little more grey in my hair this week, believe me it came from the task of finding the right dramatic material for such splended artists as Bette Davis and Spencer Tracy. In fact we considered and rejected dozens of plays before selecting the one we think is perfect, "Dark Victory." As a producer, I've always disliked the type of play known as a "vehicle," one that's designed for the actor instead of the audience. And when there are two noted players in a cast, there's a double danger that the play will turn out to be a double vehicle. But "Dark Victory" has grip and power and human appeal. And when our curtain falls on the third act, I believe you'll agree with me that this play is really a great emotional experience. Each woman in our audience will unconsciously put herself in the place of Judith Traherne; each man will wonder what he would have done as Dr. Frederick Steele.[70]

Second, his opening monologues and short closing dialogues with that evening's stars worked to promote them and their upcoming pictures, and usually worked in a very mild reference to the sponsoring product:

> Tonight even the unemotional lights in front of the Lux Radio Theatre have a special glow of pride in our players and our play, "Dark Victory." Our stage is set for a prize-winning achievement—and so is the stage in your home, when Lux Flakes is starred. Many domestic producers have discovered that casting Lux Flakes in a leading role is [chuckle] good business at the household box office.

Most Hollywood stars were not required to endorse Lux soap directly; their lines of dialogue stuck carefully to upcoming films and small items of personal promotion. DeMille lent an air of ad-libbed intimacy to these celebrity conversations, though each was in fact carefully scripted by the agency writers assigned to the show. His third important function was as narrator of the film adaptation's action. Vital due to the abbreviated form into which Lux had to condense film properties, DeMille's crossover into narrator saved him from the taint of mere product spokesman and gave him a dramatized role to play—distracting attention from the role of "Cecil B. DeMille, producer/director" that the agency actually hired him to perform.

In actuality, Danny Danker is the person most closely associated with production of *Lux*, from the decision to hire DeMille to negotiations with studios for stars and suitable properties. The programs were written and produced by JWT staff, including most notably George Wells, who served as primary writer for the first several years and moved on to script movies at MGM; and Sanford Barnett, who served first as director but took over as head writer after Wells; along with many others who wrote the commercial continuity and produced the weekly broadcast. DeMille's actual role was to show up at the final dress rehearsal to run through a final version with the cast, then to host the broadcast that night.

This strategy of "false authorization" was highly successful, as attested by articles in the press that hailed this very popular show. A review in the *New York Times* of the *Lux* production of *Love Is News*, starring Bob Hope, Madeleine Carroll, and Ralph Bellamy, credited DeMille with "smoothness of production, astute casting and judicious choice of plays" that reflected "the De Mille touch."[71] An article several months later credited DeMille with all of these functions, and allowed him to expand on them in his producer persona, a role DeMille seemed happy to play on the air and off:

> Here in Hollywood I have tried to recreate the glamour and mystery of the old stage days of handsome men and beautiful women. Selection of plays is a matter of finding one the American people will want to hear. Actors are chosen in the same way—largely, it is a matter of determining the ones favored by listeners for the roles to be played. Then we set to work to make radio translate the scene as well as sound.[72]

The Christian Science Monitor ran a lengthy piece in 1944 crediting DeMille not only as director and producer, but with having come up with the basic idea for the show:

No one could have been better prepared to take the show over its early hurdles than DeMille. To the opinion of the experts, who said no one would listen to a solid hour of drama over the air, he replied, "Let's try it, anyway." Accustomed to handling large groups of actors and the biggest, he found it easy to quiet them in front of the microphone. He was, of course, an ideal choice as liaison man between movies and the radio, since he had worked in both fields.[73]

Whether or not this misleading information was deliberately put forth by agency publicity or whether writers in other media simply absorbed it from DeMille's persona on air, it worked in much the same way as had their technique with Rudy Vallee. Not only did DeMille's persona bespeak "Hollywoodness" and lend a consistency to the weekly dramas, his active impersonation of the role of author helped to conceal the hybridity of the radio adaptation format and to lend it an aura of cultural legitimacy that this entirely mass-produced (and, indeed, second- or thirdhand) form would otherwise lack. For the audience, DeMille's persona and the already-known quality of the former feature films that the program adapted promised a preestablished relationship, a guarantee of cultural acceptability and popularity (and avoidance of the controversial and "tasteless") that other stand-alone or original dramas could not provide. The presence of Hollywood-authorized stars lent an air of established glamour and grandeur of the movie variety. In turn, DeMille's radio evocation of the stage—"the curtain goes up," "our stage is set," and so on, and the name of the program itself—borrowed a little bit from Broadway and the legitimate theater to bridge the gap between Hollywood and the more sacralized territory of live drama. DeMille had also directed Broadway productions, so his author persona could easily be extended along these lines.[74]

It is a measure of the taken-for-grantedness of DeMille's authorship that, in the throes of a union dispute in 1945, when DeMille very publicly left the air as a consequence of refusing to support AFRA's (American Federation of Radio Artists) opposition to a California anti-labor bill, organizers responded by "outing" his nominal role in the Lux program. In a rebuttal to a speech made by DeMille defending his action, broadcast on March 31, 1945, over the Mutual network, an AFRA spokesman revealed:

In paragraph seven he [DeMille] said, "I have been asked to tell you the reason I no longer *conduct* the Radio Theatre of the Air. . . ." The masquerade has been going on long enough. Mr. DeMille never conducted the program, nor did he produce it nor did he direct it. Mr. DeMille was a narrator on the program, came to dress rehearsal on Sunday, read his lines which were prepared for him, and returned on Monday evening to read them over the air.[75]

This spokesman was Orson Welles. In stripping the mask of authorship from DeMille, Welles sought to remove the facade of "Culture" from the commercial enterprise of radio, to reveal economic conditions of labor disputes and heavy-handed management politics that underlay the thin and always precarious veneer of cultural authority. Ironically, Welles himself filled a role similar to DeMille's for the radio program associated with his name. Only this time, the cultural stakes were higher.

Packaging Welles

By 1938, Orson Welles's reputation as the boy genius of the New York stage had been secured. With his repertory company, the Mercury Theater, Welles had mounted a series of acclaimed productions, including the groundbreaking "Negro *Macbeth*," *The Cradle Will Rock*, and *Dr. Faustus*, directed for the WPA. Dramatist, actor, director, and producer, in his theatrical efforts Welles truly did perform all the roles that *Lux*'s DeMille took false credit for. In addition, Welles had made his radio debut a few years earlier on CBS in the *March of Time* series, followed by several well-received performances on CBS's *Columbia Workshop* and also, in 1937, as the voice of Lamont Cranston, *The Shadow*. Shortly, Hollywood would call, with its extraordinary offer that resulted in *Citizen Kane*. Welles's personal reputation for cultural genius reached its peak in May 1938, when his face appeared on the cover of *Time* magazine; inside, a caption read "Marvelous Boy."[76]

On the radio front, President Roosevelt's exploration of radio's public address potential had resulted in increased controversy over the appropriate social and political role of the broadcast medium. The networks, at first trying "to please the administration by donating time for administration speeches and supporting the New Deal recovery efforts"[77] and allocating extensive network coverage to the president's Fireside Chats and activities of the executive branch, found themselves once again under fire as custodians of the national voice, particularly because many of their affiliates were owned by newspaper interests deeply opposed to Roosevelt's New Deal policies. In return, Roosevelt made the cross-ownership of radio stations by newpapers an issue of personal concern and closely supervised appointments to the FCC and the station licensing process. By 1938, it was clear that Roosevelt would support the reopening of the commercial network monopoly question, as indeed happened in 1940. Once again the networks sought to divert attention from radio's political pitfalls by emphasizing its important cultural function. CBS was the first to recognize the confluence of its own need for cultural standing and the value of the persona "Orson Welles" as a cultural commodity.

In the summer of 1938, CBS contracted with Welles for a weekly dramatic series to begin in July. Hailed in network press releases as "one of the youngest and ablest of this generation's actor-directors" and acknowledged as the leader of the Mercury Theater, "the most virile and exciting of the new theater movements," Welles, with his troupe, would present nine hour-length broadcasts on Monday nights at 9:00 beginning on July 11 (replacing *The Lux Radio Theatre* for the summer). According to the network:

> Welles has been given carte blanche to choose his own medium and his own subjects, and stated he will reveal the precise nature of the presentations within the near future. The programs are to have the general title of "First Person Singular" and, besides being their star actor, Welles will write, cast, direct and produce the series. The entire Mercury Theater company will be at Welles' disposal and he will have a free hand in the selection of material and technique.

To dispel any lingering doubts that the author of this series would be Orson Welles and no other, the network went on to promise: "No Columbia director will be assigned to the broadcasts, but Davidson Taylor of the CBS program department is to act as general supervisor to coordinate the resources which will be placed at Welles' command."[78] And lest the cultural mission of this enterprise be at all suspect, a second press release reassured:

> For what is believed to be the first time in radio history an entire series of programs will be devoted to the great stories of classic and contemporary literature written in the first person singular and enacted as the experience of an individual. . . . Although Welles has not yet revealed what classics he will select, he expects to explore fields of literature heretofore untouched by radio and bring to that medium the same spirit of adventure which he brought to the theater last season.[79]

This repetition of the words "classics" and "literature" sought to distinguish this dramatic program from the stuff of everyday original radio drama and comedy, and to bestow on it the same aura of cultural legitimacy that Welles's authorial presence sought to guarantee.

John Houseman's memoirs make it clear that this construction of Welles as author supreme rested at least partially on the same kind of fiction as DeMille's direction of *Lux*. At first Welles, fascinated with this new medium, exerted his authorial control over all aspects of production, from writing to sound effects. Houseman describes the process of selecting and condensing the initial *First Person Singular* broadcast. Having first selected the classic *Treasure Island*, Welles left it to Houseman—who was totally unfamiliar with radio—to educate himself in the art of radio script writing and streamline the story into something resembling fifty minutes. However, less than a week before the broadcast, Welles determined that a much more impressive debut could be had with *Dracula*—from the original by Bram Stoker. By late afternoon two days before the first scheduled rehearsal, Welles and Houseman had barracaded themselves behind a pile of cut-and-pasted excerpts at nearby Reuben's delicatessen, emerging triumphantly the next day with a completed script only hours before rehearsal: "Then, just before nine, as a few early birds appeared for breakfast and the streets outside came to life, we nailed down the Count, with a burnt stake through his heart, and rose from our table. Three days later *Dracula* went on the air as the opener of what was to become a legendary radio series."[80]

From the beginning, Welles had sought to draw on his association with the culturally legitimate to open up a sphere of aesthetics and performance unique to radio—to use his cultural credentials to create a new kind of form and, as we shall see, a new kind of authorship. Initial press releases quote him as saying:

> I think it is time . . . that radio came to realize the fact that no matter how wonderful a play may be for the stage it cannot be as wonderful for the air. The Mercury Theater has no intention of producing its stage repertoire in these broadcasts. Instead, we plan to bring to radio the experimental techniques which have proved so successful in another medium and to treat radio itself with the intelligence and respect such a beautiful and powerful medium deserves.[81]

Later, on the occasion of the first broadcast of the program under Campbell Soup sponsorship, Welles responded to the announcer's invitation to "give us a word or two about the play" by making the distinction clear: "Gladly, Mr. Hill, but if you'll pardon me it's not a play, it's a story. You see, I think that radio broadcasting is different from motion pictures and the theater and I'd like to keep it that way. The Campbell Playhouse is situated in a regular studio, not a theater. There's only one illusion I'd like to create: the illusion of the story."[82]

An even greater illusion was that of authorship itself in this new medium, as Welles would soon learn, but meantime the Mercury Theater company experimented with forms of narrative and ways of framing both dramatic storytelling and audience positioning that truly did create a unique voice in radio. For the initial production of *Dracula*, Welles, Houseman, et al. told the story in the form of diary excerpts, both read and enacted, in which Welles played the roles of both doctor and narrator. In closing, Welles replaced the usual interview or commercial plug, usually done in first person and addressed to the audience in second person, with a twist of the narrative frame. First reassuring listeners that this is just a fiction and need not worry them, Welles tells them that they can turn off the radio and go to bed. But then a wolf howls, and he goes on: "That's alright, you can rest peacefully, that's just sound effects. . . . There! Over there in the shadows— see? It's nothing . . . nothing at all. . . . But remember, ladies and gentlemen [and here Welles falls into his Count Dracula accent], there are wolves . . . there are vampires . . . such things do exist."[83] This mixture of self-conscious showmanship, direct address, and fictional frame were rarely attempted and virtually never achieved as successfully as by Welles.

For the next broadcast, an adaptation of John Buchan's *The Thirty-Nine Steps*, the production eschewed the typical first-person narrative introduction and plunged direcly into straight dramatic action. Only twenty minutes into the show did Welles turn to the microphone as combination narrator/character, saying, "This is the fellow speaking . . . the fellow with the brown paper parcel and the cut across his knuckles. This is what he [Hannay, the main character] said. . . ."[84] At this point, the narration switched to Hannay's voice, though it was performed by Welles in both cases. Here the Mercury program created a complex type of address to the audience that at once played with standard radio narrational and formal codes and used them to create an even tighter illusion of dramatic reality.

By the end of September, Welles's time and attention were far more taken up with the impending disaster of his theatrical production *Danton's Death*. Houseman continued to supervise most of the radio series's writing and editing, making selections of material with Welles's approval: "The material was chosen by Welles and myself on the basis of contrast and personal preference with occasional suggestions from the outside. In each case we would discuss the tone and mood of the production and then I would go off and write it."[85] Howard Koch had been hired as additional scriptwriter, assisted by Ann Froelich, with Paul Stewart as associate producer and working director. Already Welles, though participating at some points in selection and writing, and with all decisions subject to his approval, was fully participating in the production of the program only at the final dress rehearsal and in the actual performance. Here, however, his contributions were essential and truly characteristic:

> Sundays, at eight, we went on the air. Beginning in the early afternoon . . . two simultaneous dramas were unfolded each week in the stale, tense air of CBS Studio One: The minor drama of the current show and the major drama of Orson's titanic struggle to get it on. Sweating, howling, disheveled, and singlehanded he wrestled with chaos and time—always conveying an effect of being alone, traduced by his collaborators, surrounded by treachery, ignorance, sloth, indifference, incompetence and—more often than not—downright sabotage. Every Sunday it was touch and go. As the hands of the clock moved relentlessly toward air time the crisis grew more extreme. . . . Scripts and scores flew through the air, doors were slammed, batons smashed. Scheduled for six—but usually nearer seven—there was a dress rehearsal, a thing of wild improvisations and irrevocable catastrophes.
>
> After that, with only a few minutes to go, there was a final frenzy of correction and reparation, of utter confusion and absolute horror, aggravated by the gobbling of sandwiches and the bolting of oversized milkshakes. By now it was less than a minute to air time.
>
> At that instant, quite regularly week after week, with not a second to spare, the buffoonery stopped. Suddenly out of chaos, the show emerged—delicately poised, meticulously executed, precise as clockwork, smooth as satin. And above us all, like a rainbow over storm clouds, stood Orson on his podium, sonorous and heroic, a leader of men surrounded by his band of loyal followers; a giant in action, serene and radiant with the joy of a hard battle bravely fought, a great victory snatched from the jaws of disaster.[86]

Other properties selected for treatment the first season included the postponed *Treasure Island*, *A Tale of Two Cities*, *The Thirty-Nine Steps*, *The Count of Monte Cristo*, and G. K. Chesterton's *The Man Who Was Thursday*.[87]

The shows's ratings, though respectable, climbed to rival *Lux* only after the famous *War of the Worlds* broadcast on October 30, 1938. Welles and Houseman had selected the property and Howard Koch and Ann Froelich did the condensing and scripting, with Houseman's assistance. The Thursday before the broadcast, a recording was made of the first rehearsal, and the writing team plus director Paul Stewart made further changes: "We all agreed that its only chance of coming off lay in emphasizing its newscast style—its simultaneous, eyewitness quality."[88] Welles arrived from the theater after the Saturday rehearsal had ended, and so confronted the material for the first time on the night of the broadcast. Houseman credits Welles with the direction, pacing, and vocal emphasis that led to the very marked impact of the show. "His sense of tempo, that night, was infallible. . . . The broadcast . . . had its own reality, the reality of emotionally felt time and space."[89] This reality was attested to by the panic reaction that soon came crashing down on the heads of the Mercury Theater troupe, resolving into days of publicity, several lawsuits against the network, and, for Orson Welles, a landmark offer from RKO to direct a film in Hollywood with as much freedom and reliance on the Welles reputation as CBS had promised.

Also as a result of the *War of the Worlds* phenomenon, in December CBS managed to attract a sponsor for the program—almost simultaneously with the closing of the Mercury Theater, defeated by overly elaborate productions, poor reviews, and Welles's increasing absence. After an obligatory visit to the Camden, New Jersey, soup plant, Welles and his remaining troupe now became the spokesmen for the Campbell's Soup Company, no longer under CBS's arms-length control but supervised by Ward Wheelock, president of Campbell's ad agency. The *Mercury Theater of the Air* had become the *Campbell Playhouse*. Now the meetings to decide upcoming productions included not only Welles and Houseman but also Wheelock and other agency executives. Not only did commercials have to be worked into each week's program, Welles and guest stars were required to make product plugs along the same lines as those done on the Lux program. And pressure to popularize the program's literary selections began to be felt. Wheelock had performed a survey for Campbell prior to proposing sponsorship; according to its findings, members of the public surveyed preferred more movie adaptations featuring film stars, less use of the first-person narrative, and less Welles.[90]

The new series debuted on December 9, 1938, with an adaptation of Daphne du Maurier's best-selling novel *Rebecca*. Campbell and Whee-lock clearly had set out to walk that delicate cultural line between the popular and the authorized. The program opened with a full biogra-phy of Orson Welles, dwelling on his artistry and genius and making good use of his *War of the Worlds* fame. To emphasize further the show's cultural claims, the show's announcer—not Welles, but a com-mercial spokesman—made this appeal:

> You know the manufacturers of Campbell's soup don't believe in all this talk about the radio audience having the average intelligence mentality of an eight year old child. They think the radio listeners are the same people who go to the pictures and to the theater and who read books. They rea-son that even the most popular radio entertainment should be addressed to the adult population citizenry of America.[91]

The announcer then brought out Orson Welles, not to comment on soup or radio itself, but to introduce the evening's dramatic selection. But at the end of the broadcast, after a commercial for Campbell's soup made by the announcer, Welles introduced Margaret Sullavan, the star of the production, and with Daphne du Maurier herself con-tributing by shortwave connection, they discussed not only the up-coming Selznick film production of *Rebecca*, but the sponsor's prod-uct. Sullavan herself was required to deliver the plug, "You know, two things I like very much are good stories and good soup. And when I tell you my idea of a great soup—that's Campbell's chicken soup—that, Mr. Welles, is no story." Welles replied, "I'm glad you feel that way. Nice of you to say so." Now, as John Houseman put it:

> Welles, in addition to being "producer, writer, director, star and narrator" of the Campbell Playhouse now became its leading salesman: he assumed the role of a sophisticated world traveler who, having savored all the great-est broths and potages of the civilized world, still returned with joy and appreciation to Campbell's delicious chicken-and-rice, tomato and pea.[92]

It was a role from which Welles would increasingly distance himself.

Campbell, however, was pleased enough with the critical and rat-ings success its venture enjoyed that it renewed at the end of the spring season. Among the selections discussed for possible broadcast from June to December 1939 were *Wuthering Heights*, *The Philadelphia Story*, *The Little Foxes*, and *Make Way for Tomorrow*—an interesting list in that all were based on original novels or plays, but their marketability to audiences depended on their publicity as films recently released or currently in production in Hollywood. Yet this connection was played down in press releases announcing the new series, and its cultural legitimacy emphasized with such phrases as "the list of its broadcasts reads like a library of the world's best books" and "bringing to the microphone the great books as well as the most famous stage plays of the world."

Meantime, Howard Koch and Ann Froelich had left the program with offers from Hollywood, and Houseman and Paul Stewart resumed primary responsibility for broadcasts, with Welles appearing only on the night of the live program, now Fridays at 9:00. In June, Welles received his stunning offer from RKO and departed for the coast. Campbell's resisted the suggestion that the show's production shift to Los Angeles as well, so for most of the fall season of 1939 Houseman produced the program in New York while Welles flew in once a week for the broadcast. Not until November did Campbell's "relent" and allow the show to move West. But in December, Welles and Houseman had a dramatic and long-in-the-making falling out that resulted in Houseman's withdrawal from the program. By February 1940, despite Welles's efforts to keep the show going—and to preseve the only regular income he now had, in the wake of his now-legendary filmic difficulties—Campbell's resigned from sponsorship and Welles was off the air. His peculiar compromise between high culture and commercialism, bound up in the authorial persona, would soon come back to haunt him.

In late 1939 sociologist Hadley Cantril embarked on a detailed study of the *War of the Worlds* broadcast and its impact, under the aegis of the Princeton Office of Radio Research. Along with the results of his surveys and analysis of the panic's causes and effects, Cantril wished to publish a complete version of the radio script. As it was eventually published, the table of contents of Cantril's study contains, under its heading "The Broadcast," the attribution "Script by Howard Koch." In his introduction, Cantril mentions that "Howard Koch has kindly permitted us to publish for the first time his brilliant adaptation of the *War of the Worlds*" and further chips away at Welles's facade of authorship with this seemingly innocuous introductory narrative: "At eight p.m. eastern standard time on the evening of October 30, 1938, Orson Welles with an innocent little group of actors took his place before the microphone in a New York studio of the Columbia Broadcasting System. He carried with him Howard Koch's freely adapted version of H. G. Wells's imaginative novel, *War of the Worlds*."[93] Using the traditional means of ascribing authorship—and ignoring all that radio's unique circumstances added to the complexity of this culturally weighted definition—Cantril came down clearly on the side of Koch, reducing Welles to mere bearer of the script. When Cantril in April 1940 applied for permission to publish in this form, Welles objected vehemently to this cultural intervention, calling it "an error so grave, and in my opinion so detrimental to my own reputation that I cannot in all fairness speak well of it until some reparation is made" and "something worse than merely untrue." Cantril offered several emendations, including "Script ideas and development by Orson Welles assisted by John Houseman and Mercury Theatre staff and written by Howard Koch under the direction of Mr. Welles." This was too elaborate and still incorrect, according to Welles; after an urgent exchange of telegrams he declared bluntly: "Can see no conceivable reason for your steadfast refusal to believe *The War of the Worlds* was not only my conception but also, properly and exactly speaking, my creation. Once again, finally, and I promise for the last time, Howard Koch did not write *The War of the Worlds*. Any statement to this effect is untrue and immeasurably detrimental to me."[94] Cantril, with ample evidence to the contrary (as far as the traditional evidence of "writing" was concerned) from Houseman's secretary and the other contributors, held his ground; the attribution stood and in the end very little fallout occurred—because by the time the book achieved circulation, Welles's reputation-saving masterpiece *Citizen Kane* made good on all the postponed promise of genius. Here again, however, the problem of authorship would later rear its head.[95]

What made the matter so urgent in Welles's eyes? One of his biographers, Simon Callow, offers this explanation:

> The note of desperation is explained by his public standing at that moment. . . . He was surfing on a tidal wave of publicity which threatened to engulf him, since there was nothing visible to justify it; his most recent work in the theatre had passed either unnoticed or unloved, his radio programme, though commanding solid audience figures, generated little excitement. None of his Hollywood projects had materialised. *The War of the Worlds* was, in effect, his only real claim to widespread fame: it was the reason that he was in Hollywood at all, the real reason that he had been able to negotiate the famous contract, the only living proof of his multi-faceted genius. The revelation that he had not actually written

it would deprive his image of one of its crucial dimensions, making him look a fraud; the discovery that the whole thing had been an accident would have finished him off for good.[96]

Welles had come squarely up against the bottom-line situation of the artist as commodity: the very conditions that made his authorial persona possible worked at every moment to undercut it; his artistic viability rested on an artificial construction of singular genius, from the beginning an impossible mongrel creation of inherently oppositional circumstances. Radio's characteristic compromise between the vulgar popular and the sacralized cultural produced a hybrid constantly under attack from both sides, with Welles and the territory he had sought to carve out for himself squeezed desperately in the middle. *Citizen Kane's* impressive debut quieted this dilemma, but only temporarily.

Welles went on to do a substantial amount of work in radio, a chapter of his career that still has not been sufficiently examined. After a hiatus during which *Citizen Kane* was created, Welles returned to the air in 1941with his new *Orson Welles Almanac* for Lady Esther products. This program represented the realization of an idea Welles had developed as early as 1935, with plans to distribute via transcription through Ziv productions. The 1941 version again featured Welles as showman and personality, using his persona to unite a mixed bag of stories, dramatic readings, and guest interviews. During the 1940s he made numerous appearances on other popular radio shows, including those hosted by Jack Benny, Fred Allen, Edgar Bergen, and Bob Hope. He served as guest host on Fred Allen's show in the summer of 1943. During the war years, Welles produced and starred in *Ceiling Unlimited* and *Hello Americans*, both patriotic efforts for audiences at home and abroad, respectively. *Orson Welles Almanac* would return to the air under different sponsors and guises twice more: once in 1944, sponsored by the Mobil Oil Company as more or less a celebrity interview show, and again in 1945, as a political commentary program that ran until October 1946 under the sponsorship of Lear Incorporated. Two more programs returned to the dramatic format: *This Is My Best*, which Welles began on in March but was fired from in April, and the *Mercury Summer Theater* from June to September 1946.[97]

Yet the Welles with whom most Americans became familiar was not the actor/dramatist working, however untraditionally, in drama or discussion under the aegis of his own name, but the celebrity who made guest appearances on the most popular shows. On such programs his status as recognized cultural commodity could be gently parodied, usually by Welles himself. In this appearance on *The Fred Allen Show* in 1942, after an elaborate setup in which various Welles underlings appear to make sure conditions are exactly right for the grand star, Allen addresses Welles's genius image:

> *Allen*: I always pictured you as a man from another planet, a transcendentalist, a genius, a legend in the making—and here you are, joking and laughing with little old egg-laying me.
>
> *Welles*: Fred, I wish somebody would do something about this Superman myth the public has swallowed about me. It's embarrassing. After all, I'm just an ordinary guy.

A summary of Welles's "ordinary" childhood and early career follows, which reveals him entering Northwestern University at the age of five, majoring in Esperanto, graduating at age seven, magna cum laude, hanging around with Einstein until they fell out over the theory of relativity, then resigning from the Smithsonian Institute at the age of twelve and going into the theater. Now, at last, he is looking for a partner for his new radio program and has settled on Fred Allen. Their first production will be *Les Misérables*, which Allen agrees to run through on his program. The play is introduced:

> Orchestra (Heavy dramatic music . . . Fades)
>
> *Welles*: (Dramatic) *Les Miserables*! Victor Hugo's immortal story of a soul transfigured and redeemed, through suffering. This is an Orson Welles production.
>
> *Announcer*: Radio version of *Les Miserables* prepared by—
>
> *Welles*: Orson Welles!
>
> *Announcer*: Directed by—
>
> *Welles*: Orson Welles!
>
> *Announcer*: Starring—
>
> *Welles*: Orson Welles! During Orson Welles' presentation of *Les Miserables*, Mr. Welles will be assisted by that sterling dramatic actor of stage, screen, and radio, Mr.—
>
> *Orchestra*: (Heavy dramatic music . . . Fades quickly)

Not only is his name omitted, but as the skit progresses Allen's contributions prove to amount to a knock on the door, the blowing of a whistle, and a gurgle, while Welles carries the production.[98]

However, by 1941, pressing issues other than artistic integrity or definitions of high culture had begun to preoccupy the radio industry, and indeed the American public. These issues would not be forgotten, nor would the conflicted realm of gender, racial, and ethnic distinctions that radio so precariously controlled during its first two decades be simply set aside. Rather, the nationalizing and unifying capacities of this now established medium would be put to a new test, with higher stakes than ever before. As the war in Europe rumbled ominously on the margins of radio practice, definitions of American identity and lines of difference—not only between groups of Americans but between the United States and its enemies abroad—began to place a new set of demands on the industry, its regulators, program practices, and the listening public, now a citizenry unified by war but deeply divided by the very cultural categories and exclusions that radio itself had promoted and sustained.

EIGHT

On the Home Front: Fighting to Be Heard

The fundamental questions posed to the U.S. public by broadcasting's centralizing address from the 1920s—Who are we? Who are we not?—took on a dramatically increased urgency and public importance in the late 1930s and early 1940s as U.S. involvement in World War II began to look inevitable. Radio itself functioned to help create that inevitability, as several historians have argued. Richard Steele notes that in the wake of the NAB's 1939 "equal time" code (instituted to keep controversial speakers like Father Charles Coughlin from buying time independently to espouse political views),[1] commercially sponsored "morale-building" programs took the place of outright political commentary and debate. Although a careful attempt was made to balance interventionist and anti-interventionist political speeches and commentary, "they constituted only a small part of the vast amount of radio time devoted directly or indirectly to foreign policy issues. Most of what the public heard in that regard was 'public service' programming aimed at promoting various aspects of the administration's mobilization effort."[2]

Edward M. Kirby, chief of the Radio Branch of the Bureau of Public Relations of the War Department, emphatically confirms this perception in his account of radio's relationship to the war. By 1941, he claims, sponsored programs with strong interventionist themes that glossed over the actual politics involved were "*not only permitted but encouraged*" by the radio networks.[3] This substitution of morale building on the home front for more open and balanced political debate not only tipped the balance toward support of war mobilization, it forced attention to the question of American unity and cultural identity in a way not seen since the early 1920s, bringing radio's unique nationalizing address into the center of the task of recruiting a nation for war.

230

Steele concludes that radio's hawkish orientation resulted less from widely held political views within the industry than from the desire to cooperate, and to be seen to be cooperating, with the Roosevelt administration in order to avoid the quite explicit threat of unfavorable resolution of the chain broadcasting monopoly investigation initiated by the FCC in 1938.[4] Also operative was the never spoken but always present fear of direct government takeover of the industry as had happened during World War I:

> The insecurity that prompted that cooperation intensified in the months before the outbreak of the European war with indications that the FCC was considering new regulations and that the long-suspended antitrust ax was about to fall. Moreover, immediately after German troops swept into Poland, the White House put the industry on notice that should radio fail to serve the nation's interest in the current emergency, the administration was prepared, as [Stephen T. Early, Roosevelt's press secretary] expressed it, to "make it behave."[5]

The film industry responded to a similar situation, having been charged in 1938 with antitrust violations. In July 1940, the Hays Office established the Motion Picture Committee Cooperating for National Defense; in August, several prominent Hollywood figures offered their support for the mobilization efforts; in November, the Justice Department settled its case in a manner very favorable to large studio interests.[6]

Apprehensions along these lines motivated Edward M. Kirby, in 1940 director of public relations for the National Association of Broadcasters, to undertake an investigation of government plans for radio on behalf of his anxious constituency—perhaps additionally motivated by congressional hearings called to investigate the contested nomination to the FCC of Thadeus Brown, which had exposed "the financial manipulations of the major networks and of the RCA" to the American public.[7] Kirby later claimed that his inquiries disclosed absolutely no organized plan in place for wartime broadcasting in 1940, or even any much-discussed plan, and that the effect of his active approach was his appointment as "Civilian Advisor to the Secretary of War for Radio."[8] Later this evolved into a separate Bureau of Public Relations of the War Department, comprising several branches that included Press, Radio, and Women's Interest, with Kirby at the head of the Radio Branch. In that capacity Kirby began to involve the industry formally in defense-related work, bringing in broadcast executives to staff the Radio Branch, with the clearly recognized goal of emerging "unscathed and unshackled" by government when war broke out—or, as Kirby succinctly put it, "not with a General in the control room."⁹

In light of this enterprise, Kirby proudly points to three decisive radio undertakings that increased public support for Roosevelt's interventionist stance. First, the three radio networks participated enthusiastically in the broadcast of the so-called free training maneuvers, carried out by the U.S. Army in Louisiana and Arkansas in the summer of 1941, sending mobile correspondents to cover the action on an intensive, day-by-day basis. Furthermore, broadcasts from the war game field were intercut on network broadcasts with actual coverage of the war in Europe—brought to the United States by transcription. The purpose, according to Kirby, was "to establish *psychological parity* with the European conflict," placing American troops' war maneuvers in the same imaginary space as overseas battles and helping the American public to visualize an American army in Europe. Indeed, these cleverly edited pieces may have helped to convince some listeners that our troops were already fighting alongside the European allies, aiding the climate of interventionist inevitability.

Second in Kirby's account were the sponsored programs mentioned above, especially the broadcasts from U.S. Army camps by such major stars as Bob Hope and regular programs like Coca-Cola's *Parade of Spotlight Bands*, which featured the nation's top popular bands performing at different army bases, five nights a week. These shows, along with efforts to increase the participation of men and women in uniform on the major quiz shows, according to Kirby, "*gave the Army ready-made audiences numbering in the millions—which it would not have had otherwise.*"¹⁰ Later, these programs were joined by a host of shows produced in cooperation with government groups as diverse as the Office of War Information, the Defense Department, the Navy and Army Air Corps, the Treasury Department, and even the Immigration and Naturalization Service. Third, Kirby discusses the roots of the Armed Forces Radio Service in the shortwave broadcast of sports results to troops stationed in Iceland in the summer of 1941. This led to the rebroadcast of regular network programming abroad—at first complete with commercials, though these were later deleted as "too demoralizing"—and eventually the establishment of portable transmitting stations that the U.S. troops could set up for the rebroadcast of AFRS transcriptions as they moved overseas and into the South Pacific.

NBC's records indicate how widespread were the as-yet uncoordinated efforts toward interventionist programming by 1941 in an in-house report titled "In Defense of America: A Nation Listens." The report tallied up "defense broadcasts" from January to July 1941—months before Pearl Harbor—and arrived at a total of 627 separate broadcasts on NBC's two networks, in cooperation with the Treasury Department, the War Department, the U.S. Navy, the "US Govt. Administration," and special organizations and service groups. Of the subject matter of the programs, the largest category by far was "civilian defense and morale," with 233 programs, followed by "production for defense" with 153 and "general defense talks" with 142. The programs ranged from weekly series to special one-time reports and discussions.

Series included *I'm an American*, produced in cooperation with the Immigration and Naturalization Service, which "introduce[d] to listeners distinguished naturalized Americans who discuss[ed] the democratic way of life," aired in a lackluster Sunday noon time slot on the Blue network; *Speaking of Liberty*, produced by the Council for Democracy, in a fairly desirable Thursday early-evening (6:30–6:45) slot on the more commercial Red network, featuring well-known authors and journalists discussing "the problems facing America's democracy"; and the high-profile *Defense for America* from 7:00 to 7:30 Saturday nights on Red, whose favorable spot on the schedule reflected the buying power and interests of its sponsor, the National Association of Manufacturers. (Otherwise, it is hard to imagine how the program's "actual visits to plants where tools of national defense are now being turned out" could have proven so riveting as to compete with other Saturday-night network offerings.)[11]

Another polished and popular series in the very favorable Tuesday 8:30–9:00 slot was *For America We Sing*, a patriotic celebration of America's musical heritage, produced on behalf of the Defense Savings Bond Campaign of the Treasury Department by Frank and Anne Hummert—though this connection is never mentioned in official NBC documents. In fact, a memo from Frank Hummert to Niles Trammel of NBC in October 1941 objects to some reports of his involvement: "I know the boys were trying to be kind to me, but as you know, I do not want my name used in connection with the Treasury performance. . . . You will recall when you and I first arranged for this series, that this point was brought up then and it was agreed that no publicity connecting me with the performance would go out."[12] Whether this was natural modesty or unwillingness to extend such courtesy to every needy government bureau to come down the pike is unclear, but soon an overload of requests for this sort of assistance would prompt government and the advertising industry to enter into a much more formalized arrangement.

Other big-budget, star-studded productions in 1941 included *Listen America*, an unlikely combination of "discussions by authoritative speakers [and] dramatic sketches . . . featuring stars of stage, screen and radio" on the topic of "the importance of proper nutrition in building up bodies, as well as minds, for national defense," sponsored by the Women's National Emergency Committee at 10:30 on Friday nights on the Red network; *Spin and Win with Jimmy Flynn* on Saturdays at 9:00 (Blue), one of the above-mentioned quiz programs featuring military personnel and actually produced at various army camps; and two programs initiated by Nelson Rockefeller's Latin American coordinating office, *The Hemisphere Review*, "a kaleidoscopic picture of the Western Hemisphere in music, story, and song," with guest stars each week, and *Good Neighbors* on Thursdays at 10:30 on Red, "a series of dramatized human interest programs built around the various Central and South American countries."

For women, daytime hours provided *What Can I Do?* devoted to the "persistent question" of "women's place in national defense," and *Buck Private and His Girl* (which might appear to answer the question), "a romantic serial dealing with the trials and tribulations of Private Steve Mason, former automobile mechanic drafted into the Army." And to recruit the rising generation, NBC scheduled *From Oxford Pacifism to Fighter Pilot* on Saturdays at the child-friendly hour of 5:45. The bland title apparently obscured a fair amount of British-sympathetic excitement: "The blazing spectacular story of one of Britain's gallant air fighters, from pacifist beginnings to a fiery plunge from the skies. The true story of the actual exploits of one of the RAF's un-named heroes." Other series, such as *Defense News*, took a more straightforward informative approach, featuring different speakers on various defense-related subjects each week. Spring 1941 programs included New York's Mayor Fiorella La Guardia speaking at a meeting of the Save Freedom Citizen's Committee on the need to curtail "domestic controversy" around alien-baiting and paranoia about "fifth-columnists." A rare program mentioning African Americans was aired on June 28, 1941, addressing the Negro March on Washington being urged by the Brotherhood of Sleeping Car Porters.[13]

If such programs assisted government efforts to encourage an interventionist consensus, their avoidance of open political debate redirected attention to cultural issues, notably the problems of unity and common purpose. In order to avoid acknowledging the political divisions that split U.S. public opinion on the subject of war—and opinion polls showed that as late as June 1941, 79 percent of Americans thought that the United States should stay out of the war in Europe[14]—government propaganda efforts, enthusiastically aided by commercial media interests, placed overwhelming emphasis on justifications for war arising out of the American character, out of "natural" love for freedom and democracy, and painted those characteristics in stark contrast to Nazi totalitarianism and military rule. In order to avoid acknowledging the deep social and racial divisions that radio itself had helped to maintain on the home front, renewed efforts to broaden radio's address to include previously marginalized or ghettoized groups, or at least to mitigate the worst racial and ethnic abuses, were initiated both within the networks themselves and as a result of government agency intervention. Subaltern counterpublic groups were not slow to respond to the openings produced by such strategies, and pressures quickly began to build to allow previously unheard voices a space on the public airwaves, telling their own stories in a context of newly invigorated inclusiveness and redrawing of social boundaries.

The wartime quest for unity, by calling out American values unfortunately not fully dispersed through actual American society, had the paradoxical effect of ripping the cover of complacency off everyday practices and revealing the lack of unity and the violation of "natural" democratic precepts that lay beneath the surface. As a 1943 poll in the *Pittsburgh Courier* claimed in its headline, the "war exposed extreme discrimination," leading 41 percent of African American citizens polled to conclude that discrimination and segregation had increased during the war. Some of the 56 percent who disagreed with that conclusion still maintained that the army itself had done much to spread racial bias, because its segregated practice "takes race bias wherever it moves . . . Army traditions have revealed heretofore concealed race prejudice," so that "the question of segregation is now out in the open for the first time."[15] Newspapers such as the *Courier*, the *Amsterdam News*, and the *Chicago Defender*—always important in the African American community because of exclusion from the "mainstream" white press, but even more crucial during the war years—urged black citizens to fight on the "Double V" front: victory against the enemy abroad and against racial hatred at home. Yet, conversely, the opening of new avenues of speech for excluded groups brought with it a backlash from those invested in maintaining white dominance. One Alabama congressman, for instance, expressed the peculiar double-mindedness of those fighting for equality and freedom abroad while defending precisely the opposite qualities at home. In a letter to Roosevelt's assistant Edwin M. Watson objecting to the federally mandated employment of black workers in government agencies, Frank Boykin wrote: "It is difficult for me to express the way our people [i.e., his white constituents] feel about this matter. They are really more upset about this than they are about the war and I really believe our people would rather be dead than have to put up with the negro men giving our white women orders. As a matter of fact, I know they had."[16] Clearly, reconciling these deeply held and deeply contradictory positions would be a process fraught with pitfalls. One major arena for this battle on the home front was radio, as the American nation struggled to define who we were—a unified public committed to democracy and freedom—and who we were not, exemplified by the explicitly racialized totalitarian regimes of the Axis powers and Japan. In the process, voices were heard that had previously been suppressed, leaving a legacy that would come to slow but inevitable fruition in postwar television.

Hydra-Headed Propaganda

Most historians agree that the period of World War II managed to avoid the ethnophobic excesses leading up to and following World War I, along with the necessity for creating the kind of concentrated, though later reviled, centralized propaganda machine operated by the Creel Committee on Public Information during the earlier era. Frequently it is the nature of U.S. society itself that is credited with this happy avoidance; by 1940, the argument goes, restrictions on immigration, increasing homogenization of the American public through a rising standard of consumption, and a widely shared consensus on basic American values had worked to reduce the need for hysterical anti-alien measures and propaganda machines.[17] Yet at the same time it is obvious that the Depression years spawned greater political and social discord than any other comparable period of the twentieth century, with Communist and Socialist political parties stronger than ever before; widespread popularity of red-baiters and anti-Semites like Henry Ford, Father Coughlin, and the "Christian Right"; outright fascist organizations such as the German-American Bund gaining strength; increasingly militant conflicts between industry and labor; and general lack of faith in the American economic system that had failed millions of unemployed and desperate citizens over a period of almost a decade. Egregious violation of the rights of African American citizens continued unabated, with the black press tallying up monthly lynching counts and with very slim prospects for desegregation even in the military, which faced the prospect of fighting for a freedom and democracy conspicuously missing from its own practices. The debate around the "Smith Act," passed by Congress in 1940, seemed to presage a return to 1920s xenophobia in its provisions for the mandatory registration and fingerprinting of all foreign-born Americans, with Italians and Germans (many of them Jewish refugees) under particular scrutiny as the war in Europe gained in intensity.

The Roosevelt administration, already under fire for its heavy use of mass media to promote party policies, faced the need to coordinate government information gathering and dissemination efforts in order to monitor and control public opinion, while at the same time avoiding the creation of a centralized propaganda office, which would surely have come under strong criticism. Its response was to endorse a multiplicity of government-related offices, bureaus, and liaisons with private organizations to mold a more unified public response to the war without the appearance of direct authorization.[18] This hydra-headed approach, though marked by duplicated efforts and bureaucratic complexity, worked to disseminate (and collect) a wealth of information to and about the American public all the more effective for seeming spontaneous and collective, all the more persuasive for appearing as a "natural" outgrowth of basic American values. By 1941, according to one ingenuously enthusiastic analyst, "although today there does not exist a superagency for publicity such as the Creel Committee on Public Information of World War I days, the present system of publicity set-ups in all major governmental departments is probably only slightly less effective than a superagency following the general pattern of the CPI would be."[19] The uncoerced cooperation of the national media played an essential role in these efforts, with radio, for the reasons mentioned above, providing a particularly receptive as well as effective conduit for the numerous branches, bureaus, offices, and drives that made up the World War II propaganda apparatus. Following is an attempt to trace some of the more significant contributors to wartime mobilization, emphasizing those that made use of radio.

"Radio is the one channel of publicity which has not previously been available in a great international crisis. It lends itself with singular effectiveness to the creation of morale on a national scale."[20] So claimed the Treasury Department in 1941, one of the first and most enthusiastic agencies to mobilize public opinion in its Defense Savings Bond program. However, the story of America's redefinition of itself as a unified nation prepared to fight to defend its values begins even earlier, as Nazi propaganda and aggression reached U.S. notice in the late 1930s. Among the first to respond were those concerned with anti-Semitic activities in the United States, whose fight against such homegrown bigots as Father Coughlin and the Reverend Gerald L. K. Smith made them particularly sensitive to the success of fascist appeals in their own country. Organizations including the former Foreign Language Information Service, which in 1939 under the direction of Read Lewis and Louis Adamic changed its name to the Common Council for American Unity (CCAU), the National Conference of Christians and Jews (NCCJ), the Anti-Defamation League of the B'nai B'rith (ADL), the American Jewish Committee, and more recently formed groups such as the Union for Democratic Action, the Council for Democracy, the Council Against Intolerance in America, and the American Council Against Nazi Propaganda, rallied on the common ground of tolerance, democracy, and active resistance to appeals to prejudice and fear of difference. Campaigns begun to combat specifically anti-Semitic propaganda at home and from overseas broadened to include racial and ethnic unity more comprehensively defined.

The Council for Democracy, for instance, formed in 1940, specifically defined its goal as "unity" of "all Americans working and living together harmoniously" and spoke out against prejudice directed toward "Jews, Catholics, Negroes, the foreign-born or any other group" in our "national consciousness." This group also relied heavily on the mass media, particularly radio, and produced two regular programs,

Americans All and *Speaking of Liberty*, in the spring of 1941. According to Richard Steele:

> The patriotism promoted by the Jewish defense effort had none of the chauvinism and Anglo-conformity traditionally associated with "Americanism." It touted "diversity rather than goose-step uniformity" and argued that the nation's strength lay in "the variety of its peoples, the richness of its heritage." . . .
>
> . . . Ultimately, the same logic and organizational dynamics that had led groups initially interested in combatting anti-Semitism to espouse eventually an undifferentiated "tolerance" would draw these same groups more or less reluctantly into support of a racial justice that included blacks and other "colored" minorities.[21]

Most of these groups were anxious to work with government agencies and the media to spread their message. The ADL embarked on a controversial campaign of cooperation with the Justice Department and the House Committee on Un-American Activities, "monitoring and reporting on subversives" sympathetic to the Nazi regime.[22] Most organizations, however, funded by private sources such as the Carnegie Foundation and fund-raising in the civilian community, worked on educational campaigns in the schools, general-interest publications such as the CCAU's *Common Ground*, radio programs like the ADL's *Lest We Forget* series on America's patriotic celebrations and heritage, dissemination of articles and materials to the press, and research on race hatred and its causes. Thus, when the government began to organize itself to mobilize public opinion in 1941, it found a ready-made set of civilian groups anxious to provide advice, personnel, and assistance. Eventually, with the formation of the Office of War Information (OWI) in 1942, these efforts would come together in an expression of broad-based American values, though they would ultimately conflict with the more narrowly channeled efforts espoused by advertising-oriented media groups. Meantime, however, the government struggled to find the right response to pressing needs for information dissemination and collection.

As historian Sydney Weinberg points out, prior to 1942 a melange of government agencies contributed in overlapping and ultimately restricting ways to the government information effort. The Office of Emergency Management (OEM) formed the Division of Information in March 1941, under the direction of Robert Horton, to disseminate information acquired from the various OEM agencies to the press and public about government-private business cooperation in defense mobilization. However, the lack of clear guidelines about whether the agency's task should consist of unity and morale building or a more critical perspective on the many problems encountered by government-business cooperative efforts led to virtual paralysis. Similarly, the Office of Government Reports (OGR), under the direction of the president's close friend and adviser Lowell Mellett, primarily concerned with information gathering on the state of public opinion and the operation of public inquiry offices, found itself faced with charges of propagandizing on behalf of the administration. Congress cut the OGR's appropriation to "a new low" in 1942, severely restricting that organization's effectiveness. Under pressure from his advisers, Roosevelt created the Office of Civil Defense (OCD) in May 1941, with New York Mayor Fiorello La Guardia in charge, specifically to devise methods of building morale toward defense efforts and enhancing government public relations through the media.

However, dissatisfied with La Guardia's progress by the fall of that year, Roosevelt initiated a new branch of the OCD to be called, in line with avoidance of the appearance of propaganda, the Office of Facts and Figures (OFF), to "provide public opinion samplings and give Americans an accurate and coherent account of government policy."[23] Librarian of Congress Archibald MacLeish was placed in charge of this new bureau, giving rise to a fairly autonomous writers' group within the government bureaucracy whose interpretation of their mission would create public controversy during the two years of its existence. Also under the aegis of the OFF, a Radio Division was formed, headed by former CBS programming vice president William B. Lewis, to "give guidance to Government departments and agencies and to the Radio industry as a whole concerning inquiries . . . by the broadcasting companies and stations, and to handle certain Government programs on the networks within the U.S."[24]

Further complicating the picture was the Office of the Coordinator of Information (OCI), created in July 1941 under the leadership of Colonel William G. "Wild Bill" Donovan, primarily an information collection bureau concerned with issues of national security (later to evolve into the CIA), which in August 1941 produced the offshoot Foreign Information Service (FIS), intended to direct American propaganda outward toward the rest of the embattled world. Playwright and journalist Robert Sherwood was placed in charge of this latter branch, where, like MacLeish, he gathered around him a distinguished assembly of writers, journalists, and other figures from the media and the arts who operated under relatively little direct guidance or interference (including John Houseman, fresh from his battles with Orson Welles). Out of their efforts arose the long-lived Voice of America service, still extant in 1996.

By 1942, this welter of competing and often loudly disagreeing players in the game of information dealing had reached a level of confusion that necessitated rethinking—and, of course, with America's entry into the war following Pearl Harbor in December 1941, the task took on new urgency. Roosevelt commissioned the Bureau of the Budget under the direction of Milton S. Eisenhower (Dwight D. Eisenhower's youngest brother) to make a study of the situation and come up with a proposal for better coordination of efforts. Eisenhower, while still opposed to a Creel Committee-like centralized bureau, nevertheless produced in spring of 1942 the draft of an executive order, "Consolidating Certain Information Functions of the Government into an Office of War Information."[25]

Elmer Davis, well-known journalist and radio commentator, accepted the post of head of the new Office of War Information on June 13, 1942.[26] Davis's mission, as described in the OWI's charter, was to

> formulate and carry out, through the use of press, radio, and motion pictures, and other facilities, information programs designed to facilitate the development of an informed and intelligent understanding, at home and abroad, of the status and progress of the war effort and of the war policies, activities, and aims of the Government. . . . Review, clear, and approve all proposed radio and motion picture programs sponsored by Federal Departments and Agencies and serve as the central point of clearance and contact for the radio broadcasting and motion picture industries respectively in their relationships with Federal Departments and agencies concerning such Government programs.[27]

Yet, unlike the Creel Committee or the German propaganda ministry under Joseph Goebbels, the OWI remained primarily a coordinator rather than an originator of information, reliant on the cooperation of other agencies and outside groups, and particularly on the voluntary cooperation of the media, whose independence from government control remained sacrosanct.

The OWI, until its reorganization in 1943, divided its efforts into three branches: the Domestic Branch, under the direction of newspaper publisher Gardner Cowles Jr.; the Policy Development Branch, under MacLeish, which became known as the "writers' branch"; and the Overseas Branch, under Sherwood. Under the aegis of the Domestic Branch, various separate and sometimes overlapping bureaus flourished, including the Bureau of Intelligence, the Bureau of Publications and Graphics, the Bureau of Motion Pictures, the Radio Bureau, the News Bureau, and the Bureau of Campaigns. Whereas the Bureau of Intelligence concerned itself with the gathering of information, the latter four all involved dissemination efforts. The Bureau of Campaigns became the locus of cooperative advertising-sponsored patriotic promotion via all media, but with radio playing a primary role, working especially closely with the War Advertising Council, which had been set up by the advertising industry in 1942.[28] The Bureau of Motion Pictures (directed by Lowell Mellett) depended on the film industry for its effectivity. The News Bureau gathered press releases from other agencies and rewrote them for wider press distribution.

The Radio Bureau, under the direction of William B. Lewis, also had a primarily coordinative function, which took effect October 1, 1942:

> All plans or proposals for new or continuing series or for individual radio programs developed by or for the national headquarters of the several Government Agencies for local stations or networks will be submitted to the Chief of the Radio Bureau, OWI, for clearance. . . . At the discretion of the Radio Bureau this material will be channeled to the proper outlets.[29]

The result of this mandate was the development of the "Network Allocation Plan," which circulated "an average of three messages a week" on more than one hundred of the highest-rated sustaining and commercial programs, through submission of timely themes and campaigns to the advertising agencies and networks that produced them. The ways in which specific messages were to be incorporated into programs were left to the discretion of the producers; anything from a few lines of dialogue to a spot announcement at some point in the program, to a dramatic enactment within the show's plot served to advance wartime messages. Some messages became plot motifs that ran on for weeks, especially on the daytime serials. The Radio Bureau accomplished this through the "fact sheets" that it circulated, each of which laid out a basic problem, suggested ways to deal with it, and outlined a few possible approaches to the audience, along with a catchy slogan or two. However, at times a more selective technique was employed through the bureau's "program inventory," a comprehensive listing of all programs carried on the major networks, along with pertinent information such as scheduled time, audience, plotlines, subject matter, and the names of the writers, producers, and actors associated with them. When a topic of particular relevance or interest to one of these programs came along, messages from the OWI could be "placed at short notice with detailed knowledge of the program and even of the writer and the actor for whom it is best suited."[30] Writers and producers could also draw on the bureau's "radio background material" publications, which provided information about a variety of important subjects and themes.[31] Some of these publications came from the Bureau of Publications and Graphics.

Uniquely in the OWI, the Bureau of Publications and Graphics, rather than depending on the voluntary but self-interested cooperation of privately owned media, could itself originate and publish books, pamphlets, articles, and visual materials such as posters relatively unimpeded by supervision from within the government or by resistance from media beyond its control. Dominated by MacLeish and his independent-minded group of writers and journalists, the bureau was headed by Pulitzer Prize-winning historian Henry Pringle and included such later well-known names as Bruce Catton, Arthur M. Schlesinger Jr., Philip Hamburger, Adrienne Koch, McGeorge Bundy, and Malcolm Cowley. Most of this group had moved as a unit from the Production Bureau of OFF, where they had already produced some of the most influential and controversial propaganda of the early war years. All "shared MacLeish's conviction that the OFF's most urgent task was to explain to Americans *why* the United States would have to fight the coming war"[32] (emphasis added) and shared the inclusive, ideologically progressive orientation of the prodemocracy groups discussed above. Their distinctive sense of mission clashed with the more utilitarian, commercial media-based efforts of the rest of the OWI, and soon began to create serious conflict both within and outside of the organization.

In January 1943, Gardner Cowles determined to restructure his organization to tighten control over the disjointed jigsaw puzzle of spun-off units that made up the Domestic Branch of the OWI, with particular attention to those areas, such as the Bureau of Publications and Graphics, that seemed to operate at cross-purposes with the rest. He brought in two new directors from the media industries: James Allen, former motion picture industry executive, now to serve as assistant director in charge of policy and subject-matter development; and William B. Lewis from the OFF (and before that, CBS), as assistant director in charge of program coordination and production. Though Allen's responsibilities included the "Publications" section of the new split-apart Bureau of Publications and Graphics, Pringle's writers were moved out of that area and into the other half, the Bureau of Graphics and Printing, under Lewis. Lewis's office also subsumed the former Bureau of Campaigns, which now became a division of the assistant director's office. When Lewis named Price Gilbert, formerly in charge of advertising for Coca-Cola, chief of this new division, stifling levels of bureaucracy replaced the writers' previous autonomy, dominated by the kind of commercial advertising-based orientation resisted by the pamphleteers since the OWI's inception. Indeed, these moves seemed calculated precisely to produce the stifling of the writers, who, perceiving this, quit the OWI en masse on April 15, 1943, claiming that "the activities of the OWI on the home front were dominated by high-pressure promoters who preferred slick salesmanship to honest information."[33] The story of the "writers' war"—more accurately, the "writers and advertisers war"—within the OWI speaks to the heart of the tensions, particularly racial, surrounding the appeal to American unity and identity during World War II, as well as to the role that the commercial medium of radio played within it.

"The War That Refreshes: The Four Delicious Freedoms!"

Early on, MacLeish and his Publications Bureau in the OFF conceived their mission as the larger fight against fascism in all its forms—not the narrow goal of defense in itself, or later winning the war as an end in itself, but centrally involving the definition of what the fight against fascism meant, particularly in its implications for policy on the home front. They expressed this vision of American unity and purpose primarily in a series of pamphlets, written within the bureau and distributed not only to press and media but to civic groups, educators, military, trade organizations, community groups, and individuals. Thus, unlike any other branch of government information at this time, the pamphleteers could communicate directly with the American public without going through the screening mechanism of the commercial media—precisely the capacity that would be taken from them as a result of their very success. One early publication, produced in the OFF before its subsumation into the OWI, titled "The Four Freedoms," received widespread circulation and acclaim as a comprehensive and inspiring statement of American values in wartime. Based on President Roosevelt's January 1941 address to Congress, the "four essential human freedoms" consisted of freedom of speech and expression, freedom of worship, freedom from want, and freedom from fear, and these were used to "underscore the fundamental American aims" during the crucial mobilization period of 1941.[34]

The Treasury Department was one of the first to echo this OFF publication in its savings bond campaign, identifying the four national characteristics to be promoted in line with the four freedoms:

> Through all of the Defense Savings publicity there will be seen running a note of faith, confidence, courage and determination: Faith in our destiny, in the people and the institutions of America, in the method of freedom and in equal justice under law; courage to meet the challenge of despotism; confidence in our inner strength, in our unity and integrity of purpose, in our capacity to solve our problems by the cooperation of men standing upright, not upon their knees; determination that all of the national strength will be utilized to preserve these American values.[35]

Overall, "Tolerance and freedom and unity without uniformity" formed what these writers and others rallying the nation for war conceived as "the real essence of America."[36] Furthermore, in line with the call to definite action by the Treasury Department (to buy defense bonds), the agency expressed the kind of integrationist appeal that would later prove so troubling:

> In a democratic society, national unity can be achieved, not by force, but by persuasion, not by the liquidation of minority interest groups, but by their incorporation into the framework of the nation. This can be done only as each group comes to see that its welfare is dependent upon the welfare of the nation as a whole. To accomplish this, it is vitally necessary to give everyone a sense of taking direct part in activities which extend beyond those of his particular group but upon which its welfare depends.[37]

Though the immediate purpose of the Treasury Department may have been participation in defense bond purchase, this sort of rhetoric could be, and was, interpreted as a call to bring formerly marginalized groups into the center of the morale effort.

"The Four Freedoms" was one of the pamphlets circulated to radio networks and producers as "background material," along with other successful publications such as "Divide and Conquer," about enemy propaganda techniques; "The Unconquered People," describing resistance in Nazi-occupied countries; "The Thousand Million," informing the public about the United Nations; and "Toward New Horizons," about developing U.N. policy. Markedly not included in this list was one of the bureau's most controversial pamphlets, "Negroes and the War," released in January 1943. Though the publication that most immediately sparked the mass resignation of the writers in April 1943 concerned agricultural production, it was "Negroes and the War" that detonated a series of reactions pointing most directly to the tensions developing not only within the OWI Domestic Branch, but within the country as a whole.

The issue of race relations within the United States possessed a particular edge within the justification of American war aims, because of its uniquely powerful ability to knock the foundations out from under U.S. claims for democracy, equality, and freedom. Not only were African Americans well aware of the peculiar contradictions of their situation, especially after the promised rewards for their loyalty in World War I had failed to materialize in improved social and political conditions,[38] but so were Jewish and other groups committed to fighting Nazi anti-Semitic propaganda, including many members of the writers' group in the OFF. Later, Japanese propaganda would play directly into this gap between American rhetoric and practice, pointing out that "in the United States there is the greatest racial inequality in the world. . . . the equality slogan is hypocrisy."[39] By 1941, OFF opinion research shows that "the morale of Negroes was being depressed by discrimination and a lack of opportunity to serve."[40]

In the spring of 1941, writers within the Publications Bureau of the OFF initiated a pamphlet specifically addressing the issue of race within the "unity without uniformity" ideals described above. Its inception was prompted by a series of articles in a black weekly journal that asked the question, "What will happen to the Negro if Hitler wins?" and answered it in the grimmest terms: clearly Nazism held no promise for African Americans. The writer was Chandler Owen, an African American journalist who was hired by the Publications Bureau to write the copy of what turned into a seventy-two-page booklet, with 141 photographs showing aspects of black life in the United States, including "the Negro press, the church, the farmer, the city dweller, the Government worker, the athlete, the trade unionist, the business man, and the activities of Negroes in the Armed Services of the country."⁴¹ By the time of the pamphlet's publication, the writers' branch had moved to the OWI and was credited with authorship, though a six-page introduction prefaced the text under Owen's signature, complete with photograph. The pamphlet was intended for a black readership, including prominently the black press and black soldiers in the armed forces.

From the beginning there was trouble. Before the pamphlet's publication, the Bureau of Intelligence within the OWI objected to the entire project on the grounds that it could be taken as a "threat" to the African American community implying a "come along or else" attitude. The War Department blocked the pamphlet's distribution to black troops, though it was allowed to gain a place in camp libraries. Authorities in "Negro affairs" in other departments of the government objected that they had not been consulted, though the OWI did seek the advice of specialists in the War Manpower Commission and the Office of Strategic Services. Despite internal misgivings, demand for the pamphlet exceeded that of most others published by the OWI; more than 2.5 million copies were distributed, though many minority government specialists as well as the black press complained that the white population was in far more need of the positive picture the pamphlet painted of the African American community than were its own members, to whom it appeared more of a sop and smoke screen for discrimination. Others objected to its avoidance of the real issues of outright discrimination and racial hatred on a daily basis, especially in defense industries and in the military itself.⁴²

However, the most serious fallout occurred in Congress, where debates over funding the OWI for its next year's operations were taking place. Southern members of Congress in particular condemned the OWI for producing such objectionable material, and for using its government-funded position to create "disunity" and further undesirable New Deal social programs. And, as Gosnell points out, "The reactions in Congress to the pamphlet . . . were disastrous to the OWI."⁴³ Congressman Starnes of Alabama proposed on June 18, 1943, that funding for the Domestic Branch be cut altogether and the branch itself completely shut down, claiming that "the type and character of the domestic propaganda foisted upon the American people through publications printed and distributed at Government expense by the Office of War Information is a stench to the nostrils of a democratic people," and indicating that he "prefer[red his] information through a free and uncontrolled press on all phases of life in free America."[44] Congressman Allen of Louisiana clarified just what sort of stench Starnes was referring to:

> Elmer Davis, instead of helping the war effort domestically, I think, is hurting it. The propaganda which he has put out in the form of pamphlets and otherwise has done a great deal to foment unrest, to create disunity, and to make the minority problem worse, much worse. His propaganda stuff has hurt the South. We have a serious racial problem in this nation. We in the South understand that problem and know best how to deal with it. We understand the psychology of the race problem. Davis had 2,500,000 copies of a certain pamphlet printed and sent everywhere. . . . This pamphlet undertook to glorify one race in the war. We in the South wish to encourage that race. We are the best friends of that race. But such propaganda raises a race issue, which ought to be kept down. We want unity in this country. All over this country now we are having race riots, even in the North, and the type of propaganda which the OWI has been sending out certainly does not hold that situation down.[45]

Inspired by such rhetoric, the motion to cut funding of the Domestic Branch to zero passed, 156 to 60, though it was later modified to allow for some funding under promise of organizational revision. The OWI was reorganized and it was announced that pamphleteering would be abandoned and controversial past publications pulled from distribution. These latter decisions had already been made before the congressional funding debate, in the wake of the writers' resignation in April.

Though the controversy over "Negroes and the War" points out the destabilizing nature of racial issues within the mobilization of American national identity, it also emphasizes the perceived danger of allowing too much autonomy to those who would articulate wartime ideals untrammeled by the system of private checks and balances inherent in the commercial media system. Congressman Starnes's statement of preference for a "free press" was followed by various paeans to the commercial media. Congressman Robsion of Kentucky stated, "I would rather take my information from reports put out by the War and Navy departments and by the many able and disinterested radio broadcasting stations and the newspapers. They are less biased than Mr. Davis and Mr. Mellett." Senator Robertson of Virginia believed that funds to the OWI should be cut so that it could not "infiltrate political propaganda into the free press and radio."[46] The lesson that seemed to be learned by the OWI administration from the writers' war debacle was that dependence on the screening mechanisms of the media industries based on private commercial concerns provided the best possible protection against similar embarrassments.

This was the interpretation given to the situation by the writers themselves; they had discerned a muzzling process at work even before the flap over racial matters, linked to the increasing permeation of advertising personnel and techniques and reliance on commercial media within the OWI. In a statement released to the press, the writers summarized their objections to the course the OWI was taking:

> There is only one issue—the deep and fundamental one of the honest presentation of war information. We are leaving because of our conviction that it is impossible for us, under those who now control our output, to tell the full truth. No one denies that promotional techniques have a proper and powerful function in telling the story of the war. But as we see it, the activities of OWI on the home front are now dominated by high-pressure promoters who prefer slick salesmanship to honest information. They delude themselves that the only effective appeal to the American public in wartime is the selfish one of "what's in it for me?" . . . The promoters who are now running the domestic information policy of the OWI . . . are turning this Office of War Information into an office of war ballyhoo.[47]

As Schlesinger explained:

> The advertising men have been striking out for more and more power over the whole domestic information policy. This has meant a primary interest in manipulating the people, not in giving them the facts. It has meant an increasing reliance on advertising techniques instead of honest information. . . . It has meant an increasing conviction that any government information campaign likely to affect a vested business interest should first be approved by that interest. It has meant a steady replacement of independent writers, newspapermen, publishers, mostly of liberal inclination, by men beholden to the business community for their livelihood and thinking always as the business community thinks.[48]

Another writer, Francis Brennan, framed his objections in terms of the basic principles of advertising and its fundamental techniques as applied to the subject of war: "Those techniques have done more toward dimming perception, suspending critical values, and spreading the sticky syrup of complacency over the people than almost any other factor."[49]

Brennan and artist Ben Shahn summed up this debate in the form of a poster. Underneath a drawing of the Statue of Liberty holding up not a torch but four bottles of Coca-Cola, the slogan read, "The War That Refreshes: The Four Delicious Freedoms!"[50] This anticommercialism, though temporarily defeated within the walls of government war agencies, would resurface in the debates over television to emerge postwar. Associating progressive social values with government regulation and regressive action on social issues with the commercial interests of business, advertisers, and broadcasters, this war-established dichotomy would play heavily into the way that television would negotiate its practices in the 1950s. Yet as far as radio was concerned, advertising-based interests had won the day. Inspired by a solid self-interest, the networks, agencies, and sponsors proved themselves ready and willing to contribute to wartime morale—though without disrupting profitable practices and arrangements, and only insofar as controversy could be contained. This was just the kind of check and balance to progressive ideology that the Congress had in mind. Yet even within this careful approach, some problems just would not go away.

We, Too, Are Americans: Race Redux

As illustrated by the "Negroes and the War" debacle, an area of pressing concern as the United States headed into war was the symbolic category of race, most markedly as it affected African Americans both in the civilian population and in the military forces, but also in its customary role as mediator of ethnic tensions generally, now newly called into dispute as white America's disparate European roots became a source of division rather than unity. An active campaign to rearticulate the "Negro" (in the parlance of the times) and the relationship of race and ethnicity in general to public citizenship took place on several fronts, in which radio played a crucial role. First, anti-Nazi propaganda groups made an explicit effort to define the issue of race broadly rather than narrowly, preferring to champion tolerance and freedom from prejudice of all sorts, producing an opening into which black leaders moved with alacrity. Programs such as *Americans All, I'm an American!, Freedom's People, Speaking of Liberty,* and *America in the Air* attempted to redefine race and ethnicity within American identity and assimilation, deliberately including the claims of African Americans to full rights and citizenship along with those of Americans of European descent. Second, efforts were made to change the dominant mode of representing ethnic groups, including African Americans, on domestic radio through pressure on existing programs, initiation of special shows that addressed U.S. racial history and relations explicitly, and increased access of black groups, in particular, to direct expression on the air, which had previously been denied. Third, broadcasts directed at U.S. troops at home and overseas also began to grapple with the needs and interests of black soldiers and consequently with the very distinctions and cultural barriers that made such a separate address necessary.

Fighting a war against European enemies caused the barely subsumed struggles of assimilation of European ethnic groups to emerge once again into uneasy prominence. German, Italian, and Russian Americans suffered a certain amount of discrimination in defense industry hiring as well as in other venues, and many of radio's early efforts to address war morale took on the problem of reintegrating these nationalities into mainstream American identity. Though recent immigrants bore the brunt of ethnocentric suspicion, even second-generation descendants of "enemy" heritage could be included in the "dangerous" category—a resurrection of Anglo-American exclusionary values that frequently extended to include "Negroes, Mexicans, Orientals and Jews." This led, in some cases, as the nation geared up its defense hiring, to employment requirements that explicitly stipulated "white citizens of American nationality" or "Nordics only"—even as Americans prepared to fight for "democracy."[51] Some attempts to redress the reracializing of American identity themselves compounded the problem by reverting to a 1920s notion of "race" that, even while extending to European "races" the hand of inclusion, worked all the more effectively to obscure the more pressing, underlying problem of non-"white" racial exclusion.

For instance, a program proposed to NBC in the spring of 1941, a special episode of the INS-sponsored *I'm an American!* program called "America Answers!" spoke back to "the totalitarian dictators to democracy" by proclaiming "AMERICA ANSWERS THE DICTATORS! We are one people! We share the same blood—the blood of free men!" However, despite the program's intention to show a "pageant of all America" in the experiences of immigrants "from all lands," the show's script makes clear that the lands included only those located in the northwestern part of the Eastern Hemisphere. Colonists from "Holland, France, Sweden, and England" led off the march to America, soon after joined by Poles, Germans, Jews, and

Italians, with never a mention of those from Africa, Asia, or those already to be found upon the land before the others arrived. Despite the democratic intention behind the scenario of "men of forty races building a great America—the railways being laid across the continent with Italians singing 'O Sole Mio' as they advanced civilization through the wilderness" to "suggest the march of Americans of all races side by side through our democratic history to the present time," it is clear that the new use of the old concept of racial difference here works to obscure those even more "different," pushing them outside the rhetoric of democracy.[52]

In response to this excluding pressure, other groups worked to foreground African Americans within radio's discourse about American identity. One program also proposed in the spring of 1941 demonstrates the tensions existing between various government and public groups concerned with promoting a more inclusive definition of "American" and the trepidations of network officials in going where very few programs had ventured before. In January 1941, Niles Trammel of NBC received a letter from J. W. Studebaker, commissioner of the Department of Education, proposing a series of thirteen programs that he believed "would make a real contribution to the development of greater national unity, and to the promotion of our national defense effort." To be titled *We, Too, Are Americans*, the series was to focus on the "contributions of Negroes to American life" by covering various areas such as "science, discovery, and invention," music, literature, art, religion, "agriculture, industry and personal service," education, and "amusements," as well as public service and the military.[53] This was followed up by a letter from Ambrose Caliver, a "senior specialist in the higher education of Negroes" within the U.S. Department of Education and primary author of the series, to Phillips Carlin, by then head of the NBC Blue network, reporting that a grant had been obtained to produce the series. Caliver had spoken to Carlin of the plan as early as August 1940, but no action had been taken.

Carlin referred the letter to Dr. James R. Angell, NBC's head of public service, who in turn reported to Trammel on February 7 with a halfhearted endorsement:

> If they have some money to put into the undertaking, we could probably get a really first-class musical program; the others would be more doubtful. I fancy none of them would be popular south of Mason and Dixon's line. . . . I do not believe that, in any case, we could wisely undertake thir-

teen. . . . I am afraid, coming from Studebaker, we should get a worse headache by declining to discuss the matter further, than by letting Caliver come up again and offer more definite details.[54]

This reluctance is further demonstrated in a February 17 follow-up memo from Angell to Walter Preston Jr., manager of NBC's public service division:

> In substance the material represents an effort on Mr. Carlin's part last year either to condense into two or three programs a plan Mr. Caliver (a colored man) had in mind or to side-track it altogether. . . . It seems to all of us rather essential that in view of Caliver's position in Washington he be invited to come up and talk again about his program, even though we delay considerably taking any action.[55]

Further difficulties stemmed from NBC's 1940 dispute with ASCAP (leading to its cancellation of license for ASCAP materials), which held the rights to most of the music being proposed for the program. However, enthusiastic cooperation was obtained by Caliver, with ASCAP president Gene Buck almost gushing:

> I know of no group in America that has made a greater contribution to the musical culture of the country than the Negro. In fact, I honestly believe that the only real fundamental American music comes from the Negro. We are very glad, with this communication, to extend to your Department full authorization for you and the Department to use any and all of the works written and composed by members of our Society over any and all broadcasting networks or individual station.[56]

With this hurdle out of the way, a six-part series was approved, now to be titled *Freedom's People*. Part I aired Sunday, September 23, 1941, after another bout of stalling on NBC's part over whether the program warranted such privileged status, as it was neither "defense" nor "religious" material. Studebaker's staunch maintenance that such a program, designed to promote inclusion of black voices and experiences into the mounting dialogue on American identity and democracy, indeed constituted a part of the overall defense effort marks the limits of inclusiveness being strained by war-inspired racial definitions.[57] It also represents the kind of decision making NBC and other broadcasters were pleased to have taken out of their hands with the installment of the OWI.

The OWI embarked on a deliberate program of inclusion on several fronts. One was a handbook for writers called "When Radio Writes for War," which advised on a variety of topics. It included this reminder:

> When portraying a Negro on a radio program, avoid the Stepin Fetchit type, the minstrel man, the stooge, the dumb domestic, the guy always being chased by ghosts. And Negroes have names as commonplace as John and Mary. Seldom are they colorful as "Eight-ball," "Ironhead," "Blackboy," or "Razor." When Negro characters appear in a script, try to have them played by real Negroes—straight and intelligently—if Negro actors are available. And they *are* available in all large radio production centers.[58]

The fact that writers had to be reminded of these aspects, of course, points to the fact that even by mid-war they were being routinely violated. A 1944 article in the *Journal of Negro Education* summarizes the progress made in the improvement of radio representations; though it concludes that "radio is less unfavorable to the Negro than motion pictures," the next four pages are devoted to continuing unfavorable practices such as "the theme of the superstitious Negro"; characterizations in the minstrel tradition such as "Molasses and January," "Sunshine and Snowball," "Aunt Jemima," and even "Amos 'n' Andy" (specifically omitting Rochester of the Jack Benny show from inclusion in this category); and the continued overemphasis (to the exclusion of other representations) of "singing spirituals and folk songs and singing and playing jazz music." Even in educational or cultural programs sponsored by influential organizations such as the National Urban League and the National Negro Newspaper Publishers Association, the article notes:

> In most parts of the country, stations will not permit discussions of "Negro rights" unless such topics are so intertwined with entertainment as to make the former very secondary. Some Southern stations cut off chain programs from the North when "controversial" issues affecting race relations are injected. Thus the *Town Meeting of the Air* broadcast "Let's Face the Race Question" was not carried by the outlet in New Orleans because of "technical difficulties."[59]

Yet the progressive "unity without uniformity" movement continued to push determinedly against racial lines, often turning to the powerful medium of radio to open up previously forbidden topics.

Sometimes it is possible to see this rearticulation of race and national identity literally happening on paper. For instance, in 1942 the Union for Democratic Action, a group formed in May 1941 by prominent liberals and labor leaders expressly to further the "fight against fascism, both home and abroad," planned a panel discussion program on the proposed poll tax. A working outline exists of the proposed program. Under the heading "Effects on Country as a Whole," listing such consequences as disproportionate representation of the wealthy and the negative effects on the war effort, written in as a late consideration is "e. Negro problem." Later, the writer went back and scratched out "problem," penciling in "morale" in its place. This marks a shift in thinking, perhaps strategic on the UDA's part, about the relationship of the black minority to the newly conceptualized democratic majority. A UDA program in January focused specifically on "Negro Morale and the War," featuring James Hubert, executive director of the New York Urban League; Roy Wilkins, editor of *Crisis* and assistant secretary for the NAACP; and others. Here, black leaders were allowed to speak for themselves on network radio, a phenomenon still quite rare.

Yet this reconceptualization had to work within limits, and in the drawing of these limits can be seen some of the tensions within which postwar handling of television representation would have to work. The UDA had for some time been active in the struggle for desegregation of the armed forces, calling a conference on "The Negro and Defense" in June 1941. The letters of invitation, directed to political organizations as well as labor and civil rights groups, differ according to the group being addressed. To white groups, such as the IUMSWA, James Loeb Jr., executive secretary of the UDA, writes bluntly:

> One of the most dangerous cracks in our national unity against totalitarian aggression is the bitter, growing, and largely justified resentment of Negroes at the way in which they have been kicked around in the defense program. . . . The enemies of democracy, of effective aid to Britain and of the whole defense program are playing upon the resentment among Negroes which naturally results from this unjust discrimination with the result that Communist and anti-Semitic sentiment is growing in Harlem like wildfire.[60]

To black groups, however, such as the Brotherhood of Sleeping Car Porters, the NAACP, the National Urban League, and the Negro Labor Committee, a more disinterested, idealistic note was sounded:

> Many members and supporters of those organizations backing the defense program because they want to insure the defeat of Hitlerism with all it represents in terms of dictatorship, military aggression and a phi-

losophy of a master and slave races, are becoming more and more aware of the discrimination against Negroes here in America. They are finding it increasingly difficult to square the continued existence of such an injustice with the democratic ideals for which we are being called upon to sacrifice.[61]

Here the contradictory nature of wartime racial realignment can be clearly seen: for blacks, a rhetoric of inclusion deployed strategically that *denies* racial distinctions in favor of a transcendent democratic national identity; for whites, a discourse of fear that *depends* upon racial distinctions to motivate white participation. However, in the atmosphere of institutionalized racism of World War II—as exemplified in armed forces segregation and in the congressional debate described above—these sentiments were progressive indeed, and reflected a cautious workable position.

Many of the radio programs and panel discussions that resulted from such self-conscious political organizing were carried on local and public stations, such as the celebrated *New World A-coming*; one-time specials carried over networks, such as *America's Negro Soldiers* on NBC, sponsored by the War Department; *This Is Our War*, produced on WOR for the Mutual network; and *An Open Letter on Race Hatred*, produced and aired on CBS in the wake of the racial riots in Detroit in the summer of 1943. Network efforts that addressed issues of race on a regular basis included *These Are Americans*, a six-part series over CBS's Pacific Coast Network; *Democracy at Work*, produced by the Council for Democracy and aired over NBC; and an OWI-sponsored effort called *My People*, which debuted over Mutual in February 1943. However, the last of these debuted without the benefit of Mutual's key station, WOR, which refused to drop a fifteen-minute commercial program to make way for the OWI half hour. The *Pittsburgh Courier* noted that in other similar cases, programs had been transcribed and aired at other times; it attributed WOR's refusal to do so to "the Southern bloc within the WOR setup" and highlighted the "ream of protests" that the station's omission incurred.[62]

Riots in Detroit and other cities in the summer of 1943—manifestations of the increasing, rather than diminishing, tension over race that could not be ignored—sparked a number of radio programs that openly addressed the problem of discrimination and rising resentment in the black community. On NBC, Paul Robeson spoke out for supporting the war effort despite racial inequality on an episode of *Labor for Victory*, produced jointly by the AFL and the CIO. *America's Town Forum* presented "Let's Face the Race Question," which featured a panel of prominent African American civic and cultural leaders. On CBS, the program *People's Platform* addressed the question, "Is the South solving its race problem?"—a construction that neatly distanced what was far from solely a southern issue. On local radio, "one of the most provocative and innovative black radio series of the postwar era" debuted in 1944 on WMCA in New York: *New World A-coming*, based on the book by Roi Ottley, who wrote several of the scripts, produced and directed by Michel Grayson, narrated by Canada Lee, and with music by Duke Ellington.[63]

Many of these programs focused on the figure of the black soldier. As Matthew Murray and Donald Meckiffe argue, this heroic figure functioned as a mediation of the tensions surrounding representation of African Americans during the war. At once central to the war theme yet carefully excluding larger "civilian" issues that might provoke greater resistance, the black soldier began to make an appearance in many broadcast and film venues.[64] The OWI and the War Department actively encouraged this kind of dramatic integration. Frank and Anne Hummert, in particular, cooperated enthusiastically with suggestions for incorporating black characters into scripts, introducing soldiers, especially, into such shows as *Our Gal Sunday*, *Young Widder Brown*, *Just Plain Bill*, *Amanda of Honeymoon Hill*, and *The Romance of Helen Trent*.[65] These efforts were kept under wraps; as Louis G. Cowan of the War Department wrote to Truman Gibson in May 1942 regarding the Hummerts' cooperation: "I have a feeling that in some ways this is going to be one of the most important propaganda devices that we could begin to use. Because of the nature of the approach and the material, this must all be kept very confidential. Otherwise, its effect might be injured."[66] Later, Gibson concurred: "In my opinion this is one of the most significant of all current efforts in the field of public relations. . . . Information and facts presented as the Hummert's [*sic*] are doing in their radio scripts will go a long way toward eradicating improper attitudes based on lack of knowledge."[67]

Other programs made sporadic efforts to introduce black characters or to propagate the information on black soldiers sent out by the OWI. But despite these efforts, which began in 1942 and increased in 1943, their occurrences were few and far between in an atmosphere that still maintained minstrel representations as the standard for indicating an African American presence on the air. Even in 1943, a listener (identified as a Harlem resident) could write following a show incorporating a black character, "Your program is the only one that I have heard that gives credit to my race. All the programs that I have heard so far have tried to make my race look as if they are childish, crap shooters, razor wielders, etc."[68] And the wartime compromise of concentration on the black soldier meant that postwar representations of race, without that partially endorsed figure to contain it, could once again lapse into simple absence; the "black soldier" faded from view after the war, with few war-inspired inclusionary representations to take his place.

In addition, as Murray and Meckiffe point out, the emphasis on masculinity did little to change the inclusion of black women on the air. Black women were still mostly confined to the role of domestic servant, and pressures to "improve" this representation could even backfire. For instance, in a 1944 letter from the Knox Reeves Advertising company addressed to Carl Wester and Company, Irna Phillips's producers, an advertising executive complains:

> I think you should know that General Mills has received quite a few letters from listeners—mostly Negroes—who complain about the way we present the character of Millicent, after having set her up as one who has had some educational advantages. The Negro race is, of course, supersensitive, and we cannot hope to satisfy everybody; but since we have established the fact that the girl has had some educational background, it might be better to let her play a little more straight and not sound quite so much like the end man in a minstral [sic] show.[69]

And if we consider the two early television programs featuring African American actors that carried over from radio—*Amos 'n' Andy* and *Beulah*—little of the wartime renegotiation of black representation can be perceived.

It is also significant that both *Amos 'n' Andy* and *Beulah*, as developed on radio, employed white men playing the roles of black men and, in the case of *Beulah*, a black woman: a double erasure.[70] Black women represent the most completely marginalized group in radio's practices, and their limited inclusion in both day- and nighttime programming troubles the notions of gender representation, discussed below, because black women were often depicted as working for pay in both the private and the public sphere, usually for white women who occupied not only a different racial category but a different class.

Speaking of black women made it clear that the white middle-class construction of the category "woman" was as noninclusive as the category "public," and raised uncomfortable distinctions of class and race even as the rhetoric of gender solidarity began to make social change possible. The discourse surrounding the black soldier worked to push black women even further toward the edges of the speakable; the postwar rhetoric of the masculinized "Golden Age" would limit the recognition of the vitally important role of black women even in coverage of the civil rights struggle on television.

Pitching Morale to the Troops

But meanwhile, as domestic radio struggled to redefine American identity on the home front, the increasing number of troops abroad soon brought about an extension of the OWI's mission to include broadcasting overseas. As Edward Kirby recounts in his history of radio in wartime, the shortwave rebroadcast of sports results to troops stationed in Iceland in 1941 expanded to the formation of the Armed Forces Radio Service. Recognizing a need, early in 1942, to "reach American troops all over the world with radio news and entertainment," the Bureau of Public Relations of the War Department began to look for someone to head up this operation, and, as Theodore Delay reports, "A Hollywood man appeared to be desirable because of the probably resultant contacts with the nation's greatest reservoir of entertainers."[71] The bureau contacted Danny Danker of J. Walter Thompson, who suggested Thomas H. A. Lewis, formerly vice president in charge of radio at Young & Rubicam.

Lewis, whose radio credits included *The Kate Smith Show*, *The Aldrich Family*, and *The Screen Guild Theater*—and who was married to screen star Loretta Young—accepted the appointment and with it a colonel's commission in the army. Later, Lewis would bring in another Y&R man, Sylvester "Pat" Weaver, to head up the Program Production Services office in Hollywood.[72] Working with a "Radio Subcommittee" composed of Niles Trammel of NBC, William Paley of CBS, and John Reber of JWT, along with Arthur Page, vice president of AT&T, and Ralph Starr Butler, an executive at the General Foods Corporation, Lewis launched the AFRS with a plan "based frankly on the 'Swan' campaign'"—that is, an advertising campaign that Y&R had previously undertaken for the Swan soap company, beginning with a market research effort directed at discovering the morale needs of U.S.

troops, just as the Swan campaign had researched the soap needs of U.S. housewives.[73] Based on the results of this survey, conducted in July and August 1942, the AFRS undertook to set up a network of stations, both permanent and portable, as the fighting fronts advanced, and to provide news and morale-building entertainment from home to the troops abroad, with an emphasis on entertainment. From the Armed Forces Network set up in Great Britain in 1943 to the "Mosquito Network" in the Pacific, the AFRS relied on a combination of recorded network rebroadcasts and original programming, all with the common goal of keeping up the morale and fighting spirit of American troops, couching information and educational materials in a matrix of familiar and reassuring entertainment.

Though at first existing network programs were recorded in their entirety, it soon became apparent that listening to familiar plugs for products singularly lacking overseas actually had a detrimental effect on morale. The AFRS instituted a policy of deleting commercial announcements from programs—a process called, interestingly, denaturing—but the often integrated nature of commercial content in radio programming made for broadcasts with large and gaping holes—such as those left by the deletion of introductions in which product names were inextricably woven into the narration or of transitions performed in interior commercial spots. AFRS personnel tried various methods to compensate for the lack of commercials—substituting "gag" announcements or extended musical interludes—but for some programs complete reworking was necessary.

Out of this necessity, several AFRS productions arose that were actually compilations from several network programs. Among them were the *Front Line Theater*, which assembled assorted network dramatic programs into a weekly format; this was succeeded by the *Globe Theater*, hosted by Herbert Marshall. Another, *Mystery Playhouse*, concentrated on various mystery dramas and was emceed by Peter Lorre. These shows employed hosts to record special introductory and transition material that unified the programs' disparate dramas and eliminated commercial content.

However, the true "commercials" of AFRS programs consisted of morale messages. Thomas Lewis described the AFRS's basic sales pitch: "Morale, Americanism, security, things are going 'OK' at home, we are sending you the needed materials, we are doing all we can to help you, this is your country—America, you are the best soldier there is, the 'why' of things, and finally *you will win*."[74] To get these basic points across, a roster of original programs to be produced within the AFRS was proposed in the summer of 1942.

The AFRS had inherited a program already in the works in the Bureau of Public Relations, the program most prominently associated with the AFRS today: *Command Performance*, a star-studded variety show that featured such luminaries as Jack Benny, Bob Hope, Bing Crosby, Frank Sinatra, Kate Smith, Bergen and McCarthy, and a host of Hollywood stars as well, often in combination. Based on the premise that ordinary soliders should be able to "command" the performances of any star in the land, these programs also grew into overseas tours of military bases and helped to boost the postwar popularity of many budding stars. *Command Performance* was supervised after 1945 by Pat Weaver, who used his agency contacts to procure the cooperation of top Hollywood agents, who in turn produced the program's star power. This could lead to spectacular combinations of talent, as in a production of "Dick Tracy" organized by Weaver in 1946, in which "Bing Crosby played Tracy, Bob Hope was Flat Top, Jimmy Durante was the Mole, Judy Garland was Snow White, and Dinah Shore was Tracy's long-suffering girlfriend, Tess Trueheart."

Other programs proposed for production on the AFRS's initial schedule included such varied offerings as *Music for Sunday*, described as a weekly half hour of "undenominational hymns" performed by recognized musicians; *Your Broadway and Mine*, recordings of Broadway shows edited for radio; *The Sports Parade*, which provided important sports news from home; *Hi, Dad!*, a program featuring the activities of soldiers' children; *GI Jive with Jill*, a musical disc-jockey program that introduced one the most popular of the AFRS's regular performers, Martha Wilkerson as "Jill," who combined news items from various hometowns and letters from servicemen with popular music; *Yanks on the March*, a dramatized news story aired weekly; and *Freedom's People*, described as "a half-hour weekly Negro variety program."

Though *Freedom's People* was initially "intended to be slanted for colored troop morale," by the fall of 1942 the idea was revamped by Major Mann Holiner, whose pre-army career involved "the production of Negro theatricals."[75] The AFRS's handling of this idea demonstrates the especially destablizing role of race in wartime, and forecasts the way in which television would gingerly address the subject to its postwar audience. By mid-1942, racial tensions within the

U.S. military were building to the peak they would reach in the troubled year of 1943. It had become apparent to African Americans both within the military and in the general public that the government's recruitment efforts stopped far short of full inclusion in all activities of the armed forces. The army initially restricted the numbers of black recruits and assigned them rigidly to noncombatant positions. Blacks were barred from the Coast Guard and the marines and limited to serving in the mess in the navy. As noted above, segregation on army bases exceeded that prevalent over most of the United States; the military was a hostile environment for African American recruits, who found themselves banned from most on-post facilities, such as USOs, canteens, theaters, and even chapels. And, as Harvard Sitkoff notes, "Blacks who protested were harassed and intimidated; those who persisted in their opposition were transferred, placed in the stockade, or dishonorably discharged."[76]

Off post, with many of the largest training bases located in the South, the atmosphere was even more violent. Black soldiers in uniform were beaten and lynched. Race riots connected to military base conflicts broke out in cities across the country in 1942 and, despite the military's attempts at suppression, were covered widely in the black press. By 1943, the situation had "exploded into an epidemic of racial violence," with 242 racial battles in forty-seven cities, culminating in the Detroit riot in June, in which thirty-four were killed and more than seven hundred injured.[77] Overseas, the U.S. Army introduced segregation based on race into countries with no such native traditions, and in some places black soldiers experienced far more favorable treatment from foreign—even "enemy"—citizens than they did from their own compatriots.

Clearly, the AFRS's selling message—"Things are going 'OK' at home. . . . This is your country—America"—would be a hard sell to black troops stationed abroad; equally clearly, black soldiers, faced with both the hardship of war and the relentless barrage of racial discrimination, were in desperate need of morale-building messages. In an atmosphere in which the mere acknowledgment of racial tension was capable of undermining morale—so that racial tensions on army bases not only could not be mentioned in news reports but could not even be included on the list of censored subjects[78]—the idea of a program slanted toward Negro troops was regarded as dangerous. As Delay explains, "Slanting the program would admit the existence of colored-white conflicts within the services, and would possibly intensify the problem." However, the uneasy fact remained that *Command Performance* and indeed all of the other AFRS productions were explicitly and exclusively white. So the name *Freedom's People*, with its implication of the contested role that black identity held in the American public, was changed to the more neutral *Jubilee*, and the program was reconceptualized as "a fine Negro variety show using foremost talent which was to be selected only for its entertainment value. . . . Its entertainment value would be of morale assistance to *all* troops."[79]

Broadcast first on October 9, 1942, *Jubilee* became one of the most popular of the AFRS offerings, its recordings today preserving much of the finest in jazz music available from the 1940s. Its debut program offered Ethel Waters, Rex Ingram, Eddie Anderson, Duke Ellington and his orchestra, and the Hall Johnson Choir. Later, Ernest Whitman served as host; other featured artists included Lena Horne, the Mills Brothers, Noble Sissle, and Jesse Cryer.[80] Yet its segregated practice, as Delay notes, solidified the AFRS practice of offering no programs specifically designed to deal with the morale problems of black soldiers for the duration of the war. Even when "a colored general" (General Benjamin O. Davis) asked for an effort to be made to address the specific concerns of black troops in 1944, the AFRS declined, although "later in the war special consideration was given to 'Command Performance' requests for colored performers in order to assist a general Negro service battalion morale problem, but no special indication of the problem was made by the simple fulfillment of these requests."[81]

However, the years 1943–44 mark a high point of black voices on the national networks and specific attention to America's ongoing racial hypocrisy. Yet, as William Barlow concludes: "Never before in the history of network broadcasting had racial issues been probed so openly on the national airwaves. . . . But even as global victory was at hand, the discussion of race relations and the emphasis on black programming was disappearing from the American airwaves."[82] With the ending of the war and the lessening of the urgency constantly to encourage and support an inclusive national identity based on "unity without uniformity," network radio could return to its normal state of silence on racial matters. The issues of returning veterans, "full [white male] employment" (never conceptualized as including significant numbers of blacks or women), and conversion from defense manufacturing to production of consumer goods would occupy U.S. society and the media industry in the immediate postwar years. Television, too, loomed on the horizon, having been postponed by the exigencies of war. The postwar period would see attempts to carry over more inclusive racial representations to the new medium, but in a manner designed to defuse racial identity and deny its social consequences, rather than acknowledge it.[83] On the other hand, the networks' abandonment of radio for television (along with the simultaneous opening up of the underutilized FM band) would provide opportunities for black voices on the air in venues previously untenable, as the dominant cultural focus shifted to television.

Redefining the Public Woman

Recruiting a nation for war meant addressing its female population as well. Although the various morale-building efforts of the OWI on radio reached an increasingly feminine audience in the 1940s, it was the campaign to recruit women into wartime service in the workplace that marked the greatest change in radio's address to women and the way that women's proper role was conceptualized. Maureen Honey argues that the radical nature of the call for women to move out of the private sphere of domesticity and consumerism and into a public role in the workplace was always tempered by the persistence of competing symbolic constructions: "Two conflicting images of women existed during the war: the strong dependable patriot who could run the nation and the innocent vulnerable homemaker who depended upon soldiers to protect her way of life."[84] Nonetheless, by bringing the tensions between private domesticity and public presence into wide circulation, often in a way that made domesticity now a choice that might even be selfish and unpatriotic in certain situations, wartime media succeeded in recasting the identity of the audience to whom they appealed. The OWI's major approach to this topic was its "Womanpower" campaign of 1942.

Coordinated through the War Advertising Council, U.S. media recruited women for war work in a variety of venues. J. Walter Thompson produced a series of short dramatic spots, called "Listen Women," that ran adjacent to daytime programming on NBC and were designed to "sell" the idea of work outside the home, not only as a patriotic duty for women but as a solution to a wide range of personal and social ills. In one script, a woman contemplates applying for wartime work but worries that her husband will raise a series of objections.

Casting this debate as an imagined argument allows the woman to answer each objection, in increasingly adamant terms. As her husband argues, "Don't you think I can support you myself? Do you *have* to work?" and "Factory work is a man's job. It'll tire you out too much," and finally, "No! Definitely NO! It's a man's job. Do you think I want people to go around saying I can't support my wife!" his partner counters with appeals straight from the pages of the OWI campaign booklet, ending with, "But I don't care! I'm needed, and I'm going to work for my country if it breaks up my happy home."[85] Of course, it turns out that her husband offers no such resistance, even bringing the subject up himself and encouraging her initiative. Concluding in a direct appeal to the audience, with what may have been one of the more revolutionary concepts of the Womanpower drive—"If you can run a vacuum cleaner you can run a machine in a factory . . . easily" and promising women, "You'll get good pay . . . usually the same that a man gets for equal work"—the Listen Women campaign and others like it brought to the fore a series of issues (equal pay for equal work, the arbitrary nature of distinctions between men's and women's jobs, women's strength and ability in the workplace) that would not be forgotten after the war.

Yet the challenge to the "naturalness" of female domesticity went beyond temporary patriotic justifications; in another script, work outside the home is presented as carrying a psychological benefit for all women, war or no. In this scenario, an overwrought woman bursts into the office of "Doctor Thelma Nissen (famous woman psychiatrist)" and confides to the woman she finds there, "I'm so nervous—so unhappy. . . . I tell you, I just want to stand up and SCREAM!" She is advised that the solution lies in "work. Hard work. Work with your hands and your body that makes you forget yourself and discover how strong you really can be if you must. And you must! . . . I mean WORK in the plainest, simplest sense of the word. Work at a huge machine that weighs thirty tons . . . work in over-alls, with an hour out for lunch . . . and back to the job again." As the grateful woman goes hurrying off to the U.S. Employment Service, it is revealed that her adviser is not Dr. Nissen, but a "gray haired woman" named Mrs. Blair, a former patient whose nerves had recovered under the regime she outlined.[86] In the world created by Womanpower, women are strong, can operate heavy machinery "easily," need work for personal fulfillment, and have a well-defined duty as public citizens—and these are factors any "gray haired woman" can recognize, not just the experts. These meanings may have exceeded those intended by the OWI—and, indeed, they were hastily contained even as the war drew to a close in 1944 and 1945—but they had created scenarios for the public woman that would not fade away so easily. Yet it should be noted that all of these appeals were directed at the class of women whose lives permitted a solely domestic role, leaving many working-class and black women outside the boundaries of developing feminist address, as noted above.

Of course, the most public woman on the air in the 1940s was in a position few could hope to obtain: Senator Mary Marlin. Jane Crusinberry's character moved into wartime mode with alacrity, incorporating wartime issues and morale-building propaganda into her program even as Mary faced a constant barrage of dramatic personal problems. During her reelection as senator in 1944, the serial featured several stump speeches in which Mary emphasized the need for men and women of courage in public life, placing her own role in the context of American women who had served their country:

> All through American history, the women of America have fought for a land of OPPORTUNITY, FAITH, and FREEDOM. . . . In the year 1944, as it was in the year of 1692, this is a land of UNLIMITED future for Americans—men and women—IF . . . IF that future holds UNLIMITED OPPORTUNITY—for every individual to attain the highest achievement of which he is capable. That is the Great American Dream.[87]

This is explicitly an appeal to equality in public life in which women are included. Elsewhere, Crusinberry, through her central character, urged women to take up war work—"Now, especially, women are needed in other places, outside the home"[88]—and emphasized the importance to America's fighting troops of the work Mary Marlin did in the Senate. As another character states, "She feels it is her duty to stay in the Senate and make sure that the Great American Dream for which their sons and husbands are fighting will be waiting for them on their return from the battlefields."[89] Here was a public role for a woman on a large scale, and Crusinberry's audiences followed Mary's career avidly.

Yet already by late 1943, despite continued high ratings, Crusinberry's sponsors began to shift uneasily under the pressure of this high-profile public role. This may have been exacerbated when Kirby

Hawkes, Crusinberry's producer at Benton & Bowles for Procter & Gamble, left the agency in June 1943. Hawkes and Crusinberry had enjoyed a compatible working partnership, but Hawkes's replacement, Walter Craig, soon found numerous problems in Crusinberry's work. She resisted his criticisms in lengthy battles fought by letter, telegram, and plot outline; in August 1943, Procter & Gamble dropped its sponsorship. Standard Brands picked the show up and Crusinberry came under J. Walter Thompson supervision, at which time the serial also changed networks and leading actor, running against its Benton & Bowles/NBC replacement, which featured its former star and in its former time slot.

John Reber and Robert Colwell immediately began to seek outside advice about the direction the serial should take, consulting both Irna Phillips and Charles Christoph in the spring of 1944. Though their objective, as stated, was simply "to pump up the CAB [Crossley ratings] just like we do on night time,"[90] both objected to precisely those characteristics that had made *Mary Marlin* unique among serials: its concentration on Mary's public position and politics. Both suggested that the story line be redomesticated. Christoph wrote:

> The really basic point to remember is that quickly—immediately—Mary becomes . . . during this conflict of basic loyalties . . . not a cold big shot in Washington—but an ordinary woman with ordinary emotions and fears, in dire trouble, but doing her duty as a crusader now, for Justice gallantly, *and, fighting to protect herself and her loved ones*. This change in Mary's point of view should be clearly indicated. . . . the political matters simply highlight Mary's "every-woman" values. She's really just a woman "like you."[91]

Phillips, at that time under contract to J. Walter Thompson as a consultant on daytime programs, advised along similar lines:

> Let's get back to the plain Mary Marlin—the plain, average, everyday woman in a small town who loves her husband—a story that in many ways served as a mirror for a daytime audience in which their own lives were reflected. . . . We should know that her only consideration, her only desire is a reunion of the family. This desire is in the hearts of thousands of women today. Money, position, prestige should be out the window. The only security, the only reality, a family unit.[92]

Phillips went on to express doubts that Crusinberry should be the writer to take this on, and urged J. Walter Thompson to find a replacement. It is possible that she had her own company in mind; at any rate, the agency acknowledged that "obviously you can't give these to Crusinberry as being Irna Phillips' ideas," but they did pass along Christoph's. Crusinberry responded quickly, "Your letter of March 22nd received. Mr. Christoph's suggestions are so foreign to my contemplated plot and the background of Mary Marlin, that they would involve a complete change in the main characters as well as the entire story."[93] Though she also attached several plot outlines that would involve reuniting Mary with her long-lost husband Joe, there was no further hint of abandoning the basic Washington premise.

This obduracy resulted in Crusinberry's being removed from her position of primary writer for the serial. Though *Mary Marlin* remained under contract with Standard Brands, Crusinberry later explained that "during this time there was considerable agency plot interference and, as the best way out of a difficult situation, I allowed them to plot the show and engage their own writers."[94] The new JWT-produced version kept Mary Marlin in Washington, but a new kind of plot tension took precedence, one that now explicitly pitted Mary's duties as a public, working woman against her responsibilities as a mother and a wife. First, a series of scandals around Mary's personal life functioned to "raise questions about Mary's ability (or any woman's ability) to perform a public role. . . . As her 'scandalous' behavior is discussed and publicized, it becomes more difficult in the serial to consider Mary an effective public servant."[95] As Mary's private life becomes public, the difficulty of negotiating the "private" identity of femininity in the public sphere is brought out. Second, Mary's combination of motherhood and public life is questioned when Joe's "Aunt Elizabeth" arrives from Iowa to take custody of Mary's son, Davey, and Mary must make the age-old decision to put her child's interests first:

> If this keeps up, Davey can be marked psychologically for the rest of his life. He can't have a normal childhood—He'll have no father to depend on . . . and his mother in a glass cage for everyone to stare at. . . . I . . . I . . . won't have him grow up in an atmosphere like that. . . . my career is hurting my child and Davey means more to me than anything in the world. If I have to resign from the Senate, I will. I can't ruin Davey's life.[96]

Though Mary had been able to balance child and career in previous years, now, suddenly, the domestic imperative loomed large. As the war drew to a close and agencies and sponsors began to think of the years ahead, Mary Marlin's role as a public woman began to look less desirable, and her reintegration into the domestic sphere became an increasingly urgent goal. However, the audience did not respond to these changes as the agency hoped. Ratings plummeted precipitously, and *The Story of Mary Marlin* was canceled March 18, 1945, never to revive.

This tension that always surrounded the working women of the war period revealed itself in advertising as well. Maureen Honey cites an ad run in May 1944 in the *Saturday Evening Post* that encapsulates the conflict between private and public roles and hints of the resolution to come. An attractive young mother in overalls, about to bicycle off to work, pauses as her daughter asks, "Mother, when will you stay home again?" The ad copy for ADEL Precision Products Corp. answers:

> Some jubilant day mother *will* stay home again, doing the job she likes best—making a home for you and daddy. . . . Meanwhile she's learning the vital importance of precision in equipment made by ADEL. In her post-war home she'll want appliances with the same high degree of precision and she will get them when ADEL converts its famous *Design Simplicity* to products of equal dependability for home and industry.[97]

Here we see an articulation of women's "new" place in the postwar economy, returned to the private sphere but able to apply the lessons of wartime work to the scientific suburban home. The uncomfortable fact that, of women workers polled in 1944, more than 70 percent wished to keep their jobs outside the home would be quickly pushed to the side under the demands of "full employment" and the new consumer economy.[98] Though the commercialism of radio had been identified by some wartime critics as a force working against progressive politics, critics who had particularly condemned the "drool" of daytime radio for its failings of triviality and escapism, during the war years sponsors, networks, and government alike combined to produce a reframing of women's roles that made a strong, though always contained, argument against the gender status quo. However, these same forces could change their tune when the winds of war slackened and the demands of the postwar economy became visible. As women were urged, forcibly, out of their wartime jobs and back into the domestic sphere, television would become at once the prize and the chief selling agent of the postwar suburban promise.

Overall, the legacy of wartime radio for the policies and practices of television has been seriously neglected by broadcast historians. Three elements in particular stand out. First, the tension between commercialism and public service, arising out of the "writers' war" in the OWI among "New Deal" critics, writers, and policy makers, would carry over into discussions of television policy, culminating in the Kennedy years under Newton Minow. Second, the identification of the commercial with the feminine through the debate over daytime serials would have important consequences for network practice, as I argue in the conclusion to this volume; likewise, much of television's insistence on the domesticated female image might be read as containment of the transgressive possibilities opened up by wartime radio. Finally, the wartime policy of nonrecognition of racial differences under an increasingly strained cover of enforced assimilation into a dominant "white" norm carried over into television's early years. The otherwise peculiar double standards of early TV—a rhetoric of inclusion contradicted by the persistence of minstrel representations and almost complete marginalization—had its model in wartime contradictions and negotiations, soon to be exacerbated by the pressures of the Cold War. In an atmosphere in which the acknowledgment of any type of social difference or conflict became tantamount to an endorsement of communism, the "integration without identification" policies of NBC, for instance, ensured that only the least important aspects of social issues would be addressed. Not until the 1960s would pressure build to break through the enforced unity of wartime identity.

Conclusion: Terms of Preferment

The end of the war brought a speedy disbanding of government agencies and an equally speedy introduction of the broadcasting industry's long-delayed prize: television. By 1947, a limited schedule of network programming was available in most large population centers, and local stations filled in increasing numbers of hours each day. Little discussion of changes to the basic structure of broadcasting preceded TV's debut. Thanks to the industry's cooperation during the war years, not only in the field of broadcasting but in the manufacture of strategic defense technology, the government cooperated willingly in broadcasting's smooth transition to a peacetime economy. Development of television brought not only employment in factories converted to consumer electronic manufacture and a pat on the back for a job well done to the electronics industries, but also a prime medium of promotion and sale of the many other goods and services that would propel the postwar economy.[1] It made sense, then, that many of network television's early attractions included those so successful on radio, adapted to the new medium, such as *The Goldbergs*, *The Life of Riley*, *Amos 'n' Andy*, *The Jack Benny Show*, *The Silver Theater*, *Lux Video Theatre*, *Lights Out!*, *Easy Aces*, *Kay Kyser's Kollege of Musical Knowledge*, *One Man's Family*, *I Remember Mama*, and many more.

But contrary to some assertions, it was not advertiser abandonment of radio that motivated the rapid removal of network assets from the old medium to the new; rather, networks made a deliberate policy decision to concentrate development in the new technology, where sales potential was vast and regulatory conditions favorable, at the expense of radio. During the immediate postwar years, still-flourishing radio network profits were taken from that side of the business and applied directly to television's growth. Radio programs were broadcast simultaneously over both media, or "simulcast," often with decreasing regard for their intelligibility to radio listeners.

As radio waned as a national medium, networks broke down and local stations found themselves increasingly on their own. The rise of "music format" radio made use of the newly "discovered" FM band (its use having been suppressed by RCA prior to the war) to encourage a new local approach to radio. As the "disc jockey," previously featured in some local morning and late nighttime slots, slowly took over the entire radio schedule and network-distributed programs declined to nearly zero, in many cities a new "black format" arose, pioneered in Chicago by Jack L. Cooper. Cooper had been on the air for many years, originating one of the first shows directed at the black audience, *The All-Negro Hour* on WSBC in 1929. This was a sixty-minute variety show employing an all African American cast of musicians and comics. WSBC was an "ethnic language" station, which sold time to producers of many nationalities, who acted both as showmen and brokers, putting together a schedule of performances and selling sponsorships to local advertisers. Later Cooper originated and produced several serials aimed at the black audience, and expanded into the disc-jockey format in 1937. By 1948, Cooper was a successful radio entrepreneur, with more than forty hours of programs airing on four different Chicago stations, grossing more than $185,000 annually. This economic success allowed Cooper to lauch the program *Listen Chicago* in 1948, a news and panel discussion show on topics of the day, including the growing campaigns for civil rights.[2]

Other cities began to feature black-oriented programming during this period, often based on music, but for the first time allowing black voices a space on the airwaves in an arena uncontrolled by whites. WDIA Memphis, owned by two white men, Bert Ferguson and John Pepper, hired Nat D. Williams, a widely respected local high school teacher, newspaper columnist, and musical entrepreneur, to put together a program that would address the African American audience. His initial rhythm and blues show, called *Tan Town Jamboree*, debuted in October 1948 and led to a total conversion to a black-oriented format within the year, directed and managed by Williams. Blues player B. B. King started his career as a disc jockey on WDIA; the station also featured a daytime program hosted by Willa Monroe, known as the "Tan Town Homemaker." Most influential was a public affairs program created and hosted by Williams called *Brown America Speaks*, which focused on race issues "addressed from a black perspective."[3] The format quickly spread to such stations as WEDR Birmingham, WOBS Jacksonville, WBOK New Orleans, WSOK Nashville, WLOU Louisville, WCIN Cincinnatti, KXLW St. Louis, WABQ Cleveland, and WOOL Washington, D.C. WERD Atlanta became the first black-owned station using this format. As Barlow summarizes: "In 1949 there were only four radio stations in the entire country with formats that directly appealed to black consumers. By 1954 there were no less than two hundred stations in this category, and that number rose to four hundred by 1956."[4] These stations not only brought a kind of music to the airwaves that had previously been excluded but introduced a new style of "jive" DJ talk, soon imitated by white personalities such as Wolfman Jack and Alan Freed. One New Orleans personality, Vernon Winslow, in 1948 originated a progam called *The Poppa Stoppa Show* on WJMR New Orleans, to "showcase the city's nightlife and music" for which he developed a special way of talking based on black street English: "It came from the rhyme rap that folks in the streets were using in New Orleans. The language was for insiders, most white folks couldn't understand it so it became a unique identity and people were proud of it as a way to show solidarity and brotherhood. I wrote my radio scripts in that language and Poppa Stoppa was my mouthpiece, so to speak."[5] Winslow himself was an art professor at Dillard College, trained at the Chicago Art Institute; this language was a creation his white employers soon encouraged him to teach to white DJs. Later Winslow moved to WEZZ, where he became known as "Doctor Daddyo." The format quickly spread among urban youth, both black and white. Not only soul music but rock 'n' roll emerged out of this newly liberated radio terrain, as the dominant social and economic focus shifted to television.

In network television, economic stability rested on the carryover of the relationship among sponsor, agency, and network so successful during the previous three decades of radio. Agencies such as J. Walter Thompson and Young & Rubicam took the lead in developing television programs for their clients. JWT's *Kraft Television Theatre* was one of the first live anthology dramas, debuting in 1947. By 1955, JWT had formed the "J. Walter Thompson Company Television Workshop" to research advertising techniques for the new medium, including matching program types to products and managing scheduling and marketing research, based on their success with such programs as

Father Knows Best, The Adventures of Ozzie and Harriet, Lux Video Theater (later the *Lux Playhouse*), *Omnibus, Meet the Press,* and *The Ed Sullivan Show.* By 1956, the company had built one of the largest TV studios outside the major networks to test and preproduce the programs under its direction.[6] However, already costs were rising and soon pressure to cede the controlling position occupied by the agencies for so long began to push toward network control.

The live anthology drama, eulogized as a brief, shining moment of creative integrity and artistry in a dreary commercial process, grew out of early agency ventures into television. The format itself represents less of a change from radio practices, where live drama had become a staple, than the convergence of a set of conditions, not least of them discursive, that came together in the wake of wartime public service and high purpose. William Boddy describes in depth the way that the "golden age" was positioned in the writing of influential critics and broadcast executives as a drama of high-minded networks versus the unholy alliance of advertisers and Hollywood: high ideals of public service carried out by serious young men from the New York dramatic scene in conflict with the base commercial purposes of sponsors, whose corrupting and stifling effects brought this glorious period to a premature end, in favor of cheap, Hollywood-produced sitcoms and westerns (the fact that sponsors and their agencies had brought this period about is frequently overlooked).[7] This was a useful strategy for the networks, who were able to use it in the wake of the "quiz show scandals" of the late 1950s to justify reducing advertiser control and exerting network dominance over television production and schedules. But half the work had already been done in the discursive battles of the Second World War. The bad odor of commercialism, its resistance to progressive social views, its antithetical relationship to public service goals, its feminized shallowness and triviality, had been well established in places like the OWI, the critical media, and social science discourse during the war years. But clearly television would remain commercial; no public debate even to the extent of that over educational radio in the 1930s took place in the late 1940s. How to reconcile the basic commercialism of television with the high expectations for public service placed on it, both by critical commentators honed by the war and by favorable regulatory treatment? The point man in this debate, the person placed by the leading network, NBC, to negotiate and in some ways embody the terms of this conundrum, was a character we have met before: Sylvester "Pat" Weaver.

From his experience with Fred Allen at Young & Rubicam, to his wartime service with the AFRS, to his emergence on the television scene in charge of programming at NBC (and later in his interest in subscription television after ejection from the network),[8] Pat Weaver's career traces the high points of midcentury broadcasting, and he has been treated as a key figure by many historians. Though his position as, first, vice president of the Program Division and then president of the NBC network extended only from 1949 until 1955, his crucial role in defining and developing the emerging medium of television has become a staple assertion of broadcasting history. Three related programming practices are usually counted among Weaver's key innovations: the network "spectacular," the "magazine format" show exemplified by *Today*, *Tonight*, and *Home*, and the concept of multiple sponsorship.[9] On these three accomplishments, along with Weaver's personal charisma and overtly "intellectual" style, the Weaver myth has grown to nearly unassailable proportions. It is hard to find an account that does not speak highly of Weaver's efforts at NBC. Terms such as *professional*, *showman*, *theorist*, and *thinker* surround most invocations of his name. The leading broadcast history textbook, *Stay Tuned*, contributes to this view: "*Today*, and its sister *Tonight* show . . . are good examples of unique television formats—both devised by NBC's brilliant network chief of the early 1950s, Sylvester 'Pat' Weaver."[10] A similar comprehensive account states decisively, "Weaver conceived a new form, participating sponsorship, which allowed a number of national sponsors to carve a program into separate blocks of time, each considered its own segment."[11] Another historian concludes, "*Today* amounted to sheer innovation on Pat Weaver's part."[12]

These statements largely echo several highly strategic magazine pieces from the 1950s. In a two-part series in the *New Yorker* in October 1954, Thomas Whiteside reported that Weaver "worked out a fairly revolutionary method of advertising. . . . In defiance of the prevailing system, in which a single advertiser bought and controlled an entire program, Weaver . . . offered short segments of time on them to several advertisers, who could insert whatever commercials they chose."[13] *Harper's Magazine* repeated this assertion two years later: "Weaver's approach to sponsorship was equally original. He pioneered what he called the 'magazine concept,' by which the network sells spot advertisements on programs the way a magazine sells pages."[14]

What are we to make, then, of a memo appearing in the NBC files dated February 1954, from Davidson Taylor to Robert W. Sarnoff?[15] The memo was written in response to a letter received by General Sarnoff from Martha Rountree, a journalist and radio broadcaster (owner and producer of the long-running *Meet the Press*) who charged NBC with having stolen her idea for a magazine-style women's show. Rountree called *Home* "an almost exact copy of her suggested format for a one-hour five day per week woman's magazine of the air." In his memo suggesting an appropriate response to Rountree, Taylor states bluntly, "The idea of a woman's magazine of the air five days a week is one of the oldest ideas in radio and television." His proposed letter goes on to explain:

> I am sure you know that the idea of a woman's magazine of the air is a more or less basic one. It actually has been done on network radio and was tried on network television unsuccessfully in the early 40s. You may be interested to know that we have proposals of this kind dating back as far as the month of June, 1929, at which time a program very similar to *Home* was proposed for radio by Margaret Cuthbert, a member of the NBC Staff to Bertha Brainard in the NBC Program Department.[16]

His invocation of feminine names is significant in light of the strategy that I will argue lay behind NBC's programming strategy in this crucial postfreeze period of the 1950s. The contradiction between the public assertion of Weaver's programming genius and the in-house acknowledgment of a very different genealogy for this particular idea reveals the suppression of one of radio broadcasting's most successful and influential potential legacies to television.

Neither the magazine concept nor multiple sponsorship was a new idea, and Weaver and NBC were well aware of this. Instead, their deliberate attribution of the authorship of these concepts to Weaver was intended to remove the feminine stigma that surrounded this well-established format and elevate it to the high level of public service so eagerly pursued by NBC television during its early years. The highly successful and now almost entirely "forgotten" career of Mary Margaret McBride—one of the foremost practitioners of this format, on NBC no less—exemplifies the uses and appeal of women's magazine shows in radio, and a comparison can help to point out the very different and far more limited definition of "women's" as opposed to general interests that Weaver's *Home* and *Today* shows enforced in the new masculinist regime of network TV.

Nancy Fraser's analysis of the gendered public sphere and her notion of "subaltern counterpublics" help to make it clear that NBC employed gender distinctions strategically in this mythmaking process.[17] In network television's renegotiation of private and public roles in postwar America, television networks attempted to justify the enormous amount of public investment in establishment of the new medium by promising to bring public service into private homes. Postwar television rejected the privatized, feminized commercialism of daytime radio in particular in favor of a new public role: educational, serious, and masculine. Weaver spearheaded this approach and became at once the purveyor and leading symbol of NBC's postwar strategy—an approach that should be understood less as a mark of personal genius than as a very pragmatic response to the economic and regulatory pressures of the period, as Vance Kepley has argued.[18] Yet every mythical hero must slay his monster, and in this case the monster was the taint of feminized mass culture linked to commercialism, as embodied in the success—and excess—of Mary Margaret McBride.

Origins of the Magazine Format

As I noted in chapter 5, the magazine-format program involving multiple sponsors in segmented participation was very familiar to the American radio public of the late 1940s—or at least to half of it: the feminine half. As Taylor's memo candidly admits, magazine programs had formed a staple of daytime radio. Their popularity culminated in the extremely successful daytime magazine show of Mary Margaret McBride, on the air continuously for twenty years by 1954 and reaching more than eight million listeners per day—20 percent of the available broadcast audience. McBride's celebrity was hardly a secret confined to daytime radio listeners, either: her fifteenth anniversary celebration in 1949 was held in Yankee Stadium, the only facility large enough to hold the seventy-five thousand people who filled every seat and formed huge crowds outside. Special subway trains were arranged to handle the enormous numbers of people who gathered from all over the New York area. Five years previously, her tenth anniversary program had filled Madison Square Garden. Other indicators of McBride's high profile include her being named "outstanding woman of the year in radio" in 1950 by the Associated Press poll of U.S. women's editors, her selection by Forbes Sales Executives organization as one of the top twelve "salesmen" of the year in 1952, and the spawning of what one commentator estimated to be more than three hundred imitators on the air by the late 1940s. Yet given that her audience was mostly female, and thus existed outside the visible horizon of most honor-bestowing institutions, a more accurate indicator of McBride's popularity and cultural impact is the volume of mail she received. Estimated in 1944 at five thousand letters weekly, during a World War II paper drive she was able to donate more than three million letters that she had stored away. Fans frequently included with their letters what *Newsweek* called "bizarre gifts," and many accounts describe her Central Park South apartment as "overflow[ing] with dolls, hand-worked aprons and other homely presents."[19] Letters in the Library of Congress collection testify to the close personal relationship many in the audience felt they had with the woman they listened to daily.[20]

Yet Taylor was incorrect in naming 1929 as the date of the first women's magazine of the air, as we have seen. Station WJZ had begun a woman's half hour from 4:00 to 4:30 each weekday in 1926, featuring Mrs. Julian Heath, president of the National Housewives League, as discussed in chapter 5. By 1932, at least two of the twenty daytime homemakers' programs on the air involved multiple sponsorship: Ida Bailey Allen's *Radio Homemakers Club*, on CBS twice a week; and NBC's *Radio Household Institute*, three times a week. Both of these latter shows had been built up by producers outside the network, who purchased the time and brokered it to sponsors whose products could be featured in each day's program. The attitude of the networks toward such a situation can be seen in a memo from Margaret Cuthbert to John F. Royal in 1932 headed "An answer to the daytime broadcasting presentation from the outside":

> A little over three years ago Mr. Herbert S. Houston and Mr. Edwin Muller, Jr. assumed the development of Mrs. Ida Bailey Allen as a food broadcaster on the Columbia chain. . . . Time was secured from the Columbia chain, and she was systematically built up with the public. In three years, through the sale of her services, a revenue of over a million dollars in time sold and half a million in talent charges were obtained. The sponsors included Procter & Gamble, Royal Baking Powder, National Biscuit, American Sugar Refining, Pillsbury's Flour, Beech-Nut and about thirty other leading advertisers. If such a result could be attained by a small outside organization, working without capital, a much greater

result should be had by NBC developing such a plan with one or more leading authorities as broadcasters.[21]

The network proved unwilling to invest the kind of capital Cuthbert envisioned in her plan. Even after networks and national advertisers turned to the serial format, local stations continued their interest in the kind of home product advertising that could be tied to programming for women, and in 1934 station WOR in New York devised a format that would bring Mary Margaret McBride onto the air.

Homemaker shows hosted by fictional characters had already been tried by a few single sponsors, the most famous being Betty Crocker for General Mills. Carol Hill at station WOR decided that a similar format might work locally for that station, and set up interviews for a daytime multiple-sponsor household advice format.[22] McBride, a journalist and feature writer of national reputation whose career had been adversely affected by the Depression, auditioned and was hired to appear for fifteen minutes daily as "Martha Deane," a character she very soon abandoned. Envisioned by station staff as a "grandmotherly type" who would dispense advice in the guise of stories about her numerous grandchildren and neighbors, the Martha Deane persona interfered with McBride's conception of what a worthwhile women's program should be like. In an incident that became part of McBride's standard news release biography, she recanted her identity on air with a dramatic pause, then this announcement: "I find it necessary to kill all my family. I'm not a grandmother. I don't have any children. I'm not even married. I'm not interested in telling you how to take spots out of Johnny's suit or how to mix all the leftovers in the ice box. I'm a reporter and I've just been to the flea circus. If you would like to hear about it, I'll tell you."[23] Though maintaining the Martha Deane name, McBride continued her program as a mix of product endorsements, reports of personal experiences, current events, and social commentary. In 1937 she began a three-times-weekly broadcast over CBS under her own name, while continuing at WOR. At this point, too, she began her policy of inviting guests on the show, ranging from political figures to celebrities to common folk with stories to tell.

All of her broadcasts were unscripted and ad-libbed, but already her own (and presumably her audience's) concept of what McBride was doing on the air began to conflict with reports appearing in the mainstream press. *Newsweek* described McBride in 1938 as a "onetime

Missouri farm girl [who] rambles along in an Ozark accent, ignoring all rules of radio form and dignity . . . the woman who gabs aimlessly as if at a church social, the woman who, in other words, chatters rudderless on the radio just as most people chatter in everyday life."[24] McBride's own description of her radio technique revealed considerably more planning: "When I am on the air, I imagine that I am talking to a young married woman with a couple of children. A woman who at one time had a job and is still interested in the jobs of other people, the business world. So I talk about people who do things, the world at large. I try to give her the vicarious thrill of going places and meeting people."[25]

McBride apparently perceived little conflict between reporting on the world at large and reporting on consumer products, as long as she could test them beforehand and give informed endorsements. The ad-libbed, extemporaneous nature of her program and her endorsements allowed her to broadcast in both venues, WOR and CBS, with different sponsors. It also differentiated her program from most others on the air at the time, most of which relied heavily on scripts, and pointed in the direction NBC would take with *Tonight* and *Today*. During the war she effectively promoted drives and bond sales and was particularly effective in recruiting women for war work.[26] After the war, it was a testimony to McBride's impact that General Omar Bradley selected her show for his first radio appearance. She became known as a compelling interviewer, persuading many of her guests to speak more freely and intimately than they would with any other radio broadcaster. Eleanor Roosevelt and Mayor Fiorello La Guardia were frequent guests.

McBride was an independent radio broker, taking on sponsors—who lined up to be considered for her show—deciding on the nature of her on-air endorsements, booking talent and determining program content, and switching networks when it suited her. In 1940, McBride gave up her WOR program and went to a forty-five-minute format on NBC, aired daily at 1:00. Now producing two forty-five-minute shows per week, on CBS and NBC, McBride could handle twelve different sponsors per week on each one. Each sponsor paid roughly $150 for this weekly mention, besides paying the network directly for time. It is estimated that McBride's income reached $100,000 by 1942. Out of this she paid her on-air assistant Vincent Connolly, two women to aid her in product research and program booking, besides "two to four typists" to handle fan mail responses, all under the direction of her manager and lifelong companion, Stella Karn.[27] In 1950, when, as the *New Republic* reported, she "got mad at NBC" and left for rival network ABC, she took her seventeen sponsors with her.[28] Most of these were household products, such as Sweetheart Soap, Knox Gelatin, Wesson Oil, and Fannie Farmer Candies, but they also included AT&T, the Florida Citrus Commission, and other services. McBride's audiences seemed as accepting and even welcoming of her product endorsements as they were of her editorial content.

Discursive Positioning

Many accounts quote letters that support the idea of McBride's loyal audience as faithful consumers—and indeed they were, as sponsor testimonials prove. Yet description of this success was frequently couched in overtly disparaging terms. Unlike the flattering discourse that surrounded Weaver's portrayal in the press, adjectives such as *innocent, naive, cozy, fluttering, twittering,* and *bewildered* surround Mary Margaret McBride. One *Time* article about her was titled simply "Goo."[29] These terms frequently spilled over onto McBride's audience, usually described as all female, despite evidence of considerable male attendance at her daily broadcasts and anniversary shows. The caption under a *Life* photograph read, "Winsome and plump, Mary Margaret McBride looks like a typical Mary Margaret McBride fan. She snuggles up to the microphone, chats cozily into it."[30] Allen Churchill began a lengthy profile in the *American Mercury* with the statement: "The most publicized neuroses in the world undoubtedly belong to an ample, middle-aged lady named Mary Margaret McBride, who in days before radio might have lived a life of obscure inhibition. Thanks to a unique merger of Marconi and Freud, however, she is today prosperous and dearly beloved of some 6 million American women."[31] As with the other popular daytime format, the soap opera, McBride's relationship to her listeners was given a pathological, irrational twist by which the listeners were made to seem not only unintelligent but peculiarly susceptible and easily led (even by this naive, twittering woman). Philip Hamburger (formerly of the OWI writers' bureau) opened his damaging satire in *Life* by making the nature of McBride and her audience clear:

> Between Mary Margaret McBride and several million housewives within earshot of New York's WEAF there exists a communion that approaches the mystical. The bonds that unite Mary Margaret and her flock (who

would plunge headlong into bowls of dehydrated split-pea soup rather than call her by any other name) appear to be based on mutually shared adventures of the mind and stomach.[32]

Allen Churchill indulged in similar disparagement of both McBride and her audience, while simultaneously denying her background in journalism: "Where others in radio are content to read commercials prepared in advertising agencies, Mary Margaret is interested enough in her own products to investigate them as thoroughly as a newspaper reporter. Nothing about a product is too trivial for Mary Margaret to ferret out and pass along to her listeners, coated with the joy of discovery."[33]

The sex of the writer seemed to have less to do with an article's overall tone than its venue. Barbara Heggie, writing in the *New Yorker*, described McBride's influence on her audience in very different terms from those she later used in a *Woman's Home Companion* article: "It is certainly just as well that she draws the line at tobacco and liquor; otherwise, undoubtedly, the housewives of the Eastern seaboard would be lying about their houses in an alcoholic stupor, smoking like chimneys."[34] Interestingly, in the *Woman's Home Companion* Heggie avoided much reference to the audience, concentrating instead on McBride's hard work and successful formula; in fact, she stated, "Actually, [her] dithery facade conceals one of the shrewdest minds in radio."[35] The metaphors of addiction and hypnosis were often employed (as with the soaps), frequent mention was made of McBride's weight, age, and plain appearance, and throughout it was the commercialism of McBride's show that was stressed. Very little time was given to the intellectual, cultural, or social content of McBride's program, despite an illustrious list of interviewees; most accounts stressed the personal nature of McBride's concerns, with emphasis on the whimsical and frivolous. McBride herself was aware of these characterizations, and objected to them:

> What does make me hopping mad is when somebody assumes that there's nothing to my job except getting on the radio and rambling along, garrulously saying anything that comes into your dear little head. Men, especially, are sometimes like that. . . . they'll say: "I listen to you, but heaven knows why, the way you go on. It isn't your voice—and it certainly isn't what you say. I don't know what it is." . . . I think it IS good hard work—don't let anybody fool you. It's being a reporter, knowing a story when you see it and keeping at it until you've got that story. It's NOT talking

all the time about MY friends, MY family, MYSELF as one critic maintained. It's the stories—good solid feature stories with as much information, drama and fun as you can get out of them that make women remember, seven years afterward and almost word for word, parts of broadcasts that even I have forgotten by now."[36]

Here we begin to see clearly the divide between the publics being addressed, on the one hand, by McBride (and, I would argue, by many other disparaged daytime formats) and, on the other, by magazines such as the *New Yorker*, *Life*, *American Mercury*, *Time*, and *Newsweek*. This is precisely the distinction—and it is explicitly a gendered one— that Pat Weaver would exploit in his programming philosophy in the early 1950s.

Weaver's Magic Trick

It can clearly be seen from the above that McBride's program provided a model, in more ways than one, for Weaver's so-called innovations on NBC television. All three programs, *Today*, *Tonight*, and *Home*, draw on McBride's formula of varied guests, intensive but informal and ad-libbed interviews, a mixture of news, current events, and entertainment, within a magazine format using multiple sponsorship. Another important influence, and a program type growing in popularity in the 1940s, were the numerous radio "morning shows" that had sprung up, themselves influenced by McBride and her imitators. Often composed of husband-and-wife teams, either real-life or fictional—including Ed and Pegeen Fitzgerald, Dorothy Kilgallen and Dick Kollmar, Tex McCrary and Jinx Falkenburg, just to name a few of the East Coast practitioners—these shows featured back-and-forth banter between the hosts interspersed with interviews, news, and reviews. Frequently referred to as "Mr. and Mrs. Breakfast" programs, one article states that by 1948, "28 sets of Fitzgeralds were battling it out over the airwaves from morn till night, crunching, commercializing and shooting the breeze."[37] Pegeen Fitzgerald, often credited with originating the format, had gotten her start in radio in 1940 as one of the numerous McBride imitators, on a program called *Pegeen Prefers*. So with all these models abounding on the airwaves, hardly a secret either to the American public or presumably even to highbrow magazine writers, where do the claims for Weaver's originality come from? Can they be based simply on the transfer of the form to a new medium?

But even putting such a program on television had been tried before—

by McBride herself (along with many others). Very early on, in the fall of 1948, McBride's manager, Stella Karn, proposed a move onto the new medium. With no daytime broadcasting as yet available, McBride signed a contract for thirteen weeks of a half-hour program to be aired at night. Scheduled by NBC on Tuesday at 9:00, immediately following Milton Berle's *Texaco Star Theater* and opposite Bob Hope's program on CBS, McBride's television debut was a failure even by her own standards. Television in its early days, with awkward lighting, immovable cameras, and emphasis on the visual appearance of its personalities, proved far less flexible than radio. But the *New York Times* review of her debut also reveals an obstacle to her success indicative of the larger forces shaping programming policy at the networks:

> Perhaps the ladies in the daytime can survive Miss McBride's effusive and interminable commercials, but for the men at home in the evening they are hard to take after a day at the office. To watch Miss McBride shift—without pause or loss of breath—from a eulogy of Kemtone paint to an analysis of Russia is an ordeal not quickly forgotten. If nighttime television is to be daytime radio, away video, away![38]

Perhaps this comment gives us a clue to Weaver's accomplishment, if we consider the nature of the oppositions being presented here. Ladies/men, home/office, commercialism/serious news, daytime radio/nighttime television: these are the conceptual polarities within which 1950s television had to negotiate.

The subaltern counterpublic of female listeners responded to McBride's attempts to open up the restricted domestic sphere prescribed for women by dominant broadcasting practices. Their voices can be heard emerging in letters to the editor responding to Churchill's article. One woman wrote: "Allen Churchill's article . . . is unfair, patronizing, and certainly unkind. Mr. Churchill has written a sarcastic, farcical and superficial article about a woman who conducts the most *intelligent* woman's program on the air today." Another defended McBride's "brilliant mind" and reflected: "What makes a person rally to another's defense? . . . it is a complete respect, formed over a period of years, for one whom I feel has the courage of her convictions, as well as the integrity to represent the best. . . . After fifteen years of listening to the same trustful voice, a bond has been created that is not easily broken, regardless of any criticism or understatement that may come from an interviewer."[39]

On the other hand, both William Boddy and Vance Kepley conclusively demonstrate that a primary network goal through the mid-1950s was to position the networks as agents of the public interest, espousing programming principles that emphasized their high-minded efforts to resist the commercialism and triviality of sponsor-dominated forms. This strategy had both economic and regulatory utility. Further, as Lynn Spigel demonstrates, in the 1950s the subject of gender itself became part of television's social discourse. A fear of "feminization" of the family hierarchy and society at large runs through articles about television and the programs themselves; in order to legitimate its use and to offset fears of social disruption, the networks positioned television as "work" for women and as "education" for children.[40]

One aspect of Weaver's programming philosophy that contemporary articles stated clearly, but that has been de-emphasized by subsequent scholars, was his desire to remove, or at least to lessen, the control that advertising agencies and their sponsors still exerted over television schedules. All three of his signature contributions—spectaculars, magazine format, multiple sponsors—were primarily designed to achieve this end. Weaver wanted to carve out a space in which network program executives like himself could have the kind of autonomy and control over programming unseen since the 1920s in broadcasting. As Vance Kepley points out, these efforts were also designed to impress the FCC favorably with the network's programming responsibility.[41] In order to do this, the networks had to define themselves as less commercial, less overtly concerned with the hard sell and hucksterism associated with sponsor-driven radio and more concerned with public service, high culture, education, and disinterested information. William Boddy has demonstrated the ways in which the New York-based press picked up on this self-serving rhetoric and assisted the networks in their strategic image building.[42]

However, because NBC's finances were still heavily dependent on sponsor investment, a way had to be found to decry the excesses of commercialism, disassociate the networks from their problematic performance in radio, and carve out a new serious, public-spirited role—without alienating the sponsors who paid the bills. Here is where NBC, with Weaver as its particular spokesman, could fall back on the tried-and-true method of naturalizing strategic cultural hierarchies behind the screen of gender distinction. The kind of commercialism associated with radio could be linked to the feminine, specifically to the female world of daytime programming. What Weaver's shows did was to eliminate the feminine taint from the magazine format—literally, in the case of *Today* and *Tonight*, on which the sole female host or feminine component of the husband-and-wife breakfast team was dropped and an all-male host format instituted. Discursively, the positioning of Weaver as an innovative genius and his shows as original ideas denied the feminine daytime origins of the concepts, while placing them in a context of serious masculine invention. And what about NBC's concession to femininity, *Home*?

References to *Home* are couched in the language of elevation. From Castleman and Podrazik, we learn that "*Home* was aimed at housewives, but Weaver treated them with considerably more respect, assuming that they were intelligent, perceptive viewers. . . . *Home* avoided the glamour chit-chat formula in favor of a more down-to-earth style of dealing with fashion, food, home decorating, leisure activities, home gardening, and children."[43] In the context developed above, it is not hard to see that this formula, no matter how respectfully conceived, represents a considerable *narrowing* of interests defined as legitimately feminine. Implied here is the notion that women's interests should be confined to "home." Just to clarify the appropriate components of women's sphere of interest, as Inger Stole points out, "the program's editorial content was divided into two categories, the "emotional" and the "service" areas.[44] Even an attempt to include more serious material, *Home*'s "News from Washington" segment, was described by its creators as "a handsome guy with a compelling personality" delivering "legislative news of interest to dames."[45] References in interdepartmental correspondence contradict Weaver's staff's stated respect for the "class" female audience his show purported to attract by referring to them as "broads" and "higher type dames."[46] Here too we find the assumption, contrary to published research, that educated upper-middle-income women had not been served by "the dreck of daytime radio," and explicitly positioning *Home* in contrast to its radio forebears.[47]

The program's lack of success and eventual cancellation points to the difficulties that Weaver's strategic use of gender created for understanding actual female audiences. In a discursive system in which the lowbrow "other" was defined as feminine, reconciling television's predominantly feminine audience and formats with the networks' new improved mission proved problematic indeed. With *Tonight* and

Today, far more successful with audiences (still predominantly female), Weaver managed to remove the overtly feminine stigma of this formerly daytime format and reposition it within the polarized gender representations of the 1950s. Spigel describes some of the ways that *Today* sought to mediate this tension, in order to attract the key female audience, through carefully contained representations of appropriate female concerns such as specifically delineated "women's" segments.[48] The commercialization of these shows remained just as intense but sanitized, and did set a precedent for the loosening of sponsor control that would increase through the decade.

Thus, by slaying, or at least burying, the monsters of the feminine daytime, the Weaver myth could flourish. I hope to suggest by the argument presented in this concluding essay that television's negotiations of high and low culture, of appropriate program forms and conceptions of audience, rest on distinctions, among them gender, formed in the crucible of radio practice and refined during the discursive upheavals of World War II. And further, these distinctions carry through much of the scholarship that has sought to describe them. As a reopening of the subject of radio history suggests, alternative voices did exist on the airwaves, and our lack of awareness of their existence suggests that much research still remains to be done to uncover radio and television's subaltern counterpublics and the programs, writers, and producers who spoke to them. Until we incorporate these alternative practices into our history classes and publications, we will continue to circulate and reinforce versions of history that incorporate a very real ideology—all the more insidious because they refuse to acknowledge their own partisan position.

Voicing History

This history of the expectations, fears, functions, and uses of a medium once stunningly new, now almost forgotten, makes no claim to being a complete version of events, or of covering even all of the most significant topics. Rather, it contains a set of concerns and of voices neglected by past histories, whose importance in shaping our notions of American identity have been left to the sidelines of most broadcasting history writing to date. This shaping took place along crucial lines of gender, race, and ethnicity, debates over public authority, and the complex host of interrelated distinctions so central to our narratives of national and personal identity that our media disseminate daily. Their prominence on radio resulted from a combination of the medium's technological capacities, the way that it was understood and used by corporate and government authorities, and the relatively constricted concentration of power in the hands of a few who spoke to the many. Television, of course, continues this critical public function today, though its modes of address and narrative as well as the circumstances of its control differ.

For each "comprehensive" history of radio broadcasting or of any other subject that appears, conscientious historians must continue to investigate the boundaries between what is known and what has been excluded from knowledge, what is heard speaking loudly in our largest public forums and what remains pushed to the sidelines, silenced or muffled in our historical accounts—and must continue to analyze the purposes and effects of such selections. There is no one "true" story of the history and function of this evanescent medium called radio in the United States. Rather, a wide variety of negotiably true and differentially valuable histories exist, whose validity will have to be judged based on the depth of their evidence, the clarity of their argument, and the way they fit into the needs and uses of the present. History is always ideological; history is always on some level personal. It is written by historians whose training, purposes, and basic assumptions and selections intertwine with present-day needs and preoccupations, and it finds a readership based on similar affinities. And, as I hope I have demonstrated convincingly in this account, media narratives, structures, and audiences are produced in, and themselves help to produce, the same crucible of negotiations of social power that shapes the histories through which we later understand them. Radio as a medium of narratives of national identity has been transmuted to the visual outpourings of television, but its cultural implications remain with us still.

Ask Gertrude Berg. Having maintained a successful program for almost twenty years, Berg recounts in her memoirs her equally successful transition to television. Despite initial rejection by programming executives at both CBS and NBC in 1948, Berg's own direct appeal to William Paley resulted in an audition for *The Goldbergs* and an eventual ten-year run, at first on CBS, later switching to NBC. The radio show had become more of a domestic sitcom and less of a comedy/drama serial over time, moving to a weekly schedule and a focus on the characters' personal and familial comic difficulties, with less and less emphasis on their ethnic roots. For television this change in tone was heightened, as the Goldberg family—once again with teenage children, played by a new cast, as its original characters had grown out of the family situation—became middle-class and eventually moved to the suburbs of Long Island. According to Berg's memoirs, the television Goldbergs lived a domestic life little different from that of the other families of early television, fully assimilated and untroubled by the ethnic differences that had given the original show its unique perspective.

This facade of normalcy, both on the show and in the account published by Berg in 1961, creates its own "strategic forgetfulness," however, in dropping from its history the underlying drama that necessitated the program's move to NBC in 1952. Philip Loeb, the actor playing Jake Goldberg, found himself listed in *Red Channels* along with 151 other actors, writers, and directors—a disproportionate number of whom were Jewish—accused of Communist sympathies or affiliations in the wake of Joseph McCarthy's red-baiting campaign. Despite Loeb's denials, the network and sponsor, General Foods' Sanka Coffee, insisted that Loeb be dropped from the cast. Berg supported Loeb, refusing to fire him and publicizing his innocence. However, General Foods dropped the series "for economic reasons" in May 1951; in winter 1952 it reappeared on NBC, as Erik Barnouw puts it, "under another sponsor and without Philip Loeb."[49] Loeb's career ended with this widely publicized incident; unable to find work in television, radio, or theater, he committed suicide in 1955. In Berg's account, this entire event becomes the bland statement, "We had very loyal audiences who followed us from CBS to NBC and on to film." Later, she goes on to declare: "For the most part the sponsor and agency hardly bothered me. . . . I have always had amiable relationships with my sponsors. Their products sold—even to me. I still use the toothpaste I first started to advertise on radio. I still drink the coffee without caffeine before I go to bed—and in the morning I use another coffee I advertised but this one has caffeine."[50]

In the reassuring normalcy promoted by national television in the 1950s and 1960s, such real-life events, despite their importance and links to some of the central dramas of the twentieth century, had no place, could not be spoken. It is important that we not let the misleadingly realistic but always motivated and partial representations of our national media stand unchallenged as historical documents. As statements, they are remarkable both for what they say and what they leave unsaid. Once again, the drama behind *The Goldbergs* says more about American culture and politics than the bland face it turned to the world. Those who would use television images of the "peaceful" decade of the 1950s as a blueprint for America's future would do well to remember this central tension.

Notes

Introduction: The Nation's Voice

1. "When we speak of a *field* of position-takings, we are insisting that what can be constituted as a *system* for the sake of analysis is not the product of a coherence-seeking intention or an objective consensus . . . but the product and prize of a permanent conflict; or, to put it another way, that the generative, unifying principle of this 'system' is the struggle, with all the contradictions it engenders." Pierre Bourdieu, *The Field of Cultural Production* (New York: Columbia University Press, 1993), 34.

2. See Susan Douglas, *The Invention of American Broadcasting 1899–1922* (Baltimore: Johns Hopkins University Press, 1987).

3. Radio's "soul" is a concern in an editorial on radio written by Gertrude Berg, which I discuss in chapter 1.

4. See, for example, Lizabeth Cohen, *Making a New Deal: Industrial Workers in Chicago, 1919–1939* (Cambridge: Cambridge University Press, 1990); M. Willey and S. A. Rice "The Agencies of Communication," in *Recent Social Trends in the United States*, ed. President's Research Committee on Social Trends (New York: McGraw-Hill, 1933); Jeanette Sayer Smith, "Broadcasting for Marginal Americans," *Public Opinion Quarterly* (Winter 1942): 588–603; Douglas Czitrom, *Media and the American Mind: From Morse to McLuhan* (Chapel Hill: University of North Carolina Press, 1982).

5. See, for instance, Lynn Spigel, *Make Room for TV: Television and the Family Ideal in Postwar America* (Chicago: University of Chicago Press, 1992); Lynn Spigel and Denise Mann, eds., *Private Screenings: Television and the Female Consumer* (Minneapolis: University of Minnesota Press, 1992); Julie D'Acci, *Defining Women: The Case of Cagney and Lacey* (Chapel Hill: University of North Carolina Press, 1994).

6. Robert W. McChesney, *Telecommunications, Mass Media, and Democracy: The Battle for the Control of U.S. Broadcasting, 1928–1935* (New York: Oxford University Press, 1993); William Boddy, *Fifties Television: The Industry and Its Critics* (Urbana: University of Illinois Press, 1990).

7. Warren Susman, *Culture as History: The Transformation of American Society in the Twentieth Century* (New York: Pantheon, 1984).

8. "A discursive formation is not, therefore, an ideal, continuous, smooth text that runs beneath the multiplicity of contradictions, and resolves them in the calm unity of coherent thought; nor is it the surface in which, in a thousand different aspects, a contradiction is reflected that is always in retreat, but everywhere dominant. It is rather a space of multiple dissensions; a set of different oppositions whose levels and roles must be described." Michel Foucault, *The Archaeology of Knowledge and the Discourse on Language* (New York: Pantheon, 1972), 155.

9. Benedict Anderson, *Imagined Communities: Reflections on the Origin and Spread of Nationalism* (London: Verso, 1983).

10. Homi K. Bhabha, *The Location of Culture* (London: Routledge, 1994); Toni Morrison, *Playing in the Dark: Whiteness and the Literary Imagination* (Cambridge: Harvard University Press, 1992); David Roediger, *The Wages of Whiteness* (London: Verso, 1991); Ann Douglas, *Terrible Honesty: Mongrel Manhattan in the 1920s* (New York: Farrar, Straus & Giroux, 1995).

11. Nancy Fraser, "Rethinking the Public Sphere," in *The Phantom Public Sphere*, ed. Bruce Robbins (Minneapolis: University of Minnesota Press, 1993).

12. Lawrence W. Levine, *Highbrow/Lowbrow: The Emergence of Cultural Hierarchy in America* (Cambridge: Harvard University Press, 1988).

13. See Gene Fowler and Bill Crawford, *Border Radio* (New York: Limelight, 1990).

14. Jannette L. Dates and William L. Barlow, eds., *Split Image: African Americans in the Mass Media* (Washington, D.C.: Howard University Press, 1990).

1. Radiating Culture

1. Gertrude Berg, "Radio Is Eulogized by One of Its Most Noted Characters," *Cleveland Press*, (n.d., box 21, folder 29, "Correspondence—Rise of the Goldbergs—1933," NBC. (See "Collections Consulted" for explanations of abbreviations used in notes.)

2. Senator James Watson, *Congressional Record*, November 5, 1927, 1792; Joseph K. Hart, "Radiating Culture," *Survey*, March 18, 1922, 948.

3. The following information and quotes (with page numbers given in parentheses in the text) come primarily from Gertrude Berg, *Molly and Me* (New York: McGraw-Hill, 1961).

4. Gertrude Berg, *The Rise of the Goldbergs* (New York: National Broadcasting Company, 1933), 14–15.

5. Memo to M. J. Woods, "Pepsodent Mail Response—the Goldbergs," January 27, 1932, box 13, folder 1, NBC. See also "A Brief Study of the Appeal and Popularity of 'The Goldbergs,'" NBC Statistical Department, July 25, 1932, box 13, folder 58, NBC.

6. M. Willey and S. A. Rice, "The Agencies of Communications," in *Recent Social Trends in the United States*, ed. President's Research Committee on Social Trends (New York: McGraw-Hill, 1933), 215.

7. Warren Susman, *Culture as History: The Transformation of American Society in the Twentieth Century* (New York: Pantheon, 1984), 228.

8. Lizabeth Cohen, *Making a New Deal: Industrial Workers in Chicago, 1919–1939* (Cambridge: Cambridge University Press, 1990), 325, 330.

9. Quoted in Christina S. Drale, "From Maritime to Showtime: Popular Perceptions of Radio in the 1920s," (paper presented at the meeting of the Popular Culture Association, New Orleans, March 23–26, 1988), 11.

10. Benedict Anderson, *Imagined Communities: Reflections on the Origin and Spread of Nationalism* (London: Verso, 1983), 36.

11. J. C. W. Reith, *Into the Wind* (London: Hodder & Stoughton, 1949) p. 103.

12. Robert W. McChesney, *Telecommunications, Mass Media, and Democracy: The Battle for the Control of U.S. Broadcasting, 1928–1935* (New York: Oxford University Press, 1993); on the BBC, see Paddy Scannel and David Cardiff, *A Social History of British Broadcasting*, vol. I, 1922–1939, *Serving the Nation* (Oxford: Basil Blackwell, 1991).

13. J. Fred MacDonald, *Don't Touch That Dial! Radio Programming in American Life from 1920 to 1960* (Chicago: Nelson-Hall, 1979), 2.

14. Susan Smulyan focuses on this debate in *Selling Radio: The Commercialization*

of *American Broadcasting 1920–1934* (Washington, D.C.: Smithsonian Institution Press, 1994).

15. Joseph H. Jackson, "Should Radio Be Used for Advertising?" *Radio Broadcast*, November 1922, 72.

16. Bruce Bliven "How Radio Is Remaking Our World," *Century Magazine*, June 1924, 149.

17. "Radio: The New Social Force," *Outlook*, March 19, 1924, 465–66.

18. K. B.Warner, "The Washington Radio Conference," *QST*, April 1922, 7–12.

19. "About the Radio Round-Table," *Scientific American*, December 1922, 378–79.

20. Raymond Francis Yates, "What Will Happen to Broadcasting?" *Outlook*, April 9, 1924, 604–6.

21. "Radio," 466.

22. McChesney, *Telecommunications*.

23. NBC announcement reprinted in Erik Barnouw, *A Tower in Babel* (New York: Oxford University Press, 1966), 187.

24. Though NBC's announcement also makes prominent mention of the constitution of an advisory council, this board existed largely for cosmetic purposes and had no impact on day-to-day operations, as many critics have noted. See Barnouw, *A Tower in Babel*, 206; McChesney, *Telecommunications*, 70, 118–19.

25. See McChesney, *Telecommunications*; Susan Douglas, *The Invention of American Broadcasting 1899–1922* (Baltimore: Johns Hopkins University Press, 1987); Michele Hilmes, *Hollywood and Broadcasting: From Radio to Cable* (Urbana: University of Illinois Press, 1990).

26. Anderson, *Imagined Communities*, 35.

27. Ibid., 36.

28. Ibid., 42–43.

29. Ibid., 204.

30. For discussion of these issues in film, see Lester Friedman, ed., *Unspeakable Images: Ethnicity and the American Cinema* (Urbana: University of Illinois Press, 1991).

31. Douglas, *The Invention of American Broadcasting*, 306–7.

32. Stanley Frost, "Radio Dreams That Can Come True," *Colliers*, June 10, 1922, 16.

33. Frank Leroy Blanchard, "Experiences of a National Advertiser with Broadcasting," April 15, 1930, station files—KDKA, BPL.

34. M. J. Caveney, "New Voices in the Wilderness," *Colliers*, April 1920, 18.

35. Lynn Spigel discusses popular fears of the invasive qualities of TV in undermining paternal authority in the family in *Make Room for TV: Television and the Family Ideal in Postwar America* (Chicago: University of Chicago Press, 1992).

36. Bruce Bliven, "The Legion Family and the Radio: What We Hear When We Tune In," *Century Magazine*, October 1924, 813.

37. Ibid., 818.

38. For the cultural precedents of this phenomenon, see Lawrence W. Levine, *Highbrow/Lowbrow: The Emergence of Cultural Hierarchy in America* (Cambridge: Harvard University Press, 1988).

39. Roland Marchand, *Advertising the American Dream: Making Way for Modernity 1920–1940* (Berkeley: University of California Press, 1985), 88–94.

40. Joseph H. Jackson, "Should Radio Be Used for Advertising?" *Radio Broadcast*, November 1922, 76.

41. At the extreme of cultural deviance, even after the standardization caused by networks and frequency regulation following the 1927 Radio Act, a few broadcasters managed to escape the disciplinary reach of official regulation by moving across the Rio

Grande into Mexico. See Gene Fowler and Bill Crawford, *Border Radio* (New York: Limelight, 1990).

42. Anderson refers to "languages of power": "Certain dialects inevitably were 'closer' to each print-language and dominated their final forms. Their disadvantaged cousins, still assimilable to the emerging print-language, lost caste, above all because they were unsuccessful (or only relatively successful) in insisting on their own print-form." *Imagined Communities*, 45.

43. Kitty Parsons, "Announcers' English," *Scholastic Magazine*, January 11, 1936, 13, 27; S. H. Hawkins, "Here's the IDEAL Announcer!" *Radio Age*, April 1925, 50, 52; "The High and Mighty Place of the Announcer," *Radio Broadcast*, December 1926, 180–81.

44. "Pussy Willow English," *Saturday Review of Literature*, June 16, 1934, 752. On Roxy, see James C. Young, "New Fashions in Radio Programs," *Radio Broadcast*, May 1925, 83–89.

45. Don E. Gilman, quoted in Arthur Garbette, "Interview with Don E. Gilman," *San Francisco Police and Peace Officers' Journal*, February 1929, 28–29.

46. Charles M. Adams, "Radio and Our Spoken Language: Local Differences Are Negligible, But Radio Shows Up Personalities," *Radio News*, September 1927, 208.

47. See Robert H. Wiebe, *The Segmented Society: An Introduction to the Meaning of America* (New York: Oxford University Press, 1975), 30–33; Marchand, *Advertising the American Dream*, 208–17; Stuart Ewen, *Captains of Consciousness: Advertising and the Social Roots of Consumer Culture* (New York: McGraw-Hill, 1976).

48. See Matthew Murray, "Television Wipes Its Feet: The Commercial and Ethical Considerations behind the Adoption of the Television Code," *Journal of Popular Film and Television* 21 (Fall 1993): 128–38.

49. William A. Orton, *America in Search of a Culture* (Boston: Little, Brown, 1933), quoted in Levering Tyson, "Where Is American Radio Heading?" in Levering Tyson and Judith Waller, *The Future of Radio and Educational Broadcasting* (Chicago: University of Chicago Press, 1934), 18.

50. Waldemar Kaempffert, "The Social Destiny of Radio," *Forum* 71 (June 1924): 771.

51. Pierre Bourdieu, *The Field of Cultural Production* (New York: Columbia University Press, 1993), 129; Pierre Bourdieu and Loic J. D. Wacquant, *An Invitation to Reflexive Sociology* (Chicago: University of Chicago Press, 1992), 90–91.

52. Stewart Ewen and Elizabeth Ewen address the relationship of immigration and mass culture explicitly in *Channels of Desire: Mass Images and the Shaping of American Consciousness* (Minneapolis: University of Minnesota Press, 1992).

53. Stow Persons, "The Americanization of the Immigrant," in *Foreign Influences in American Life*, ed. David F. Bowers (Princeton, N.J.: Princeton University Press, 1944), 44.

54. See David Roediger, *The Wages of Whiteness* (London: Verso, 1991); also Eric Lott, *Love and Theft: Blackface Minstrelsy and the American Working Class* (New York: Oxford University Press, 1993).

55. Roediger dismisses economic competition arguments in his "wages of whiteness" theories.

56. In *Making a New Deal*, Cohen details the ways in which ethnic and racial division could both threaten and, handled properly, be used by management to defuse union organization in the 1920s and 1930s.

57. Michael R. Winston, "Racial Consciousness and Mass Communication in the United States," *Daedalus* 111 (1982): 173.

58. David Brion Davis, "The American Dilemma," *New York Review of Books*, July 16, 1992, 14

59. Leonard Dinnerstein and David M. Reimers, *Ethnic Americans: A History of Immigration and Assimilation* (New York: Harper & Row, 1975), 40.

60. Robert N. Bellah, *The Broken Covenant* (New York: Seabury, 1975).

61. Quoted in Dinnerstein and Reimers, *Ethnic Americans*, 70.

62. M. R. Davie, *World Immigration* (New York: Macmillan, 1946), 13.

63. Frances Kellor, *Immigration and the Future* (New York: George H. Doran, 1920), 50.

64. Wiebe, *The Segmented Society*.

65. By the end of the war, fully one-third of American forces were foreign-born. Kellor, *Immigration and the Future*, 58.

66. John Higham, *Strangers in the Land: Patterns of American Nativism 1860–1925* (New York: Atheneum, 1968), 275. On the assumption that intelligence tests, which supposedly did not reflect level of education, were therefore neutral in regard to all environmental influences, this new "scientific" evidence for the superiority of northern Europeans and "native" Americans was used to influence impending restrictions on immigration. Higham shows how these "scientifically proven" ideas trickled down into such diverse nativist manifestations as the passionate defense of literary traditionalism (shades of Harold Bloom!), the resurgence of the Ku Klux Klan, and the rise of anti-Semitism in the 1920s.

67. T. J. Jackson Lears, *No Place of Grace: Antimodernism and the Transformation of American Culture, 1880–1920* (Chicago: University of Chicago Press, 1994); T. J. Jackson Lears, "From Salvation to Self-Realization: Advertising and the Therapeutic Roots of the Consumer Culture, 1880–1930," in *The Culture of Consumption: Critical Essays in American History 1880–1980*, ed. Richard Wrightman Fox and T. J. Jackson Lears (New York: Pantheon, 1983).

68. However, the Lynds were also children of their times: ethnic diversity was played down considerably in the Middletown study because the Lynds' vision of an organically "whole" culture could not incorporate the idea of ethnic difference and tension. This is shown particularly in the fact that "Middletown"'s black population was deliberately excluded from the study at the outset: "In a difficult study of this sort it seemed a distinct advantage to deal with a homogeneous, native-born population, even though such a population is unusual in an American industrial city. Thus, instead of being forced to handle two major variables, racial change and cultural change, the field staff was enabled to concentrate upon cultural change. The study thus became one of the interplay of a relatively constant native American stock and its changing environment. In the main this study confines itself to the white population and more particularly to the native whites." Robert S. Lynd and Helen Merrell Lynd, *Middletown* (New York: Harcourt Brace Jovanovich, 1929), 8–9. Here African Americans, many of whose ancestors probably came to American shores long before those of the "native white" population, are considered as existing outside "native American stock" from the beginning. Obviously, too much difference could not even be considered part of this community, thus problematizing the very idea of "community" itself in a way that the Lynds were incapable of addressing.

69. Letter to the editor, *New Republic*, 1924, as cited in Higham, *Strangers in the Land*, 264.

70. Susman, *Culture as History*, xx–xxi.

71. Kathy Peiss, *Cheap Amusements: Working Women and Leisure in Turn-of-the-Century New York* (Philadelphia: Temple University Press, 1986); Roy Rosenzweig, *Eight Hours for What We Will: Workers and Leisure in an Industrial City, 1870–1920* (Cambridge: Cambridge University Press, 1983); Ewen and Ewen, *Channels of Desire*.

72. Marchand, *Advertising the American Dream*, 67.

73. Marchand, ibid., discusses the formation of the "consumerist caste" (to use Eileen Meehan's term) in the perception of advertising executives. He concludes that they represented only about 30 percent of the U.S. public, that fraction just below the 5 percent wealthy. By this calculation, most working-class and immigrant families would fall outside the intended scope of advertising. However, I would argue, first, that this definition is contradicted somewhat by the venues in which advertising actually appeared, and second, that intention does not limit influence. Ad men may have thought they were talking to a relatively affluent minority, but the majority could listen in and be influenced. "Consumerist caste" is a term used by Eileen Meehan to denote the group primarily addressed by U.S. commercial media. Eileen Meehan, "Heads of Household and Ladies of the House: Gender, Genre, and Broadcast Ratings, 1929–1990," in *Ruthless Criticism: New Perspectives in U.S. Communications History*, ed. William S. Solomon and Robert W. McChesney (Minneapolis: University of Minnesota Press, 1993), 204–21.

74. To cite just a few: Lewis Jacobs, *The Rise of the American Film* (New York: Columbia University Press, 1939); Garth Jowett, *Film: The Democratic Art* (Boston: Little, Brown, 1976); Robert Sklar, *Movie Made America* (New York: Vintage, 1976); Ewen and Ewen, *Channels of Desire*.

75. Cohen, *Making a New Deal*, 132–33.

76. Douglas Czitrom, *Media and American Mind: From Morse to McLuhan* (Chapel Hill: University of North Carolina Press, 1982), 192.

77. Ibid.

78. Roediger, *The Wages of Whiteness*, 134.

79. Dale T. Knobel, *Paddy and the Republic: Ethnicity and Nationality in Antebellum America* (Middletown, Conn.: n.p., 1986), 178–79, quoted in ibid., 143.

80. Lott, *Love and Theft*, 95.

81. Toni Morrison, *Playing in the Dark: Whiteness and the Literary Imagination* (Cambridge: Harvard University Press, 1992), 5.

82. Ibid., 38.

83. Ibid., 66.

84. George Lipsitz, *Time Passages: Collective Memory and American Popular Culture* (Minneapolis: University of Minnesota Press, 1990), 64.

85. David Roediger claims that after racial superiority, women's rights was the second most frequently addressed (and denigrated) political issue. *The Wages of Whiteness*, 125–26.

86. Marchand, *Advertising the American Dream*, 193.

87. As to advertising representations of other "ethnic" groups, their existence was subsumed altogther into the "white" norm; as Marchand observes, "To immigrants, the message of advertising was implicit: only by complete fusion into the melting pot did one gain a place in the idealized American society of the advertising pages." Ibid.

2. How Far Can You Hear?

1. Bruce Barton, "This Magic Called Radio," *American Magazine*, June 1922, 72.

2. John Higham, *Strangers in the Land: Patterns of American Nativism 1860–1925* (New York: Atheneum, 1968), 316.

3. See, for example, Christopher Sterling and John Kittross, *Stay Tuned: A Concise History of Broadcasting in America* 2d ed. (Belmont, Calif.: Wadsworth, 1990); Tom Lewis, *Empire of the Air: The Men Who Made Radio* (New York: HarperCollins, 1991).

4. Alvin H. Harlow, *Old Wires and New Waves* (New York: Appleton-Century, 1936; reprint, New York: Arno, 1971), 468.

5. S. E. Frost Jr., *Education's Own Stations* (Chicago: University of Chicago Press, 1937), 464–74; Werner J. Severin, "WHA-Madison: Oldest Station in the Nation" (paper presented at the meeting of the Association for Education in Journalism, Madison, Wis., 1977).

6. Susan Douglas, *The Invention of American Broadcasting 1899–1922* (Baltimore: Johns Hopkins University Press, 1987), 206.

7. Quoted in Lowell Ames Norris, "The World's First Radio Program," *Yankee*, December 1965, 179.

8. Douglas, *The Invention of American Broadcasting*, 293.

9. Westinghouse Corporation, "Radio's First Fifty Years," part I: pre-1920s (recording) (New York: Westinghouse, 1970), General Library no. 933, SPERDVAC.

10. Douglas, *The Invention of American Broadcasting*, 174–76.

11. Ibid., 196.

12. For a discussion of female amateurs, see chapter 5. For evidence of Chicago's black radio amateurs, see the *Chicago Defender*'s radio columns, September 1926 through September 1928. My thanks to Lisa Parks, University of Wisconsin-Madison, for her research in this area. Lizabeth Cohen discusses working-class and ethnic amateurs in *Making a New Deal: Industrial Workers in Chicago, 1919–1939* (Cambridge: Cambridge University Press, 1990), 132–33.

13. "Radio Gets a Policeman" (oral interview of Herbert Hoover), Oral History Collection, Columbia University, *American Heritage*, August 1955, 76.

14. See also "To Calm the Jarring Radio Waves," *Literary Digest*, March 18, 1922, 12–13: "'The most gratifying result of the Conference,' as the New York *Evening Mail* sees it, 'is Mr. Hoover's determination that the inventive genius of the American small boy shall not be restrained.' 'Other and greater interests never get anywhere with the Secretary when they "pick on" the American small boy,' reports Frank J. Taylor, in the New York *Globe*."

15. "Strays," *QST*, September 1921, 47.

16. "The 'Phones and Amateur Radio," *QST*, March 1922, 32.

17. K. B. Warner, "The Washington Radio Conference," *QST*, April 1922, 9.

18. "Holding Our Own," *QST*, July 1922, 33–34.

19. "What Bothers the B.C.L.," *QST*, January 1924, 7–8. See also "Let There Be Justice!" *QST*, February 1924, 68–69.

20. "The Third Conference," *QST*, November 1924, 7–8.

21. "Strays," 47.

22. "With the Radiophone Folks," *QST*, December 1921, 31.

23. For a sampling, see "With the Radiophone Folks," *QST*, January 1922, 27–29; "With Our Radiophone Listeners," *QST*, March 1922, 48–49, 51; April 1922, 56–58; September 1922, 38–39, 41.

24. S. M. Kintner, "Pittsburgh's Contributions to Radio," *Proceedings of the Institute of Radio Engineers* 20 (1932): 1857. BPL.

25. Public Relations Department, Westinghouse Broadcasting Company, "History of Broadcasting and KDKA Radio," news release, n.d., in *American Broadcasting: A Source Book on the History of Radio and Television*, ed. Lawrence W. Lichty and Malachi C. Topping (New York: Hastings House, 1976), 105.

26. Kintner, "Pittsburgh's Contributions," 1857.

27. Tom Kneitel, *Radio Station Treasury, 1900–1946* (Commack, N.Y.: CRB Research, 1986), 23.

28. These figures are from a chart compiled by *Radio Broadcast*, April 1923, 524.

29. Quoted in "How Radio Increased Good-Will for 9 Concerns," *Radio Topics*, January 1923, 26.

30. This quote and the next are found in Marvin R. Bensman, "Regulation of Radio

by the Department of Commerce, 1921–1927," in *American Broadcasting: A Source Book on the History of Radio and Television*, ed. Lawrence W. Lichty and Malachi C. Topping (New York: Hastings House, 1976), 548. Bensman gives his sources as "Memorandum from Mr. Carson to Assistant Secretary Huston, National Archives Record Group 173, January 27, 1922" and "Memorandum from Mr. Carson to Mr. Hoover, NA RG 40, February 20, 1922," respectively.

31. Douglas, *The Invention of American Broadcasting*, 313.

32. Neil Leonard, *Jazz and the White Americans* (Chicago: University of Chicago Press, 1962), 102.

33. Ibid., 91–92.

34. Milton Mezzrow and Bernard Wolfe, *Really the Blues* (Garden City, N.Y.: Doubleday, 1946), 61.

35. "The Appeal of the Primitive Jazz," *Literary Digest*, August 25, 1917, 28–29. See also Kathy J. Ogren, *The Jazz Revolution: Twenties America and the Meaning of Jazz* (New York: Oxford University Press, 1989).

36. Here I do not mean to make the claim that this is the "actual" origin of jazz. The history is much more complex than this account allows, as many writers have discussed. Rather, this anecdote is interesting for the way that jazz's origins are accounted for in the public media of the white, middle-class United States and the underlying distinctions and assumptions it reveals.

37. Henry O. Osgood, *So This Is Jazz* (Boston: Little, Brown, 1926), 5–6, quoted in Leonard, *Jazz and the White Americans*, 33.

38. Anne Shaw Faulkner, "Does Jazz Put the Sin in Syncopation," *Ladies' Home Journal*, August 1921, 16, 34.

39. It makes a fascinating footnote that one practice particularly decried by Faulkner was the increasingly popular phenomenon of "corset checks" at dances: young women would remove their restricting corsets in the ladies' cloakroom and check them for the duration of the dance, in order to free their movements for jazz dancing. Faulkner laments the current decline in standards not only at "hotels, clubs and dance halls" but even at "one of the biggest fraternities of a great college," which "thought it necessary to print on the cards of invitation to the 'Junior Prom' that 'a corset check room will be provided.' Nor would the girl who wore corsets in [former] days have been dubbed 'old ironsides' and left a disconsolate wallflower in a corner of the ballroom." Ibid., 34.

40. Quoted in John R. McMahon, "Unspeakable Jazz Must Go!" *Ladies' Home Journal*, December 1921, 34.

41. Ibid., 34. This strategy bears close resemblance to the functioning of middle-class morality within the division of public and private spheres in Joan Landes's discussion of the French Revolution: marking out the privileged class of democracy—white middle-class men—from both the lower, racially degraded classes and the "corrupt" aristocracy, through the process of "feminizing" these groups and placing both them and women as a gender outside the parameters of full citizenship. See Joan Landes, *Women and the Public Sphere in the Age of the French Revolution* (Ithaca, N.Y.: Cornell University Press, 1988). It also strikingly prefigures the use of feminized cultural hierarchies in the later debates over daytime radio serials and their listeners, down to the recommendation of the "purifying" effects of listening to "good, legitimate" nighttime programs such as those starring Jack Benny and Edgar Bergen. See John Hutchens, "Are Soap Operas Only Suds?" *New York Times Magazine*, March 28, 1943. I discuss this subject in chapter 6.

42. All of these examples are from Leonard, *Jazz and the White Americans*, 29–46, except where otherwise noted.

43. Peter Dykeman, quoted in the *Philadelphia Public Ledger*, as quoted in "Kind Words for Jazz, But—," *Literary Digest*, November 18, 1922, 33–34.

44. "Letter from Mr. Huston to radio inspectors, NA RG 40, January 11, 1922" in Bensman, "Regulation of Radio," 548.

45. Testimony of William Terrell, chief radio inspector for the Department of Commerce, *Hearings before the Committee on Interstate Commerce*, U.S. Senate, 71st Congress, 1st session, May 24, 1929, 1071.

46. "Western Electric Broadcasting Stations in the U.S.," *Radio Broadcast*, January 1923, 256.

47. See Susan Smulyan, *Selling Radio: The Commercialization of American Broadcasting 1920–1934* (Washington, D.C.: Smithsonian Institution Press, 1994), 122–24.

48. "Letter from Mr. Tyler to Mr. Edwards, NA RG 173, December 16, 1921," in Bensman, "Regulation of Radio," 547.

49. June 4–11, 1922, as printed in *Radio Broadcasting News*, June 3, 1922, 9, 10.

50. "Radio Wedding Impressed Listeners," *Radio Broadcasting News*, December 9, 1922, 1.

51. Lynn Spigel, *Make Room for TV: Television and the Family Ideal in Postwar America* (Chicago: University of Chicago Press, 1992), 136–42.

52. Though I have selected precisely those stations whose innovative negotiations had an impact on the developing hegemony in radio—excluding those more marginal, counterhegemonic, and thus in many ways more interesting and unfamiliar but less influential practitioners—I hope to show that these stations' decisions and definitions responded to the same kinds of pressures and tensions that ran generally through the field of radio broadcasting. Their successes and adaptations over time point clearly to preferred negotiations; we will examine them closely from both sides to arrive at a broad picture of developing dominant practices.

53. Roland Marchand, *Advertising the American Dream: Making Way for Modernity 1920–1940* (Berkeley: University of California Press, 1985), 91.

54. Gleason L. Archer, *The History of Radio to 1926* (New York: American Historical Society, 1938), 260.

55. George H. Douglas, *The Early Days of Broadcasting* (Jefferson, N.C.: McFarland, 1987), 26.

56. Archer, *The History of Radio*, 278.

57. Quoted in ibid., 303 n.

58. Ibid., 303.

59. Most of the following is taken from the WJZ and WJY logs, box 98, NBC.

60. Warren Susman, "Personality and the Making of Twentieth Century Culture," in *Culture as History: The Transformation of American Society in the Twentieth Century* (New York: Pantheon, 1984), 274.

61. Ibid., 283.

62. William E. Harkness, "Speech—AT&T," February 1923, box 1, folder 2, EPH James.

63. Though these qualifications could as easily fit women as men, and indeed did characterize the many female announcers on the air during this period, the assumption of masculinity in Harkness's description of the relationship between announcer and audience would have a severely limiting effect on women's roles on the air, as will be discussed in chapter 5.

64. Douglas, *The Early Days*, 52.

65. Especially at the larger stations heard across the country, the first radio personalities shaped national perceptions of broadcasting. One of the earliest was Harold Arlin at KDKA in Pittsburgh. Like several others during this period, Arlin was an engineer with

an interest in radio who just happened to be in the right place at the right time to emerge from the background into the limelight. At WJZ, Thomas H. "Tommy" Cowan was selected in the fall of 1921 as its organizing voice, due largely to a background in music, which, given that the schedule consisted mostly of phonograph records, stood him in good stead. In 1922 Bertha Brainard joined the staff, as described above. All three of these New York pioneers would eventually leave the air for executive and managerial posts in radio. Others, entering the field as the role of announcer began to take shape as a specialized profession, would go on to become household familiars.

WJZ's Milton J. Cross was a singer with a "mellifluous voice" and a knowledge of classical music, who could fill in the empty spots by playing the organ. His best-known role was as host for the Metropolitan Opera broadcasts on NBC from 1931 into the 1940s. Norman Brokenshire, hired by WJZ in 1924, represents one of the first of the self-consciously constructed on-air personalities: "He believed that an announcer should get his individual charm and personality on the air, and he became an ad-libber and show stealer, to the annoyance and admiration of the studio bosses." Ibid., 63. Other WJZ personalities included Major J. Andrew White, one of the earliest sportscasters, later to become famous for his role in founding what would become the CBS network; and Ted Husing, whose fabrication of a B.S. degree from Harvard helped to get him the job but whose specialization in sports would keep him on the air for decades. On WEAF, Graham McNamee also made his name "through his vivid and breathtaking accounts of sporting events of all kinds." Ibid., 63. See also Ted Husing, *Ten Years before the Mike* (New York: Farrar & Rinehart, 1935).

66. For letters from listeners, see the Wendell Hall collection, SHSW; also see the Mary Margaret McBride collection, Library of Congress. Many radio biographies contain accounts of this relationship with fans, including Husing's, McBride's, and Berg's; for an early description, see Julia V. Shawell, "Lopez Speaking," *Radio News*, January 1928, 741–851.

67. William Peck Banning, *Commercial Broadcasting Pioneer: The WEAF Experiment, 1922–1926* (Cambridge: Harvard University Press, 1946).

68. William E. Harkness, "Radio Broadcasting in the Metropolitan Area," February 1923, box 1, folder 2, EPH James.

69. Banning, *Commercial Broadcasting Pioneer*, 113–17.

70. Scrapbook—Roxy and His Gang, New York Public Library, Center for Film and Theater Research, Lincoln Center. Also Lucille Husting, "Hello, Everybody! A Trip Backstage Elicits Roxy's Personal Story," *Radio News*, December 1927, 604ff.; "Roxy Decides Not to Fight Radio," *Radio Age*, April 1925, 24; James C. Young, "Broadcasting Personality," *Radio Broadcast*, July 1924, 246–50; "Roxie" (S. L. Rothafel), "A Bit about Myself," *Radio Broadcast*, October 1923, 459–64.

71. James C. Young, "New Fashions in Radio Programs," *Radio Broadcast*, May 1925, 83.

72. Archer, *The History of Radio*, 358.

73. "Broacast Miscellany," *Radio Broadcast*, October 1925, 758.

74. George C. Furness, "Program Pioneers: The Eveready Hour and Its History," *Radio News*, December 1929, 510. See also Julia V. Shawell, "The Eveready Hour," *Radio News*, May 1928, 1273–74.

75. Furness, "Program Pioneers," 581.

76. Later themes included a traveling showboat, film director Merian Cooper relating his experiences "sharing the trials and privations of a nation or people who migrate semi-annually with all their possessions," Arthur Young's tales of lion hunting in Africa, and an annually repeated program centered on the tales of a New York taxi driver, "Red" Christianson, and his adventures while shipwrecked on the Galápagos Islands.

77. F. G. Fritz, "Wendell Hall: Early Radio Performer," in *American Broadcasting: A Source Book on the History of Radio and Television*, ed. Lawrence W. Lichty and Malachi C. Topping (New York: Hastings House, 1976), 277.

78. Ibid., 278.

79. Ibid., 279.

80. All of the following letters—and there are many more—come from box 3, folder 3, Hall, SHSW.

81. Fritz, "Wendell Hall," 282.

82. "WWJ 'Firsts,'" WWJ file, BPL. See also "The Detroit News Radio Broadcasting Station," *Radio Topics*, May 1922, 5–6.

83. From the *Detroit News*, September 1, 1920, as quoted in Radio Staff of the Detroit News, *WWJ—The Detroit News* (Detroit: Evening News Association, 1922), 8.

84. Quoted in Winfield Barton, "What Broadcasting Does for a Newspaper," *Radio Broadcast*, February 1924, 346.

85. Quoted in ibid., 344.

86. Robert M. Lee, "Who Is to Be All Highest of Radio World?" *Chicago Tribune*, December 19, 1923, 6. The first three articles in the four-part series appeared December 16 (pp. 1, 16), 17 (p. 3), and 18 (p. 5).

87. Quoted in Daniel D. Calibraro and John Fink, *WGN: A Pictorial History* (Chicago: Tribune Company, 1971), 14.

88. Ibid., 11; "Reminiscences of Quin Ryan," May 16, 1965, BPL, 21.

89. Eugene MacDonald retained the WJAZ station license, however, soon applying for a new frequency. The disputes that followed would result in the famous court decision in 1925 that delegitimated all broadcasting regulation up to that point and led to the Radio Act of 1927.

90. Bruce A. Linton, "A History of Chicago Radio Station Programming, 1921–1931, with Emphasis on Stations WMAQ and WGN." (Ph.D. diss., Northwestern University, 1953), 94. See also E. F. McDonald Jr., "What We Think the Public Wants," *Radio Broadcast*, March 1924, 382–84, for similar results.

91. "Interview with Judith Waller, by Mr. Frank Ernest Hill, on June 1, 1951, at NBC, Merchandise Mart, Chicago, Ill.," Waller collection, SHSW, 8.

92. Ibid., 15–16.

3. Who We Are, Who We Are Not: The Emergence of National Narratives

1. Homi K. Bhabha, *The Location of Culture* (London: Routledge, 1994), 236.

2. Ann Douglas, *Terrible Honesty: Mongrel Manhattan in the 1920s* (New York: Farrar, Straus & Giroux, 1995).

3. Ibid., 420.

4. Burton W. Peretti, *The Creation of Jazz: Music, Race and Culture in Urban America* (Urbana: University of Illinois Press, 1992), 154.

5. Philip K. Eberly, *Music in the Air* (New York: Hastings House, 1982), 41–50; William L. Barlow, "Commercial and Noncommercial Radio," in *Split Image: African Americans in the Mass Media*, ed. Jannette L. Dates and William L. Barlow (Washington, D.C.: Howard University Press, 1990), 175–250.

6. Douglas, *Terrible Honesty*, 421.

7. Gilbert Seldes, "Toujours Jazz," *The Dial*, August 1923, 160.

8. Virgil Thomson, "Enter: American-Made Music," *Vanity Fair*, October 1925, 124.

9. James Lincoln Collier, *Louis Armstrong: An American Genius* (New York: Oxford University Press, 1993), 23.

10. "Sepia Band Given Discs; Whites Radio," *Chicago Defender*, April 22, 1939, 21.

11. Peretti, *The Creation of Jazz*, 185.

12. Ibid.

13. *Fleischmann's Yeast All Colored Show*, as-broadcast scripts, April 9, 1937; April 16, 1937; scripts, reel 16, JWT. This program was also known as the "Harlem Revue"; *Variety Radio Directory 1937–1938* (New York: Variety, 1937), 57.

14. *Radio Broadcasting News*, December 9, 1922, 10.

15. Barlow, "Commercial and Noncommercial Radio." For NBC's estimation of audience appeal, see "Gentlemen, Be Seated," promotional brochure for *Dutch Masters Minstrels*, 1930, box 3, folder 6, "NBC-Advertising Promotion-NBC-'Case Histories' 1928–1938," James.

16. *Aunt Jemima*, scripts, January 17, 1929; January 24, 1929; February 7, 1929; JWT.

17. *The Cream of Wheat Menagerie*, script, January 7, 1929; January 8, 1929; JWT.

18. "*Radio Talk Number One—To be given for Brer Rabbit Molasses*—Under the auspices of *The National Radio Home-makers Club*, Ida Bailey Allen, President—'The Gingerbread Man' by Jessie Gaynor," scripts, n.d. 1930, JWT.

19. George Lipsitz, *Time Passages: Collective Memory and American Popular Culture* (Minneapolis: University of Minnesota Press, 1990).

20. *Brer Rabbit Molasses* script, 4.

21. J. Fred MacDonald responds to this subterranean but deeply felt omission by including a final chapter titled "Blacks in Radio Programming" in what remains the best book yet written on the cultural aspects of radio, *Don't Touch That Dial! Radio Programming in American Life from 1920 to 1960* (Chicago: Nelson-Hall, 1979). Its position as a seeming afterthought reflects the displaced centrality of the disuniting factor of race in a medium that did more than any other to unify cultural discourse in the United States. MacDonald is a thorough and sensitive enough historian to at least include a well-developed chapter; other histories pass over the subject entirely. As Toni Morrison states, "In matters of race, silence and evasion have historically ruled literary discourse"; the same is true for broadcast history. *Playing in the Dark: Whiteness and the Literary Imagination* (Cambridge: Harvard University Press, 1992), 9. MacDonald is also the author of *Blacks and White TV: African Americans in Television since 1948*, 2d ed. (Chicago: Nelson-Hall, 1992).

22. Most of the information in this section on the *Sam 'n' Henry* and *Amos 'n' Andy* programs comes from the bound scripts and scrapbooks of the Freeman Gosden and Charles Correll Collection, Department of Special Collections, Doheny Library, University of Southern California, Los Angeles (abbreviated hereafter as USC). Major book-length sources on *Amos 'n' Andy* include Melvin Patrick Ely, *The Adventures of Amos 'n' Andy: A Social History of an American Phenomenon* (New York: Free Press, 1991); and Arthur Frank Wertheim, *Radio Comedy* (New York: Oxford University Press, 1979). Other useful sources, besides the ever-perceptive *A Tower in Babel*, include MacDonald's *Don't Touch That Dial!* and Raymond W. Stedman's *The Serials: Suspense and Drama by Installment* (Norman: University of Oklahoma Press, 1977). Articles and other materials that provide useful historical and biographical information are cited in the notes. Sources for other areas of research—vaudeville, immigration and assimilation, and radio history in general—are also cited at the appropriate points in the text. For overall theoretical perspectives, Toni Morrison's *Playing in the Dark* provides valuable insight into the role of race in literary discourse. Robert C. Allen's *Speaking of Soap Operas: Film Style and Mode of Production in 1960* (Chapel Hill: University of North Carolina Press,

1985) provides a clear and useful outline for a cultural studies approach to media texts; *The Classical Hollywood Cinema* by David Bordwell, Janet Staiger, and Kristin Thompson (New York: Columbia University Press, 1985) sets a standard for examining institution-text linkages. Along with scripts and written materials, my analysis of the shows themselves is based on the tape collection of the Society to Preserve and Encourage Radio Drama, Variety, and Comedy (SPERDVAC), Los Angeles, and on recordings in the Recorded Sound Collection of the Library of Congress, Washington, D.C.

23. B. Blackbeard and M. Williams, eds., *The Smithsonian Collection of Newspaper Comics* (Washington, D.C.: Smithsonian Institution Press, 1977), 15; J. Robinson, *The Comics: An Illustrated History of Comic Strip Art* (New York: G. P. Putnam's Sons, 1974).

24. Stedman, *The Serials*, 8–9.

25. Bordwell et al., *The Classical Hollywood Cinema*.

26. For an excellent overview of the minstrel show tradition and the Joe Bren Company's place in it, see Melvin Patrick Ely, "Jefferson Snowball, Traveling Minstrel," in *The Adventures of Amos 'n' Andy*. Most accounts of *Amos 'n' Andy*'s development, including Ely's, emphasize the personal backgrounds of Freeman Gosden and Charles Correll. Though this is relevant information, space does not permit a detailed examination here. Instead, I refer the reader to Ely and to Wertheim's *Radio Comedy*. I would also argue that, though the original inspiration for the program came from these two men, they were operating within the cultural context of their times. Other sources providing biographical information on Gosden and Correll are Thomas Meehan, "WEAF, 7:00–7:15: 'Ow wah, ow wah, ow wah,'" *New York Times Magazine*, December 31, 1972, 5–7, 26, 28, 31, 33; Max Wylie, "Amos and Andy—Loving Remembrance," *Television Quarterly* (Summer 1963): 17–24.

27. Daniel D. Calibraro and John Fink, *WGN: A Pictorial History* (Chicago: Tribune Company, 1971), 29–30.

28. Wertheim, *Radio Comedy*, 23–24.

29. Rockford *Register-Gazette*, October 5, 1926, scrapbook 1, USC .

30. Quoted in Ely, *The Adventures of Amos 'n' Andy*, 54.

31. Indeed, much of the show's early humor must be seen as arising from the dialect itself, as the early shows move slowly, carefully developing the characters of Sam Smith and Henry Johnson, two country bumpkins who are lured from Alabama to Chicago by the promise of jobs and money. In the scripts preserved in the USC library, both parts are typed in dialect, but the first two months show many words crossed out and even deeper dialect penciled in—substituting "mo'" for "more," "heah" for "here," "fas'" for "fast." The characters' reactions to unfamiliar situations and occasional malapropisms (later to become much more heavily emphasized), along with the dialect, supplied all the humor in the early shows; aside from the opening theme there is no music, no sound effects supplemented the action, and all voices were supplied by Gosden and Correll. Not until 1935 did other actors get involved in the production.

32. Scrapbook 1, USC.

33. Both titles for the program seem to echo a reference with which most Americans would be well acquainted: the comic pair Sam and Andy from Harriet Beecher Stowe's *Uncle Tom's Cabin*.

34. Ruth Adams Knight recounts Judith Waller's interview with a network executive: "A blackface comedy team had been enjoying a vogue over her Chicago station. Miss Waller decided their popularity was great enough to justify the interest of a national sponsor, an entirely new plan at the time. She went to New York and presented the idea to an official of a broadcasting company. He looked at her with open amazement. 'Are you suggesting that we attempt to broadcast this program over *several* stations at the

same time *every night in the week?*' he demanded. 'That was my idea,' Miss Waller replied mildly. There was a long silence. Then: 'You must be crazy,' was his only comment. Not long afterward Miss Waller sold Amos and Andy to a rival network." Ruth Adams Knight, *Stand By for the Ladies: The Distaff Side of Broadcasting* (New York: Coward McCann, 1939), 42–43. Also see Catharine Heinz, "The Voice of Authority, or, Hurrah for Christine Craft," *Feedback* (Spring 1984): 3–6.

35. Wertheim, *Radio Comedy*, 48–49.

36. Blackbeard and Williams define the comic strip as "a serially published, episodic, open-ended dramatic narrative or series of linked anecdotes about recurrent, identified characters, told in successive drawings regularly enclosing ballooned dialogue or its equivalent and minimized narrative text." *The Smithsonian Collection*, 13. Eliminate the purely visual elements and this perfectly describes the form developed in *Amos 'n' Andy*. Its content, too, owes much to the comic strips. From Outcault's "Yellow Kid," run in the Hearst papers in the 1890s, to "Doonesbury," the subject matter of the strips has been social satire and commentary, usually from the position of the "outsider," set in a lower- to lower-middle-class milieu. Frequently employing ethnic humor—the "Katzenjammer Kids"—and often dealing with the equally pressing problem of gender and domestic relations—"Gasoline Alley," "The Gumps"—comic strips took on the problems and contradictions of society and daily life in a humorous form.

37. Both Ely, in *The Adventures of Amos 'n' Andy*, and Wertheim, in *Radio Comedy*, examine *Amos 'n' Andy*'s roots in the minstrel show. In addition, Ely does an excellent job of placing the show's subject matter within the historical moment of the "great migration" of southern blacks to northern cities. Wertheim focuses on *Amos 'n' Andy*'s commentary on the Depression, which, he argues, accounted for much of the program's widespread acceptance. This tradition of social satire and commentary points out *Amos 'n' Andy*'s debt to the comic strip narrative.

38. Morrison, *Playing in the Dark*, 6.

39. Scripts, book 1, USC.

40. That these characterizations were in wide circulation can be seen in the results of a poll of Princeton students in 1932, in which they were asked to identify the characteristics most closely associated with three ethnic groups—Chinese, Japanese, and Negroes. The results for "Negroes" are as follows:

Characteristic	Number of respondents agreeing
Superstitious	84
Lazy	75
Happy-go-lucky	38
Ignorant	38
Musical	26
Ostentatious	26
Very religous	24
Stupid	22
Physically dirty	17
Naive	14
Slovenly	13
Unreliable	12

By comparison, heading the list of Japanese characteristics were intelligent, industrious, progressive, shrewd, and sly, whereas Chinese were characterized as superstitious, sly, conservative, tradition-loving, and loyal to family ties. Cited in S. Lieberson, *A Piece of the Pie: Blacks and White Immigrants since 1860* (Berkeley: University of California Press, 1980), 367. Also, the numbers agreeing on characteristics were much smaller for

Asians than for blacks—the highest number agreeing was forty-five for the top-listed Japanese traits and thirty-four for the Chinese. The extremely high rate of agreement for the top two "Negro" traits—superstitiousness and laziness—reflects very closely the traits suggested as dominant on *Amos 'n' Andy*.

41. The same was true for *The Goldbergs*, in which gentile characters hardly ever appeared.

42. In this *Amos 'n' Andy* bears a certain resemblance to some more recent popular programs featuring African American characters. Herman Gray points out this tendency in *The Cosby Show*, in which "the characters are never presented in situations where their racial identity matters. This representation of racial encounters further appeals to the utopian desire in blacks and whites for racial oneness and equality while displacing the persistent reality of racism and racial inequality or the kinds of social struggles and cooperation required to eliminate them." Herman Gray, "Television, Black Americans, and the American Dream," *Critical Studies in Mass Communication* 6 (1989): 383.

43. It should be mentioned here that the concept of ethnicity is itself a relatively recent one. Previously, the various cultural and geographic groups of the "new immigrants" were conceived as "races"—the Italian race, the Irish race, the Jewish race—and thus the "special" status of the so-called Negro race, by existing in popular consciousness as a race like any other, yet so significantly "different," exacerbated the "otherness" of African Americans. See Lieberson, *A Piece of the Pie*, 5.

44. Alfred F. McLean, *American Vaudeville as Ritual* (Lexington: University of Kentucky Press, 1965), 121–22; see also D. Gilbert, *American Vaudeville: Its Life and Times* (New York: Dover, 1940); and Joe Laurie Jr., *Vaudeville: From the Honky-Tonks to the Palace* (New York: Holt, 1953).

45. They were also performed primarily *for* white working-class men, as Jannette L. Dates and William Barlow point out in their incisive introduction to *Split Image*. The irony and suppression of black performers made to conform to white stereotyped expectations both in vaudeville and in music are traced by William Barlow in his chapter on the early music industry titled "Cashing In: 1900–1939" in the same volume.

46. Morrison, *Playing in the Dark*, 47.

47. In fact, as Jacqueline Jones points out, the majority of immigrants from the rural South to the cities of the North were white, though the proportion of American blacks living in the South fell from 90 percent to 50 percent between 1910 and 1960. Jacqueline Jones, *The Dispossessed: America's Underclass from the Civil War to the Present* (New York: Basic Books, 1992). For a discussion of the historical context of black Americans and the "great migration," see Ely, *The Adventures of Amos 'n' Andy*, chap. 5.

48. *Amos 'n' Andy*'s varying use of accent almost deserves a study in itself. As noted previously, supporting characters, particularly professional ones, often exhibit a minimal use of dialect. Interestingly, most women—especially those presented as "worthy" love interests, such as Amos's girlfriend, Ruby Taylor—speak with no accent at all. In the cartoon run in the *Daily News*, women in general are drawn with few of the caricaturing "blackface" features that are used to represent the male characters, including being considerably lighter skinned. The more comic—and less intelligent and desirable—the character, the heavier the accent and the darker the skin.

49. *Amos 'n' Andy*, "Democrats and Republicans," from the SPERDVAC collection, n.d.

50. James Baldwin, *Nobody Knows My Name* (New York: Dell, 1962), 133–34.

51. Letters in the Gosden and Correll collection at USC provide ample opportunity for further research into diverse audience interpretations and uses of the program. It is interesting to note that, as Ely points out in *The Adventures of Amos 'n' Andy*, the pro-

gram appeared to support and confirm both racist attitudes and more sympathetic "these people are just like us" readings simultaneously.

52. See Bishop W. J. Walls, "What about Amos 'n' Andy?" *Abbott's Monthly*, December 1931, 38–40, 72–74. See also ibid., chap. 9, for a detailed exploration of popular debate over the radio program; also William L. Barlow, "Commercial and Noncommercial Radio," in *Split Image*. Barnouw, in *A Tower in Babel*, cites an interview with black writer William Branch, who said that he enjoyed the show until he learned, "those people were supposed to be 'us.'" (230).

53. Morrison, *Playing in the Dark*, 17.

54. What happened in 1951, when NBC attempted to transfer the program to television? Ely's *The Adventures of Amos 'n' Andy* provides a thorough and very interesting account of the process of objection, negotiation, and conflict that eventually led to its being removed from the 1953 season. I believe that *Amos 'n' Andy*'s unsuitability to television arose from several factors. First, the visual component of television forced the symbolic quality of *Amos 'n' Andy*'s "blackness" to take on a literal form: television's "overdetermination" wrecked the delicate balance the radio program had achieved between racial and ethnic/country humor by visually emphasizing its racial aspects. Suddenly, it became quite apparent that these characters were in no way "black" but white projections, and insulting ones.

Second, after thirty years of restrictions on immigration—not eased until the 1950s, despite the terrible consequences, for eastern European Jews in particular, of these restrictions during and after World War II—*Amos 'n' Andy*'s form of humor based on "difference" was quickly becoming irrelevant to the overwhelming "normalcy" of the postwar years. Other "ethnic" shows made their TV debut—*The Goldbergs*, *The Life of Riley*, *Life with Luigi*—and quickly lost favor to the *Donna Reed Show*, *Father Knows Best*, *Leave It to Beaver* genre of mainstream middle-class lifestyles. A society that had fought a war for the American system of values set out to demonstrate just what those values were, beginning an era of denial of diversity that lasted until the 1970s.

55. Meehan, "WEAF, 7:007:15," 33.

56. Of course, race and skin color have never been equivalent in the complex of identity in the United States, but it is a trope of racial discourse to define it as such. As Robert H. Wiebe writes: "Within this larger framework skin color found its special place in American society. In colonial America, red and black were synonymous with those qualities of culture that were usually considered most radically at odds with white communities. Africans and Indians were not necessarily the primary danger to a white community's integrity, but they marked the greatest social distances from white society. Even if skin color itself did not arouse horror, it blended with judgments of such a vast cultural separation that an easy intermingling within the community was almost impossible. When readily observable characteristics became the standard measure of acceptability early in the nineteenth century, skin color, already a clue to profound differences, emerged as central in its own right, as the substance of these differences and therefore as the threat to purity most fearfully avoided. Along with such secondary traits as the curl of the hair and the slant of the eyes, color provided a sovereign test that all Americans of all shades learned as part of a common heritage." *The Segmented Society: An Introduction to the Meaning of America* (New York: Oxford University Press, 1975), 74.

57. W. E. B. Du Bois, *The Souls of Black Folk* (New York: Fawcett, 1961), 16–17.

58. Henry Louis Gates Jr., "An 'Amos 'n' Andy' Christmas," *New York Times*, December 23, 1994, A35:2.

59. Margo Jefferson, "Seductified by a Minstrel Show," *New York Times*, May 22, 1994, 2:1.

60. Jessie Parkhurst Guzman, ed., *Negro Year Book* (Tuskegee, Ala.: Tuskegee Institute, 1946), 446.

61. Estelle Edmerson's master thesis, "A Descriptive Study of the American Negro in U.S. Professional Radio, 1922–1953" (University of California, Los Angeles, Theater Arts Department, 1954), much drawn upon in subsequent studies (see MacDonald, *Don't Touch That Dial!*; Dates and Barlow, *Split Image*), tells a remarkable story of the intervention of academic study in real-life racial politics. In the course of her thesis research, Edmerson revealed to the members of the AFM's Local 767, all "Negro," that contracts for radio and television work were being made only with the local white chapter, Local 47, and that Los Angeles station and agency hiring practices specifically excluded the Negro chapter from consideration: "Words cannot express the tremendous effect which this information of Los Angeles radio stations' hiring procedure had on the participants of the first forum discussion at Local 767. Like a small balloon that bursts with over-filling, most of the participants, seemingly filled with experiences of limitations and disadvantages resulting from their racial separation, concluded that the segregated arrangement of their union activities had to be discontinued" (272). This revelation resulted in a merging of the two locals in April 1954, after a highly charged series of meetings that revealed stark racism at the highest levels of the AFM.

4. Eavesdropping on America: Kitchen Table Conversations

1. Robert Sauder, "Program Coming In Fine. Please Play 'Japanese Sandman,'" *American Heritage*, August 1965, 27.

2. NBC commercial representative to Mr. C. B. Donovan, Acme Apparatus Company, November 26, 1926, box 2, folder 3, NBC; Gleason L. Archer, *Big Business and Radio* (New York: American Historical Company, 1939), 289, 299, 311.

3. John F. Royal, "The Network Program Department," box 13, folder 27, NBC.

4. Harrison B. Summers, ed., *A Thirty-Year History of Programs Carried on National Radio Networks in the United States 1926–1956* (New York: Arno, 1971).

5. See Robert Ernst, *Weakness Is a Crime* (Syracuse, N.Y.: Syracuse University Press, 1991); John Hunt, *Body Love: The Amazing Career of Bernarr Macfadden* (Bowling Green, Ohio: Bowling Green State University Press, 1989); Mary MacFadden and Emile Gavreau, *Dumbbells and Carrot Strips* (New York: Holt, 1953).

6. A memo from John Royal to Bertha Brainard dated May 30, 1932, indicates that tensions existed, including Royal's demands that "all profane words regardless of dramatic license" must be eliminated from *True Story* and other dramatic programs because "we are getting too many letters of complaint." Box 7, folder 6, NBC.

7. Ernst, *Weakness Is a Crime*, 77.

8. George Gerbner, "The Social Role of the Confession Magazine," *Social Problems* 6 (1958): 37.

9. Wilbur Schramm, "The World of the Confession Magazine" (unpublished manuscript, University of Illinois, Institute of Communications Research, 1957), cited in ibid., 37.

10. Quoted in Ernst, *Weakness Is a Crime*, 81.

11. *Memory Lane*, brochure, October 1931, box 3, folder 5, EPH James.

12. Ibid., 5.

13. Ibid., 7.

14. Ibid., 15.

15. *The Real Folks of Thompkins Corners*, program brochure, January 1931, box 3, folder 5, EPH James, 17, 19.

16. Ibid., 9.

17. Ibid.

18. Charles Stumpf and Tom Price, *Heavenly Days! The Story of Fibber McGee and Molly* (Waynesville, NC: The World of Yesterday, 1987).

19. Ibid., 43.

20. Quoted in ibid., 51.

21. Arthur Frank Wertheim, *Radio Comedy* (New York: Oxford University Press, 1979), 238. Silly Watson's character is very similar to that of Lightnin' on *Amos 'n' Andy.*

22. John Dunning, *Tune In Yesterday* (Englewood Cliffs, N.J.: Prentice Hall, 1976) 152.

23. Stumpf and Price, *Heavenly Days!* 33.

24. "Interview with Judith Waller, by Mr. Frank Ernest Hill, on June 1, 1951, at NBC, Merchandise Mart, Chicago, Ill.," Waller collection, SHSW, 28.

25. *Clara, Lu and Em*, January 6, 1936. Chicago Museum of Broadcasting collection.

26. Raymond W. Stedman, *The Serials: Suspense and Drama by Installment* (Norman: University of Oklahoma Press, 1977), 507–8.

27. *Gangbusters*, June 9, 1944, SPERDVAC collection, reel G384.

28. J. Fred MacDonald, *Don't Touch That Dial! Radio Programming in American Life from 1920 to 1960* (Chicago: Nelson-Hall, 1979), 159.

29. Roland Marchand, *Advertising the American Dream: Making Way for Modernity 1920–1940* (Berkeley: University of California Press, 1985), 88–94.

30. H. A. Batten, speech transcript, January 5, 1938, N.W. Ayer, 9.

31. William Peck Banning, *Commercial Broadcasting Pioneer: The WEAF Experiment, 1922–1926* (Cambridge: Harvard University Press, 1946), 103.

32. "How Advertising Came to Radio—and Television, 1900–1932," from "History of Radio" file, N. W. Ayer archive, 31–32.

33. "Why Don't We Use the Radio?" *J. Walter Thompson Newsletter*, February 5, 1925, 4–7. Box 7, JWT.

34. "Two J.W.T. Clients Use Radio Advertisements," *J. Walter Thompson Newsletter*, February 19, 1925, 5. Box 7, JWT.

35. Minutes of representatives meeting—Wednesday, July 11, 1928, box 1, folder 5, JWT.

36. H. Calvin Kuhl, "The Grim Reber," Writings and Speeches, JWT, 25–27.

37. Minutes of group meeting, Assembly Hall, April 16, 1930, JWT.

38. For a rather disdainfully critical acknowledgment of this claim, see Ben Bodec, "Ad Agencies and Radio Theories," *Variety*, January 3, 1933, 62.

39. Dorothy Dwight Townsend, "Mrs. Wilkins Reads the Ladies Home Journal," *JWT News Bulletin*, June 1923, 1–5. JWT.

40. Minutes of representatives meeting, September 8, 1927, box 1, folder 4, JWT, 6.

41. Minutes of representatives meetings, April 9, 1929, JWT, 6–7.

42. JWT Officers and Staff—Sidney Bernstein—JWT Personnel Information—Daniel Danker, RG3, JWT.

43. Robert T. Colwell, "Theme Song Days," RG3, box 3, folder 9, Sidney Bernstein papers, Officers and Staff, JWT Personnel Information: Robert Talcott Colwell, JWT, 3.

44. JWT Officers and Staff—Sidney Bernstein—JWT Personnel Information—Daniel Danker, RG3, JWT.

45. Susan Smulyan, *Selling Radio: The Commercialization of American Broadcasting 1920–1934* (Washington, D.C.: Smithsonian Institution Press, 1994).

46. John F. Royal to Roy C. Witmer, June 15, 1932, Correspondence files, 1932, NBC.

47. Bertha Brainard to Roy C. Witmer, May 16, 1933, Program—Commercial, 1933, NBC.

48. Matthew Murray, "Television Wipes Its Feet: The Commercial and Ethical Considerations behind the Adoption of the Televison Code," *Journal of Popular Film and Television* 21 (Fall 1993).

49. Witmer to Shaw, October 23, 1935, box 92, folder 11, NBC.

50. Burke Boyce to George F. McClellan, "Program Deletions," 5–12–33, box 16, folder 60, NBC.

51. William C. Erskine to John F. Royal, July 5, 1933, box 16, folder 50, NBC.

52. Burke Boyce to George F. McClellan, "Program Deletions," 5–27–33, box 16, folder 50, NBC.

53. Bertha Brainard to George F. McClellan, "Program Deletions," 6–6–33, box 16, folder 50, NBC.

54. Bertha Brainard to George F. McClellan, "Program Deletions," 6–14–33, box 16, folder 50, NBC.

55. Burke Boyce to John F. Royal, "Chase and Sanborn (Fanny Brice)—May 24th, 1933," box 16, folder 50, NBC.

56. Burke Boyce to John Royal, "Policy Reading," 10–13–33, box 90, folder 17, NBC.

57. For a history of the Hollywood-radio connection, see Michele Hilmes, *Hollywood and Broadcasting: From Radio to Cable* (Urbana: University of Illinois Press, 1990).

58. C. L. Menser to Sidney N. Strotz, September 9, 1936, box 92, folder 17, NBC.

59. Janet MacRorie to Bertha Brainard, October 1, 1936, box 92, folder 1, NBC.

60. Janet MacRorie to "Messrs. Royal and Witmer," February 24, 1937, box 92, folder 42, NBC.

61. Bertha Brainard to Roy C. Witmer, March 22, 1937, box 93, folder 2, NBC.

62. Roy C. Witmer to Bertha Brainard, "Daytime Dramatic Scripts," March 24, 1937, box 93, folder 2, NBC.

63. Roy C. Witmer to Janet MacRorie, April 23, 1937, box 93, folder 2, NBC.

64. Janet MacRorie to Lenox R. Lohr, February 28, 1938, box 90, folder 37, NBC.

65. William Boddy, *Fifties Television: The Industry and Its Critics* (Urbana: University of Illinois Press, 1990); Christopher Anderson, *Hollywood TV: The Studio Systems in the Fifties* (Austin: University of Texas Press, 1994).

66. "Operations Report for Studio and Office Sections, April 20, 1947," box 355, folder 59, NBC.

5. The Disembodied Woman

1. Gwen Wagner, "A Girl Reporter-Announcer Speaks Up: Radio in Days of Yore," *Radio Age*, September 1925, 30.

2. One writer, E. P. J. Shurick, nicely summarizes this misconception; introducing a chapter titled "The Woman's Role in Broadcasting," he exclaims: "Women have had a surprising lot to do with broadcasting and its development. Not in the scientific laboratory, where the woman's delicate touch is in little evidence! Nor especially in an executive sense with making the wheels go around in a radio station! But when it comes to a subtle feminine influence from the receiving end as listeners, women have had everything to do with broadcasting." *The First Quarter-Century of American Broadcasting*, (North Branch, N.J.: Midland, 1946), 140.

3. For a partial and tentative listing of some other early women in broadcasting, see Catherine Heinz, "Women Radio Pioneers," *Journal of Popular Culture* 12 (1978): 305–14. Also see Francis Willard Kerr, *Women in Radio* (Washington, D.C.: U.S. Department of Labor, Women's Bureau, 1947); Earl Chapin May, "Women on the Air," *Pictorial Review*, October 1934, 22, 50–51; letter from Henriette K. Harrison to Eliza-

beth Bain, December 14, 1965, file 36, item A, BPL; note attached to clipping re: Pattie Field, February 1974, box 9, folder 10, EPH James; John B. Kennedy, "Ladies of the Air Waves," *Colliers*, July 9, 1932, 14, 44; Morleen Getz Rouse, "Daytime Radio Programming for the Homemaker 1926–1956," *Journal of Popular Culture*, 12 (1978): 315–28.

4. However, some recent studies, such as Christopher Anderson's work on Hollywood-influenced television, *Hollywood TV: The Studio Systems in the Fifties* (Austin: University of Texas Press, 1994); Michael Curtin's reexamination of television documentary during the Cold War, *Redeeming the Wasteland: Television Documentary and the Cold War* (New Brunswick, N.J.: Rutgers University Press, 1995); and Nina Leibman's exploration of the overlapping concerns of television and film during the 1950s, *Living Room Lectures* (Austin: University of Texas Press, 1995), look more specifically at the complex web of interactions, institutional as well as audience related, that helped shape this new medium.

5. This same dynamic seems to be operating with new technologies, such as the Internet. It is also interesting to note that the imbrication of gender and race, always a highly charged conjunction, operated even in the 1910s, as witnessed in a cartoon from *QST* in which a young woman meets several of the male amateurs with whom she has been communicating. Each clearly "unsuitable," for reasons ranging from age to race to general nerdishness, they represent the dangers faced by gender-bending activities such as wireless. Particularly emphasized is the distorted racially stereotyped representation of a black man in the group.

6. Abbye M. White, "Hearing North America," *Radio Broadcast*, September 1923, 421–25.

7. Alfred M. Caddell, "A Woman Who Makes Receiving Sets," *Radio Broadcast*, November 1923, 29–33; "Some Girls Build Their Own," *Radio Digest*, November 4, 1922, 5; Irving Vermilya, "QRX for a New O.W.," *QST*, July 1921, 29–31; M. Adaire Garmhausen, "WWV at Home," *QST*, March 1924, 25–26; "Who's Who in Amateur Wireless," *QST*, October 1922, 58–59. Also see brief profiles in *QST*, March 1924, v.; June 1924, vi; July 1924, vi.

8. "Girls to Study Wireless," *QST*, August 1916, 201.

9. "Who's Who," *QST*, August 1916, 302–3.

10. "The Ladies Are Coming," *QST*, August 1917, 19.

11. "As If We Can't Train 'em Too!" letter from H. J. Burhop, 9ZL, Manitowoc, Wis., *QST*, July 1920, 53.

12. "Beginning at the End," *QST*, September 1920, 10.

13. "Give the Fair Sex a Chance," letter from Edward T. Jones, New Orleans, *QST*, November 1920, 2.

14. "The Radio Ladies," *QST*, March 1921, 64.

15. "Give the Fair Sex a Chance," 51.

16. See "Who's Who in Amateur Wireless" and *QST* March and June, 1924. Under a photo of Jesse E. Koewing, announcer and manager of WOR, the *Radio Digest*, February 3, 1923, 5, saw fit to add: "Miss Koewing is single—she hopes not for long." *QST* featured a photograph in July 1924 of Mildred S. Lorenton, an operator from Providence, Rhode Island, with the caption, "If the fellows in amateur radio averaged up anywhere near as good-looking as the girls there would be a lot more stations in Hollywood" (vi).

17. "Fifth District O.W.'s," *QST*, December 1921, 65.

18. See Shaun Moores, "The Box on the Dresser: Memories of Early Radio and Everyday Life," *Media, Culture & Society* 10 (1988): 23–40.

19. See, for instance, Oliver H. P. Garrett, "Broadcasting as an Industry," *American Review of Reviews* (November 1927): 517–23, prepared in consultation with NBC ex-

ecutives; memorandum 11/3/27 from G. W. Johnston to G. F. McClelland, department files—press relations 1927–29, box 90, folder 1, NBC.

20. Wagner, "A Girl Reporter-Announcer," 30.

21. "Women in Advertising," JWT house advertisement, 1918; "Importance of Women as Consumers and Employees," memo from Marianne Keating to Ruth Ritenour, October 19, 1964, RG 3, box 8, folder 19; officers and staff, Sidney Bernstein, JWT history: Women, JWT. See also E. P. H. James collection, box 1, folder 12, SHSW, for NBC promotional brochures in late 1930s and 1940 emphasizing these statistics.

22. Two studies of women in broadcasting, done in the 1940s, briefly delineate the careers of other female broadcasters, whose functions ranged from the traditional (homemaker advice programs, children's shows, and public service) to the obscure (writers for radio's ubiquitous daytime serial dramas) to the unusual (such as Jill Jackson, sports reporter for New Orleans station WWL). Ruth Adams Knight, *Stand By for the Ladies: The Distaff Side of Broadcasting* (New York: Coward McCann, 1939); Francis Willard Kerr, *Women in Radio: A View of Important Jobs in Radio Held by Women* (Washington, D.C.: U.S. Department of Labor, Women's Bureau, 1947). Their existence points not to the lack of women in this field—indeed, both studies have trouble encompassing the magnitude of their tasks—but to the conflicted status of women and women's programming within the broadcasting institution.

23. WJZ logs, NBC collection, box 98, SHSW; see also Frances Drewry McMullen, "Bertha Brainard, Radio Producer," *Woman's Journal*, November 1928, 18–19; "Women in Business III," *Fortune*, September 1935, 86; Herndon Green, "What Is Woman's Place in Broadcasting?" *Radio News*, November 1927, 477; "We Pay Our Respects to—Bertha Brainard, *Broadcasting and Broadcast Advertising*, September 1, 1937, n.p.; Asa Bordages, "Stars of the Payroll," *New York World Telegram*, February 1, 1937, n.p.; Ruth Arell, "Silent Voices in Radio," *Independent Woman*, November 1927, 342ff.; Kathleen McLaughlin, "Woman Builds High Place in Organizing Air Programs," *New York Times*, January 22, 1939, 2:4.; "Program Director," *American Magazine*, April 1933, 41. See also reminiscences of Raymond F. Guy, Broadcast Pioneers Collection, 326, and "Reminiscences of Mark Woods," Oral History Research Office, Radio Unit, 41–47.

24. Bertha Brainard, "Women Listeners Are Good Critics," *New York Times*, September 18, 1927, 16:1.

25. Green, "What Is Woman's Place?" 537. See also "Radio Sets Are Heralded as Ideal Christmas Gifts," *New York Times*, December 9, 1928, 20.

26. Memorandum from Bertha Brainard to Roy C. Witmer, August 23, 1932, department files—programming—commercial, 1932, box 90, folder 13, NBC.

27. Department files, box 90, folders 12, 13, 31, NBC. See also Bertha Brainard, "No Formula Is Found for Radio's Theatre," *New York Times*, October 19, 1930, 10:12.

28. "The Reminiscences of William S. Hedges," Oral History Research Office, Radio Unit, Broadcast Pioneers Microfilms, SHSW.

29. "Interview with Judith Waller, by Mr. Frank Ernest Hill, on June 1, 1951, at NBC, Merchandise Mart, Chicago, Ill.," Waller collection, SHSW, 36.

30. Catharine Heinz briefly describes several examples in "Women Radio Pioneers": Myrtle Stahl at WDAP (later WGN) in Chicago, hired as general program director in 1922; Dorothy Gordon at WEAF in 1923; Madge Tucker at WRC, Washington, D.C., in 1924; and many more.

31. In Popenoe's and the other managers' comments and in Codell's somewhat skeptical summary we see clearly expressed the dangerous qualities possessed by this upstart nonvisual medium, specifically linked to the feminine: what Amy Lawrence calls "the problem of the speaking woman." Building on work previously done by Mary Ann

Doane and Kaja Silverman, Lawrence identifies various ways in which women's voices have been contained and subordinated within classical Hollywood cinema: "Women's voices are positioned within narratives that require their submission to patriarchal roles. . . . female characters are made to use language that silences them. . . . the cinematic conventions of visual and audio representation convert woman to spectacle, precluding her status as subject, and [place] women on the weak end of sound/image hierarchies. . . . The authorial voice is rarely heard as a *woman*'s voice in classical cinema." *Echo and Narcissus: Women's Voices in Classical Hollywood Cinema* (Berkeley: University of California Press, 1991), 169.

Radio offered another sphere of purely aural representation in which women's voices would be similarly contained. These concerns go back to nineteenth-century popular entertainment, as Robert C. Allen has shown. Tracing the process by which burlesque, originally populated by transgressive "talking women" who dressed in men's clothing and took male parts in satirical sketches, became transformed into a medium of female physical spectacle, Allen concludes: "The burlesque performer's transgressive power was circumscribed by her construction as exotic other, removed from the world of ordinary woman. Her power to reordinate the world was similarly limited by largely depriving her of speech. . . . the appeals of burlesque became increasingly bifurcated: verbal humor provided usually by male comedians and sexual display provided by female performers." *Horrible Prettiness: Burlesque and American Culture* (Chapel Hill: University of North Carolina Press, 1991), 237–38. Popenoe's summary of WJZ's survey and the comments of the station managers that precede it indicate a need to impose similar restrictions on women's voices in radio. With their insistence on women's bodies, appearance, and sexualized physical presence, these comments demonstrate that radio awoke the same culturally subversive possibilities as women's representation in classical Hollywood cinema.

32. "Women Announcers—Why Not? Weaker Sex Heard Often in European Air, but Only Few Make Grade Here," Martin Codell collection, scrapbook 60, 1933, SHSW. See also Louis E. Bisch, "Why Women Don't 'Click' on the Air," *Radioland*, February 1934, 29, 65.

33. "The Largest Clinic of Advertising Experience in the World," RG 1, box 9, folder 1, Corporate Administration: New Business, JWT, 45.

34. In 1945, J. Walter Thompson accounted for 7.9 percent of all radio advertising billings on NBC, ABC, CBS, and Mutual, second only to Young & Rubicam's 9.45 percent, according to Llewellyn White, *The American Radio*, (Chicago: University of Chicago Press, 1947), 59.

35. Stockholder's affidavit, Helen Resor, March 20, 1924, RG 2, box 7, folder 123, Officers and Staff Members, Biographical Information: Resor, Helen Lansdowne, JWT.

36. "Re: Mrs. Resor and Separation of Women's from Men's Editorial Groups," RG 3, box 4, folder 21, Officers and Staff, Sidney Bernstein, JWT Personnel Information: Ruth Waldo, JWT.

37. Ibid.; "J. Walter Thompson Company," *Fortune*, November 1947, 205.

38. Robert T. Colwell, "Theme Song Days," RG 3, box 3, folder 9, Sidney Bernstein papers, Officers and Staff, JWT Personnel Information: Robert Talcott Colwell, JWT, 3–4.

39. Michele Hilmes, *Hollywood and Broadcasting: From Radio to Cable* (Urbana: University of Illinois Press, 1990); Colwell, "Theme Song Days"; Calvin Kuhl, "The Grim Reber," RG 3, box 7, Sidney Bernstein papers, Officers and Staff Members, Biographical Information: John U. Reber, JWT.

40. Aminta Casseres, "Radio Today Is Not Just a Good-Will Medium," *JWT News Bulletin*, October 1929, JWT.

41. See WJZ logs, for instance, NBC collection, box 98, folders 11 (1924) and 25 (1927), SHSW.

42. Christine Frederick, "Radio for the Housekeeper," *Good Housekeeping*, 1922, excerpted in *Literary Digest*, September 9, 1922, 28–29.

43. It is interesting to contrast her proposal with a similar format adopted in 1932 by NBC. Called *The Woman's Home Magazine of the Air*, this daily program featured commercially sponsored fifteen-minute segments with subject matter restricted to those household and personal care topics most easily related to product sales, rather than providing a complete informational service. Fact sheets 1931–34, box 4, folder 4, NBC, E. P. H. James, SHSW.

44. Morleen Getz Rouse, "Daytime Radio Programming for the Homemaker," *Journal of Popular Culture*, 12 (1978): 315–27.

45. "Throngs of Radio Pals Attend Our Radio Tea," *People's Gas Club News*, April 2, 1923, file 36–JJ, BPL.

46. "Radio for Women," *Literary Digest*, November 28, 1925, 20.

47. "Ida Bailey Allen's Radio Career through the Years," summary prepared by Charles Premmac, April 29, 1966, file 36, item L, vertical file "Women in Broadcasting," BPL, 4.

48. Ibid., 6. See also memo from Margaret Cuthbert to John F. Royal, December 5, 1932, Central Files, "Cosmo Broadcasting Company—1928–31." box 2, folder 116, NBC; Mary Jordan, "Housekeeping by Radio," *Radio News*, January 1928, 742ff.; Betty McGee, "Opened Doors," *Radio Digest*, September 1930, 90ff.

49. Fact sheet, "The Woman's Radio Review," fact sheets 1931–34, box 4, folder 4, NBC, E.P.H. James, SHSW.

50. Harrison B. Summers, ed., *A Thirty-Year History of Programs Carried on National Radio Networks in the United States 1926–1956* (New York: Arno, 1971), 29. Already by the next season, 1932–33, the number of homemakers' talks had declined to eight; the following seasons fluctuated between eight and twelve. This does not, however, take into account local radio, where such programs remained popular.

51. Margaret Cuthbert, "Daytime Broadcasting," Central files, box 2, folder 116, NBC, 6.

6. Under Cover of Daytime

1. Edgar A. Grunwald, "Program-Production History, 1929–1937," *Variety Radio Directory 1937–1938*. (New York: Variety, 1937) p. 28.

2. Roland Marchand, *Advertising the American Dream: Making Way for Modernity 1920–1940* (Berkeley: University of California Press, 1985), 69.

3. Ibid., 162.

4. Andreas Huyssen, *After the Great Divide: Modernism, Mass Culture, Postmodernism* (Bloomington: Indiana University Press, 1986), 47, 62.

5. Robert W. McChesney, *Telecommunications, Mass Media, and Democracy: The Battle for the Control of U.S. Broadcasting, 1928–1935* (New York: Oxford University Press, 1993).

6. Ibid., 115–16.

7. I should emphasize here that "only women were listening" characterizes a set of attitudes and discursive constructions of the audience, not necessarily the actual constitution by gender of people listening. In fact, by most estimates, men consistently made up a proportion of the daytime audience between 20 and 30 percent (especially during the Depression, when many were unemployed and at home), and women, of course,

have always made up the majority of the nighttime audience—between 55 and 65 percent.

8. Robert C. Allen, *Speaking of Soap Operas* (Chapel Hill: University of North Carolina Press, 1985), 24, 18.

9. See ibid. as well as Ellen E. Seiter, "Women Writing Soap Opera: The Careers of Irna Phillips and Jane Crusinberry" (paper presented at the meeting of the Society for Cinema Studies, Bozeman, Mont., June 1988). See also the Irna Phillips collection, SHSW.

10. "Plan Presentation Montgomery Ward," n.d., box 4, "Proposed Programs, 1931–48," Phillips.

11. *Broadcasting*, March 1, 1935, 12, cited in Allen, *Speaking of Soap Operas*, 114.

12. Seiter, "Women Writing Soap Opera," 32.

13. Ibid.

14. Memorandum from Willis Cooper to Sidney Strotz, August 8, 1934, box 62, "NBC Correspondence, December 1933–December 1948," Phillips.

15. Irna Phillips, "In Defense of Daytime Serials," box 63, "Miscellaneous Correspondence," 1937–49, Phillips. A female editorial writer in the *Pittsburgh Press* echoed these sentiments in a very different setting. Condemning in no uncertain terms the bulk of daytime fare as "the cheapest, trashiest, falsest, slushiest, corniest TRIPE that ever proceeded from the mind of man," the author went on to indict the serial producers' conception of their "Monday through Friday" audience as different from that on weekends: "And on those two days, that others, more intelligent, are apt to be around the house, listening. What an admission for housewives to accept! What an insult is implied! These trashy serials are good enough for them through the week when they are working alone in the house; but in the evenings, and on Sunday, when the MORE INTELLIGENT members of the family are home, oh No! THEN, on with the fine programs that invite the cultured listener!" Florence Fisher Parry, "I Dare Say,—" *Pittsburgh Press*, September 6, 1944, n.p., box 5, folder 4, Crusinberry.

16. Hobe Morrison, "Analyzing the Daytime Serials," *Variety*, August 19, 1943, n.p., box 63, "Miscellaneous Correspondence, 1937–49," Phillips.

17. Letter from Ken Robinson to Carl Wester, May 24, 1940, and letter from Ken Robinson to Carl Wester, June 7, 1940, box 62, "NBC Correspondence, December 1933–1948," Phillips.

18. Letter from Irna Phillips to Hobe Morrison, August 23, 1943, box 63, "Miscellaneous Correspondence, 1937–49," Phillips.

19. Allen, *Speaking of Soap Operas*, 140–50.

20. Seiter, "Women Writing Soap Opera."

21. Nancy Fraser, "Rethinking the Public Sphere," in *The Phantom Public Sphere*, ed. Bruce Robbins (Minneapolis: University of Minnesota Press, 1991), 1–32; see also Stephanie Coontz, *The Way We Never Were* (New York: HarperCollins, 1992), especially 42–67.

22. "NBC Press Conference, New York," May 29, 1945, box 63, "Miscellaneous Correspondence, 1937–49," Phillips, 8.

23. *Today's Children*, Episode 65, September 16, 1932, box 5, "Today's Children 1932 August-December," Phillips.

24. Lawrence W. Levine, *Highbrow/Lowbrow: The Emergence of Cultural Hierarchy in America* (Cambridge: Harvard University Press, 1988). In chapter 7, I will examine these developments in radio.

25. Constance Rourke, *American Humor: A Study of the National Character* (1935; reprinted New York, 1953), 96–97, cited in ibid., 30.

26. Allen, *Speaking of Soap Operas*, 18–44.

27. Phillips admitted to employing "collaborating" writers, whose names she claimed were never kept secret, as her critics charged, but had been published in *Variety* itself. She objected vehemently to their characterization as "a stable of ghost writers" and emphasized her constant and continuing involvement as primary author. She was always listed as primary author for *Today's Children.*

28. Raymond W. Stedman, *The Serials: Suspense and Drama by Installment,* (Norman: University of Oklahoma Press, 1977), 267.

29. Ibid., 236.

30. Irna Phillips, "Why Can't We Do Something Besides a Daytime Serial?" 1942, n.d., box 63, "Miscellaneous Correspondence, 1937–1949," Phillips.

31. "Hummerts' Mill," *Time,* January 23, 1939, 30.

32. This information is compiled from several sources: Stedman, *The Serials;* Harrison B. Summers, ed., *A Thirty-Year History of Programs Carried on National Radio Networks in the United States 1926–1956* (New York: Arno, 1971); *Variety Radio Directory 1937–1938* (New York: Variety, 1937); Frank Buxton and Bill Owen, *The Big Broadcast* (New York: Viking, 1972).

33. Michael Mok, "Radio Script-Writing Factory Outdoes Dumas Pere's Plant," *New York Post,* January 30, 1939, n.p., clipping file, "Hummert—Mr. and Mrs. Frank," NYPL-LC.

34. Stedman, *The Serials,* 313.

35. Ibid., 318.

36. James Thurber, "Soapland," in *The Beast in Me and Other Essays* (New York: Harcourt Brace, 1948), 220.

37. Maurice Zolotow, "Washboard Weepers," *Saturday Evening Post,* May 29, 1943, 48.

38. "Story of Mary Marlin," promotional booklet for television, box 5, folder 5, n.d., Crusinberry.

39. Seiter, "Women Writing Soap Opera," 26.

40. Letter from John Taylor, Compton Advertising Inc., to Jane Crusinberry, July 7, 1938, box 2, folder 5, Crusinberry.

41. Telegram from Gil Ralston, Compton, to Crusinberry, March 19, 1940, box 2, folder 7, Crusinberry.

42. Letter from Gil Ralston to Crusinberry, August 2, 1940, box 2, folder 7, Crusinberry.

43. Letter from Gil Ralston to Crusinberry, November 14, 1940, box 2, folder 7, Crusinberry.

44. Letter from John E. McMillin, Compton Advertising, to Crusinberry, June 13, 1938, box 2, folder 5, Crusinberry.

45. Letter from Sidney Strotz, NBC, to Crusinberry, May 24, 1939, box 3, folder 3, Crusinberry.

46. Telegram from Kirbey Hawkes, Benton & Bowles, to Crusinberry, May 5, 1942, box 2, folder 1, Crusinberry.

47. All of the quotes from the letter summaries below are taken from two of the lists, randomly selected: "Fan Mail July 12 to 26 (1935) Inclusive" and "Radio Fan Mail August 13th to August 27th Incl.," both in the Jane Crusinberry collection, box 4, folder 1, SHSW. Each of these summaries is three to five pages long and contains approximately fourteen synopses per page.

48. This plot summary is taken from the *Cedar Spring Times,* a promotional vehicle for the program dated September 1936, in an article titled "Mary Marlin 'Highlights,'" box 5, folder 2, Crusinberry, 2ff.

49. Mary Marlin was played first by Joan Blaine, then by Anne Seymour. Seymour

dropped out briefly and Betty Lou Gerson took over the role, but upon the move to New York production Seymour once again stepped in, from 1937 through 1943. Though Blaine had her supporters, many felt that Seymour's "patrician" tones provided the "true" Mary Marlin. However, three other actresses played the part in its declining last two years: Muriel Kirkland, Eloise Kummer, and Linda Carlton.

50. "Ratings and Facts of Interest," box 5, folder 5, Crusinberry.

51. "Story of Mary Marlin."

52. George A. Willey, "The Soap Operas and the War," *Journal of Broadcasting* 7 (1963): 341.

53. Phillips, "Why Can't We Do Something Besides a Daytime Serial?"

7. The Disciplined Audience: Radio by Night

1. However, see Eileen Meehan, "Heads of Household and Ladies of the House: Gender, Genre, and Broadcast Ratings, 1929–1990," in *Ruthless Criticism: New Perspectives in U.S. Communications History*, ed. William S. Solomon and Robert W. McChesney (Minneapolis: University of Minnesota Press, 1993), for a critique of the biases and hidden inaccuracies of these measurement methods.

2. "Radio I: A $140,000,000 Art," *Fortune*, May 1938, 47–52, 112, 114, 117–18, 120; "Radio II: A $45,000,000 Talent Bill," *Fortune* May 1938, 53–55, 122.

3. See Susan Smulyan, *Selling Radio: The Commercialization of American Broadcasting 1920–1934* (Washington, D.C.: Smithsonian Institution Press, 1994), 122–24, for a history of the use and conflicts over recorded programs, called "transcriptions."

4. Ad agencies' creative role was never acknowledged in on-air credits, and most fan and consumer publications overlooked agency personnel's and sponsors' contributions to radio production. This was a deliberate policy on the part of the agencies, as we shall see, and one important strategy in the critique of radio that arose in the late 1940s (in the wake of the FCC's "Blue Book" report) was the indignant revelation of the agency role in radio. For instance, Jack Gould of the *New York Times* attempted to rip aside the "veil of anonymity which always has enshrouded the advertising agency" in an article in 1948, claiming that "those responsible for the preparation of the overwhelming majority of commercial programs are virtually unknown to the listening public" and as such their important role as "a trustee of national values" was being exercised without recognition or oversight. Jack Gould, "Matter of Credit," *New York Times*, April 18, 1948, sec. 2, p. 9.

5. Harrison B. Summers, ed., *A Thirty-Year History of Programs Carried on National Radio Networks in the United States 1926–1956* (New York: Arno, 1971).

6. Lawrence W. Levine, *Highbrow/Lowbrow: The Emergence of Cultural Hierarchy in America* (Cambridge: Harvard University Press, 1988), 177.

7. Ibid., 176.

8. Ibid., 219, 222–23.

9. Early on, these regulations worked to "increase the distance between the amateur and professional" (ibid., 139), one of the hallmarks of sacralization, and radio's handling of race by exclusion and selective representation reinforced the racialization of cultural hierarchies.

10. Ibid., 195.

11. Ibid., 235.

12. A. M. Sullivan, "Radio and Vaudeville Culture," *Commonweal*, December 13, 1935, 176.

13. Margaret Cuthbert, "Women's Activities Division Report," November. 9, 1938,

box 93, folder 43, NBC; Margaret Cuthbert to Horton Heath, "History of Women's Programs 1926–1948," March 26, 1948, box 335, folder 1, NBC.

14. For discussion of Alice Keith's role, see Robert W. McChesney, *Telecommunications, Mass Media, and Democracy: The Battle for the Control of U.S. Broadcasting, 1928–1935* (New York: Oxford University Press, 1993), 221.

15. Also beginning their radio careers at this time were Al Jolson for Chevrolet, Burns and Allen, Ed Wynn, Jack Pearl, the Marx Brothers, and Stoopnagle and Bud. Summers, *A Thirty-Year History*, 31.

16. Arthur Frank Wertheim, *Radio Comedy* (New York: Oxford University Press, 1979), 135–36.

17. Jack Benny and Joan Benny, *Sunday Nights at Seven* (New York: Warner, 1990), 37.

18. Wertheim, *Radio Comedy*, 144.

19. Memo from E. R. Hitz to John F. Royal, 4/6/32, box 7, folder 40, NBC.

20. Obviously, many radio and television programs used similar premises, from *Burns and Allen* to *The Adventures of Ozzie & Harriet*.

21. Benny and Benny, *Sunday Nights*, 111.

22. Milt Josefsberg, *The Jack Benny Show* (New York: Arlington House, 1977), 139.

23. Benny and Benny, *Sunday Nights*, 107.

24. Florence Murray, comp. and ed., *The Negro Handbook*, (New York: Wendell Malliet, 1942), 223; Jessie Parkhurst Guzman, ed., *Negro Year Book* (Tuskegee, Ala.: Tuskegee Institute, 1946), 446.

25. Josefsberg, *The Jack Benny Show*, 184.

26. Benny and Benny, *Sunday Nights*, 103–4.

27. Margaret T. McFadden, "America's Boyfriend Who Can't Get a Date: Gender, Race, and the Cultural Work of the Jack Benny Program, 1932–1946," *Journal of American History* (June 1993): 131. The implicit homoeroticism of Jack Benny's show has been discussed by several writers, including Alexander Doty in *Making Things Perfectly Queer: Interpreting Mass Culture* (Minneapolis: University of Minnesota Press, 1993). As early as 1935, Bertha Brainard of the NBC Programming Department noted this trend on the show: "I felt that there was a definite tendency toward effiminate [*sic*] characterizations, particularly by Frank Parker. I feel strongly about this, especially when a tenor with a high voice has the line. I'd like to see anything of the lavendar [*sic*] nature all out. Jack doesn't need this sort of material to get his humor." Memo from Bertha Brainard to John W. Swallow, June 17, 1935, box 34, folder 33, NBC.

28. Benny and Benny, *Sunday Nights*, 134.

29. Ibid., 132.

30. Josefsberg, *The Jack Benny Show*, 159.

31. Much of the material in this chapter on Allen's life and radio progams comes from Alan Havig's perceptive and well-researched study, *Fred Allen's Radio Comedy* (Philadelphia: Temple University Press, 1990). Other sources include Fred Allen, *Treadmill to Oblivion* (Boston: Little, Brown, 1954); Wertheim, *Radio Comedy*; Robert Taylor, *Fred Allen: His Life and Wit* (Boston: Little, Brown, 1989); Pat Weaver with Thomas M. Coffey, *The Best Seat in the House* (New York: Knopf, 1994); and Beverly Smith, "Want a Job at a Million a Year?" *American Magazine*, December 1945, 24–25.

32. Wertheim, *Radio Comedy*, 161.

33. Allen, *Treadmill to Oblivion*, 5.

34. Havig, *Fred Allen's Radio Comedy*, 61.

35. See ibid., 72, for a complete listing and chronology.

36. From *Town Hall Tonight* script, June 15, 1938, 6, cited in Wertheim, *Radio Comedy*, 175.

37. Weaver, *The Best Seat in the House*, 76.

38. From *Town Hall Tonight* script, January 11, 1939, cited in Havig, *Fred Allen's Radio Comedy*, 177.

39. Letter from John E. McMillin to Niles Trammel, June 4, 1940, box 74, folder 90, NBC.

40. Letter from Niles Trammel to John E. McMillin, June 12, 1940, box 74, folder 90, NBC.

41. Allen, *Treadmill to Oblivion*, 91.

42. Havig, *Fred Allen's Radio Comedy*, 82.

43. Ibid., 193.

44. Letter from Max Wilk to Niles Trammel, November 17, 1948, box 115, folder 28, NBC. Jack Gould recommended in 1946 that Ajax Cassidy "should be forthwith exiled to WHN [New York's ethnic broadcasting station]." Jack Gould, "Programs and People," *New York Times*, October 13, 1946, sec. 2, p. 9.

45. Kenny Delmar audition tape, June 22, 1949, Recordings, series L, NBC.

46. See Howard Zinn, *The Southern Mystique* (New York: Knopf, 1964), 217–18; C. Vann Woodward, *The Strange Career of Jim Crow* (New York: Oxford University Press, 1957), 99–100; Jack Temple Kirby, *Media-Made Dixie* (Baton Rouge: Louisiana State University Press, 1978); and Thomas R. Cripps, "The Myth of the Southern Box Office: A Factor in the Racial Stereotyping in American Movies, 1920–1940," in *The Black Experience: Selected Essays* (Austin: University of Texas Press, 1970).

47. George Sessions Perry, "Backstage in Allen's Alley," *Saturday Evening Post*, January 4, 1945, 14–15, 34, 37.

48. Gene Cook, "Senator Claghorn," *Life*, March 18, 1946, 62.

49. Allen, *Treadmill to Oblivion*, 202–3.

50. Cook, "Senator Claghorn," 64.

51. Gag Writers Wanted," *Newsweek*, October 15, 1945, 100.

52. Havig, *Fred Allen's Radio Comedy*, 186–87.

53. Allen, *Treadmill to Oblivion*, 27.

54. Perry, "Backstage in Allen's Alley," 15.

55. Memo to Mr. I. E. Showerman from Janet MacRorie, December 20, 1938, box 59, folder 28, NBC. See also I. E. Showerman to Janet MacRorie, December 19, 1938; Edward R. Hitz to I. E. Showerman, December 16, 1938; and Dorothy Kemble to Ken R. Dyke, May 3, 1938; all box 59, folder 28, NBC.

56. "Allen Sees Red Again," *Variety*, January 1, 1947, 21.

57. "Allen to Stay On Despite Censors," *Variety*, February 5, 1947, 1.

58. Allen's 'Dead Air' Hook Cues CBS Bid; NBC to Swing Mop Freely as Before," *Variety*, April 23, 1947, 1.

59. Letter from Clifford Forster, acting director, ACLU, to Niles Trammel, May 7, 1947, box 115, folder 13, NBC.

60. Perry, "Backstage in Allen's Alley," 15.

61. Ibid., 99–100; Benny and Benny, *Sunday Nights*, 130.

62. Smith, "Want a Job at a Million a Year?" 24.

63. "Fred Allen Gets Peabody Nod, So Does LaGuardia," *Variety*, March 21, 1945, 26.

64. "Fred Allen Discusses Mr. LaGuardia," *New York Times*, April 15, 1945, 2:7.

65. Havig, *Fred Allen's Radio Comedy*, 83.

66. Ibid., 92.

67. Frank Buxton and Bill Owen, *The Big Broadcast* (New York: Viking, 1972), 86.

68. Minutes, Creative Staff meeting, December 21, 1932, JWT, 9.

69. "Harvard Boy Scores: Story of Danny Danker," *Variety*, November 3, 1943, 38.

70. *The Lux Radio Theatre*, "Dark Victory," January 8, 1940. For a more extensive

treatment of *The Lux Radio Theatre*, see Michele Hilmes, *Hollywood and Broadcasting: From Radio to Cable* (Urbana: University of Illinois Press, 1990).

71. R. W. Stewart, "A Drama in Retrospect," *New York Times*, September 22, 1940, 10:4.

72. T. R. Kennedy Jr., "'Grand-Daddy' Show," *New York Times*, November 24, 1940, 12:1.

73. Frank Daugherty, "He Sells Soap!" *Christian Science Monitor Week*, March 25, 1944, 8. Many later historical articles have uncritically repeated this misinformation. Bernard Lucich writes, "Later in 1935, the production of the show was handed over to Cecil B. DeMille, who moved the show to Hollywood." Bernard Lucich, "The Lux Radio Theater," in *American Broadcasting: A Source Book on the History of Radio and Television*, ed. Lawrence W. Lichty and Malachi C. Topping (New York: Hastings House, 1976), 391. Alan Barbour repeats this and several other errors: "Apparently tiring of the stage-play format, CBS moved the program to Hollywood, hired famed film director Cecil B. DeMille as host and director." Alan G. Barbour, "Lux Presents Hollywood," in *The Old Time Radio Book*, ed. Ted Sennett (New York: Pyramid, 1976).

74. Though DeMille happily played along with the fiction of authorship in interviews and on air, in his own autobiography he is careful to speak of his *Lux* experience only in terms of hosting the broadcast—though nowhere does he actually refute the much larger role he was so often given credit for. See Cecil B. DeMille, *Autobiography*, ed. Donald Hayne (Englewood Cliffs, N.J.: Prentice Hall, 1959), 346–48.

75. "In reply to Cecil B. DeMille," March 31, 1945, box 12, folder 43, Welles.

76. *Time*, May 6, 1938.

77. Betty Houchin Winfield, *FDR and the News Media* (New York: Columbia University Press, 1994), 109.

78. Columbia Broadcasting System, "Orson Welles, Mercury Theater to Present Nine 1–Hour CBS Broadcasts, " June 9, 1938, box 7, folder 22, Welles.

79. CBS, "Welles to Dramatize Great First Person Stories in CBS Series," June 15, 1938, box 7, folder 22, Welles.

80. John Houseman, *Run Through* (New York: Simon & Schuster, 1972), 364.

81. Columbia Broadcasting System, "Orson Welles."

82. *Rebecca, Campbell Playhouse* broadcast, December 9, 1938, tape 11–1, Welles.

83. *Dracula, Mercury Theater of the Air* broadcast, July 11, 1938, tape 1–1, Welles.

84. *The Thirty-Nine Steps* (rehearsal), *Mercury Theater of the Air* broadcast, August 1, 1938, tape 3–1, Welles.

85. Houseman, *Run Through*, 368.

86. Ibid., 392.

87. Ibid., 368.

88. Ibid., 393.

89. Ibid., 402.

90. Report on survey, *Campbell Playhouse* 1939–40. box 7, folder 24, Welles. Previously, the Mercury Theater had tried to distance itself from movie adaptations; it was careful to declare the broadcast of *The Thirty-Nine Steps* as "from the book itself and solely for radio presentation." Box 7, folder 22, Welles.

91. *Rebecca, Campbell Playhouse* broadcast.

92. Houseman, *Run Through*, 413.

93. Hadley Cantril, *The Invasion from Mars: A Study in the Psychology of Panic* (Princeton, N.J.: Princeton University Press, 1947), 3.

94. Quoted in Simon Callow, *Orson Welles: The Road to Xanadu* (London: Jonathan Cape, 1995), 490, 491.

95. A similar conflict arose over Welles's collaboration with Herman J. Mankiewicz

and the *Citizen Kane* script. See Pauline Kael, *The Citizen Kane Book: Raising Kane* (Boston: Little, Brown, 1971).

96. Callow, *Orson Welles*, 491–92.

97. One biographer attributes Welles's precipitous departure from *This Is My Best* to a "personality conflict" with an agency executive who accused Welles of conflict of interest in selecting properties to adapt with an eye to future film projects "and not because it was 'good radio.'" Frank Brady, *Citizen Welles* (New York: Scribner's, 1989), 381. By far the best source of information on Welles's radio career is the Museum of Broadcasting's *Orson Welles on the Air: The Radio Years* (New York: Museum of Broadcasting, 1988).

98. Allen, *Treadmill to Oblivion*, 135–51.

8. On the Home Front: Fighting to Be Heard

1. Edward M. Kirby to the Board of Directors of the National Association of Broadcasters and the Code Committee, "Re: Father Coughlin's Broadcasts," September 24, 1940, box 78, folder 7, NBC.

2. Richard W. Steele, "The Great Debate: Roosevelt, the Media, and the Coming of the War, 1940–1941," *Journal of American History* 71 (June 1984): 84. Even earlier, two prominent anti-interventionist news commentators had been removed from the air by networks fearful of their opposition to administration policies; this left only strongly pro-mobilization commentators such as H. V. Kaltenborn, Edward R. Murrow, and Raymond Gram Swing, along with the extremely popular gossip columnist Walter Winchell, who was outspoken in his support for Roosevelt's mobilization efforts and in his disdain for those who disagreed. The two isolationist commentators were Hugh Johnson, taken off the air by NBC in 1937, and Boake Carter, removed from CBS in 1938. According to Steele, "NBC took action against Johnson without prompting from the administration, although the network kept officials informed; the White House initiated the removal of the immensely popular Carter" (83). See also America First Committee, press release, "John T. Flynn Speaks at America First Rally at Madison Square Garden," October 31, 1941, and subsequent correspondence with NBC, box 81, folder 53, NBC.

3. Edward M. Kirby, "References and Recollections of Historic Highlights: American Broadcasting in World War II," box 1, folder 1, Kirby, 12.

4. And this was not the only threat. By 1941 the broadcasting industry and its regulatory body, the FCC, faced investigation by Congress under resolutions passed in every legislative session since 1936, charged with monopoly, undue influence, corruption, concentration of ownership, stock racketeering, license trafficking, and overly close relationships with certain politicians. Carl J. Friedrich and Evelyn Sternberg, "Congress and the Control of Radio Broadcasting, I," *American Political Science Review* 37 (1943): 797–818.

5. Steele, "The Great Debate," 76. Indeed, several of the president's advisers in 1941 proposed just such a government takeover of media to serve a central propaganda effort modeled after the German Ministry of Information, including Vice President Henry Wallace and John J. McCloy, assistant secretary of war. See Richard W. Steele, "Preparing the Public for War: Efforts to Establish a National Propaganda Agency, 1940–41," *American Historical Review* 75 (1970): 1640–89.

6. Steele, "The Great Debate," 75.

7. Friedrich and Sternberg, "Congress and the Control," 811.

8. Kirby, "References and Recollections."

9. Ibid., 5.

10. Ibid., 13.

11. "In Defense of America," box 82, folder 67, "Defense Programs, 1941," NBC.

12. Letter from Frank Hummert to Niles Trammel, October 16, 1941, box 83, folder 17, NBC.

13. All of the above program descriptions are from "In Defense of America."

14. "Gallup and Fortune Polls," *Public Opinion Quarterly* (Fall 1941): 487.

15. "War Exposed Extreme Discrimination—Poll," *Pittsburgh Courier*, January 2, 1943, 4.

16. Letter from Frank Boykin to Edwin M. Watson, March 6, 1943, Franklin D. Roosevelt Papers, official file 93, reprinted in Richard Polenberg, ed., *America at War: The Home Front, 1941–1945* (Englewood Cliffs, N.J.: Prentice Hall, 1968), 114–15.

17. See Richard W. Steele, "The War on Intolerance: The Reformulation of American Nationalism, 1939–1941," *Journal of Ethnic History* 9 (1989): 3–35. Steele cites Stephan Thernstrom, *A History of the American People*, vol. 2 (San Diego, Calif.: Harcourt Brace, 1984) as an example of the common textbook approach. See also J. Fred MacDonald, *Don't Touch That Dial! Radio Programming in American Life from 1920 to 1960* (Chicago: Nelson-Hall, 1979), for a similar view applied to radio, especially 61–80.

18. Steele, "The War on Intolerance."

19. Cedric Larson, "Publicity for National Defense: How It Works," *Journalism Quarterly* 18 (1941), 255.

20. Peter H. Odegard and Alan Barth, "Millions for Defense," *Public Opinion Quarterly* (Fall 1941): 405.

21. Steele, "The War on Intolerance," 27, 30.

22. Ibid., 24.

23. Sydney Weinberg, "What to Tell America: The Writers' Quarrel in the Office of War Information," *Journal of American History* 55 (1968): 75. Other sources useful for tracing the labyrinth of government propaganda organizations include Allan M. Winkler, *The Politics of Propaganda: The Office of War Information 1942–1945* (New Haven, Conn.: Yale University Press, 1978); and Steele, "Preparing the Public for War. The spring 1943 edition of *Public Opinion Quarterly* published a series of articles on the OWI; see particularly Lester G. Hawkins Jr. and George S. Pettee, "OWI: Organization and Problems," *Public Opinion Quarterly* (Spring 1943): 15–33. See also Larson, "Publicity for Natonal Defense."

24. Letter from Stephen Early to Archibald MacLeish, December 27, 1941, as quoted in Charles A. Siepmann, "American Radio in Wartime," in *Radio Research, 1942*, ed. Paul F. Lazarsfeld and Frank N. Stanton (New York: Hawthorn, 1944; reprinted New York: Arno, 1979), 114. See also memo from Frank E. Mullen to all department heads, division heads and managers of M&O stations, January 26, 1942, box 89, folder 4, NBC.

25. This new organization would include and/or supersede most of the above-mentioned agencies, with the exception of Donovan's OCI, now regrouped as the Office of Strategic Services (OSS), and with the further inclusion of Nelson Rockefeller's Coordinator of Inter-American Affairs office, a group that had focused on maintaining favorable relationships with Latin America and counteracting Nazi propaganda there.

26. Winkler, *The Politics of Propaganda*, 23–31.

27. Executive Order of June 13, 1942, "Consolidating Certain Information Functions of the Government into an Office of War Information," as quoted in Siepmann, "American Radio in Wartime," 114.

28. For an extended history and critique of the War Advertising Council, see Gerd

Horten, "Radio Goes to War: The Cultural Politics of Propaganda during World War II" (Ph.D. diss., University of California, Berkeley, 1995). A book based on this dissertation is to be published by the University of California Press in 1997.

29. OWI Regulation No. 2, September 9, 1952, cited in Siepmann, "American Radio in Wartime," 115.

30. Siepmann, "American Radio in Wartime," 131.

31. All of these strategies were aimed at network programs and stations. To reach the hundreds of nonaffiliated stations, an area admittedly neglected by the OWI, a few other tactics were used, such as periodic publication of the "Radio War Guide," which listed important topics and graded them by urgency (AA, A, B, C, and D priorities). A "National Spot Allocation Plan" was also devised to allocate one government message a month to major spot advertisers, to be broadcast on their programs. Additionally, baseball and football broadcasts were recognized as particularly effective for reaching the highly desired male audience (in this time of active recruiting), and stations carrying the more than three hundred sports broadcasts per day (!), along with their advertisers, were solicited to include at least two government messages during each event. Finally, a series of transcribed programs, produced by or in conjunction with the OWI, was circulated to local stations, most of them repeats of network broadcasts; examples include the *Treasury Star Parade, You Can't Do Business with Hitler,* and the OWI's "Victory Front" and "Victory Volunteer" series. See Siepmann, "American Radio in Wartime."

32. Weinberg, "What to Tell America," 76.

33. Harold F. Gosnell, "Objections to Domestic Pamphleteering by OWI in World War II," *Journalism Quarterly* 23 (1946): 362, quoted in ibid.

34. Winkler, *The Politics of Propaganda,* 5.

35. Odegard and Barth, "Millions for Defense," 403.

36. Ibid., 404.

37. Ibid., 409.

38. Matthew Murray and Donald Meckiffe, "Radio and the Black Soldier during World War II" (paper presented at the meeting of the American Studies Association, Pittsburgh, November 1995); see also David Levering Lewis, *When Harlem Was in Vogue* (New York: Knopf, 1981).

39. Saul K. Padover, "Japanese Radio Propaganda," *Public Opinion Quarterly* 7 (Summer 1943): 197.

40. Gosnell, "Objections to Domestic Pamphleteering," 364.

41. Ibid., 363.

42. Reaction to "Negroes and the War" was discussed on the House floor during appropriations hearings in June 1943. U.S. Congress, House Committee on Appropriations, "Hearings on the National War Agencies Appropriation Bill, 1944," 78th Congress, 1st session, 896–97.

43. Gosnell, "Objections to Domestic Pamphleteering," 367.

44. *Congressional Record,* House, 78th Congress, 1st session, June 18, 1943, 6133–34.

45. Ibid., 6136.

46. *Congressional Record,* Senate, 78th Congress, 1st session, June 30, 1943, 6826–28.

47. Lewis Wood, "Writers Who Quit OWI Charge It Bars 'Full Truth' for 'Ballyhoo,'" *New York Times,* April 16, 1943, 13. See also "Explanation Given on Split in OWI," *New York Times,* April 14, 1943, 25; "Sole Aim Is Facts, Says Davis of OWI," *New York Times,* April 15, 1943, 9.

48. Letter from Schlesinger to Bernard DeVoto, April 1943, in the DeVoto papers, Stanford University, quoted in Weinberg, "What to Tell America," 88.

49. Letter from Brennan to Elmer Davis, April 6, 1943, in the Henry Pringle papers, Manuscript Division, Library of Congress, cited in Weinberg, "What to Tell America," 86.

50. See Weinberg, "What to Tell America," 86.

51. Richard W. Steele, "NO RACIALS: Discrimination against Ethnics in American Defense Industry, 1940–42," *Journal of Labor History* (Winter 1991): 65–90. See also a letter from the Union for Democratic Action to several other groups, dated June 1, 1941, rallying them for a conference on "the Negro and Defense," which states, "Very few of the defense industries, practically none in the New York area, hire Negroes, and a definite and frankly avowed policy of exclusion from employment has been adopted by the most important airplane manufacturing companies and some others of vital importance in defense. So serious is the denial of employment opportunities to Negroes in the defense program that the proportion of Negroes among the people on relief in New York has gone up very markedly, not because more Negroes are on relief, but because almost literally none of them have gotten jobs from the defense program while a considerable number of white persons have." The writer goes on to detail similar violations of rights in the armed forces. "UDA Administrative File," box 21, Americans for Democratic Action.

52. Memo to Carleton D. Smith, March 31, 1940, box 84, folder 17, "I'm An American—1941," NBC.

53. Letter from J. W. Studebaker to Niles Trammel, January, n.d., 1941, box 83, folder 22, "Freedom's People—1941," NBC.

54. Memo from James R. Angell to Niles Trammell, February 7, 1941, box 83, folder 22, NBC.

55. Memo from James R. Angell to Walter Preston Jr., February 17, 1941, box 83, folder 22, NBC.

56. Letter from Gene Buck to J. W. Studebaker, September 8, 1941, box 83, folder 22, NBC.

57. In a telegram on September 11, Studebaker urgently communicated to Trammell: "Negro program is regarded here as exceedingly important aspect of general national defense program. It was conceived primarily for purpose of developing the national unity essential to defense. For other types of programs we would not make the same argument but are convinced this is distinctly a program you can defend on basis of its direct contribution to defense." September 11, 1941, box 83, folder 22, NBC.

58. "When Radio Writes for War," n.d., box 5, folder 5, Dick Dorrance Collection, BPL, 10.

59. L. D. Reddick, "Education Programs for the Improvement of Race Relations: Motion Pictures, Radio, the Press, and Libraries," *Journal of Negro Education* 13 (1944): 384.

60. Letter from James Loeb Jr. to G. MacPherson, June 11, 1941, box 21, "UA Administrative File, Na-Ne," ADA.

61. Letter from James Loeb Jr. to Brotherhood of Sleeping Car Porters, June 1, 1941, box 21, ADA.

62. "Radio Station Refuses OWI Race Program," *Pittsburgh Courier*, February 20, 1943, 20.

63. See William L. Barlow, "Commercial and Noncommercial Radio," in *Split Image: African Americans in the Mass Media*, ed. Jannette L. Dates and William L. Barlow (Washington, D.C.: Howard University Press, 1990), especially 189–209; see also J. Fred MacDonald's chapter titled "Blacks in Radio Programming," in *Don't Touch That Dial!* 345–58.

64. Murray and Meckiffe, "Radio and the Black Soldier." See also Clayton R. Koppes and Gregory D. Black, "Blacks, Loyalty, and Motion Picture Propaganda in World War II," *Journal of American History* 73 (1986): 383–406, for a discussion of similar tactics in film.

65. "Hummert Radio Scripts," box 212, RG 107, National Archives; also see Erik Barnouw, *The Golden Web: A History of Broadcasting in the United States*, vol. 2, *1933 to 1953* (New York: Oxford University Press, 1968), 162.

66. Letter from Louis G. Cowan to Truman Gibson, May 5, 1942, box 184, "Bureau of Public Relations, 1942," RG 107, entry 188, Secretary of War, Office, Assistant Secretary of War, Civilian Aide to the Secretary, Subject File, 1940–47, National Archives.

67. Letter from Truman Gibson to Edward Kirby, July 2, 1942, "Hummert Radio Scripts," box 212, RG 107, National Archives.

68. Letter from Mrs. James E. Bright to "Mr. Harum," n.d., box 212, RG 107, National Archives.

69. Letter from H. K. Painter to Kay Brennan, September 20, 1944, box 62, "Knox Reeves," Phillips.

70. *Beulah*, a spin-off from *Fibber McGee and Molly*, was created and the title character performed for its first few years by Marlin Hurt, a white actor.

71. Theodore S. Delay Jr., "An Historical Study of the Armed Forces Radio Service to 1946" (Ph.D. diss., University of Southern California, 1951), 84–85. The following section on the development of the AFRS is based on Delay's work, except where otherwise specified.

72. Weaver later claimed that, when he reported to AFRS headquarters at Gower Street and Santa Monica Boulevard in Hollywood, he found "a staff loaded with so many Young & Rubicam people, I almost felt I was back on Madison Avenue." Pat Weaver with Thomas M. Coffey, *The Best Seat in the House* (New York: Knopf, 1994), 147.

73. Ibid., 90.

74. Interview with Thomas H. A. Lewis, July 19, 1950, in Delay, "An Historical Study," 108–9.

75. Delay, "An Historical Study," 150.

76. Harvard Sitkoff, "Racial Militancy and Interracial Violence in the Second World War," *Journal of American History* 58 (1971): 667.

77. Ibid., 671–75.

78. Memo from J. H. Ryan to Byron Price, April 9, 1942, Office of Censorship, box 388, "Racial Discrimination," National Archives. In reference to the riots at Fort Dix, Ryan writes, "This is one type of story that I should like very much to keep off the air. Obviously it does not run counter to any suggestions in the Code because it relates to something that we cannot specify in the Code for obvious reasons. It can do quite a considerable amount of harm, lends itself most readily to axis counter-propaganda and does not seem to be an important enough news story to overbalance the dangers it contains."

79. Delay, "An Historical Study," 150.

80. "Race Artists Broadcast to Our Armed Forces Overseas," *Pittsburgh Courier*, February 20, 1943, 21.

81. Delay, "An Historical Study," 151–52.

82. Barlow, "Commercial and Noncommercial Radio," 192.

83. See NBC's files on the "integration without identification" policy adopted in the postwar years and its application to television; box 129, 569. Essentially defining the inclusion of persons of color as a "problem," NBC attempted to integrate more black actors into programs where race as a social issue could be ignored—as background characters in public settings, in non-race-specific walk-on parts, and in the well-established category of musical performance as entertainers on variety shows—while avoiding those programs that focused on race as an issue: that is, anything that dealt with actual African American experience or that ran the risk of offending the delicate sensibilities of advertisers and racist viewers. This denial of overall differential treatment under a well-meaning cover of carefully delimited inclusion bears a close resemblance to radio policy

during the war, and left the networks open to the maximum amount of interference: even a very small number of objections functioned to point up race as a "problem"; once that happened, NBC's policy mandated removal from the airwaves. My thanks to Lisa Parks, University of Wisconsin-Madison, for her research in this area.

84. Maureen Honey, "The 'Womanpower' Campaign: Advertising and Recruitment Propaganda during World War II," *Frontiers* 6 (1981): 53. These women were always depicted as white. For other discussions of women during World War II, see Maureen Honey, *Creating Rosie the Riveter* (Amherst: University of Massachusetts Press, 1984); Karen Anderson, *Wartime Women: Sex Roles, Family Relations, and the Status of Women during World War II* (Westport, Conn.: Greenwood, 1981); Susan Hartmann, *The Home Front and Beyond: American Women in the 1940s* (Boston: Twayne, 1982); D'Ann Campbell, *Women at War with America: Private Lives in a Patriotic Era* (Cambridge: Harvard University Press, 1984); and Ruth Milkman, *Gender at Work: The Dynamics of Job Segregation by Sex during World War II* (Urbana: University of Illinois Press, 1987).

85. "Listen Women—Womanpower—5 Minute Dramatized Spot Series," no. 2, March 25–26, 1943, microfilm scripts, reel 204, JWT.

86. Ibid., no. 6.

87. *The Story of Mary Marlin*, episode 2507, November 8, 1944, scripts, Crusinberry. I am grateful to Jennifer Wang, University of Wisconsin-Madison, for her research in this area.

88. *The Story of Mary Marlin*, episode 12, January 2, 1945.

89. *The Story of Mary Marlin*, episode 1986, November 2, 1942.

90. Letter from Robert Colwell to John U. Reber, January 13, 1944, box 62, "J. Walter Thompson—Correspondence 1940–47," Phillips.

91. Memo from Charles Christoph to John Reber and Robert Colwell, March 22, 1944, box 2, folder 11, Crusinberry.

92. Letter from Irna Phillips to Robert Colwell, March 6, 1944, box 62, "J. Walter Thompson—Correspondence 1940–47," Phillips.

93. Letter from Jane Crusinberry to John U. Reber, March 24, 1944, box 2, folder 11, Crusinberry.

94. "Ratings and Facts of Interest," box 5, folder 7, Crusinberry.

95. Jennifer Wang, "Are Soap Operas Only Suds?" (paper presented at the Telecommunications Colloquium, University of Wisconsin-Madison, fall 1995).

96. *The Story of Mary Marlin*, episode 2, January 2, 1945, Crusinberry.

97. *Saturday Evening Post*, May 1944, reproduced in Honey, *Creating Rosie the Riveter.*

98. Anderson, *Wartime Women*, 163.

Conclusion: Terms of Preferment

1. See Mary Beth Haralovich, "Sitcoms and Suburbs: Positioning the 1950s Homemaker," in *Private Screenings: Television and the Female Consumer,* ed. Lynn Spigel and Denise Mann (Minneapolis: University of Minnesota Press, 1992); George Lipsitz, *Rainbow at Midnight: Labor and Culture in the 1940s* (Urbana: University of Illinois Press, 1994); George Lipsitz, *Time Passages: Collective Memory and American Popular Culture* (Minneapolis: University of Minnesota Press, 1990); Lynn Spigel, *Make Room for TV: Television and the Family Ideal in Postwar America* (Chicago: University of Chicago Press, 1992); William Boddy, *Fifties Television: The Industry and Its Critics* (Urbana: University of Illinois Press, 1990); Christopher Anderson, *Hollywood TV: The*

Studio Systems in the Fifties (Austin: University of Texas Press, 1994); Michele Hilmes, *Hollywood and Broadcasting: From Radio to Cable* (Urbana: University of Illinois Press, 1990).

2. Mark Newman, "On the Air with Jack L. Cooper: The Beginnings of Black-Appeal Radio," *Chicago History* 12, no. 2 (1983): 51–58.

3. William L. Barlow, "Commercial and Noncommercial Radio," in *Split Image: African Americans in the Mass Media*, ed. Jannette L. Dates and William L. Barlow (Washington, D.C.: Howard University Press, 1990), 210–11.

4. From Mark Newman, "Capturing the Fifteen Million Dollar Market: The Emergence of Black Oriented Radio," (Ph. D. diss., Northwestern University, 1984), cited in ibid., 214.

5. Quoted in Barlow, "Commercial and Noncommercial Radio," 218.

6. See "Television Workshop" files, JWT.

7. Boddy, *Fifties Television*.

8. See Hilmes, *Hollywood and Broadcasting*.

9. A recent article by Pam Wilson suggests a fourth contribution: the documentaries *Operation Frontal Lobes*. See Pam Wilson, "'Operation Frontal Lobes': Cultural Hegemony and Fifties Program Planning," *Historical Journal of Film and Video* 15, no. 1 (1995): 83–104.

10. Christopher Sterling and John Kitross, *Stay Tuned: A Concise History of Broadcasting in America*, 2d ed. (Belmont, Calif.: Wadsworth, 1990), 280.

11. Harry Castleman and Walter J. Podrazik, *Watching TV: Four Decades of American Television* (New York: McGraw-Hill, 1982), 48–49.

12. James L. Baughman, "Television in the Golden Age: An Entrepreneurial Experiment," *Historian* 47 (February 1985): 185.

13. Thomas Whiteside, "Profiles: The Communicator," Part II, "What about the Gratitude Factor?" *New Yorker*, October 23, 1954, 66. See also Part I, "Athens Starts Pouring In," *New Yorker*, October 16, 1954, 37–64.

14. Martin Mayer, "Television's Lords of Creation, Part I: Strategic Thinking at NBC," *Harper's Magazine*, November 1956, 27. Lynn Spigel begins to deconstruct this myth in her acknowledgment of multiple-sponsor, magazine-format programs being tried during the late 1940s and early 1950s on stations around the country. See *Make Room for TV*, 80.

15. Memo from Davidson Taylor to Robert W. Sarnoff, February 19, 1954, box 123, folder 26, NBC.

16. Ibid., 3.

17. Nancy Fraser, "Rethinking the Public Sphere," in *The Phantom Public Sphere*, ed. Bruce Robbins (Minneapolis: University of Minnesota Press, 1993).

18. Vance Kepley, "The Weaver Years at NBC," *Wide Angle* 12, no. 2 (1990): 46–63.

19. "Gossip of the Kilocycles: Miss McBride (also Miss Deane) Gets Annual Gift Shower," *Newsweek*, November 21, 1938, n.p. (from McBride collection, Library of Congress, box 4); Barbara Heggie, "Mary Margaret McBride: A Profile," *New Yorker*, December 19, 1942, reprint, no page numbers, box 4, McBride.

20. See Jacqueline D. St. John, "Sex Role Stereotyping in Early Broadcast History: The Career of Mary Margaret McBride," *Frontiers* 3, no. 3 (1978): 31–38; Douglas J. Carr, "Selling without a Script: The Overlooked Radio Career of Mary Margaret McBride" (paper presented at the meeting of the Popular Culture Association/American Culture Association, New Orleans, March 1988); Barbara Heggie, "Mary Margaret's Miracle," *Woman's Home Companion*, April 1949, 37ff.; "Gossip of the Kilocycles"; Philip Hamburger, "Mary Margaret McBride," *Life*, December 4, 1944, 47–53; Allen Churchill, "Mary Margaret McBride," *American Mercury*, January 1949, 7–14.

21. Memo from Margaret Cuthbert to John F. Royal, December 5, 1932, central files—Cosmo Broadcasting Company, 1928–31, box 2, folder 116, NBC.

22. Bennett Cerf, "Here Comes McBride," *Saturday Review*, March 1, 1947, 4–6.

23. Quoted in St. John, "Sex Role Stereotyping," 33.

24. "Gossip of the Kilocycles."

25. Quoted in St. John, "Sex Role Stereotyping," 43.

26. Enid A. Haupt, "Recruiting Women for Vital National Service," *Philadelphia Enquirer*, July 2, 1944, n.p., box 4, McBride.

27. Heggie, "Mary Margaret McBride."

28. Saul Carson, "On the Air: Soap and the Roosevelts," *New Republic*, December 25, 1950, 21.

29. "Goo," *Time*, November 25, 1940, 56–57.

30. Hamburger, "Mary Margaret McBride," 47.

31. Churchill, "Mary Margaret McBride," 7.

32. Hamburger, "Mary Margaret McBride," 47.

33. Churchill, "Mary Margaret McBride," 9.

34. Heggie, "Mary Margaret McBride."

35. Heggie, "Mary Margaret's Miracle," 80.

36. Quoted in St. John, "Sex Role Stereotyping," 35.

37. Ted Shane, "Mr. and Mrs. Breakfast," *Pageant*, June-July 1948, 43.

38. "Miss McBride," *New York Times*, September 26, 1948, 2:1.

39. "The Open Forum," *American Mercury*, April 1949, 509–10.

40. Spigel, *Make Room for TV*, 36–72.

41. Kepley, "The Weaver Years."

42. Boddy, *Fifties Television*.

43. Castleman and Podrazik, *Watching TV*, 87.

44. Inger L. Stole, "Capturing the 'Ideal' Audience: The Emergence of Network Daytime Television, 1948–1954" (M.A. thesis, University of Wisconsin-Madison, Department of Journalism and Mass Communication, 1992), 15.

45. Memo from Ted Mills to Charles Barry, July 30, 1953, box 133, folder 68, NBC.

46. Memo from Ted Mills to Sylvester L. Weaver, September 11, 1953, box 377, folder 6, NBC.

47. Memo from Ted Mills to Sylvester L. Weaver Jr., September 11, 1953, "Today's Home," box 123, folder 26, NBC.

48. Spigel, *Make Room for TV*.

49. Erik Barnouw, *The Golden Web: A History of Broadcasting in the United States*, vol. 2, *1933 to 1953* (New York: Oxford University Press, 1968), 269.

50. Gertrude Berg, *Molly and Me* (New York: McGraw-Hill, 1961), 245.

Collections Consulted

(Abbreviations in parentheses are used in notes.)

Duke University Library—John W. Hartman Center for Sales, Advertising and Marketing History
    J. Walter Thompson (JWT)
Indiana University, Bloomington—Lilly Library
    Orson Welles
Broadcast Pioneers Library—College Park, Maryland (BPL)
Library of Congress—Manuscript Division (LC)
    Mary Margaret McBride
    Ogilvy and Mather
    Jane and Goodman Ace
Museum of Broadcasting—Chicago
Museum of Radio and Television—New York
N. W. Ayer Company, New York
National Archives, Washington, D.C. (NA)
New York Public Library—Lincoln Center Library of the Performing Arts (NYPL)
Society to Preserve and Encourage Radio Drama, Variety, and Comedy (SPERDVAC)
State Historical Society of Wisconsin, Madison (SHSW)
    Martin Codell
    Jane Crusinberry
    Theodore S. Delay
    Wendell Hall
    William S. Hedges
    E. P. H. James
    Edward M. Kirby
    Carlton Morse
    National Association of Broadcasters (NAB)
    National Broadcasting Company (NBC)

Irna Phillips
Paul Rhymer
Rosser Reeves
Union for Democratic Action (UDA)
Judith Waller
University of Southern California (USC)
Freeman Gosden and Charles Correll

Index

Compiled by Laura Moss Gottlieb

331

Michele Hilmes is associate professor of communication arts at the University of Wisconsin-Madison. She is the author of *Hollywood and Broadcasting: From Radio to Cable* (1990) and numerous articles on broadcasting history.